FREEDOM AND COMMUNITY

Freedom
and Community

A STUDY OF SOCIAL VALUES

NICOLAS HAINES

MACMILLAN

London · Melbourne · Toronto

ST MARTIN'S PRESS

New York

1966

MACMILLAN AND COMPANY LIMITED
Little Essex Street London WC2
also Bombay Calcutta Madras Melbourne

THE MACMILLAN COMPANY OF CANADA LIMITED
70 Bond Street Toronto 2

ST MARTIN'S PRESS INC
175 Fifth Avenue New York NY 10010

IN MEMORY OF

Constance Frances Mitchell

late Head Teacher at East Ham Grammar School for Girls

Contents

PART THREE: JUSTICE

PART FOUR: COMMUNITY

Preface

(mainly for tutors)

THIS is a book for beginners. Beginners, that is, in methodical discussion of social values. Professional philosophers, for instance, or those seeking to be, will gain from it little more than a chance to exercise their analytical equipment. The book is intended for beginners and sets out to avoid both the jargon and the arrangement of problems in academic philosophy. The alternative was to provide for a very small number of professionals further 'in-group' discussion when the need (as we see it) is to provide the literate multitudes who now serve society with some equipment for thought about the values to which their work in our society commits them.

Yet the book has some 'textbook' features. The Notes and References draw attention to the literature in ethics, epistemology, social and political philosophy and at the same time, having in mind the cultural limits imposed upon many students by their formal education, some care is taken to indicate other areas of inquiry and even to give facts which the specialist in one of these areas might consider trivial and unworthy of mention.

More important than any other feature of the book (from the teacher's vantage-point) are the Questions for Discussion. Those actually provided at the end of each chapter should, of course, be regarded as examples of what might be done, not as an exhaustive list of possibilities. Thought of the kind to which this book is dedicated *is* discussion — it is part of the endless conversation, creating what has been called in this book 'community of meaning'. Then there are the incidental benefits of such discussion — the facility it may develop for critical activity in other fields.

It is hoped then that tutors and leaders of discussion groups in many places of many kinds will use the book as a basis for a course of tutorials, seminars, or discussion-classes. In adding some suggestions about the use of Discussion material in this book the author has in mind, of course, tutors and leaders whose experience has not so far encompassed discussion of this kind. Besides, there are in many parts of the world, even today, groups who meet for conversation without benefit of government grants or 'specialist' leadership and some of these may welcome suggestions about the organization of discussion.

Philosophy is primarily an activity — sometimes solitary, sometimes social — best a little of each. But when it is both social and regular as in a discussion group which has to meet weekly or at more frequent intervals it is best to *prepare*. Discussion groups are subject to two maladies: *aphasia*, or speechlessness, (common in Anglo-Saxon communities) *polylogy*, or much-speaking, a disease akin to group-hysteria, sometimes met with east of Suez, not unknown even in the West. To these perils tutors in modern institutions of higher (or further) education will add those of *bibliophobia*, or fear of reading, said to be encouraged by the student-grant system, leading to restrictive practices and a premature onset of trade-union inertia, and *microergonia*, a development of these tendencies consisting in an inability to do more than the minimum in any occupation. Against the last two of these modern diseases there is only one remedy — agreement with the major conclusions of this book; but against the first and the second the tutor himself has some defence: preparation.

Take the Questions for Discussion at the end of Part Two. Let us say the group-leader, or tutor, intends the group to discuss *each* of the questions based on Chapter 10. He will find that the questions differ as to complication and amount of preparation needed but not one of them can be undertaken without preparation of some kind (if only the reading of Chapter 10). But to come to details.

He himself, poor man, will have to read or know about the material in the chapter. Then for Question One, he will ask one student (a week before or more) to read up all the references to 'nature' in Heraclitus and give an account of these. Another will read the Declaration of Rights and the text of Chapter 10 and give an account of this. (Say ten minutes or so each.) A third (or the two students who have done the other) will read Popper and all three will be asked to relate their comments to the question 'what part does the concept of 'nature' play in the discussion of human good?' The tutor (according to the type of group — sixth form, undergraduate, W.E.A., etc.) can save himself work by confining his own preparation to the everyday uses of 'nature' and using these as the talking-points for the rest of the group. Having read this book he will have in mind the larger question (at the beginning of Part One) of man's 'anxious' approach to his two worlds, and so forth. (Beyond ecology to philosophy, of course.)

The second of the questions calls for less reading. This is an opportunity for more free discussion and the leader's task will be to keep the discussion moving around the group as freely as he can without losing sight of the important questions involved. He needs to have some formulation of the final and interim conclusions he wishes to reach in his mind if he is to avoid attacks of polylogy. For instance, the question in parenthesis: Is *man* born at all? is a most important one and can start a much more profound inquiry into the nature of man as the subject of values and so on. But it would (in our experience) be fatal to insist on this if it does not arise spontaneously or as the result of careful, unforced guidance. Better to start off with 'unschooled' discussion of freedom in relation to children even at a personal level but not, of course, without efforts continuously to move the talk 'up' as opportunities arise.

The third question gives plenty of scope for further teaching and it would probably be sound advice not to allow 'free discussion' until such teaching has been done in accordance with the particular interests of the group. Tutors young and in-experienced (or old and ditto — the two categories are by no means inseparable) may fly from aphasiac conditions to the temptations of such questions as these and achieve nothing except a lot of noise. Questions about faith are catalysts. Hence the suggestion for detailed breaking-down of the discussion on alienation. Best, perhaps, have three or four separate comments prepared by several members of the group (two to each?).

Perhaps discussion gives no trouble to most. Perhaps it is of less value than we are suggesting. Perhaps all 'perhapses' vary from place to place and time to time. And then again, perhaps it would be helpful if we could find out and, using this book as a 'whipping boy', discuss both discussion in general and the 'social values' in particular and in such ways cross the red (or black) brick frontiers between the wide variety of groups for whom such discussion is intended and create our own community of interest. The author would be glad to be engaged in such an exchange of experiences and to hear of what happens where such matters are discussed for the first time and of particular difficulties in this kind of activity.

Acknowledgements

HELP received from other writers is acknowledged in references to their books throughout. A 'non-specialist' book of this kind owes most to the people who suggested the need for it: students of all ages, in a wide variety of institutions and in several parts of the world whose considerable if unspecifiable contribution the author gratefully acknowledges.

List of Titles

abbreviated in footnotes and Discussion notes

Benn and Peters, *SP*: S. I. Benn and R. S. Peters, *Social Principles and the Democratic State*, Allen & Unwin, 1959.

Burnet, *EGP*: J. Burnet, *Early Greek Philosophy*, A. & C. Black, 1948.

Copleston, *CH*: F. C. Copleston, *A History of Philosophy*, vols i–vi, 1947–60, Burns, Oates & Washbourne 1946.

DL: Diogenes Laertius, *Lives of Eminent Philosophers*, with an English translation by R. D. Hicks, in the Loeb Classical Library, Heinemann, 1950.

Freeman, *AP*: K. Freeman, *Ancilla to the Pre-Socratic Philosophers*, Oxford, Blackwell, 1952.

Freeman, *CP*: K. Freeman, *Companion to the Pre-Socratic Philosophers*, Oxford, Blackwell, 1953.

Freud, *BW*: *The Basic Writings of Sigmund Freud*, New York, Random House, The Modern Library, 1938.

Gomperz, *GT*: T. Gomperz, *Greek Thinkers, a History of Ancient Philosophy*, vols. i–iv, trans. Laurie Magnus, and G. G. Berry, John Murray, 1901–12.

Russell, *HWP*: Bertrand Russell, *A History of Western Philosophy*, Allen & Unwin, 1946.

Sabine, *HPT*: G. H. Sabine, *A History of Political Theory*, Harrap, 1937.

Introduction: Social Service

'THEM' AND 'US'

'WE, the people', have seldom lacked champions to defend our cause against 'them', our rulers. If history is the story of liberty,[1] it is also the story of a few men here and there who for one reason or another have chosen to speak up for the many against the few — the many subjects against the few rulers. The 'people' have grown used to separating themselves from their governments; they have grown used to thinking of themselves as 'Us' apart from 'Them'.

Not that the demagogues, the people's champions, the liberal thinkers and writers had no good reason to fence us off from our rulers like sheep from their shepherds: rule, government itself, however just, however benign, wields a sceptre, grasps the weapons of power in its hands: it would not be government, else. Besides, rulers have in the past claimed privilege beyond what the work of government seemed to require. Those who enjoyed political power have often made free also of far more goods — the wealth of the whole nation — than seemed fair or fitting. When your governing class retires to its castles and palaces, surrounded by rich park-lands, and defends its blatant privileges by force under the guise of justice it needs no liberal penman to make plain to the impoverished that there are two nations, not one: 'Them', the rulers, 'Us', the ruled.

Habits can outlive their usefulness, however, and even persist

---

[1] The phrase is Hegel's. See also Benedetto Croce, *History as the Story of Liberty* (Meridian, 1955; first published in English by Allen & Unwin, 1941). Ch. 12 is relevant.

In addition to books referred to in these footnotes students of social philosophy should use throughout:

Benn, S. I., and Peters, R. S., *Social Principles and the Democratic State* (Allen & Unwin, 1959).

For the notion of social service as a 'devolution' or 'decentralization' of social and political power the work of L. Duguit at the beginning of the century is of interest. For a summary of his theories in the realm of jurisprudence see C. K. Allen, *Law in the Making* (O.U.P., 1958), pp. 574 ff.

to the point where they aggravate the very evils which called them into being. So with this habit of separating rulers from ruled: if our age in our Western civilization is but half as democratic as it claims to be, the time has long since passed when it is useful to do our thinking about society wholly or even largely in terms of 'Them' against 'Us'. For 'democracy' means the spread of power among the people, and where there is power there is also responsibility. The champions of the people in the past never tired in their efforts to summon the rulers to the bar of 'history', of 'opinion', or even of the divine judgement to answer for the use they were making of their power. To date, however, they have said considerably less about what it means to the people to be answerable for their own fate.

For it is inconvenient to be told that there is no one to blame but oneself. Demagogues know that well enough. Many young men and women leaving home for the first time have moments when they know only too well how hard a thing it is to have to answer for oneself, with no parents to turn to and none to blame if a decision goes wrong. It may be that in our modern mass democracies some of us at least are still at this stage. We have left 'home', having rid ourselves of paternal government, have gone into the Far Country of democratic rule, but have yet to grasp that we cannot turn back every time there is trouble to 'Them' at home — for 'They' are now, to a large extent, 'Us'.[1]

The 'people' has no doubt at all times *been* the community in the sense that far more people directly or indirectly are involved in certain political acts than those men who are called the 'government'. Who, for instance, made the French Revolution possible? Louis XVI? His Austrian Queen with her notorious belief in *gâteau* for the poor? Turgot? Necker? Calonne? The Third Estate? The *sans-culottes* who stormed the Bastille? Or have we to include all landlords and clergy as well as the nobles of eighteenth-century France who behaved in ways which made the decisions of their superiors inevitable?

[1] Sir Francis Galton, pioneer of intelligence-measurement, said: 'The vast majority . . . have a natural tendency to shrink from the responsibility of standing and acting alone' (quoted by H. L. Mencken, *Notes on Democracy*, New York, 1926).

Let us say that there is 'social' as distinct from 'political' power. If we admit that there always is social power impinging upon political decisions, we may also admit that the conversion of the one into the other is likely to be more regular, systematic, and at the same time complicated in a mass democracy. Far more of us will be involved in much more of what government does, though the terms and nature of our involvement may be far from clear. One thing is clear, however: the old habit of looking to 'Them' when in reality 'They' are partly 'Us' can only deprive us of understanding what we are at. Such habits may also threaten democracy by inclining us to 'leave it to them' without our knowing exactly what is being left to political decision.

Social power is organized within the ideas we have about our work, our associations, the 'goods' we prize for ourselves and others, the values we put upon institutions and various ways of conducting our relations with each other, the ends we think we ought collectively to pursue. All such ideas or concepts are the concern of the social philosopher. All philosophy is in this sense 'social'. The philosopher works in the skin of society, the conceptual skin, the fabric of ideas we have about how we want to conduct our affairs.

There are aims in doing such work. If we can set out what seem to be prevailing concepts involved in our social power, we may be able to come to some decision about them. We may, for instance, once this has been done, decide to *reject* certain ideas of freedom because these are seen to involve uncomfortable amounts of responsibility. We may say: 'This is not what we want at all'; but the aim is that we shall say so knowing what is at stake. Or we may say of 'equality', 'Yes, that is what we want', but be bound to add because we have thought about it, 'and therefore we must change our ways, giving up this and that which hitherto we thought we could have'. More than social philosophy will be necessary if this kind of decision is to reach beyond concepts to action; but the philosophy must come first if we are to *understand* social power and not to allow ourselves to drift mindlessly from a brief moment of democracy into a new and possibly more lasting separation of 'Them' and 'Us'.

POWER AND 'PYRAMIDS'

Think of power as like a pyramid and there is at least one reason for attending to the lower levels: the pinnacle without the base would fall. This book is meant for every member of a democratic community able, if he wishes, to see himself as part of the 'power-structure'. (And this could mean *every* member.) Two large groups may, however, be distinguished and upon them in particular rests the burden of thought in this time and place. They are in the first place those more immediately involved in political decisions; they are in the second place men and women — a large and growing number — whose whole careers are devoted to the construction and reconstruction of 'society' through their intimate, face-to-face engagement in other people's personal lives. Let us call these for the time being 'civil' and 'social' servants but with the warning that we shall be giving to these names a meaning they would not ordinarily have in daily use.

Civil servants

Who are our 'rulers' today? Are they the men who happen to hold office in the government last elected? Or perhaps the leaders of political parties to which these men belong? Are they the leaders of trade unions? The City men; Wall Street; the Bourse? Should we look for our 'real' rulers in the upper ranks of the civil or military services? Do they own newspapers, broadcasting networks, cinemas? None of these so much, perhaps, as a managerial or even an intellectual *élite*: the men of the board rooms, the directors, the university senate, or the top-technologists and research-workers? Or all these at once? Or some of them *more* than others — nearer to the apex of the pyramid?

Such questions are not our business except that they do suggest the *spread* of power (political-social) downwards and away from the pinpoint moment of decision and the man who happens to be in the appointed place with the qualifications appropriate for the making of it. We would do well to reflect that 'decision-making' itself falls most to the lot of those who represent large and powerful associations and *therefore* — by implication — to the members of those associations. Already power is broadly based and it is likely that if full use were made now of what membership in such associations entails the distinction between social and political power would be much less.

Our interest now is in the people who stand closest to the making of decisions and more particularly in their education.[1] For while decisions can be classified in terms of the professional qualifications needed in their making, political decisions are also, and at the same time, utterances (so to speak) of the community, not just of a professional or party association. The people who stand closest to them are those we mean at the moment by 'civil servants' and if these civil servants are to make decisions for the community they must have ideas, concepts to appeal to other than those which are the special monopoly of any professional group.

These civil servants (including many of those who ordinarily answer to this name) have need of something more than administrative or technical efficiency. They need to *belong* to the community, to live within its skin, even as by their decisions they help to bring about changes in the life and thought of the people.

To serve a community is not simply to do what its members severally or by majority-vote may seek to command. It is to interpret the community to itself and if possible ensure that its 'commands' are in keeping with this interpretation. This is as risky an undertaking as it sounds and would not appeal to some security-minded, career-conscious servants. For to 'serve' in this sense means that the servant must commit himself to a view of what the group is and take the chance that others will oppose him, taking the pleasures of office and decision from his hands.

The community can only be served if it has at its command men with a firm grasp on the ideas it lives by, men who have dedicated themselves to the conclusions they have reached after long (and endless) enquiry, reflection, discourse, and careful critical analysis. This is where social philosophy enters into the basic education of the civil servant. It does not offer him statistically based information about 'what the public thinks', for what is 'the public' and how can it be said to 'think' except through men who are authorized to speak for 'it' because they have spoken to each other and thought through the community's concepts?

[1] For recent comment on the education of 'rulers' in the United Kingdom see, for example, Sir Leon Bagrit's 'Reith Lectures' in *The Listener*, Nov.–Dec. 1964.

All such concepts having a prima facie claim to be part of the social integument must come under review, critically, analytically, constructively. Such questions as an inquiry of this sort — the sort undertaken in this book — provokes, may from time to time prove suitable to investigation by the sciences but this is secondary to the principal work of social philosophy. The civil servant, the man who dares to come closest to acts of political decision, has first to understand what is meant by the ideas by which his community has lived for generations. Such are the ideas we represent by 'liberty', 'justice', 'equality', and so on. To make decisions at the peak of the pyramid without some such preparation is to make them without proper respect for the community and in despite of the communal life.

Social servants

From Pope to parish priest social power was once distributed 'downwards' and 'outwards' toward whatever its base might have been. On Chaucer's pilgrims' way[1] from the Tabard Inn to the shrine of Becket in Canterbury we glimpse the lower levels — the knight, the squire, the priests themselves; and even, perhaps, the lowest — the cook, the shipman, and the ploughman. Through all ranks and orders moved priests of various kinds, conveying in their persons and through their offices some notion of what the community was *about*. The crudest of them bore about in his squalid habit some tokens of the Church and that universe the Church discerned by faith and revelation. Priestly rites kept men in that universe, joined them by their souls to its community, regulated their conduct and their relations with each other, their art, morals, and private ambitions in accordance with the 'whole' of which they were an active, constructive part.

Well into our own time priests, clergymen of one denomination or another, formed by far the largest part of that company we propose now to call 'social servants': the people who through their intimate, whole-time, face-to-face engagement in other people's personal lives make a career of social construction and reconstruction below the levels of political decision. Then during the nineteenth century they began to be joined by growing

[1] In addition to the *Canterbury Tales* see, for example, Eileen Power's *Mediaeval People* (Penguin, 1937; 1st ed., 1924), ch. 3.

numbers of newly, no doubt partially, but differently educated lay people voluntarily concerning themselves with the special needs of the poor, the sick, the exploited; social servants prompted by conscience who sometimes found themselves at odds with the clergy, with different ideas of what the community was about and therefore very different notions of what their social service should entail.

Today our social servants are hard to count;[1] they are an ever-growing army — teachers, social workers, medical men and women, police; if these are our modern priesthood, then it is likely that already they represent a proportion of the total population as great as that of the Church's agents in the Middle Ages. The differences, however, will show us why the modern social servant has need of a social philosophy. For example, we could say that as our modern civil servants would once have been in clerical orders, so many of our modern social servants are likely to become civil servants in the sense that they are paid by central or local government and directed by political institutions.

On the other hand, neither the civil nor the social servant today is 'built in' to a pyramidal structure like that of the medieval Church. If we must talk of 'pyramids' at all, it would be as well to think of many such organizations each reaching a different point according to the kind of decision which has to be reached. (Compare, for instance, the 'vertical' structure of decision-making in the police with that in the teaching profession.) Put this another way and say it is much harder even to *conceive* of a 'whole' when relating modern social service to the 'community' than we find it when imagining what things might have been like in the days of Chaucer. However the more thoughtful of his contemporaries envisaged their society, few social servants today can see themselves as conveying, from the 'top' downwards, what the community is about. Many social servants would resent the bare suggestion.

Would it not be curious, therefore, if social workers were busily constructing human relations on principles at odds with those which guide the decisions of civil servants? Curious and

---

[1] Some specimen figures: 20,000 social workers according to Baroness Wootton (see p. 8). I think it was she who suggested 'one to every two barmen'. The *Robbins Report* mentioned 22,500 graduate teachers in universities and called for 59,000 in 1980. Other suggestions call for 80,000 teachers in training by 1970.

possibly trouble-making. What are we to say, for example, of a school dedicated to the enjoyment by children of unbridled spontaneity if, in fact, as soon as the child leaves school he is compelled to come to terms with a wider society which has no respect for his undisciplined impulses? Or how would it be if social work dispensed with responsibility[1] and encouraged increasing numbers of people to attribute their faults and failings to 'sickness' in a society still governed on the understanding that more and more people could stand on their own feet[2] and make decisions for which they would answer?

Civil servants, on the other hand, may make use of our conceptual confusions in order to foist upon us arrangements which satisfy bureaucratic efficiency but do harm to habits and activities we would value if we knew what we were at. Social philosophy should help us to instruct them. We shall now consider a few occupations which do social service, showing for whom this book is meant, and at the same time having something to say about their connexions with civil service.

SOCIAL SERVANTS

When so many serve the community, where is the community apart from its servants? This question becomes more than a tease when on the one hand (as in the United Kingdom) many social servants are paid by the State, and on the other hand they themselves belong to more-or-less powerful associations, pyramids in their own right, capable of reaching collective decisions which in their turn press upon government. Thus is social converted into political power and social service into civil service.

Consider, for example, the united action of the Belgian doctors against the Loi Leburton leading to amendments to that law in July 1964. Consider further the presence in the British trade union organization of civil servants' associations and the part these might play in blocking or promoting an 'incomes policy'.

Here attention will be paid to certain professions properly called 'social service' which have, none the less, a manifest political role.

---

[1] The phrase was Baroness Wootton's in her *Social Science and Social Pathology* (Allen & Unwin, 1959), part ii, ch. 8.

[2] See the quotation from H. L. Mencken, p. 2, above.

This is done in order that we may get on with our social philosophy untroubled by the backward tug of that habit social servants share with others — the habit of dubbing themselves 'Us' (the people) not 'Them' (the rulers).

One corrective for such habits is the shocking discovery that the social servant himself is regarded by the people as on 'their' (the rulers') side. Work done for and paid for by the community seldom provokes gratitude: the social worker is more likely to be suspected than thanked. All the more necessary for her to come to terms with her role, to know what it involves. Admit at least she *is* involved. She shrinks from this because she, unlike many civil servants, works face to face with people at odds with the laws, the conventions, with the whole wearing necessity to get on with other people. Her task might be easier if she had a clearer notion of what community *might* be.

Teachers

Teachers — surely the most powerful group of social servants — have a marked inclination to become civil servants, given half a chance. Whether they do so or not, whether they forsake the classroom for the office or even for the legislature, they belong to powerful associations with direct political access. Their salaries may come either from the national or the local exchequer. The work they do in schools and universities serves (however grudgingly) the national economy. They, more than any other single class of social servants, probe the morals of the young. At higher levels at least teachers determine in large measure whether a generation shall think for itself or indifferently embark on careers incapable of further critical participation in the common life.

Many teachers hold that their obligations are defined by their students' interest in the academic subject. Yet no subject is socially neutral. The *method* of teaching, at least, is decisive. Compare, for instance, the authoritative with the evocative[1] method where these are both conceivable in the 'same' subject.

At all levels, whenever the teacher strikes an attitude, provokes or answers a question, invites confidences or repels them,

---

[1] The 'authoritative' is the method of 'because I say so'; the 'evocative' method elicits a child's response in question and answer by discussion.

comments on the news, challenges or propagates an opinion, he is doing social service, well or badly. In the most trivial detail of work and play he demonstrates standards or the lack of them, calls for rules to be respected or despised, stands for the community or else bows himself out, abdicates his own authority (as the child's parents may have done), or in one way or another discounts the community in which his charges live. Social service or social disservice, he ought at least to know what he is at.

Social workers

The group of professions which explicitly call themselves 'social work' include social case-workers, psychiatric social workers, probation officers, almoners (or medical social workers), youth-leaders, and some others. The generic title 'social work' does rather tend to monopolize functions we have for this reason gathered together as 'social service'. For the social worker has been known to see herself as manifesting attitudes and interests which separate her on the one hand from 'Them' (the supposed rulers) and on the other hand from other social servants — such as teachers, the police and the medical services.

Since 'social work' in the United Kingdom at least is inseparably associated with the social services — that is, with the aid the community through the State gives to cases of special need — it is very hard indeed for the social worker to keep herself apart from the community. On the other hand, she may see very little reason to interest herself in social and political values if she can prove to her own satisfaction that her business is with individuals and their immediate relations, not with the whole community.

This kind of distinction, however, ignores much of what we have learnt lately about man as a 'social' animal. That is, to distinguish between 'individuals' and their attitudes on the one hand and the 'community' and its values on the other is misleading if we think the one has nothing to do with the other. Social workers, for instance, are among our professional social teachers. Suppose they accept (to take one possibility) the view that men do not *do* wrong but merely *suffer* what 'society' does to them, suppose they accept such a view — are they not likely to encourage those they serve to be passive, rather than active, with respect to their faults and failings? Suppose a social worker takes the view that all

crime is the fault of 'society' not of the criminal. This could lead
to vigorous political action for social reform, but it could lead as
well to an indulgent attitude to wrong-doing which would teach
her client self-pity and dependence rather than self-criticism and
responsibility. Sometimes social workers talk as if all that mattered
was getting on with other people, being liked, having easy
relations, and so forth. This can lead to the view that anyone who
does not share popular opinions or do pretty much as his
neighbours do, any eccentric, any nonconformist, is 'sick' and in
need of 'cure'. Take this too far and you have in social service a
dangerous discouragement to the very enterprise and innovation
which in the past inspired social service as well as other advances
in civilization.

The social worker is a maker of social values as well as a
distributor.[1] She should say what she is making and invite
criticism and discussion.

The police

Prisons, handcuffs, and cold, cold cells put many social servants
off the police and certainly social workers would prefer not to be
classed with them. If this is because the social worker thinks she
has a good feeling toward delinquents which the policeman does
not have, we have at least the right to ask just how 'good' this
feeling is and what ends it is meant to serve. In any case, a feeling
of moral superiority is not by itself an adequate basis for the
classification of social servants. If social servants of all kinds would
do well from time to time to see themselves as in some sense
'Them', the whole community, social and civil servants included,
might gain from a periodical review of the police force as 'Us'.
The police are servants of the community directly engaged in the
maintenance of sufficient order for the peaceful conduct of our
affairs.

If, of course, our social science has brought us to the conclusion
either that peace and order do not matter over much or that they
can be maintained apart from law and its officers, then this is a

[1] 'The Social Worker is concerned today with the fundamental personal and family
problems of all classes and sections of the community' (Sir Charles Morris, source
not traced). For the United Kingdom see also the Younghusband Report on *Social
Workers in the Local Authority Health and Welfare Services*, 1959. For the Social
Worker as moralist see Paul Halmos, *The Faith of the Counsellors* (Constable, 1965).

very interesting conclusion indeed and we should be told about it. Many people, no doubt, dislike all thought of force exerted on their behalf and prefer not to think about the pain some people suffer as punishment for offences against the law. This again is understandable and relates, moreover, to some interesting views put forward in the past about the meaning of a 'good' society.

In the meantime it can only be harmful for one group of social servants to feel itself shut off from the rest as well as from the community it serves. The policeman has as much need as any man to understand the community he serves and to appreciate its values.

Medical men

The healing arts are important to social philosophy by reason of the standards they set, the goals they elevate, and the methods their practitioners use. Nurses, physicians, and psychiatrists in particular have considerable social power quite apart from the political power their professional associations can exercise by reason of the demand they have created for their services.

A nurse working outside a hospital may have more social power than her colleague in the wards. She finds people at their weakest; she penetrates their privacy; she explores and invariably comments upon their neighbourhood as well as their more intimate relations. It is hard at times not to relate her authority to that of the Last Enemy himself and sometimes she acts as if she agreed. The physician who lives in the locality and knows his patients well has still more power and may well set standards which have little or nothing directly to do with medicine. Yet he is not always remarkable for his insight into moral and social values; he may know little and care less about the way power is used on his behalf or even about the influence he has upon his clientèle.

The ethics of medicine, according to one authority in the profession,[1] may be endangered by the growth of science. The conduct and character of a doctor, he said, were at least as important as, perhaps more important than, his learning. 'No one is responsible for the patient as a whole', he complained. Human sympathy and understanding were being whittled away. A common discussion of social philosophy, including moral questions which

[1] Sir George Pickering, Regius Professor of Medicine at Oxford, in a Presidential Address to the British Medical Association.

are a part of social philosophy, may do something to correct these tendencies in the healing arts.

As for the psychiatrist, the healer of the mind, his is in some ways the most important and significant of all the new additions to social service. Psychiatry has extended the meaning of 'health' and 'sickness' to include matters we once thought to be in the province of priest or moralist if not of the sufferer himself. Such extensions of the healing art could work a revolution in social values, in our concepts of community, in such values, for instance, as justice (with respect to punishment), responsibility, and, by implication, liberty. The psychiatrist may know full well what he is at, but whether he does or not *we* would like to know, for we cannot lightly permit large areas of our common thought to be eroded or transformed unless we are given time to evaluate the possible consequences.

'CRISIS'

All times are critical to those with an interest in crisis. Preachers warn of Judgement; social scientists indent for grants 'urgently' needed for research to avoid national calamity; politicians in search of votes thunder about the balance of payments, a Communist conspiracy, or the lamentable state of the nation's defences. Social philosophers can hardly be left out: they must surely argue the necessity of their work and create a crisis if they have to compete for funds and interest. To be fair, British philosophers at least usually resist this temptation. On the contrary, they show remarkable modesty in the importance they attach to their own work.[1] To talk of the *need* for social philosophy as we have been doing is to run the risk of seeming brash if not positively inelegant.

Yet there it is: there is little doubt that the territories of social and political power do have features which distinguish one age from another and there seems little point in calling philosophy 'social' if we are to take no account of them.

Taking those parts of Europe and North America we often call

[1] For typical British detachment in such discussions see Professor Oakeshott's Inaugural Lecture, 'Political Education', published in *Philosophy, Politics and Society*, ed. Peter Laslett (Oxford, Blackwell, 1956).

'the West' as our area, we may summarize certain changes which are taking place either in or around the area and impinging upon it and then say that whatever philosophy we do has this for its setting.

Population

In twelve centuries of its history Europe's population (taking the continent now as a whole) rose to one hundred and eighty million. From 1800 to 1914 this became *four hundred and sixty million*.[1] The process continues here and throughout the world at an appalling rate. Too many are being born; too few are dying in time. If the West should take steps to reduce its horrifying fertility, it might well be overwhelmed in the end by the crushing weight of Eastern man. If, on the other hand, we do nothing, we may for all our desperate techniques choke our homelands, force down our standards of living, and destroy each the other's soul with the noise, smell, and insatiable appetites of too many human animals on our shrinking meadows.

The huge populations of our Western nations cannot in a century of so-called 'universal education' have taken in anything like enough of their cultural inheritance to make it their own and defend the best of it against erosion. As for the training of men in sufficient numbers to take part critically and constructively in the government of these communities, this is a matter we have not even begun to attempt.[2] To introduce our social and civil servants to some of the ideas at least by which we think our people have lived is all the social philosopher can attempt in his own right.

The problems set by a rapidly swelling population are for the scientist and the technologist to face; but those who do such work need at least to have some feel for priorities and some skill in arranging them.

[1] Figures quoted from Ortega y Gassett's *Revolt of the Masses* (Unwin paperback ed. 1961; first published in Spanish 1930).

[2] Despite such suggestions as that of Lord Bryce early in the century that education should be suited to the obligations of democracy. See his *Studies in History and Jurisprudence* (1901), and *Modern Democracies* (1921). See also E. M. Burns, *Ideas in Conflict* (Methuen, 1963), ch. 1, and compare Lord Bryce's suggestion with the work of Alexis de Tocqueville, *Democracy in America*, especially ch. xxvi of the abridged edition in English (O.U.P., World's Classics, 1946). *De la démocratie en Amérique* was first published in two parts, part i in 1835, part ii in 1840.

Automation

This revolution in human industry is far advanced and a nation bent upon keeping pace with its neighbours and rivals may have to undergo a revolution in its own heart and mind before it can exploit to the full all the possibilities of automation. Such an *inner* revolution will come hardest to the communities which have the longest industrial traditions behind them and the least space in the homelands for manœuvre, as well as the well established ways of conducting their affairs which such communities usually enjoy. Some would say this is the problem facing the United Kingdom.[1] Students used to critical and analytical discussion of the kind for which this book provides may help to break up the hard ground of settled ways and mental habits among themselves and those they serve.

Automation has possibilities of great interest to social philosophy: first, through the increase of leisure, second, through the access of new power to government. In morality, as leisure increases, work will no longer seem the 'good' it was, industry will not be a virtue; effort may cease to be the morally desirable prelude to reward and men who come to think like this may not be men as we have known them. Automation could create a new and much wider gulf between 'Them' and 'Us', the rulers and the ruled, between political and social power. This could come about by putting into the hands of government machines comprehensible only to those who mind them and feed them. On the other hand, and together with the various media of communication already available as well as increased leisure to enjoy them, direct democracy might once more become practicable even as it was among the Athenians who had women and slaves to work for them while they got on with their politics.

The rejection of Europe

The Berlin Wall, the iron curtain, and now in Africa a rejection of European ways, following upon the making of new nations out of old colonies — these are just the conditions for a rediscovery of European ideas sharpened by attack and gripped more firmly in response to momentary loss of nerve. Both Europe and North

[1] Recently stated by Sir Leon Bagrit. See p. 5 above.

America, to say nothing of other communities, have a common fund of ideas which have for centuries been part of that conceptual fabric which binds them together. Some of these ideas will be the subject matter of this book, for there is a sense in which social philosophy has nothing new to say — the way of saying it is all.[1]

A people long engaged in war, conquest, expansion, and the weariness of imperial rule may when drawing back within its frontiers take one of two courses: it may turn sour and vent disappointment or frustration upon its own traditions or it may reflect more deeply and creatively upon them. If there are Western ideas of lasting not to say universal value, their rejection by other peoples at the very time when those same peoples are more than willing to accept the skills and the produce of the West is double reason for guarding them in the only way ideas can be 'guarded' — by discussion with constructive intent.

New morality

Is it possible? Alexis de Tocqueville more than a century ago saw morals imperilled by the swift advance of egalitarian democracy in America. 'The time is fast approaching', he said, 'when freedom, public peace, and social order itself will not be able to exist without education.'[2] He could hardly have meant what we have come to call education in the past century — or at least not this alone. How, then, are men to be 'taught' to live together once they have thrown off ancient custom or the standards of a ruling caste? We do not know. Perhaps, as the naturists used to say, men have a grain of good sense in them and will co-operate in their own interests however they use the moralities of the past. Perhaps de Tocqueville exaggerated even as anxious moralists do today and the world, after all, is not going to the dogs each time a cynic speaks.

Or if it is, if men are not so bad as they are painted but far, far worse, then we may have to look to the gene-engineer for 'our' salvation: he may very soon be able to produce mutations in the unborn making them subject to discipline. A partnership between

---

[1] That is, no discoveries to make about 'nature'. Even so, the restatement of (so-called) 'old' values may amount to discoveries about 'human nature', which is, in a sense, always changing.

[2] *Democracy in America.* See also p. 14.

geneticists and the tranquillizer manufacturers was, after all, the basis of success in Aldous Huxley's *Brave New World*.

But by such desperate remedies *what* will be saved? Manifestly not the men we knew. It is true that in this book we deal in ideas about men as they *might* be rather than with what the empirical social scientist would call 'social facts'. But note the syntax: we deal with *men* (the creatures we know) and our ideas are ideas *of* those men in two senses. For they are ideas that men have had and dwelt upon and they are ideas of what those same men could make of themselves. To purpose genetic change in the human race in order to 'solve' its social problems would seem to us not solution but failure just as much as if our civil servants some centuries hence started to depopulate Earth while it was still habitable and to bring in creatures from another planet more amenable to their systems.

Make no mistake, biochemical engineering might produce a community (if that is the word) capable of lifelong euphoria such as in the past was only dreamed of in Sunday-school fantasies of the paradise to come. It is not for us to say that this could or could not be. We are entitled to say, however, that we prefer to make the best we can of that 'bad' job we call 'man' rather than throw him away and begin again at the draughtsman's drawing-board. Any 'new' morality will at least, therefore, be 'morality' and that is an idea at least as old as what we mean by 'man'.

Social service and social thought

If the growth of social service is in any sense the spread of social power, if it will not do any more to conduct our thinking about our human relations solely in terms of 'Them' and 'Us', then there are two academic subjects which we shall have to bring together: politics and ethics. Of course this is nothing new. For Aristotle, Plato, and many ancient thinkers it could be taken for granted that the problems of politics were ethical and the problems of what we would call ethics were also political. What we are doing is to return to this view for our own purposes — the purposes of social service. We will not deal with political questions except as these relate to the aims and values of social service; we will deal with moral problems only as these arise from the attempt to think about what we are at as social servants.

At the same time it would be ambitious to attempt at this stage an introduction to all the questions usually covered by the term 'social philosophy'. For instance, we shall do no more than refer in passing to the methodological questions started by the social sciences and of interest to the social philosopher. Our interest is primarily in values — in the general question, 'What are worthwhile aims in social service?' or 'What kind of society ought we to prefer?' or 'What kind of people ought we to be?'.

This is a book for those who may have no time or facility for the more complicated theoretical problems such questions provoke. It seems to us much more important that a lot of people doing social service should discuss — if possible, together — the kind of questions raised here than that a few should be diverted from social service to a lifetime's preoccupation with the logical and methodological problems of academic philosophy. The job this book sets out to do has been done if it has been used to nudge groups of people into talk about social values — not any kind of talk, but systematic, reasonable discussion which they are able to follow up, once dissatisfied, by further reading. On the other hand, those who wish to go a lot further will find indicators which they can follow even if they are not at the moment engaged in full-time study.

Technical terms and professional jargon have been avoided. The writer has made his own approach wherever possible, not because his is better than others, but because this seems to give the best chance of writing a book which will start others thinking and not leave them at ease with a collection of sayings by renowned authorities to excuse them from further effort.

Anyone may excuse himself from arguing with Plato, Locke, Hegel, Rousseau, Marx, or any other great name in the history of thought; but when the argument is started by an unknown who has not even — at the time of going to press — the distinction of being dead, the provocation is surely difficult to resist. To make quite sure, however, questions suggested for discussion will from time to time point out views different from those upheld in the text.

Summary

Part One, 'Varieties of Experience', is about knowledge itself, about truth and other social regulations of experience. Not only the particular values we discuss but the whole activity of discussing them, perhaps the whole notion of 'values' are wished upon us today partly at any rate because of a long and painful phase of European experience sometimes described as the conflict between faith and science. This is why we start here. Social service is service in a society bedevilled by such problems.

Then we go on to values indicated by such well-known titles as 'freedom', 'justice', and 'community'. But here each of these familiar names covers also a discussion of certain contemporary values which may or may not seem to us compatible with other uses, other values. Thus 'freedom' above all has to be looked at in relation to 'permissiveness' on the one hand, 'health' on the other. 'Justice', again, may mean something else than 'equality' and such distinctions may in their turn have a bearing upon social service.

The whole book has its own axe to grind, however, and even if the author could have ground it less he is unrepentant, for it seems to be necessary to a book of this kind that a definite commitment should be undertaken. In this case the writer is preoccupied with freedom and what he considers to be its neglected dimension — responsibility. This has obvious implications for social service and ought therefore to provide the kind of irritant which is necessary if the social servant is to be stung into looking at his work from the point of view of its value and the values he thinks it serves.

QUESTIONS FOR DISCUSSION

1. 'Them' and 'Us': What distinguishes 'Them' from 'Us'? When? Make a list of the categories indicated by 'Them'. Does it include social servants? Members of Parliament? managers? scientists? teachers?

2. 'The fact is that the number of officials and the quantity of work are not related to each other at all.' Professor Parkinson was talking about civil servants. Could the same be said of social servants? (See C. Northcote Parkinson, *Parkinson's Law or the Pursuit of Progress*, John Murray, 1958.)

3. When C.N.D. campaigners imprisoned for disturbing the peace in England began a hunger-strike, a psychiatric social

worker attending an extension lecture was heard to say 'They must be sick'. Discuss.

4. How would you expect 'education for democracy' to differ from other kinds of education?

5. 'Today, if we know where we are going and if we use the slave services of automation intelligently and courageously we have the chance of building a really high civilization for ourselves.' (Sir LEON BAGRIT.) What place has social service in this process? If it has a place what kind of equipment does it need?

Part One

VARIETIES
OF
EXPERIENCE

I

The Invention of Ignorance

CROWS, crayfish, men, and cocker-spaniels depend for their lives upon a universe which tolerates them. All, too, save perhaps the neutered domestic pet, have to reckon with their own kind as well as with the natural enemies of their species. On the animal 'drift line' along the shores of Lake Michigan[1] aquatic animals washed up by the receding tide lie in heaps with those in the lower levels kept moist by their comrades above long enough for them to survive until the tide comes back. Men do such things with more finesse. They have, none the less, to come to terms both with their universe and with their own kind if they are to survive. In common with other animals they have to make their way in two worlds — their habitat and their community.

Worrying, however, may well be a human monopoly; it may well be that only man worries about his place in the sun, his relations with his fellows. Sparrows *may* hold seminars in the quickset hedge; reflection on time, space, and infinity *may* absorb the rookery; wild geese may worship and even maggots have their moral code but, so far, the worry-world, the inner, subcutaneous world of 'why?' and 'how?' appears to be man's distinctive achievement. *Homo anxius*, man the solicitous, the uneasy, may well seem to some future species resembling us in other respects a tormented creature who invented awareness several millennia before he discovered the antidote.

Worrying becomes 'inquiry' when it starts to ask specific questions. Methodical inquiry is called 'learning'; the end product which allays unease we call 'knowledge', though men have hesitated to use this word in the past except for certainty.

[1] W. C. Allee, in 'Animal Sociology' in the *Encyclopaedia Britannica*, 1958 ed.

In the following chapters of Part One we shall be reflecting on the varieties of experience and also the attempts to regulate experience; for from these arise the problems of social philosophy. By 'experience' we mean what men say happens to them; by 'learning' their methodical attempts to understand; by 'knowledge' the beliefs (descriptions, explanations, theories, and so on) they arrive at. And so we are led to the regulation of experience — to meaning, to truth, and to the notion of what is 'good' for us.

Collective freedom[1]

The universe has tolerated men of a sort on our earth for, let us say, a million years. For a bare fraction of that time men in communities have lifted up their eyes and begun to see more of their habitat than a forest clearing, using a variety of names in a variety of languages to say what they saw, and to live forthwith, in their groups, according to their interpretations of experience. Here is freedom, of a sort. Collective freedom, perhaps; for the universe to each new generation has been seen as their fathers saw it, which may be only another way of saying 'in the language of their community'. Freedom, none the less; for though ancient mythologies may resemble one another in many ways, there are differences, too, and no step-by-step, one-for-one transition from stage to stage uniformly throughout the whole race of man. In the sense that the human organism in its collectives has both put the universe to speech and done so in a wide variety of ways man can be said to have been born (collectively) free.

Here is a 'freedom' we are losing.[2] To the extent that we accept the findings of the physical sciences and notwithstanding that these are themselves a human activity, we are bound to give up variety in the constructions we put upon the universe; men may in this sense, throughout their habitat, become, after a space, one community in so far as the way we look out upon the world can make us one.

Collective freedom, on the other hand, has had another side: the

[1] The word 'freedom' is used in Part One without excuse or explanation. A proper discussion of the word is provided in Part Two.
[2] But see below, Chapter 5, 'Science and Freedom'.

freedom communities have enjoyed to regulate relations within the community and to do so in part at least according to the community's view of the world. Where each new generation accepted without question the myth-poem which depicted the universe as a vast concourse of gods whose wills were defined in, or whose whims were placated by, the rules and conventions which the ruling priest-kings administered, answers were given to questions which would never be asked and there was order in all things both within the city walls and without. No need, then, to worry. Anxiety, there, would appear only as sporadic insanity, easily expelled either by outlawry or by worship. (For to worship the madman is at least to do *something* about him.)

If, on the other hand, the community ceases in the opinion of many to contain the universe within its rites, its folklore, its *mores* and institutions, then these 'answers' lose their potency,[1] their force as 'knowledge'; men will seek other answers and, perhaps, other associations either within the ancestral community or elsewhere. In the process we may hear such men demanding to be 'free'. Other kinds of demanding there may be; the connexion between 'knowing' and 'freedom' cannot be ignored.

The Milesians

'Inventors of ignorance' would be a good name for those who at different moments in our history have clearly shown their dissatisfaction with the communal view of the universe. In the sixth century before Christ a group of men born in the city of Miletus on the coast of Ionia turned their backs on ancient mythology and started inquiries[2] of a kind we now take for granted. Thales, Anaximander, Anaximenes, and their unknown friends are regarded as pioneers of European philosophy and science. Whether we regard them as 'knowing' or as 'not-knowing' (ignorant) depends on the point of view. In respect of the 'answers' about man's place in the universe or about the universe itself which were to be found in the myths of Babylon, Egypt, and

[1] The Aryan root of the word 'know' has, according to H. C. Wyld, the sense of 'mental potency' (*Universal English Dictionary*).

[2] Or what has been called 'thinking in the Greek way'. See J. Burnet, *Early Greek Philosophy*, 4th ed., hereafter referred to as *EGP* (A. & C. Black, 1948: 1st. ed. 1930), preface to 3rd ed.

the ancient Greeks themselves the Milesians[1] were not-knowing: they were uneasy about these answers; they were dissatisfied with them. As to the conclusions they reached, few modern scientists would give much for them as 'knowledge' in our terms. Yet they started *our* ways of thinking; they created new ways of coming to terms with the universe; those same ways of thinking in other times and among other men spelt revolution and talk of freedom. Their methods must, therefore, be important.

For modern, scientific man the phenomenal world is primarily an 'It'; for ancient — and also for primitive — man it is a 'Thou'.[2]

Thales took a long step to this end when he turned rule-of-thumb methods for measurement he found in Egypt into general rules. Mathematical methods and instruments, methods for weighing, measuring, numbering — these *objectify*. To objectify is, for the purpose in hand, to detach, to separate as far as possible from one's feeling-self, whatever it is one wishes to understand. Even the most intimate friend, the delight of one's life, would lose some of her wonder if whisked constantly from the scales to the measuring-rod and back again. To objectify is to treat as a 'thing' that which hitherto has been imperfectly separated from a felt unity. Such separating processes are fundamental to science; they are also an important part of the process by which men come to talk of themselves as 'free' or 'not free'.

Measures of all kinds ('rulers' in this sense included) once invented and accepted by more than the inventor himself can settle arguments and silently issue or adamantly support judgements impervious to all other human authority. You can *say* the

[1] The Milesians: see K. Freeman, *Ancilla to the Pre-Socratic Philosophers*, hereafter referred to as *AP* (Oxford, Blackwell, 1952; 1st ed. 1948). The fragments are in chs 11, 12, and 13. For comment, see K. Freeman, *Companion to the Pre-Socratic Philosophers*, 3rd ed., hereafter referred to as *CP* (Oxford, Blackwell, 1953; 1st ed. 1946), chs 11, 12, 13. See also Burnet, *EGP*, ch. i; Bertrand Russell, *A History of Western Philosophy*, hereafter referred to as *HWP* (Allen & Unwin, 1946), ch. ii; F. Copleston, *A History of Philosophy*, hereafter referred to as *CH* (Burns, Oates & Washbourne, vol. i 1946; revised ed., 1947), vol. i, chs ii, iii; T. Gomperz, *Greek Thinkers*, hereafter referred to as *GT* (John Murray, 1901–12), vol. i, bk i, introduction and ch. i; R. J. Forbes and E. J. Dijksterhuis, *A History of Science and Technology*, 2 vols (Penguin 1963), vol. i, chs i–iii; Becker and Barnes, *Social Thought from Lore to Science*, 3rd ed. (Dover, 1961), vol. i.

[2] Henri Frankfort and others, *Before Philosophy* (Penguin, 1949), ch. i, p. 12; originally published as *The Intellectual Adventure of Ancient Man* (Chicago, 1946).

scales are wrong, but to carry conviction you have to produce another instrument of the same kind. When Thales measured the pyramids, estimated the distance of ships at sea, possibly did something about the calendar, introduced the Greeks to the usefulness of Ursa Minor in navigation, and then generalized his methods, he put certain checks on all future *human* rulers. Henceforth men would be ruled by comprehensive, governing myths of the universe on one of two conditions: either the myth would have to measure up to the impersonal method, the non-human 'ruler', or they would have to be men ignorant of or indifferent to mathematics.

Thales, very probably, did not himself regard the universe as an 'it'.[1] He merely introduced objectifying methods in the pursuit of ends typical of our technology rather than of pure science. His *economic* motives were doubtless of the same kind as those which gave rise to written symbols among the priests of Sumer.[2] A special kind of relation between men and their universe appears in such work — an economic relation side by side with, when not supplanting, the family or 'I–Thou' relation sustained in the ancient myth. When men are thus given the means to *use* their habitat and, at the same time, their wants and several ambitions are no longer contained within a community-myth 'explaining' the universe to them, the way is open for the economic relation to become a demand for economic freedom, for the consumer-relation with the universe to reshape human relations.

The Pythagoreans

The 'inventors of ignorance', however, may give us a false impression of what Greek ways mean for freedom. Close to the time of Thales and not far from the Ionian shore Pythagoras gave another meaning to *philosophia* and another use to mathematics.

[1] It has been said that Thales called the universe (*cosmos*), the 'workmanship of God'. See Diogenes Laertius, *Lives of Eminent Philosophers*, trans. R. D. Hicks, 2 vols (Heinemann, Loeb Classical Library; Harvard University Press), i. i. 35. This work is referred to hereafter as *DL*. The saying ,'All things are full of gods', sometimes attributed to Thales, is doubtful both as to meaning and as to authorship — see Burnet, *EGP*, sec. xi. Freeman, *CP*, records the tradition that Thales was a pantheist 'seeing the life-force which he equated with the divine, in the Whole and in every part' .

[2] For the invention of writing see R. J. Forbes and E. J. Dijksterhuis, *A History of Science and Technology*, vol. i, p. 14.

Philosophy to the Pythagoreans was a way of life or, more precisely, a way of salvation. This and the formation of Pythagorean societies or 'brotherhoods' are of interest to us.

The Pythagorean way — of mathematic and music — owed a great deal to the religion of Orpheus: he whose

> lute was strung with poets' sinews
> Whose golden touch could soften steel and stones,
> Make tigers tame and huge leviathans
> Forsake unsounded deeps to dance on sands.[1]

From the Orphics and Pythagoras through such philosophers as Plato and Plotinus to the Christian theologians we can trace the notion of the *soul* (*psyche*) — an object of intelligent concern to priests and philosophers before it was taken over by professional soul-healers (psychiatrists) and soul-scientists (psychologists), a notion which, as we shall see, has added a great deal of complication to our ideas of freedom. For the soul becomes the man in a sense that the body (*soma*) is not; as such it is thought to be in danger both from the body's habitat and from ordinary society.

The Orphics feared the 'wheel of life' — endless reincarnations of the soul in other forms of plant and animal life. From this they sought freedom or salvation. As the Milesians objectified, separating the observer from his universe of objects by their mathematical methods, so the Orphics separated the soul from its menacing environs by music, by rites of cleansing and *ecstasy* — a 'standing-out' of the soul from the body and its habitat.

To similar ends Pythagoras devoted mathematics. Secret societies sworn to silence about the Master's teachings on pain of excommunication are presumed to have benefited from his way of life, though it is just as likely that this secrecy was a legend created later to explain the lack of written records. Transmigration of souls was hardly original to Pythagoras. We may take this as a belief with two principal facets: on the one hand a profound sense of kinship with other forms of life, and on the other a powerful, even a desperate bid to escape, to be free, to be separated. The Pythagorean way was an ascetic mode of life based on a system of

---

[1] *Two Gentlemen of Verona*, III. ii. On the Orphics see J. Harrison, *Prolegomena to the Study of Greek Religion* (New York, Meridian, 1955; 1st ed., C.U.P., 1903), ch. ix; Burnet, *EGP*, ch. ii; Freeman, *CP*, p. 73 ff.

taboos. Mathematician, scientist, he may have been, but by no means in the sense we mean today.

His system was meant fully to occupy the rational faculty, but not less to satisfy the non-rational faculties of the soul in a way that ordinary philosophical and logical ethics could not do.[1]

Numbers, their relationships and harmonies as the first principle of all reality, had a great deal to do with the Pythagorean way. Contemplation of number and the harmony of opposites led the soul to a higher life. In Pythagoras it is tempting to see *homo anxius* seeking an antidote to the pains to which the colder curiosity of such men as Thales exposed him, and an antidote at that which plainly dealt with the three worlds of man — the inner world of thought, the universe, and (through the Brotherhood) the world of human relations.

The mathematical methods of the ancients may 'liberate' men from the myth-making or the myth-made community; but if there is insight in Pythagoras it is his recognition that freedom begets new bondage. Each 'breaking free' brings awareness of other restraints. Separated on the one hand from the 'known' universe of the myth and on the other from the knowing community, the freedman, the inventor of ignorance, has no alternative but to remake his universe, to come to fresh terms with it and in doing so to reconstruct an association around him of like-minded men.

Since the sixteenth century of our era 'knowing' has exposed men to the consequences of freedom with increasing rigour. No understanding of our European and American social values is adequate without an appreciation of what it has meant since the Renaissance to *know*.

QUESTIONS FOR DISCUSSION

1. Would it be 'good' if we worried less about our place in the universe and our relations with each other? Read Aldous Huxley, *Brave New World* (Chatto & Windus; Vanguard Library, 1952), and then ask whether we seem to be making progress toward such an order.

[1] Freeman, *CP*, p. 81.

2. Has there been loss of freedom caused by progress in science? Read F. Hayek, *The Constitution of Liberty* (Routledge, 1960), ch. ii.

3. Read the quotation from Frankfort's *Before Philosophy* on p. 26. Is there any way of saying that the 'it' of modern science is 'more real' than the 'thou' of mythopœic thought?

2

Knowledge and the Church

'KNOWING is what learning does.' The end-product, 'knowledge', is to some extent shaped from the start by the process, 'learning'. If, then, our knowledge is our world-picture, our view of the universe, and if this in its turn determines how we live our lives and conduct our public relations, it will all be there in the ways of learning, the learning and knowing habits of the community, the civilization.

Knowledge in Europe since the Middle Ages has been dominated by conflict between several levels or kinds of human experience: art, poetry, religion, on the one hand, science, technology, on the other, and morals with politics somewhere in between. The least social philosophy can do is to recognize such levels of experience, for in such variety lies the condition of freedom, widely distributed and making itself felt both in human relations and in the need to 'make himself'[1] which each man confronts.

During this period different people have explained how they propose to 'come to terms with' their universe. We will review some of these explanations, the varieties of experience they represent, the methods of learning (if any), the knowledge they propose as their end, and what they have to teach us of freedom and the making of men in society.

Sacred texts
Mahmut Makal, Turkish teacher and author, describes the difficulties he faced as a modern, European-style Turkish teacher

[1] 'Neither heavenly nor earthly, neither mortal nor immortal have we created thee, so that thou mightest be free according to thy own will and honour, to be thy own creator and builder.' (Pico della Mirandola, *Oratio de Homine Dignitate*, 1486. A modern edition of Pico's works by E. Garin was published in Florence at intervals from 1942 onwards. Thomas More translated some of his letters and the biography. For further reading see P. Kilbre, *The Library of Pico della Mirandola*, New York, 1936.)

in a village where old ways still prevail. Here is his account of the
old Muslim village school:

The Hoja [teacher] was reciting at the top of his voice chapters of the
Koran which he knew by heart. He spelt out the words, one by one
and the children repeated them after him.[1]

The method is familiar. Not the Bible only and not only in our
Sunday-schools, but Latin texts, the dates of kings and battles,
arithmetical tables, verse, and other such material has been
handled in our schools by similar methods in the not-so-distant
past. We can hardly ask children still taught in this way to explain
themselves; they have no choice but to do as they are told. The
Hoja who knows his business might say something like this:
'Al Q'rān is sacred. To learn and repeat its holy language is
enough.'[2] Here is a magical view of the sacred texts which need
not detain us long. It has, however, something in common with
other, more sophisticated, explanations: the community (through
teacher and text) imposes a way of learning because it already
knows how to manage the universe and regulate its own affairs.
The universe or Allah has through his Prophet and the sacred
word provided a talisman. Nothing more is required of each new
generation but the acquisition of an elementary skill — making
the right sounds at the right time.

The *authority* of the community is 'referred back' to its own past
in the person of the Prophet (or some other such figures) and this
in its turn to the divine source of the inspiration unalterably fixed
in the text. It is assumed that no one could ask to go further than
that. We will call this, then, the way of divine authority and take
it as our starting point for other ways which may or may not
conflict with it.

The Church . . .

The sacred texts in our own Middle Ages and after were not
generally treated quite so crudely. On the other hand, their divine
authority was vouched for and insisted upon by men and
institutions often so much a part of the community that they

[1] *Bizim Köy (Our Village)* translated into English by Wyndham Deedes as *A Village
in Anatolia* (Vallentine, Mitchell, 1954).
[2] A. Guillaume, *Islam*, 2nd ed. (Penguin, 1956), ch. iii.

could not only claim to 'speak for' it, imposing their ways upon its learning, but could call upon all or a considerable part of its organized power to ensure obedience. This done, other 'ways of knowing' could be deployed within the community, though in their attempts to do so it may be argued that theologian-philosophers like Saint Thomas Aquinas were already preparing the way for radical changes and challenges to the authority of the Church.

Europe, then, *was* the Church in so far as the hierarchy could claim spiritual authority over all its peoples together with such implications for other kinds of authority they could successfully pursue. If we now suppose not a sacred text repeated parrot-fashion by helpless school-children, but a vast and growing mass of rules and propositions all turning for explanation, when challenged, to the authority of sacred persons who in their turn would doubtless appeal, if challenged, to the authority of sacred texts, we can see in what sense it was true, then, to say that the ways of learning presupposed what was to be 'known' and these together enclosed the church-community like a skin — a conceptual skin difficult, if not impossible, to break through.

The community 'knows best'. But the community was people. What was it that was 'known', that shaped the ways of learning and so satisfied the interest of men in their place, their hopes, their destiny, as to make of them to some significant degree one community, one Church?

. . . *creeds* . . .

Men knew where they stood in the universe, what they could expect, and how to come to terms with God and man. 'What is man?' 'What hopes have we?' 'How ought we to live together?' 'What is truth?' Questions of a kind the modern philosopher shudders at — perhaps not to be understood as questions at all in that sense — were answered even when they were not formulated and this may well be what most people then and now require: to be safe, free or unfree, beyond the need to inquire.

The bare presence among men of priests, sacred texts, and holy buildings was not enough. The knowledge (or confidence?) necessary to peace of mind and security had to be acquired. Or if you assume as some did that it was in some sense 'innate' it had to be realized and sustained against doubt, misgiving, fear, and pain. The rites of the Church, prayers, confession, and the counsel of the 'social servants' (as we called them) as well as such scripture as was known and could be quoted — all were *learning* and for the majority learning enough. It was the few who asked for more and in so doing upset the rest.

The knowledge the Church wrapped around the community, so to speak, was about the two concerns with which we began the last chapter: having to do with the universal environment and with human relations. The universe was *known* through the Creator and more particularly through His Incarnation — Jesus Christ — and the perpetuation of Christ in his 'body' — the Church. This was not, of course, the universe as the scientist would want to know it, as Copernicus, Kepler, Galileo, Newton, Darwin, Freud, and the rest would want to know it. But it was the universe as most people wanted to know it — the universe that tolerated man, decided his destiny, judged and determined his eternal fate. The well-known credal phrases say it all: 'I believe in God ... Maker of Heaven and Earth', '... who for us men and our salvation came down ...', and so on. With this knowledge, acquired by the methods such knowledge dictates, methods which determine that it shall be such knowledge they acquire, men can sleep safely in their beds, go about their business and even endure the 'slings and arrows of outrageous fortune' not only with fortitude but with hope.

Provided they keep the rules.

... and freedom

For in revealing Himself the Creator made known in human symbols, through human agents, and in modes acceptable to human understanding, that man's special place in the universe, so far from absolving him from its government, *obliged* him, as no other living thing could be obliged, to regulate his affairs in accordance with the divine will. Here was man's freedom. He could learn the divine will and obey it or knowingly disobey and fall into sin. There was no excuse for ignorance: the Church and its servants could instruct him as its sacraments could enable him to obey.

'Knowing is what learning does'; and if you learnt as you were required to learn within the Church you would know how to act. Morals public and private were subordinate parts of theology — the science of God. No need, then, for a separate social philosophy. Morals were and continued to be well down into our own time based upon theological axioms. Politics broke away sooner because the Church was never wholly successful in containing political power within its spiritual authority.[1]

Yet here, too, are conditions making for freedom — for political and moral freedom, for individuality and that awareness, often painful, of social space which these conditions bring. For the authority of the Church is ultimately derived from Heaven and it can appeal, therefore, directly to man's 'conscience', to his spiritual as distinct from his economic and political need. This teaches men to set themselves apart from their rulers and to question their temporal power let alone the authority of their laws over conscience. On the other hand, the conflict between kings and popes, priestly and secular authorities, prepared men long before the Reformation to divide, to set apart, to argue about relative rights, to debate legitimacy in governments and in these ways to separate themselves from their rulers, to feel free. The 'City of God' is not the 'City of Cecrops'[2] and men asked to live in both cities at once are inclined to set the one against the other as it suits them. 'One Church, one Faith, one Lord', but even so a variety of experiences and included in them a variety of possible allegiances, though not yet or not clearly a variety of ways of learning and knowing.

Faith

'Faith' is a name often given to the habits, beliefs, comforts, and assurances which, as knowledge, derived from the authority of the Church. The European conflict we spoke of at the beginning of this chapter is sometimes called a conflict of 'faith and reason' or

[1] For the history of the conflict between Church and State see G. H. Sabine, *A History of Political Theory*, 3rd ed., hereafter referred to as Sabine, *HPT* (Harrap, 1948; a paperback ed. is now available), part ii. For a more detailed study see R. W. and A. J. Carlyle, *A History of Medieval Political Theory in the West*, 6 vols (Blackwood, 1950), seriatim.

[2] *Civitas Dei*, the title of Saint Augustine's work, *Cecrops*, a legendary ancestor of the first king of the Athenians. Athens was sometimes called *Cecropia* after him. On Augustine see Sabine, *HPT*, ch. x.

'faith and science'. Of reason, science, and the conflict more later; what now, of faith?

Faith as a set of beliefs ('the faith' or sometimes 'my faith') is nothing less than the knowledge available if one 'learns the Scriptures' or sits down at the feet of priests and preachers. Where Renaissance believers thought that the Earth's central and immovable position in the universe was essential to such beliefs, the work of Copernicus and his successors presented itself as a menace. Similarly, in the nineteenth century, other believers regarded the theories of Darwin and Freud as contradictions of the sacred texts and therefore of beliefs derived from them. Far worse, as we shall see, the growing power and appeal of other ways of learning leading to other kinds of knowing seemed to many like an attack on the very foundations of the authoritative Scriptures and the authoritative Church inasmuch as these other ways did not lead to God but to propositions which cast doubt upon His reality.

When beliefs are challenged or doubts arise within the knowing-community, the community of faith, 'faith' itself takes on a new meaning: it comes to mean if not a way of learning in its own right a way of not-learning in the new and dangerous mode. 'Have faith!' may go even further and propose a special quality the manifestation of which is precisely this — that he who has faith either refuses other ways of learning or refuses to accept their conclusions, their knowledge.

Now where 'faith' means persistence with a certain line of inquiry, with a certain hypothesis or working idea in spite of contrary evidence, it plainly presupposes other methods, other ways of learning, and acts as their aid, their auxiliary. Auxiliary faith is of no interest to us at the moment, though it is a most important concept indeed in all kinds of learning. It is where faith is regarded on the one hand as a special, personal quality, and on the other as (in a sense) *authorizing* repudiation of the knowledge belonging to other ways of learning that we must move with some care. For faith in this sense must intend one of two things: either a community irrevocably shut off from other communities which accept other ways of learning, or else 'private knowledge' — and this may mean no more than a refusal to learn in any sense.

The Church of the Middle Ages cannot be said to have been a 'community of faith' in the sense we now mean. For while there were no communities formed by ways of learning not under its authority, such other ways as we are presently to review were to a large extent contained within the Church and even encouraged by it. Copernicus was a Canon of Frauenberg, his heliostatic theory anticipated to some extent by Francis of Meyronnes and Nicholas Oresme.[1] It was not the conclusions these men proposed that, during the Counter-Reformation, brought Galileo to the dock, but rather Galileo's use of the Copernican hypothesis to challenge the Church's authority as interpreter of the universe and the will of its God.

It is later on, and among the smaller Protestant sects in particular, that we find the sacred texts being used as the basis of a 'community of faith' quite explicitly opposed to other ways of learning, quite openly repudiating other kinds of knowing. The fundamentalist, for instance, who refuses to believe anything that is 'not in the Bible', can create, if others will follow him, a community in this sense. That in maintaining their position such people have to employ crude logic and their own personal judgement is a difficulty they often overlook.

That is not to say, of course, that the 'way of faith' in this sense — in the sense of rejecting other kinds of knowledge — is necessarily mistaken in what it proposes. We can hardly discuss this now but this much may be said: if the 'community of faith' is, in fact, defending kinds of knowing which it feels would be set aside by pursuing other ways of learning, then we have no good reason *not* to insist on the varieties of experience and the social and political freedom necessary to protect them.

We shall talk more later about faith in the sense of 'private knowledge'. As such it is hard to see how faith could ever get along with authority, though it may sometimes suit the interests of one or the other to seek each other's aid.

Authority

Authority is necessary to most kinds of learning though the nature of the authority may differ very much from the divine authority of the Church. Many have tried to build knowledge

---

[1] For these people see Copleston, *CH*, vol. III, ch. x. Copernicus was of course anticipated by Aristarchus of Samos in the third century B.C. and by the Pythagoreans, whose influence he admitted.

from the 'foundations' — Descartes, for instance, as we shall see.
Few have got far without using what others have said and even
taking it on trust. This is an appeal to the community — to the
dead as well as to the living. Copernicus, for example, started a
'revolution' but he drew heavily upon the thought of ancient
Hellas. Too much, some say — even his revolutionary system was
dependent upon methods of deduction he learnt from Aristotle.
Someone has spoken of Copernicus's 'almost hypnotic submission to authority' as his undoing, both as man and as scientist.[1]
Kepler said, 'Copernicus tried to interpret Ptolemy rather than
nature'.

Then came the years when authority counted for much less in
science than it had in the work of Copernicus. Today may it not
count, again, for *more*?

The scientific kind of knowledge needs specialists who master
fragments of a branch of a special science. Non-specialists must
take virtually the whole of what they are permitted to call learning
'on trust' somewhat as the faithful did, by and large, in the
churches of yesterday. True (though students may sometimes
cynically think otherwise), our texts are not sacred and are
constantly exposed to criticism and revision, but only by the few,
for only the few are competent and he who is an expert in his
allotment is a fool like the rest abroad. Does this make for 'variety
of experience'? Or does it intimidate, inhibiting interest in all but
the trivia which merit higher academic degrees and frustrating yet
further any persistent interest in the 'whole' universe, the 'whole'
man, the 'whole' society?

Suppose that the way of authority for reasons of economy and
educational mass-production becomes the typical way of learning
for the majority; we may then have to reckon with a rapid decline
in other ways, ways which in the past challenged authority and
modified it, kept it in check, with the further possibility that what
is true in this respect of our learning and knowing will also be true
of our human relations — our social and political life. The
condition of our freedom was variety and, with variety, choice;
and with choice, responsibility and its cares. If men do not like
freedom enough to put up with its responsibilities, they may

[1] A. Koestler, *The Sleepwalkers, A History of Man's Changing Vision of the Universe*
(Hutchinson, 1959), pp. 149 ff.

welcome the way of authority and forget, after a while, that there were other ways to come to terms with the universe and themselves.

QUESTIONS FOR DISCUSSION

1. Set out the arguments ordinarily used to say that the *Hoja*'s methods (p. 32) are (*a*) inferior, (*b*) bad. Compare the use of similar arguments about the teaching methods of the medieval Church.

2. 'Knowing is what learning does.' Compare 'knowing about' poetry with 'knowing about' mass, energy, etc.

3. Instead of saying 'Faith is . . .' and trying to give a definition in that way, make a list of the kinds of attitude, knowledge, etc., which are called 'faith'. On this method of definition read K. Popper, *The Open Society and its Enemies* (Routledge, 1952), ch. xi, sect. 2.

4. How much learning have we taken 'on authority' (*a*) in school, (*b*) in higher education? Does this matter? If so, why? Read B. Russell, *Authority and the Individual* (New York, Simon & Schuster, 1949); W. P. Montague, *The Ways of Knowing* (Allen & Unwin, 1925), ch. i.

3

Private Knowledge

CAN there be private knowledge? Pythagoras, according to one story,[1] is supposed to have sworn his disciples to secrecy and Copernicus to have followed his example. If by 'private knowledge' was meant special knowledge claimed by a group as its own, with barriers to communication, there would be no lack of examples. The ancient Gnostic sects on the one hand, not-so-ancient Freemasons on the other make such claims.

Then there is another possibility: is there a sense in which the knowledge peculiar to particular sciences and branches of sciences is rapidly becoming exclusive to their specialists? To some extent necessarily so, inasmuch as the symbols, the formulas, whole systems of hypotheses or theories which constitute such special knowledge require, as was said in the last chapter, *all* the time and intellectual application of their experts, and since only a few men can so dedicate themselves to any one science, only a few will, to this extent, understand.

If, moreover, experts of this order begin to say (as some have said they are saying[2]) that their 'knowledge' is only of the formulas, the mathematical patterns, and so forth, and expressly *not* of an objective universe common to us all, then 'private knowledge' in this sense together with the authoritative methods for teaching what can be taught to the majority may have far-reaching significance for the community.

[1] Said by some to have been invented later in order to explain the lack of written records. See Freeman, *CP*, pp. 74 ff., and compare with Burnet, *EGP*, p. 92. Burnet says Pythagoras preferred the oral method of teaching. On the secrecy of Copernicus see Koestler, *The Sleepwalkers*, pp. 149 ff.

[2] K. Popper, *Three Views Concerning Human Knowledge*, in *Contemporary British Philosophy*, 3rd series (Allen & Unwin, 1956). On this matter see also Chapter 5, below.

So far we have taken the social character of learning for granted: we have, at least, given pride of place to authoritative learning. More, the main theme of these first chapters will be the conventional presuppositions of most learning and the implications of these for a free society. Therefore we ought now to ask what may be intended by 'private knowledge' apart from esoteric claims by small groups or the possible developments of specialism in the sciences.

Who has not at some time said: 'I *know* this for myself. I can't explain, but I know it . . .'? Then there is what was called in the last chapter 'private faith' — a rare challenge to sacred authority as we shall recall. Even 'professionals' like René Descartes have attached great importance to 'intuition' and though Descartes's philosophy can hardly be called 'private knowledge', the place he gives to intuition in it was, from one point of view, its most revolutionary element. Are such private experiences delusions? Verbal deficiencies? Ought they to be deprived of the title 'knowledge'? If so, upon what grounds? Who is entitled to pass such a law?

The privacy of knowing

Is all knowledge private? The question belongs to a field of study we can do no more than introduce.[1] The problem must at least be appreciated. No man can be said to *know* anything until *he* knows it: that is, until what is said to be 'known' is in some way under his skin, part of him. The crude, magical view of sacred texts we attributed to the Hoja in the last chapter is objected to by pedagogics (the science of teaching) on the ground that by mouthing unintelligible words in a foreign language the children *learn* nothing. Nothing goes in to *them*. The least we would require if we were to support such practices as the repetition of otherwise meaningless 'mumbo-jumbo' is that the one who uses them should 'have faith' in such words — that in this sense at least the 'magic' should call forth a response.

On another and very different view of teaching the argument is that the teacher should strive not to put information or ideas 'into' the learner but rather use such devices as he can to 'bring it all out'.

[1] Epistemology. For an introduction to this field see, for example, A. J. Ayer, *The Problem of Knowledge* (Penguin, 1956); C. E. M. Joad, *A Guide to Philosophy* (Gollancz, 1936), part i; D. J. B. Hawkins, *Crucial Problems of Modern Philosophy* (Sheed & Ward, 1957), part i; and in Russell, *HWP*, the chapters on Locke, Berkeley, and Hume.

We have already called this the *evocative* alternative to the authoritative way of learning. Socrates was supposed to have been a master of it. Rousseau's Émile was meant to learn in this way. The evocative way of learning, however, is not necessarily a way to 'private' knowledge; on the contrary, a teacher may use this method with every intention of putting a child's 'private' thoughts into 'public' language and may only feel she has done her teaching well when this has been accomplished. After all, with examinations in view, private experience must be presumed to be publishable — or (on this criterion) worthless.

But to return to the informative ways of learning. We agreed that nothing is learnt until it has been 'put in' to the learner and is in this sense 'his'. The difficulty then, from the theorist's point of view, is that we can no longer talk with any certainty about the 'same' idea or the 'same' fact being in the textbook, the teacher's exposition, and, finally, in the 'mind' of the student. The mind, so far as we know, does not learn by making photostat copies of the objects studied; we are more inclined to the view that mental life differs from person to person. Each epidermis is the frontier of a 'territory' within which, perhaps, the language of the community is not spoken or at any rate is subject to dialectical changes which make significant differences to the reception 'social' knowledge gets once it has crossed the frontier.

Note what is happening: on this line of reasoning before we know where we are we have passed from the question 'Is there private knowledge?' to a doubt whether there is any other knowledge, any that is *not* private. Nor is this merely a parlour-game for idle philosophers. For though we talk easily of knowledge as 'stored up' in libraries, on tapes, in films, this is only a figure of speech. There is no knowledge apart from knowing persons. Imagine what our warehouses of information, our encyclopedias, archives, and the rest would 'mean' either if the planet were evacuated or if the facility for reading and understanding perished with the nations who produced them. We may talk if we will of *potential* or *available* knowledge and while the means for communication, discussion, research, and the sharing of ideas persist this makes sense, but it makes sense because at a given time and under specific conditions some one person may come to *know* what is available and so render the otherwise meaningless symbols concrete and actual. Knowing is what learning does. If there is no appropriate method and procedure called 'learning', then even to talk of potential knowledge is meaningless.

To this extent, and in this sense, *all* knowledge is 'private' and it is worth while making the point as a corrective to overmuch loose talk about the 'community' as if there were here a collective armed with 'all the knowledge there is' independently of individuals and so authorized by virtue of this communal knowledge to impose 'its' will upon individuals.

The senses

To go on from this, however, and argue that therefore there is no such thing as knowledge of the universe is to jump out of the collective frying-pan into the individualistic fire. And that is what philosophers were on their way to doing before the newly emerging sciences in the seventeenth and eighteenth centuries restored public confidence in public knowledge.

When Descartes[1] set out 'to accept nothing as true which I did not clearly recognize to be so', he started a habit of thinking about knowing which had consequences he, doubtless, would not have approved. John Locke[2] faced the problem of showing how we have knowledge of other things than sense and the operations of our own mind. Since the mind of a new-born infant is a blank (with no innate ideas), since the only contact he has with things outside himself is through his senses, can he be said to know anything but his own sensations? Locke did not answer this question very satisfactorily but he said we have *intuitive* knowledge of our own existence (as Descartes had said) and *demonstrative* knowledge of God (a way of learning considered below).

Bishop Berkeley[3] followed Locke, but made his theory of knowledge into a statement about the nature of the universe. He

[1] René Descartes (1596–1650). See his *Discourse on Method*, trans. Haldane and Ross (Dover, 1955), part ii. See also Russell, *HWP*, bk iii, ch. ix.

[2] John Locke (1632–1704), *An Essay Concerning Human Understanding*, hereafter referred to as Locke, *Essay* (Dent, Everyman's Library, no. 984, 1947). Locke's purpose was 'to inquire into the original, certainty and extent of human knowledge, together with the grounds and degrees of belief' (*Essay*, bk i, ch. i). See also Russell, *HWP*, bk iii, ch. xiii.

[3] George Berkeley (1685–1753), *The Principles of Human Knowledge* (Thomas Nelson, 1945); *A New Theory of Vision*, and other philosophical writings (Dent, Everyman's, 1910); *Three Dialogues between Hylas and Philonous in Opposition to Sceptics and Atheists* (Everyman's). See also Russell, *HWP*, bk iii, ch. xvi.

wrote at a time when Newtonian theories seemed to threaten faith by giving a picture of the 'real' world which was different from that which the Church gave. Berkeley replied with a theory of knowledge proving that we do not see 'matter' but only qualities and that as these are qualities of the senses we 'know' nothing of any world apart from our own sensations. But he went further: there *is* no matter; all reality is mental. There is no existence apart from perception and the whole reality depends upon the perceiving Creator who, by implication, is the only possible source of a knowledge other than that of our own sensations.

David Hume, who carried all this to its logical conclusion, was, like his predecessors, an 'empiricist': that is, he held that all we call knowledge is derived from experience and not from ideas, which are independent of experience. Where Locke and Berkeley intentionally or not encouraged the view that all knowledge is private, Hume, by following their arguments in the same direction, left us with no possibility of knowledge. The 'self', for instance, was nothing but a bundle of different perceptions and therefore not a subject for knowledge. 'Causation', belief used as a basis for prediction, has no logical necessity. So-called causal relations are nothing but impressions arising from the habitual association of certain sensations following each other in close connexion.

The epidermis may be a frontier; all knowledge may have, in some sense, to be private; but it seems that if you attempt to explain knowledge solely from this private (and empirical) point of view you end up with no knowledge left to explain. The wholly private self (as the sociologists would all too readily agree) is no self at all and therefore can have no knowledge. Before taking this further let us go back to René Descartes and his intuition. For what we undertook to do in these chapters was to make a man's own account of what he meant by 'learning' our constant point of reference.

Cartesian doubt

Descartes belongs to the time of Galileo, and he would doubtless have supported the Copernican revolution publicly but for the condemnation of Galileo. The experiment in private knowledge we are about to describe is itself a revolution only to be fully appreciated if we recall what was said earlier about the authoritarian society into which he was born. Copernicus was a revolutionary largely because he 'kept company with' ancient Greek scientists; but the Cartesian revolution came out of a truly solitary experience—a deliberate experiment in 'private knowledge'.

'The simple resolve to strip [himself] of all opinions and beliefs formerly received . . .'[1] came to Descartes when he reflected that there was very often less perfection in works 'carried out by the hands of various masters' than in those done by one man alone, and, by analogy, that a man would himself be a better product had he been guided by his own reason from birth instead of being at the mercy of 'our appetites' and 'our teachers'.

. . . how very different the self-same man, identical in mind and spirit, may become, according as he is brought up from childhood among the French or Germans, or has passed his whole life amongst Chinese or cannibals.[2]

The first step in rebuilding his own intellectual house was 'to accept nothing as true which I did not clearly recognize to be so'; for this he used the method of doubt. He used it until he met something sure. Having rejected all the evidence of his senses and the content of his memory as doubtful, he came at last to this bedrock:

I am, I exist, is necessarily true each time that I pronounce it, or that I mentally conceive it.[3]

This final certainty he reached by *intuition*:

the conception which an unclouded and attentive mind gives so readily and distinctly that we are wholly freed from doubt.[4]

Cogito, ergo sum: I think, therefore I am.

---

[1] Descartes, *Discourse on Method*, part ii.   [2] Ibid.

[3] Descartes, *Meditations on First Philosophy*, ii.

[4] Descartes, *Rules for the Direction of the Mind*, iii. For a criticism of Descartes the beginner may turn to Copleston, *CH*, vol. iv, or to the relevant chapters in Russell, *HWP*, or to A. K. Rogers, *A Student's History of Philosophy*, 3rd ed. (New York, Macmillan, 1932), pp. 236 ff.

'Certainty' is one difficulty in Descarte's concept of knowledge. 'Clarity', too, can mislead as a test for private judgement. The clearest idea may be erroneous. Then there is the *non sequitur* in the *cogito*. It ought to have read 'thinking — therefore — thinking'. Again, 'existence' is neither a quality nor a relation; it cannot be the subject of 'proof'. It is a noun which can be replaced by a translation of the sentence which dispenses with the need for proofs. For example, 'God exists' does not mean 'There is an entity, "God", which among other qualities has that of existence'; but rather 'there are qualities *a, b, c*, etc., and we call them "God"'. But see also D. J. B. Hawkins, *Crucial Problems of Modern Philosophy* (Sheed & Ward, 1957), ch. i, sec. 3.

This is the rock. This is the foundation. Now Descartes, demolition complete, can begin to build again.

The way of learning is clear. Clear, too, to us at least is this: what is to be known (Descartes's existence as the subject of thought) is assumed already in the way of learning. That is, *thought* is to be known, and doubting is a kind of thinking. The private knowledge which rewards Descartes is not quite so interesting as the experiment in doubt itself. For Descartes thinks that he is able once he has 'proved' his own existence to restore the principal beliefs held in his time by 'custom and example'.[1] We might say that what Descartes got for his pains was satisfaction that the ideas he had taken from public knowledge were tenable now in some sense not true before — as part of him: they are now Cartesian knowledge and not simply European, Jesuitical, scholastic, or whatever they may have seemed before.

Unimpressed as we may be by the end-product, knowledge, the proclamation of such a method, such a way of learning, ought to impress us. What a *liberty* he took! This man who, good Catholic that he was, suppressed his support for the Copernican theory when he heard that Galileo was condemned, turns faith upside down and rejects authority by making the belief in God depend upon a demonstration of his, Descartes's, existence. The Earth may, through Copernicus, have lost its central position but this blow to man's pride is softened by the Cartesian experiment. True, he takes care to point out that such activities are not for every man; but once one man has shown that the individual intellect can systematically doubt all that the community believes and then by its own unaided efforts make all such belief rest solely upon the individual's belief in himself, a venture on behalf of the race has been made from which there can be no easy drawing back.

Descartes has demonstrated that men of a certain sort can question God and the community. He has also suggested that no beliefs are worth calling 'knowledge' unless they have first been subjected to some such personal scrutiny. Finally, he has put all into doubt and uncertainty save one thing — the existence of the thinking individual so long as he is thinking.

[1] *Discourse*, ii. On the connexion between Descartes and 'Formalism' in sociology see D. Martindale, *The Nature and Types of Sociological Theory* (Routledge, 1961), pp. 215 ff.

Poetry

'For us the winds do blow,'[1] wrote a Christian poet and, getting on for a century after Copernicus's death, he added, 'The earth resteth, heav'n moveth, fountains flow ...' Poetry comes closest to what many people mean by 'private knowledge' but we have first to ask whether Herbert's declaration ought to be called 'private faith' — that is, deliberate repudiation of the Copernican world-picture. The Professor of Astronomy in Padua who refused to look through Galileo's telescope also deliberately repudiated Galileo's way of learning, but one would hesitate to call this private faith: he was, after all, acting as he thought himself obliged to act as a servant of the Church. George Herbert, too, was a servant of the Church, but a poem is not the place where one would ordinarily look for an official attitude. It is reasonable to assume that the author intends knowledge of another kind and therefore learning of a different sort from that which led Copernicus, Galileo, and others to their conclusions.

One way of getting round the difficulty is to 'rewrite' what a poet says on such a matter. For instance, we could say that what Herbert *meant* was, 'The earth is Man's home and the whole universe has been made by God to provide for him'; and there is nothing in Copernicus to gainsay *that*. True. And there is nothing in *that* (the rewriting) to resemble Herbert's poem. This 'rewriting' or 'interpretation'[2] is a common device for the removal of the discomfort caused by friction between different levels of experience and it ought always to be suspect for the same reason — the 'rewriting' puts the private experience (whatever its logical status) into public language and in so doing deprives the original of its distinction.

'Truth', 'falsity', and other ways of grading or evaluating experience (including the attempt to say what is and what is not 'knowledge') are not now before us, except that we want to resist any attempt to dogmatize about knowing. And to say that the utterance of any private experience only has 'meaning' or knowledge-value if and when it is 'translated' into the language of other ways of learning, other levels of experience, *is* to dogmatize.

[1] George Herbert, 1593–1633.
[2] Compare what is said here with B. Russell, *Human Knowledge its Scope and Limits* (New York, Simon & Schuster, 1948) part i, ch. 1.

Poetry, on the other hand (and Herbert's is not necessarily the best example), together with other arts, is public evidence of private knowledge. What are we to say, then, when in the language of poetry the conclusions of other ways of learning are not merely ignored but flatly contradicted? Certainly not that in private knowledge 'everything goes', for that would leave us with no distinctions between delusion, self-deception, and genuine knowledge. We can also admit that 'flat contradiction' in one generation can undergo considerable change in another. Are 'rest' and 'motion', for instance, anything like the exclusive terms they once seemed? Or who would say today that Berkeley's denial of matter was a 'flat contradiction' of conclusions in nuclear physics?

The claim to private knowledge, whether by poets, seers, or schizoids, is on the one hand a declaration of independence and on the other a challenge to the community to look to its tests, its criteria, if it would prevent their turning into repressive instruments, endangering the varieties of experience.

Mysticism

Mystics might be described as people who lay claim to private knowledge of 'reality', whether or not they call reality 'God'. The mystic, it has been said, 'lives at different levels of experience from other people: and this . . . means . . . he sees a different world . . .'.[1] Such people are to be found among all races and religions and their presence *within* the Church of the Middle Ages warns us against exaggerating the believer's submission to authority. The mystic might come into conflict with the rules, but not necessarily so. After the Reformation, however, and outside the Roman Catholic Church, claims to private knowledge of God such as might conceivably be called 'mystical' proliferate and we may regard them in several ways. For example, we might see the claim of ordinary men to come to terms with God by themselves and apart from any authority as an illustration of the increasing individualism of those times. We must surely allow that such claims, however they come about, add new depths to the idea of human freedom.

[1] E. Underhill, *Mysticism, A Study in the Nature and Development of Man's Spiritual Consciousness* (1st ed., 1910; Meridian, 1955), pp. 75 ff.

Hesitation is called for, however, when we try to relate such private knowledge to distinctive types of human relations.

... if each individual's destiny hangs on a private transaction between himself and his Maker, what room is left for human intervention?[1]

What room indeed! Yet for a season men who enjoyed the 'direct relation' with God through religious conversion showed a passion for 'fellowship' and formed vigorous new associations — 'knowing-communities' — of those who had enjoyed or who hoped to enjoy the private knowledge of God. The Methodist movement in England during the eighteenth century is an outstanding example. The Methodist entered his new association through an intensely personal 'experience of God'.

> And can it be that *I* should gain
> An interest in *my* Saviour's blood?[2]

sang the delighted convert, but he sang it, more often than not, in one of the groups to which the methodical John Wesley directed him. Private knowledge of this sort was soon socialized as the personal experience began through contact with the society. On the other hand, the movement soon divided against itself and lost its drive as it lost its power to recreate the private experience in new generations.

It may be that mysticism has a great deal to teach us about all 'private knowledge'. The mystic who is deemed by ecclesiastical or theological authority a 'heretic' may nevertheless, with or without martyrdom, provide through his private knowledge a useful criticism of the religious community's rules and beliefs. On the other hand, the religious movement which is founded on private knowledge of the mystical kind may in time cut off the mystic from his sources by failing to provide him with an adequate *rule*, a reliable community. So with all private knowledge. We hesitate, indeed, to speak of 'learning' unless intuition, private knowledge, or whatever we call it is hedged about with rules and

---

[1] R. H. Tawney, *Religion and the Rise of Capitalism*, the Holland Memorial Lectures for 1922 (Pelican, 1938), p. 229. Elsewhere the same writer warns us against hastiness in relating such knowledge to distinctive types of social relations; see the same work, pp. 92 ff. See further, M. Weber, *The Protestant Ethic and the Spirit of Capitalism*, trans. Talcott Parsons (New York, 1952).
[2] One of Charles Wesley's hymns in *The Methodist Hymn Book*, no. 371.

can lead to reliable beliefs. Thales confronted the ancient myths with devices for measurement; Descartes turned from intuition to what he called 'mathematic'; Copernicus relies too much on old authorities, but Galileo experiments, sites his telescope and bids the professor look and see. Even art after the romantic mood of rebellion against 'form' and rule has a way of creating new forms, new rules, though these may be seen and understood as such by the very few. We turn then to the ways of learning which decide what shall be known or what shall be called 'knowledge' with due regard for rule and reliability.

QUESTIONS FOR DISCUSSION

1. What does the scientist know *about*? In attempting an answer compare a 'physical' with a 'social' science and read K. Popper, *Three Views Concerning Human Knowledge*, in *Contemporary British Philosophy*, 3rd series (Allen & Unwin, 1956); A. J. Ayer, *Problem of Knowledge* (Penguin, 1956), ch. iii.

2. Examine the Cartesian 'experiment'. Should you try it? Read Descartes, *Discourse on Method*, part ii, first. Discuss the importance of such words as 'certain', 'clear', 'probable', to his aims.

4

Tools and Language

FREEDOM is never a sinecure. To be *sine cura* is to be without the 'cure' — or care — of souls. Private knowledge may free a man from authority, but if he has still to come to terms both with nature and with society he has still to care for his 'soul' and his knowledge will not do if it falsifies nature and fails to win the consent of those with whom he has to live. That is not to say that every dreamer, every mystic, is 'wrong' or that the common sense which regards them with suspicion is 'right'. Here is the problem: how can we relate the need to act to our various levels of experience without indecision on the one hand, precipitate, blind activism on the other?

Action — centuries of it — came before speculation and reflection. Primordial man crouching in his forest clearing seized a flint to attack his foe long before he shaped a tool, much, much longer before, in the leisure of city life, he could afford to talk about tools. Grunts and squeals graduated through centuries of modifications into a primitive language long, long before grammarians and logicians surveyed these instruments of communication and discovered the order, the principles of order in them. Free of his world the primitive may have been; but no more than any other animal could he afford to sit scratching himself beneath a tree weighing alternatives, indulging in a formal disputation about truth and goodness. He could not afford to. He was not able to. He was not that kind of man, yet. This was not his kind of freedom. Only cities would build walls high enough to give some enough respite for this kind of freedom; only in cities would men make words enough to speculate.

c

Tools as teachers

Tools and language were ways of 'learning' long before men *conceived* of either as such. To some extent they are such still for each new generation long before a child is aware — if indeed he ever becomes aware — of what is done to him through these techniques.

Man became man through tools.[1]

Made the tools, that is, and in so doing 'made' himself. To watch a hemiplegic using tools in order to assist the recovery of his brain is enough to modify any extreme views we may have held about the status of tools as mere 'instruments'. The naïve view that we make things in order to advance by clear and irreversible stages our 'mastery' of nature ought now to be untenable. Our new tools may no longer modify biological structure; it can hardly be denied that, for instance, the internal-combustion engine, not to say the computer, introduced far-reaching modifications in every other aspect of human life.

So far from bringing us simple mastery of our environment there is something to be said for the view that tools increase our exposure to the universe. For in harnessing our human skills to stone, iron, wood, then steam, electricity, nuclear energy, we *involve* ourselves and our posterity far beyond our ability to predict the consequences of such involvement at the time we engineer it. If, then, it is reasonable to say that early speculation came upon the scene far too late to influence the very tool-making processes which prepared the way for it, we may well feel inclined to say that thought today about the ends and purposes of our advanced technology must always emerge 'too late' — when the critical decisions have already been taken without consultation, and without much foresight.

This would not be the same as saying that our values were *determined* by our techniques, however, though it might seem to come to the same in the end. We need only conclude that we have not yet devised ways and means of evaluating and directing the

---

[1] E. Fischer, *The Necessity of Art: A Marxist Approach*, trans. A. Bostock (Penguin, 1963), p. 15; first published as *Von der Notwendigkeit der Kunst* (Dresden, 1959).

results of our learning commensurate with the ways of learning themselves. On the other hand, a recent and terrifying instance of technological precipitancy — the nuclear bomb — gives us, paradoxically perhaps, some reason to believe that co-operation can still divert such disasters and so give men time to cope with the unpremeditated results of their freedom. This is another way of saying that there may still be some reason to attempt the containment of technology within a social philosophy.

On the other hand, some make claims for technology which can only be sustained if we accept without questions values which they have built into their claims without regard for the distinction between decision-making, moral judgement, and the science of tools.

... all races and nations, in their ardent espousal of technologically directed industry appear to be awaiting a common signal to slough off most of their outmoded ideological differences — encumbrances inherited from an uncomprehending past — and assume instead a unanimity of outlook and purpose that will be totally new in the world, and no doubt as revolutionary as it will be new.[1]

We quote this as evidence that still, today, tools and technology may provide a way of learning which, in common with others, has its own values and attracts its own community with a threat to other kinds of community, other sorts of learning, where there is no basis of agreement between the different levels upon which men may come to terms with the universe.

Language and logic

Descartes, hacking away at all his teachers and other contemporaries had taught him, was a typical 'inventor of ignorance', a free man falling upon the conceptual fabric of his society in pursuit of private certainties. Resolute as he was, however, to doubt his own senses, alone as he was, meditating in isolation from other men's opinions, *language* (like the wooden horse Epeios

[1] R. W. King, 'Technology and Social Progress', in the *Political Science Quarterly* (Columbia, March 1963), vol. lxxxi, no. 1. The author was for years an engineer with the American Telephone and Telegraph Co. and with Bell Laboratories. Note (*a*) the pseudo-empirical statement 'all nations . . . appear'; (*b*) the 'loaded' words: 'slough off', 'outmoded', 'encumbrances', 'uncomprehending', 'ardent'; (*c*) the value assumptions: unanimity, newness; (*d*) the typical modernistic prejudice.

made for the invasion of Troy) could no more be left outside the room than could the Doubter's own skin.

'Cogito, ergo sum',[1] he said at the moment of ultimate certainty. No special language,[2] this, of the kind some logicians hanker after; not indeed Descartes' mother-tongue, but Latin — the formal language in which Europe did so much of its thinking and talking about religion, science, philosophy, and law.

Our language can be seen as an ancient city: a maze of little streets and squares, of old and new houses, and of houses with additions from various periods; and this surrounded by a multitude of new boroughs with straight, regular streets and uniform houses.

. . . to imagine a language means to imagine a form of life.[3]

We live in our languages rather as ancient or primitive man lived in the language of myth. Compare the language of love and logarithms, poetry, politics, polo, and the apostolic succession. In the language-city a man may enjoy numerous ways of life but, as Wittgenstein said, the time comes for building new suburbs the *plans* for which are, in a sense, a criticism of the ancient city-centre which has been 'there' from time immemorial.

Aristotle's logic was a kind of new suburb: a critical attempt to redevelop the ancient city of speech. The dialogues of Plato often show us men wrestling with the old language in attempts to solve the problems it created. 'What *is* "Justice"?' 'What *is* "Good"?' and we would say they were defeated from the start by language-habits — the habit, for instance, of assuming that every name meant a *thing* in the same sense as 'table' and 'chair' can be said to mean the things you would point to in explaining them to a child or a foreigner.

Nevertheless, Aristotle systematized the forms reasoned discourse could take and this was like planning a new suburb within the city boundaries. More than that, these logical forms

---

[1] In the Latin sentence there is no verbal sign for 'I' separated from the verb form 'to think', or the verb 'to be'. *Cogito* and *sum*, on the contrary, assume the agent unless a special effort is made, when using them, to do otherwise.

[2] For special languages see the work of Russell and Whitehead in mathematical logic. See also P. F. Strawson, *Introduction to Logical Theory* (Methuen, 1952; paperback ed. used here, 1963).

[3] L. Wittgenstein, *Philosophical Investigations*, trans. G. E. M. Anscombe (Oxford, Blackwell, 1953), pp. 18, 19.

were such because they were applicable to discourse in other languages than Greek. Take a commonplace of Aristotelian logic, that principle of the syllogism which says, 'a term distributed in the conclusion must also be distributed in the appropriate premiss'. Suppose I say, 'all foreigners are nasty men' and, challenged, give as the ground for my conclusion, 'X is a foreigner' with it being understood that 'X is a nasty man': my argument now takes the *form* of a syllogism:

> X is a nasty man;
> X is a foreigner;
> ∴ All foreigners are nasty men.

By the principle we have quoted, however, the conclusion is now shown to be invalid for syllogistic reasoning in any language because 'foreigner', in the conclusion and by the addition of the word 'all', is distributed (used to the whole extent of its denotation), whereas in the premiss (as shown by the word 'a') it is not.

There is no need, then, to produce examples of charming foreigners in order to refute my argument; there is no need for empirical methods. On the other hand, we might today, still without reference to 'examples', arrive at the same refutation by discussing the function of such a word as 'foreigner'. We might say, for instance, that this is the name for a class of men who are put in the same class for one reason only — their not-being-of-our-political-community. But X's nastiness may be a quality attributable to men irrespective of their nationality and therefore not relevant to the status 'foreigner'. By such an analysis, however, we do little more than confirm the value of Aristotle's forms for this kind of discussion, showing how such 'ways of learning' do indeed free men somewhat from the limitations of their own language, making community of discourse possible and putting some restriction on the wilder excesses of private judgement.

Formal logic, however, lives 'within the city' in the sense that its rules may be followed, as we saw, without need of observation and therefore without adding anything to our knowledge of the world apart from the structure of language and the logical forms of reasoned discourse. Saint Thomas Aquinas was able to marry Aristotelian logic to Catholic theology. The Schoolmen could be experts in disputation. Faith and logic had no quarrel so long as the faithful remained content with what faith had to say about the universe.

For the rules of the logic demanded only that the conclusion of an argument should follow from the premisses. That is not to say that the logic was a *mere* convention in the sense that any other rules would do for reasoned discourse. Men would not have followed for so long rules unsatisfactory to their common sense nor, for that matter, would they have been able to respect a logic which plainly had 'nothing to do with' reality. It was because the logic worked in some sense by removing baffling obstacles to discourse that it was acceptable — and still is, within limits. Besides, by means of the logic you could put irrational authority out of countenance if you chose. Men were liberated by their logic and we can still have the same experience; but at the same time, then as now, this is possible only by putting argument under rule — human rule — deriving its authority from what seems reasonable.

Mathematics

Mathematics resembled formal logic by demonstrating the validity of a theorem deduced from an axiom but the validity of the axiom itself was another matter. Axioms in mathematics like the major premises in a logical form might be statements about the universe but they might have to be taken on trust, attributed to intuition, or traced to revelation by faith or the authority of Church or sacred text.

Yet mathematics differed from formal logic in its 'distance' so to speak from the centre of the language, in being virtually a language in its own right, and one designed, at that, not for *all* the ends of that organic life we call 'society', but primarily for measurement, weight, quantification, the fractioning of 'wholes' rather than for their classification (as in logic) or their creation and enjoyment (as in the arts).

Pythagoras, it is true, found number in music or music in number. He left later Greek philosophy not with the measuring rod so much as the 'notion of the perfectly tuned string'.[1] 'I have admired the mystical way of Pythagoras and the secret magic of numbers,' said Sir Thomas Browne,[2] 'pleading', it has been said,

---

[1] See Burnet, *EGP*, p. 112.   [2] (1605–82), *Religio Medici*, part i, sec. 12.

'for religion in an age which was beginning to be dominated by science'.[1] The 'mystery' of numbers, however, is no more obvious than the facility with which mathematical methods can dissolve mystery for those inclined that way.

If logic was a well-planned suburb of the ancient language-city, mathematics was more like a new town and the beauty of it was that once men fulfilled the immigration requirements they were free to go where the streets led without bothering very much about the old city or the outside world. Descartes was a good mathematician as well as a good Catholic. His respect for the Church prompted him to suppress support for the Copernican hypothesis when Galileo was condemned. His mathematics gave him some private independence of the theological and scholastic authorities as well as a readiness to accept Copernicus. Neither mathematics nor theology, however, could decide whether or not to make his views public — only Descartes could decide; he showed his freedom *and* its cares in the choice he had to make.

Aims of learning

Before philosophy, before science, in their collective freedom men strung their mental fences and drove in their stakes with artless poetry — the myth — 'a dramatic conception of nature which sees everywhere a strife between divine and demoniac, cosmic and chaotic powers'.[2]

Man . . . arranged his life, or at least the life of the society to which he belonged, in such a manner that a harmony with nature, a co-ordination of natural and social forces, gave added impetus to his undertakings and increased his chances for success.[3]

With freedom, order; or with freedom the necessity for order. And when the science of ancient Hellas seemed to threaten the ancient order — Aristarchus, for instance, threatening the 'hearth' of the Stoic universe — science itself withers away and we hear little of it until our own era.

Are we to presume identical aims in modern ways of learning? 'Harmony with nature', 'co-ordination of natural and social

[1] B. Willey, *Seventeenth Century Background* (1st ed. 1934; New York, Doubleday, Anchor, 1955), ch. 3.
[2] Attributed to Wensinck by Frankfort in *Before Philosophy* (see above, p.26), p. 34
[3] Ibid., p. 35.

forces' — are these the purposes of ancient and modern learning, the criteria of 'success'? Nothing so simple, in our view. To make all our learning serve a common, simple end or purpose we would have to over-simplify to such an extent that a great deal of what is most important would be left out or underrated. The aim of these chapters is rather to illustrate the varieties of experience and the problems they pose for social philosophy — the problems, we may call them, of freedom.

QUESTIONS FOR DISCUSSION

1. Discuss the quotation on p. 53. Read E. Gellner, *Thought and Change* (Weidenfeld & Nicolson, 1964), and especially what the writer has to say about the Industrial Revolution as philosophy. Go back to the quotation on p. 53 and note the value words. Is the writer justified in using them as he does?

2. 'To imagine a language means to imagine a form of life' (L. Wittgenstein). How much of formal education consists of acquiring a language and to what extent is this at the same time a 'form of life'? See also the use of language in 'moral education' in Huxley, op. cit., ch. ii, etc. ('hypnopaedia').

5

Science and Freedom

By inventing ignorance men took advantage of nature 'with her back turned' and freed themselves from ancient myth and its authorities. They could not free themselves of language, nor, indeed, of the habits acquired from long centuries of tool-making and tool-using. What would such 'freedom' mean, anyway, but the disintegration of man as he had made himself? Nor were their methods of learning — logic, mathematics — made only for the destruction of old beliefs. They could help in construction and, some would say, in containing men within new beliefs, so, on this argument, reducing their freedom.

What, then, of our classical and modern science? Is not every fresh discovery bound to limit us at least in our freedom to make what we will of the universe? Men, after all, are 'of' nature, and their slow, spasmodic progress in knowledge could be seen as the universe winning an inevitable victory over fancy, so bringing to an end man's freedom under the stars. Man as Europe has known him since Thales would (on this view) be coming to the end of his days. The hours of his many-sidedness at large in a habitat where poet and seer were the equal of the mathematician and the logician are numbered. Even as the 'revolt of the masses' swamps differences of culture and taste, so must the science of the few through the education of the many deprive the visionary of his privilege — that of being alone with *his* world.

There is little doubt that many in recent centuries have looked upon certain scientific discoveries as drastic attacks on their freedom. In this chapter we shall recall such discoveries (or three typical examples), but suggest that in each case the decision to treat them in this way has been freely taken and not forced upon men by some 'necessity' of the ways of learning.

The mechanical universe

> Nature and Nature's laws lay hid in night.
> God said, 'Let Newton be!' and all was light.

Newtonian physics, paradigm of the new scientific knowledge, did not strike everyone in that way. In *Principia* Newton brought together rational proof and experimental–observational evidence, and from the three laws of motion (Kepler's) and the law of gravitation explained the movement of the solar system by the ways of mathematical deduction. The ways of knowing had been fused for the purpose of putting a mechanical universe in place of medieval picture of a divine concourse in the heavens.

In a discourse given thirty years after Newton's death Rousseau[1] pictured the sciences flinging 'garlands of flowers over the chains which' weigh men down. The sciences and the arts alike 'stifle in men's breasts that sense of original liberty for which they seem to have been born'. Here is an historian of science describing the effect of Newton's theories on the scientist's contemporaries:

The world that people had thought themselves living in — a world rich with colour and sound ... speaking everywhere of purposive harmony and creative ideals — was crowded now into minute corners in the brains of scattered organic beings.[2]

Bishop George Berkeley's is, however, the most remarkable contemporary response to Newtonian theories.[3] Natural philosophy (as science was called) made mankind, he said, 'appear ignorant and low' by declaring that men were blind to the 'true and real nature of things'. Berkeley denied the existence of 'matter' — which the Newtonians, on the contrary, took for granted. The 'great mechanical principle' of attraction signified nothing, Berkeley held, 'besides the effect itself'. What could science legitimately claim to do?

... by a diligent observation of the phaenomena within our view, we may discover the general laws of nature, and from them deduce the other phaenomena, I do not say *demonstrate*; for all deductions of that

---

[1] *A Discourse on the Moral Effects of the Arts and Sciences* (1750). Note: Newton was born in 1643 and he died in 1727.

[2] E. A. Burtt, *The Metaphysical Foundations of Modern Science* quoted by B. Willey, *The Seventeenth Century Background* p. 20.

[3] See above, p. 43 . See A. A. Luce, *Berkeley's Immaterialism* (Nelson, 194.5)

kind, depend on a supposition that the Author of nature always operates uniformly, and in a constant observance of those rules we take for principles . . . which we cannot evidently know.[1]

Berkeley protests against any claim by the Newtonians to know the *real* world and therefore to describe or explain it. The scientist, like other men, knows only the phenomena — the immediate objects of perception — and his theories are no more and no less than instruments for handling these. This was the view Andreas Ossiander set out in the preface to Copernicus's work *On the Revolution of the Heavenly Spheres*; it was the view Bellarmine urged Galileo to take of the Copernican *hypothesis*.

Berkeley complained that the Newtonians mistrusted the senses, whereas all their theories could do was to describe sensory experience.

The term 'attraction' describes the phenomena, the fall of the stone, the flow of the tide, the cohesion of bodies, etc., but does not indicate *how* each is done, nor explain it, nor name the cause.[2]

Some say that it is Berkeley, not the Newtonians or Galileo, who comes closer to what modern physicists think of their science. This view, sometimes called 'Instrumentalism',[3] would mean that the physicist admits to knowing (or caring?) nothing about a 'real' world. Yet if at the same time his ways of 'handling the phenomena' are virtually unintelligible to other men it is difficult to see how he can make 'sense' of our world for us or explain his in ways which would make it ours.

Berkeley was concerned to protect the faith and morality of the Christian from the damage he thought would be done to both if the authority of the Church as the only source of real knowledge was undermined. He certainly shows us that men need not be driven by the theories of the day into headlong abandonment of their own constructions. But then it may be that 'coming to terms with reality' is not and never has been the business of science. Whatever 'reality' could seem to mean within the myth the invention of ignorance, the distribution of freedom is also a

---

[1] *Principles of Human Knowledge* (see above, p. 43 n. 3), 101, 103.

[2] Ibid., 107. On 'deducing phenomena' from 'laws of nature' see S. Toulmin, *The Philosophy of Science* (Hutchinson, 1953; reference here to Arrow Books, ed., 1962), pp. 90 ff., but especially pp. 92 f., and what he calls the Lockean theory 'that laws of nature are principles of necessitation'.   [3] See above, p. 40 n. 2.

distribution of responsibility for decision about what is or what is not the 'real' world.

Darwin and the 'life-order'

To the question, 'What is man . . . ?'[1] the ancient poet replied, 'but little lower than God . . .' and this seemed privilege enough whatever its implications for freedom. When Charles Darwin set sail on the *Beagle*[2] in December 1831, however, he was at the start of a journey which was to end in another kind of answer to the psalmist's question — an answer given twenty-eight years later in the *Origin of Species by Means of Natural Selection*. 'What is man?' 'A descendant of other forms of life, not a great deal higher than the man-like apes.'

Modern physics not only observes and describes regularities in nature, it seeks to explain them by discovering the *form* of the regularity;[3] that is why physics has a special language and seems to construct a special world. The record of Darwin's observations in the *Naturalist's Voyage Round the World*, on the other hand, leaves us in no doubt that this is *our* world, though few of us observe it as carefully as he observed it.

I have steadily endeavoured [said Darwin] to keep my mind free so as to give up any hypothesis, however much beloved (and I cannot resist forming one on every subject) as soon as facts are shown opposed to it.[4]

Without this love of hypotheses, of course, Darwin's descriptions would scarcely have amounted to more science than, say, Gilbert White's observations around his home in Hampshire, England. The giving up of hypotheses requires an effort and it may be that it is this which distinguishes scientific inspiration from the private knowledge of the mystic or the poet.

Here, certainly, was a way of knowing which most men could understand and which seemed to belong to their world — too much so. For Darwin's theory of evolution seemed to some a harsh attack on human dignity, though others used it as a basis for social action.

[1] Psalm viii.

[2] See *A Naturalist's Voyage round the World* (Murray, 1882; 1st ed. 1845).

[3] On the difference between physics and natural history see S. Toulmin, *The Philosophy of Science* (above, p. 61), ii. 6, ii. 7 f.

[4] From Charles Darwin's *Life and Letters*.

Man may be excused for feeling some pride at having risen, though not through his own exertions, to the very summit of the organic scale.[1]

'Risen', he says. Anaximander of Miletus also had an evolutionary hypothesis but he does not use such a word.

Man was like another animal, namely a fish in the beginning.[2]

But Darwin had to reckon with a concept of human nature by contrast with which (despite the Fall of man) his view of the life-order would look like a fall indeed. Observation and description of 'phenomena' are an activity apart from man's self-assessment, his concept of his own dignity. Darwin had created a situation by his theories comparable to one in which a Victorian gentleman would feel himself if at the height of his social success it was made public knowledge that his parents were not noble but, on the contrary, nameless paupers. Darwin's is a *levelling* view; it deprives man (apparently) of privilege in the life-order as the Copernican view had deprived his home of a privileged position in the cosmic order.

Yet Darwin himself did not take this view. Why not take pride in having come so far from such humble beginnings? Men were, it seems, free to choose the conclusions they based upon Darwin's biological theories. So where, for instance, Hobbes, Hume, Helvetius, Holbach, and others had tried to bring human relations under the same laws as those of the 'mechanical universe', the Social Darwinists interpreted the theory of evolution in terms of social action.[3] Progressives and optimists, activists and reformers drew strength from Darwinism just as others felt depressed, cast down, cut off from whole ranges of possibility which — for them — had depended upon an estimate of man now seemingly discredited.

Natural selection, Darwin himself concluded, was of little relevance to civilized man because he has developed distinctive qualities and so delivered himself both from the governance and from the protection of this law of nature. Or, as we might put it, he has made himself in some measure responsible for his own destiny.[4]

[1] *The Descent of Man*, 2nd ed. (John Murray, 1885), part i, ch. 21.

[2] Anaximander: see Burnet, *EGP*, p. 70, and references in Freeman, *AP* and *CP*.

[3] On Social Darwinism see D. Martindale, *The Nature and Types of Sociological Theory*, pp. 162 ff., 174, and 187. See also below, chapter 11, pp. 120 ff.

[4] *The Descent of Man*, part i, ch. 5.

Freud and mental health

The work of Sigmund Freud has been described as a 'further infliction of an outrage on human self-love'. Freud, unlike Darwin or Newton, was personally committed from the start of his investigations to the ends of *healing*. The word 'healing' today has a sanctity among the social services it did not have a century ago; this is a matter to which we shall return.[1]

In other respects Freud's work resembles that of the naturalist: he observes where others merely see; he creates hypotheses to explain what he sees. On the other hand, he is interested inevitably in the kind of people who go to others for help with their mental functions — people whose behaviour we might describe as 'abnormal'. Freud and his followers, in fact, extend the category 'abnormal' to include a great deal of the behaviour the layman would not otherwise have placed in the healer's province.

For Freud's best-known hypotheses had to do with 'such stuff as dreams are made on', with introspective account of what a patient might think was happening in her mental life, with concepts such as the 'ego', the 'unconscious', the 'Oedipus complex', to say nothing of the 'death wish' and the all pervading 'libido' — all of which must have seemed as appropriate to everyday mental experience as the characters in Bunyan's *Pilgrim's Progress* to a normal day about town. Freud's attempts to explain mental 'sickness' led him to make new pictures of the mental life, to invent a language, and in due course to provide answers to questions such as the plain man had never thought to ask.

All this was seen to be an attack on human dignity and (by many) on human freedom. Where Darwin had admitted that man possessed superior qualities — of intellect on the one hand, sociality on the other — Freud seemed to many to be undermining the first of these and denigrating the second.

Imagine a Victorian English gentleman, a man of 'quality', at home in a fine, spacious, well-appointed house where he entertains all the 'best' people, men of wit, women of grace and elegance, the choicest offspring of a civilization at its height. Then in a nightmare he is alone in one of the topmost attics — used by his humblest

[1] M. Birnbach, *Neo-Freudian Social Philosophy* (Oxford, 1962). For an introduction to this subject see J. A. C. Brown, *Freud and the Post-Freudians* (Penguin, 1961), chs. i and ii.

servants — in the dark except for one flickering candle, burning low. Below him in the darkened house are all the riff-raff of London's underworld, thieves and prostitutes; while in the cellars, to judge by the stench, must be not his finely bred domestic animals but inmates of the local zoo together, it seems, with raving lunatics.

Some such change in the concept of human nature seemed to have been caused by Freud's theories as most men understood them. A man was a prisoner in his own mind-house and not, as he once imagined, its enlightened master.

The unconscious [Freud wrote] is the larger circle which includes the smaller circle of the conscious.

The unconscious is the true psychic reality; in its inner nature it is just as much unknown to us as the reality of the external world, and it is just as imperfectly communicated to us by the data of consciousness as is the external world by the reports of our sense-organs.[1]

When Freud explores the unconscious, moreover, he finds little to encourage the moral idealist's exalted picture of human possibilities.

As for human art, morals, law, religion, all the accumulation of habits and tastes upon which Western men prided themselves, Freud at one point traced the lot back to a sinister incident in pre-history: a sex riot in the primal horde leading to the murder of the father-leader by his sons and their own incestuous enjoyment of his women the beginning of race guilt. Hence the 'Oedipus complex' and hence, too, its effects — man's most cherished cultural achievements.[2] We would be a lot worse off without our civilized habits and conventions, but if we judge them by their origins they are not much to be proud of.

Yet Freud 'from the very outset . . . considered mental health and individual freedom as well-nigh identical'.[3] He looked upon mental health as 'liberation' and, so says the same authority, tried to build within the individual 'freedom and strength against the impact of this world'.[4] We shall have to ask later whether this

[1] *The Interpretation of Dreams*, quoted from *The Basic Writings of Sigmund Freud*, hereafter referred to as 'Freud, *BW*' (Random House, Modern Library, 1938), p. 542.
[2] *Totem and Taboo*, Freud, *BW*, p. 917. See also Freud's *Civilization and its Discontents*.
[3] G. Zilboorg, *Sigmund Freud* (Scribner's, 1951), pp. 26 f.   [4] Ibid.

identification of 'mental health' and 'individual freedom' was an advantage — for freedom — or whether, on the contrary, the grave doubt it cast on human responsibility, the increased dependence it called for upon the 'healer', are not much more significant. Another healer once said, 'They that are whole need no physician';[1] but part of the Freudian revolution was the eradication of the hitherto clear distinction between the healthy and the neurotic.[2] The dividing line betwen 'normal' and 'abnormal' was no longer a 'cliff' but a 'slope'.[3]

If a choice, then, has to be made among all the varieties of activity we have come to call 'science' of one which has pointed more directly than another toward the reduction of human freedom, we would ourselves be inclined to choose the work of Sigmund Freud or at least the inferences many have drawn from it, whether the Master would have supported them or no. For this reason, when we come to discuss the social values, we shall spend some time considering mental health and its implications for our thinking about responsibility.

For our notions of what we *might* be, to say nothing of what we *ought* to be, whether as persons or as a community, cannot be decided by a scientist's account of what we *are* or have been. That is not to say we cannot use (for instance) an account of the origin of species, an anatomy of the unconscious, to support or lend conviction to our efforts at personal or social construction. We very often do just that. Nor is it to deny that our interest in becoming must be informed by our scientific accounts of what is the case. An 'ideal' for human conduct which ignores what the science of man has to say is bad not because it is an ideal, not because it will not 'work', but because it is dishonest — it fails to face the facts before it attempts to change or modify them.

But that is not to say that there is an account of 'the facts' such that once we have it and accept it all decisions are ended, all responsibility for choice obsolete. No account of what 'is', however faithful, can deliver us from concern for what might and ought to be.

[1] Matthew, ix. 12.
[2] M. Birnbach, *Neo-Freudian Social Philosophy*, p. 7.
[3] H. D. Lasswell, quoted by Birnbach, ibid. Freud himself spoke of 'liberation' from 'neurotic symptoms, inhibitions, and abnormalities of character' (a mixed bag). See *Collected Papers*, vol. v, paper xxx.

To understand what we are at in a book of this kind it may help now to distinguish between the language and viewpoint on the one hand of the *observer* and on the other of the *participant*. As scientists we usually make every effort to talk and behave like observers. What we do experimentally is to protect our observers' role against unwitting participation in what is going on around us. What we say — in hypotheses and theories — is observers' talk, so far as we can make it so.

'Look!' we say, 'This is what we see . . .'

> Three blind mice, See how they run . . .
> They all run after the farmer's wife,
> She cut off their tails with the carving knife . . .

And there, as scientists, we stop: it is not our business to make such wondering exclamations as

> Did ever you see such a thing in your life . . .

But plainly the scientist would be at a loss without the mice, the farmer's wife, her carving knife, and above all their activity and hers. Somebody, mice or men, has to do something if there is to be a science of man and most of us, most of the time, are participants. We have to *do* things, and to do this rather than that. We have to become somewhat — and become this rather than that. In the sense that we give pride of place to the problems not of description and explanation but of participation we, in this book, are not being observers. We are taking part: whether running blindly like mice or tail-chopping or some more exalted part we leave to others to say in their role of observer.

QUESTIONS FOR DISCUSSION

1. Discuss the quotation from Charles Darwin's writings on p. 63, contrasting the 'pride' Darwin feels with the pessimism and humiliation his theories caused some people. Was Darwin in order when he spoke of the 'very summit of the organic scale'?

2. 'The unconscious is the true psychic reality.' (Freud, *Interpretation of Dreams*, quoted on p. 65 above.) Criticize the words 'true' and 'reality'. What are (*a*) the optimistic, (*b*) the pessimistic possibilities in this statement?

6

Meaning

WE men are meaning-makers. When people ask whether the universe (or 'life') 'means' anything they are asking one of two questions. First, can we men make a meaning out of the universe? Can we, that is, systematize events into a whole, find some worthwhile purpose in the system for creatures like ourselves, discover some end apart from aimless and unending change? Second, quite apart from what men may think or do, has the universe declared its interest either in men or in some ends or purposes of which men may or may not be a part? Philosophy in all its activities has to do with answering the first of these two questions and as such it has to respect all knowledge, for all learning is meaning-making and, while the separated conclusions of different disciplines may fail to satisfy, philosophy hopes to bring these together and make some meaning of the whole.

The second question, then, is not strictly our business. If the question is about what the universe has had to say for itself apart from human reasoning and inquiry, all we will say here is that we see no contradiction between the faith that the universe is meaningful in this sense and our own view of men as the meaning-makers. Christians say that man is made 'in the image of God' and that the Creator made men 'for himself'. Take these two statements in turn. Take the first to mean at least that men are *of* their universe (a proposition which all the ways of learning we have been reviewing would support) — 'of' it, that is, just as other animals as well as the so-called 'inanimate' is of it; and then add such qualities as Darwin, for instance, agreed took men beyond the range of natural selection — intellect, language, sociality, technical skill — and postulate that these are 'in the image of God'. Then let us say that these special qualities can be seen fulfilled in all those activities we now call 'meaning-making' — learning and the social regulation of learning — and are we not, in view of the second statement, bound to say that this must be so if indeed the Creator purposed a society He could enjoy? Men experiencing are in a sense the universe knowing itself. Men knowing, choosing, deciding, men free and therefore responsible, are in microcosm what the believer thinks of as the universe in large in the person of its Creator. Could a Creator so conceived have 'fellowship' with men who were anything less than what we have called 'meaning-makers'?

'Free of the universe', so to speak, for the duration of their history men might conceivably be seen as intended 'from their end' to become responsible for good and evil in such manner as to fit themselves for the divine community. By such arguments those who choose could draw out the lines of a free, responsible society into the fascinating no man's land of metaphysics. But we are concerned only with 'meaning' in human society.

Is meaning 'found'?

Even so do we not want to say we *find* meaning? From Thales to Einstein and beyond are men *looking for* those regularities in nature, those relations between the apparently unrelated which we call their meaning? An analogy from the philosophy of law may help in answering this question.[1] Some writers on jurisprudence say that the essence of law is that it is imposed on society by a sovereign will. Others oppose this and say that law develops within society. On the first view the law is handed *down* by a superior authority; on the second, it grows *up* and has itself authority over those who administer it. On this second view we talk about *finding* law; on the first about *making* it. But surely both views are possible, even necessary, in understanding law. Certainly it seems that there could be no point in talking of what is 'found' from a study of customs as 'law' unless this subsequently *was* imposed by authority. Let us say this is logically necessary to the concept of law and that the other view, the 'finding' of law, may have a political, or sociological necessity.

This, then, is the view we are taking of meaning: whatever it is

[1] For this analogy see C. K. Allen, *Law in the Making*, 6th ed. (O.U.P., 1958), introduction.

we look for and find in nature assumes the status of meaning only because it has not only been found but has been found by recognized methods, fitted into authorized schemes, rendered intelligible by one or more of a number of conventions: in short, brought under the régime of man's reason. If no more than this is allowed, it is enough.

'To make', in any case, does not mean to 'create out of nothing' (whatever that *could* 'mean'), any more than to 'make law' intends the creation of regulation without recourse to previous custom, habit, institution. We, the meaning-makers, make our meanings out of and within the universe, being ourselves its offspring.

Meaning and language

Problems of meaning may often be resolved into problems of language and tackled in that way. No doubt a dictionary and a universal translator could together solve a number of issues between people and even clear up some major social problems. There is excellent reason for the prominence which has been given lately to the study of language, but not, we think, sufficient reason to expect such a study to solve all problems — unless, that is, we agree to drop all problems which dictionaries, translators, and the methods of semantics and linguistic analysis will not solve. Some people might be prepared to do this. If, for instance, you want to make a place for yourself in academic philosophy, you would be well advised to root out some teasing problem of language and fix your undivided attention upon it, for that way lies a short-term objective, and the possibility of making some positive (if minute) contribution to scholarship of sufficient elegance and finesse to merit distinction. Once, however, you allow your imagination to be caught by what we called just now the problems of participation, such academic achievements may prove less satisfying and the relation between language and meaning not nearly so neat and precise.

Language, nevertheless, has the power not only to amaze and bemuse but to construct a world of its own — a residential suburb, so to speak, sealed against the noise and confusion of the ancient metropolis where its residents can pass their days persuaded that what they do and what they are has value though they have, in truth, less and less communication with the outside world. For as we said earlier there are many languages and some danger that the philosopher (like other men) may do no more than make one for himself even when he supposes he is busily and usefully engaged in analysing the language of others.

Sounds uttered, their symbols printed, do not make language; neither do words singly or in groups have meaning except in *use*, which is why the philosopher of language must constantly listen and avoid mistaking his professional usages or even anecdotes from classical literature for what users of the living language mean in a wide variety of situations. Meaning other than in the formal dictionary sense of definitions is not a quality of words but primarily of persons — of persons recognizing, affirming, wishing, commanding, thinking, feeling, choosing, judging, enjoying, and so on.

So wide is the variety of experience and the possibilities of 'meaning' that there may in the end be only one safe generalization we can make: that it is *never* safe to dogmatize about meaning or more particularly to say of any utterance or any experience: 'It is meaningless', unless you add, 'to me' or 'to us'.

Take a commonplace location — Charing Cross, in London. Here are four things said which have 'something to do with' it.

> The memorial of the Queen Eleanor Cross, which was destroyed by the Puritans, was erected in 1863 in the yard of Charing Cross Station.
>
> (A guide-book)

> London, Charing Cross, dep. 7.10 (detached from 7.10 from Charing Cross).
>
> (A railway time-table)

> And when so sad thou canst not sadder,
> Cry! And upon thy so sore loss
> Shall shine the traffic of Jacob's ladder
> Pitched betwixt Heaven and Charing Cross.
>
> (A poet: Francis Thompson)

ANGLOPHIL: Mmmmmm!
FRANCOPHIL: Ugh!

> (*Two travellers, returning*)

Oddly, the last of these would have most chance of being understood by someone who spoke no English. Newcomers to such
matters may reflect on the variety of meaning these utterances
represent.[1] To call any one 'meaningless' would be to deny the
reality of its level of experience. To appreciate the meaning one
has to imagine the situation and in doing this, for sure, one needs
to imagine more than the squalid precincts of the railway terminus.
On the other hand, if we wish to 'grade' these utterances in some
way, it would be better to do so by such criteria as 'true', 'useful',
'correct', 'beautiful', or their opposites. For 'meaningless'
presumes far more than any of us is able say of others' statements,
except relatively.

Meaning and 'wholes'

Meaning is a value we accord to *relations* whether as felt,
cognized, ordered, constructed, wished for, or merely imagined.
Or else it is a value attached to a person, a thing, a concept in
virtue of the part it has in a relation. Various kinds of relation are
isolated for special study by the different sciences and arts. It has
become customary for learned people to deal with relations rather
as a central post office handles mail — sorting them out into the
pigeon-holes or baskets appropriate to the various disciplines.
Tempting, then, to treat as 'dead letters' or 'embarrassing packages'
alleged relations not easy to classify. Yet not only is it improper to
reject as 'meaningless' what the academic world cannot classify;
there is a sense in which classification itself robs a relation of
meaning or changes it so that, to the academic, it does not mean
what it means to others. Some inkling of this came our way when
we were talking about the ways of learning: it is a point important
enough to look at again now.

Take a man in his sickness; consider first what part his ill health
might play in all the intricate patterns of his normal activities and

---

[1] Note that not one of the examples is properly or wholly descriptive. The first
relates a specific object (*a*) to the (alleged) past time when it was put there, (*b*) to a
still more remote date, another object, and a whole range of alleged experiences
leading to its destruction. The second looks like a description but is more like a
warning, a prophecy, a prediction. The third comes closer to 'private knowledge'.
Does it 'mean' what it 'says'? (The answer depends partly on what you think it says.)
Was he talking 'about' Charing Cross? (In answering do you not have to enter his
'community of meaning'?) What were the travellers talking 'about'?

throughout the network of his human relations. Now observe the 'same' condition as it is handled from Reception at the hospital entrance through the various 'units' which examine him, the wards where he receives treatment and so on until, if he is lucky, he leaves the hospital 'well' at the end. Which of the many experts to whose pigeon-hole the 'case' or some part of it is passed is even *expected* to understand the experience the sick man brought with him? Professionally, perhaps, only some medical social worker is under any obligation to approach it, though the hospital chaplain might be and (with luck) some nurse or even some physician may have both time and ability to 'understand what it *means*' to the patient.

Or take the relation called 'love' between parents and children and tot up all those who may consider themselves in one way or another qualified to 'handle' such a relation. Then consider what will be 'handled', say, by a child psychiatrist, an 'in-law', an ambitious politician, a local government officer, a teacher, to say nothing of a parson, a philosopher, a poet, a biologist, a psychologist, a sociologist, a leader-writer for the highbrow press, a television interviewer, or a film-script writer.

All such *atomizing* of meaning is essential to our (scientific) ways of learning: this is part of what was meant by saying 'knowing is what learning does' — there is some reason to suspect that what we 'know' by such process, and again what *we* know (in any given department) may have to disperse the original human experience, squeeze out its meaning, before what has been 'learnt' has any meaning at all to individuals. This is reason enough for philosophers to retain methods which, whatever they may lack in efficiency and precision, have the virtue of staying close to *whole* meanings and, perhaps, mediating between them and the findings of special sciences. If, on the contrary, we turn ourselves, as philosophers, into specialists in special meanings with a language of our own to play with, the only hope for the individual will be with the poets and the music-makers and they, left to themselves, have a temptation to *romanticize* — that is, to abstract feeling from other ways of learning and so aggravate the problem. 'I feel you have a feeling which I feel you feel as well...' is all very well, but a little limiting, perhaps, as a basis for extending understanding.

Dimensions of meaning

The meaning of an experience (and therefore of its expression verbally or otherwise) can be 'measured' on two dimensions — the number of persons who understand or share the meaning of the relation and the range of the meaningful experience itself. 'Measurement' in this figurative sense is not to be taken as 'evaluation'. 'Meaning' itself is a value: this is involved in saying we make meaning — that is, our 'finding' of regularities in nature is a bestowal of significance or worth just as much as a lyric beginning 'All you mean to me' is putting a 'price' on the head (at least) of the lady addressed. But we can talk of 'meaning more' and 'meaning less' and here our two dimensions are of help.

In this book we shall talk frequently of the attempt to 'extend agreement' about social values and this is the same as saying that we wish to increase the number of persons to whom 'freedom', 'responsibility', and the like will *mean* what these words mean to us — the prospect of certain kinds of human relation and the social institutions which sustain them. Compare this with, say, an attempt to extend the meaning of the relations recognized in Einstein's special theory of relativity. On the one hand the physicist *could* not extend it except among people understanding the appropriate language; on the other hand the 'meanings' involved would probably not seem of great urgency beyond a small circle. By contrast, the relation between alcohol, the efficiency of the cortex, and road-safety provoked in Great Britain, during 1964, an expensive and desperate attempt to 'extend the meaning' of this relation to all motorists intending to use the highways during the Christmas season. Even so, the Safety Campaign, if successful, would extend only part of the meaning this relation has to chemists and other scientists.

As social philosophers we run the risk either of increasing the numbers of those who give approving nods at such words as 'democracy' or 'freedom' without sharing the meaning these words have for us or else of retiring into an exclusive club, a restricted 'community of meaning', an association of those who enjoy each other's company too much to run the risk of being misunderstood by the Great Outside. We choose to take the first of these risks, though not without hedging our bets: if so many more people today are training to be 'social servants' and if, moreover, they are doing so only after completing an academic education, it should be possible to increase the number of those who share — more or less — the philosopher's meaning while preventing him (and themselves) by their practical commitments from retreating to a larger, but still exclusive, retirement behind the opaque walls of a special language.

Is meaning like jam? The further you spread it the thinner it gets? 'Private knowledge', we said, could be lost through the attempt to put it into public language, and there is possibly more danger of this today than ever before in the West. Nothing 'means' anything if it is not understood by everybody. Popularize or perish. Speak not, except in the jargon of the group, and if you have had a new thought, forget it or dress it up in old-fashioned clothes. Now that it is possible to take any individual experience and break it down into meanings, into relations dealt with by the right departments, any man who tries to hold on to what has happened to him or what he has done as if it were unique runs the risk of being treated not as a knave but, worse, far worse, as a fool. Thus Dostoevsky:

I say, gentlemen, hadn't we better kick over the whole show and scatter rationalism to the winds, simply to send these logarithms to the devil, and to enable us to live once more at our own, sweet, foolish will.[1]

The philosophy which has no time for that mood has come to critical conclusions about social values. Social engineers who aim rather to eliminate such moods than to provide for them may be more to be feared than old-time destroyers like Attila or Genghis Khan. Our only hope is little better than despair: that such engineers will provoke a rebellion which will make the worst of both worlds — theirs and Dostoevsky's.

If, on the other hand, we agreed to do no social philosophy rather than risk the kind of over-rationalizing Dostoevsky was on about, then again we would have come to critical conclusions about social values. We would be saying, in effect, that there is no way of holding the ring between private experience and public good. We would be saying that since all attempts to give value to

[1] F. Dostoevsky, *Notes from Underground* (1st ed., 1864), in W. Kaufmann, *Existentialism from Dostoevsky to Sartre* (Meridian, 1956), part i.

community end in depriving experience of its personal meaning we must leave the ordering of community to those powerful enough to impose their own personal experience upon the structure of human relations. This is a critical decision about social values. It is not new. It was reached centuries ago by the conclusion 'might is right', which is only another way of expressing defeat — intellectual, moral defeat. We can accomplish this defeat either by converting all private knowledge into public language or by giving up the attempt to find some common ground between community and private knowledge — by retiring, for instance, to enjoy our own insights with no further attempt to create a community of meaning. To go on doing social philosophy is to go on insisting that neither of these alternatives is satisfactory.

QUESTIONS FOR DISCUSSION

1. Is it possible to lay down rules for 'meaning'? If so, what are their limitations? Read the passage from Dostoevsky's *Notes from Underground*, from which the quotation on p. 75 is taken.

2.   'That is not it at all,
      That is not what I meant, at all.'

      'It is impossible to say just what I mean.'

      T. S. Eliot: *The Love Song of J. Alfred Prufrock*

Of what kinds of experience are we likely to reach a similar conclusion?

7

Is Knowledge 'Good'?

In April 1633 the Holy Office in Rome brought to trial one Galileo Galilei who had, among other offences, followed 'the position of Copernicus', 'contrary to the true sense and authority of Holy Scripture'.[1] If men were free, corporately, to make their own pictures of the universe, they were also free to preserve them from attack. Or at least to try. The *regulation* of experience — by Church or State or some other powerful group on the one hand, by rules which may be independent of authority on the other — is what we have now to consider with respect to social values. Social science classifies regularities such as *mores*, customs, laws, habits, fashions, in much the same way as the physical sciences describe regularities in (non-social) nature. We aim to take part in regulation by discussing the *value* of experiences and at the same time the justification for various kinds of regulation. This requires us to go back, for the moment, to the 'meaning of meaning'.

An experience may have meaning only within a given 'field' explored or even created by the man who enjoys it. Quite apart from 'private knowledge' many people have successfully made over for their own enjoyment available 'fields' within which experiences can have a meaning they would not otherwise have. The scholar does this. He may begin the study of Greek drama (for example) only as a means to an honours degree, but with time his studies may become an end in themselves. They may bring years of satisfaction and give to other experience a meaning it would otherwise lack. All this irrespective of the usefulness of such studies — they may be of no help to the national economy

[1] The sentence on Galileo is given in full in translation by A. Koestler, *The Sleepwalkers*, pp. 602 f.

and may keep the scholar a poor man. At the same time if he tries to explain the relations he has discovered, the meaning his work has created, his explanations may fail, his meanings seem meaningless to others.

This helps us to understand two different kinds of regulation we try to impose on experience: regulation in terms of usefulness and regulation intrinsic to the experience itself such as that we signify by 'truth' or 'beauty'. 'Is this study useful?' 'Will it do any good apart from the enjoyment it gives the student?' These are applications of what we can call the 'utility regulator'. 'Truth' is another matter. In any given field of study (for example) there may be rules which have nothing directly to do with the usefulness of that study as a means to some end outside itself. When we ask questions which mean 'Do such beliefs or experiences follow the rules of the field?' we are applying regulators which have to do with the field of study or experience regarded as itself a 'whole', under its own government, so to speak. 'Truth' is this kind of regulator. That is why the question 'Is it true?' is wholly independent of the question 'Is it useful?', though some people think otherwise and try to subordinate the first question to the second — we shall say more of this when we talk about 'pragmatism'.

Knowledge and the Fall

The Biblical story of the Fall[1] illustrates a kind of utility test for experience. God said that Adam and Eve might eat fruit from every tree save one: '. . . of the tree of the knowledge of good and evil thou shalt not eat of it'. But they did; so Paradise was lost.[2]

The forbidden knowledge was of the kind we may call 'moral'. That is, it consisted not in recognition, classification, or description of objects, but in learning to distinguish between various possibilities and to evaluate them, some good, some not good.[3] Knowledge in this sense presupposes variety of experience;

---

[1] Genesis iii.

[2] Compare Milton's *Paradise Lost*, especially bk viii, where Adam is rebuked by Raphael for taking too much interest in the problems of seventeenth-century science.

[3] The question whether the 'good' is an object is of importance to ethics. See, for example, G. E. Moore, *Principia Ethica* (C.U.P., 1903; paperback ed., 1959), who holds that this is the case. See also S. Zink, *The Concepts of Ethics* (Macmillan, 1962), ch. i; G. E. Moore, *Ethics* (O.U.P., 1912), chs 3, 4; E. Carritt, *The Theory of Morals* (Oxford, Clarendon Press, 1930), chs 7 and 8.

innocence is the absence of such variety. Only with variety is there the need to choose, to decide, or, in a word, to be free. The Fall of man is a fall into freedom.

But this is a utility test for some kinds of knowing. The prohibited experiences are bad because they put an end to certain 'goods' and initiate certain evils. Before the Fall man has no need for anxiety — his world supplies him with food. After the Fall he is *afraid* of God, ashamed, with woman, of his nakedness, compelled to work in order to survive and to see his wife bear children in pain.[1]

This story becomes something of a 'regulator' when it takes its place in Christian theology. The doctrine of original sin (comparable in some respects with Freud's account of the Oedipus complex) is a tragic[2] estimate of human effort, but the evil can be erased by the work of Christ through the Church. Some consequences of this regulation of experience have been seen in earlier chapters. The trial of Galileo may be considered in this context.

The Myth of Protagoras

The Myth of Protagoras[3] should be compared with the Biblical story of the Fall as a further example of the utility regulator.

The Sophist Protagoras, challenged by Socrates to show that virtue is teachable, adapts an old Greek myth to his purpose. The

[1] Laborious work is being reduced by automation, pain by anaesthetics and other methods. What is happening to the curse?

[2] The development of tragedy is relevant to ideas of freedom. Aeschylus, for example (524–456 B.C.), makes man responsible for his own troubles whereas the Homeric writings (possibly appearing in the ninth century B.C.) see man helpless in the hands of fate or the gods. On tragedy generally see Aristotle, *Ars Poetica*, sec. xvi; A. C. Bradley, *Shakespearean Tragedy*, 2nd ed. (Macmillan, 1905; 1st ed., 1904), lecture i; A. C. Bradley, *Oxford Lectures on Poetry*, 1st ed. (Macmillan, 1909; paperback ed., 1959), lecture iii (on Hegel). On the Greek development see B. Snell, *The Discovery of the Mind*, trans. T. G. Rosenmeyer (Oxford, Blackwell, 1953); originally *Die Entdeckung des Geistes*, 2nd ed. (Hamburg, 1948). The likening of the 'Oedipus complex' to original sin is called by Birnbach (op. cit.) 'an invidious allegation'.

[3] For one view of the connexion between myth, drama, and man's relations with the universe see A. Toynbee, *A Study of History*, abridged by D. C. Somervell (O.U.P., 1946), I, v, which deals with the concept of challenge and response.

For the myth of Protagoras I have used the Everyman edition of Plato's *Protagoras*. For a detailed study of Protagoras see M. Untersteiner, *The Sophists*, trans. K. Freeman (Oxford, Blackwell, 1954), pp. 58 ff. Note this writer's comment on the use Protagoras makes of myth.

gods formed man and gave to Prometheus and Epimetheus ('Forethought' and 'Afterthought') the task of equipping him along with other animals for what we today would call the 'struggle for existence'. Epimetheus was left to it and forgot man until he had run out of equipment. Prometheus came to the rescue. He stole inventive skill 'together with fire' from the gods Hephaestus and Athene. Man became the tool-maker. But as such he could not survive; for men lived scattered — 'cities there were none' — and their tools could not save them against the superior strength, cunning, and speed of other animals. So Zeus, father of the gods, sent his messenger, Hermes, to equip men with the *social* arts.[1]

'. . . whosoever', said Zeus, 'is incapable of partaking in shame and justice let him be put to death as a pest to the city.'

Dike, *aidos* — the social virtues — a sense of shame, a sense of fair play: these were the basic necessities of survival and because they were distributed *equally* they provided, according to Protagoras (who made a good living at it) the capacity for social education.

Technical skill by itself, then, was useless as a means to survival. What of other kinds of knowledge? This takes us beyond the Myth to Protagoras' other teaching (so far as we can tell what it was). The myth, however, makes one thing clear and this provides an interesting contrast with the story of the Fall. Once equipped both with his technical skill and with his social arts man is 'on his own' and, what is more, this is intended by Zeus. Within his cities he can work out his own salvation; there is no original curse and no need for him to depend on supernatural aid to save him.

As for other kinds of knowledge, Protagoras held that since nothing could be known with certainty what mattered was to choose between beliefs and to adopt those which *worked*. 'Nothing could be known with certainty' for there were at least two opposing points of view on any question addressed to nature. Beliefs *worked* if they gave a man success in his human relations. This deprived experience of that kind of meaning we said it could

[1] Hermes should be appointed guardian angel to social workers and Protagoras has some claim to be the founding father of social science.

have 'within wholes' except and in so far as these were agreeable to a given society.

'How to make friends and influence people' may be a crude interpretation of Protagoras' *pragmatism*,[1] but it comes somewhere near to what he meant. Protagoras' students would for the most part be well-to-do young men who wanted to get on and 'getting on' in ancient Hellas meant public life and this in its turn required, above all, success in rhetoric, in the arts of persuasion. Their teacher's experience of the courts had impressed upon him the fatuity of 'truth' as a guarantee of success in putting a case — a good orator could put opposite cases with equal conviction and persuasive power. One could not speak of the *truth* of a belief — there were no adequate proofs — the universe did not impress itself upon the minds of men; on the contrary, it left everything to disputation. Usefulness was another matter: the city was all around and no one could complain that 'society' was not interested in one's beliefs. Better, then, to come to terms with the reality one knew, than try to keep faith with a reality one could not even know well enough to call 'real'.

Knowing 'the good'

The story of the Fall, the myth of Protagoras, illustrate characteristic attempts to regulate experience. Note first what they have in common: they both take for granted a kind of knowing or at least something known which takes precedence over all other experience. This supreme knowledge is what moral philosophers discuss when they talk about 'good' or 'the good', 'the end' or even 'the highest good'. In everyday language, and as the two examples clearly present it, this is 'knowing what is good for you'.

'If you know what is good for you . . .' is a clause which very often goes before such advice as '. . . you will mind your own business', or '. . . you will keep your mouth shut', or '. . . you'll "toe the line" ' — in other words, clichés of one kind or another with the same intention: to regulate human relations by suppress-

[1] 'Pragmatism': the word was introduced by Charles Pierce in the nineteenth century. He afterwards changed it to 'pragmaticism' to distinguish his theory of meaning from William James's corruption of it. See W. B. Gallie, *Pierce on Pragmatism* (Penguin, 1952), especially the introductory chapter. William James, *Pragmatism*, 1st ed., 1907, is available in a paperback edition with others of his essays (Meridian, 1955). See also Russell, *HWP*, book III, chs xxix and xxx.

ing trouble-making views, beliefs, conduct, or more generally, experiences which don't 'fit'.

All such advice takes for granted that in the circumstances the person addressed is capable of 'knowing' — with the same certainty as the speaker 'knows' — what is *good* for him. Such assumptions may be justified or they may not; the point is, they are taken for granted. Nor are they taken for granted only by the unsophisticated. Or put it another way — so well equipped are we, today, with the jargon of half a dozen social sciences that it is becoming increasingly difficult to make such assumptions look as crude as in fact they often are. This gives the utility regulator an unaccustomed power over our thinking about 'what is good for us', as little or no provision is made in the education of many people for introducing them to the *ethical* questions such jargon obscures. In this book we shall examine several examples of what *status vocabularies* can do to the social values. Here is one:

In the United States Senate during the ninth week of the debate on the Civil Rights Bill a young Negro stood up in the public gallery to protest at the poor attendance. 'How can you say you are protecting the black man when there are only five of you there?' he asked. He was taken to hospital for 'mental observation'. An officer of the Metropolitan Police said that the young man was apparently 'mentally disturbed' and would not be charged with disorderly conduct.[1] This incident is too interesting to be dismissed with a sentence or two. All we want to do now is to point to the underlying assumption of 'what was good for' the Negro protestant and see how this is obscured by the 'status vocabulary' of psychopathology. It seems to have been assumed that it was good for the Negro not to be 'charged with disorderly conduct'. On the other hand, this course of action could be defended as 'in the public interest'. Either way the assumption has been made and the original protest, by means of it, deprived of purpose, dignity, responsibility. Provision has deliberately to be made for the critical examination of 'what is good for' us if men are not to be frog-marched out of rationality into institutions for the 'mentally disturbed'. Ethics as the critical analysis of 'goods' — ends proposed as regulators — is integral to social philosophy. Where

[1] Report in *The Times*, 5 May 1964. The Negro was Kenneth Washington of Passaic, N.Y.; the officer was Captain James Powell.

language in such special forms as we mean by 'status vocabularies' is depriving us of such provision the need is more urgent. We are more likely to hoodwink ourselves, to use the jargon of the sciences as a thought-preventive, comfortably taking it for granted that people who invent such impressive words as 'maladjustment' and 'pathological' *must* know, severally or in chorus, what is good for us.

We shall now consider separately the two examples of utility regulator.

The 'outside' test

The story of the Fall could be used to regulate what happens *inside* society by assuming a supreme good dependent upon forces or agencies *outside*. Outside, at least, such customs, laws, and institutions as prevail in the society under attack; for we have not lacked men who make such an appeal to ultramundane laws in order to justify revolution, the setting up of new institutions supposedly as means to the ends they understand. Calvin[1] in Geneva just as much as the Catholic Church throughout Europe in the Middle Ages claimed to know what was good for men in society by virtue of 'outside', ultramundane knowledge of the very kind (in these instances) the story of the Fall illustrates.

Nor are such ways of settling questions of social values confined to religious argument of the kind the story of the Fall illustrates. 'Natural Law'[2] — an idea handed on by the Stoics to the Romans and so to the later development of European political thought — was a critical instrument of the existing social life which appealed to a good dependent upon 'nature', upon what lay outside the prevailing standards of society. We shall see later that some users of this idea intended an appeal to 'reason' and 'conscience' of a kind which distinguishes them sharply from believers in divine 'election', 'predestination', and so on. At the same time others have claimed to see either in history itself or in history as the manifestation of supernatural forces processes which lie 'outside' the facilities of existing society yet which determine man's good beyond question and must therefore be understood and complied with.

[1] For an introduction to Calvin's political activities see Sabine, *HPT*, ch. xviii.

[2] For an introduction see A. d'Entrèves, *Natural Law* (Hutchinson, Universal Library, 1916).

D

The name 'historicism'[1] has been given to arguments of this kind. The historicist may claim to have discovered regularities in man's development which the laws or the morals of a time and place may reveal or even conform to but which men in society cannot deliberately, rationally construct or reconstruct. When a writer like Karl Marx[2] goes further, however, and makes it clear that the next stage in such a development is *good* and ought to be encouraged, so to speak, we may be tempted to think we are being fooled and that someone is trying to overwhelm our critical abilities by making resounding appeals to ultramundane or at least extra-social regulators which reflect his own preferences just as much as those of the class he hated were reflected in a true ultramundane picture once displayed in Sunday schools and elsewhere in the following ditty:

> The rich man in his castle,
> The poor man at his gate,
> God made them high and lowly,
> And ordered their estate . . .
>
> All things bright and beautiful
> The Lord God made them all.[3]

We are not now discussing the relative merits of these two views of what is good for us; all we are doing is to illustrate a general method in such things to be borne in mind when we discuss the social values later.

The 'inside' test

The myth of Protagoras differs from the story of the Fall in one important respect: it proposes to submit human experience to the tests only of what is good 'within the city'. We have seen how admirably this might suit the purposes of any modern social or

---

[1] The best-known recent treatment is by K. Popper in his *The Poverty of Historicism* (Routledge, paperback ed., 1961). See also the same writer's *The Open Society and its Enemies*, 2nd ed. (Routledge, 1952; a paperback ed. is now available), vol. 1, ch. i. Benedetto Croce, *History as the Story of Liberty* (New York, Meridian, 1955; 1st Eng. ed., 1941).

[2] Hegel's dialectic itself is an equally good example: he develops the whole universe to the point where it fulfils itself in the new Prussian State.

[3] Cecil Frances Alexander (1823–95). This most interesting stanza is usually omitted (I am told) in modern versions. Some see in F. H. Bradley's essay, *My Station and its Duties*, a more elegant rendering of the same theme. This essay is published in *Ethical Studies*, 2nd ed. (Oxford, 1927; 1st ed., 1876; paperback ed. is now available).

civil servant who wanted to make laws, administer systems, engineer institutions, or even do social work untroubled by misgivings about the *value* of what he is doing. Oh, to dispose of such anxieties once and for all! And how better than by looking no further than the city walls — the prevailing customs, norms, *mores*, and so forth not only of the political community but of the various existing associations to which people may be said to belong. We have to make clear our position with regard to such a utility regulator before we begin to talk in more detail about social values or even before we ask anyone to assume that such a discussion is itself worth while. For if 'values' have to do with decisions and if all we have to decide is whether a given law or course of conduct is in accordance with the prevailing customs, then the kind of discussion we do in social philosophy must be regarded as a subordinate branch of the sociological inquiry into what constitutes the prevailing customs. This is very different from a debate which assumes the customs themselves to be subject to criticism.

To look for the *ends* or *goods* which are to regulate experience inside society rather than outside in a non-human order has this to commend it: the variety of human experience is not put in danger by claimants to 'special' knowledge, claimants who thus put themselves beyond criticism. An ultramundane good such as that suggested by the story of the Fall is likely on the one hand to back up the claims of those who enjoy lordship and on the other hand to depress our confidence in what we ordinary mortals can do with our world. There are other ways of despairing about humanity, but one way is certainly the kind of ultramundane 'good' which the way of Protagoras rejects. In doing so he rejects the possibility of *depending* upon extra-human agencies and their (so-called) human representatives. As a constructive approach to society we find this acceptable.

On the other hand, to make 'getting on with people' a *means* to 'social success' as the *end* is either argument in a circle (with the 'means' the same as the 'end') or it is a way of concealing that 'social success' is a means to such other goods as wealth, power, fame, which ought to come out into the open and not hide themselves under such plausible covers as 'getting on with people'. By such a device Protagorean pragmatism is up to date in its readiness to ride roughshod over what we called earlier certain of those 'wholes' which may or may not be 'socially' successful. Take as the most important example of such 'wholes' the notion of 'being oneself'. This notion is subject to all kinds of abuse, but it has, nevertheless, an importance in ethics and thereby in social philosophy which is fundamental. Now whatever 'being oneself' entails there is no *obvious* reason why the 'whole' it conceives should be *the same as* what we achieve by the acquisition of things, of wealth, of social status, of power. It does not follow that such acquisition is incompatible with such goods; it does follow that we want to know, that we must not be misled by such a plausible device as 'getting on with people' into assuming that this includes 'being oneself'.

The other difficulty with Protagorean pragmatism is that already described as 'social relativism'. If experience is to be regulated by the 'good' of getting on with people there is good reason why this should come to mean getting on with people in this or that group, and equally good reason why *this* should mean keeping the rules of the group, doing as others do, *conforming*. Now if by 'conforming' we mean prudently doing, when in Rome, that which the Romans do, this may be sound advice — advice, at that, which we all follow through a great deal of our lives. But if prudence were all that concerned social philosophy, we would, once more, be back in a position of subordination to sociological inquiry, and *that* is undesirable because there is no reason why sociologists should know 'what is good for us' unless they have good reason to say that the prevailing customs at any given time are (by some mysterious law) the best. To take up such a position the sociologist would have to go well beyond the disciplines of his science. He would have to find some *essential* or *necessary* connexion between the names we use to signify our membership of groups ('English', 'Baptist', 'student', 'mother', and so forth) and the habits which characterize such groups at any given time in any given place. Or else he would have to adopt some fundamental ethical axiom such as this:

'Good' means adjustment between member and group such that there is no tension between them.

'Tension' would then be the only evil; change would be prohibited or else some device would be necessary for bringing it about without tension — but on whose advice? Perhaps the sociologist's — he alone would be able to say that this was not the best of all possible worlds but that the habits of the group must be changed in this direction or that. Whereas in reality groups conflict with each other and tension arises within them because of the variety of experience, and the Protagorean formula has nothing to offer to a 'community of meaning' crossing the frontiers of existing groups, nothing to say about personal experience at odds with the group except prudently to counsel conformity.

The moral question

Morality has to do with keeping the rules in society or at any rate with keeping some kinds of rules. But moral thought, at least since men like the Sophists discovered the variety of social groups and the corresponding variety of rules, has also challenged the rules, refusing to accept without question that the definition of the good life they collectively represent is final or exhaustive. Morality has to do with the regulation of *behaviour* rather than of experience in general. But the moral philosopher who challenges prevailing norms or the claims to knowledge of the 'good' with which they may be defended, raises the kind of question we have been discussing in this book — about the varieties of experience and their regulation. These are fundamental social questions and we cannot discuss them further until we have turned from the utility regulator to a way of regulating experience which claims to transcend the limitations of particular groups on the one hand, special times and places on the other — the regulator we call *truth*.

QUESTIONS FOR DISCUSSION

1. Discuss the kind of 'knowing' condemned by the myth of the Fall. Read S. Zink, *The Concepts of Ethics* (Macmillan, 1962), ch. i and other references in the footnotes. What do we know when we know what is 'good'?

2. Discuss the incident recorded on p. 82. Could the phrase 'mentally disturbed' be justified on pragmatic grounds (in Protagoras' sense) quite apart from any scientific validation?

8

Truth Conventions[1]

TRUTH is 'the majority vote of that nation that can lick all others'.[2] As a good democratic application of the Protagorean approach to human relations this sentence deserves pride of place at this point. For it tells us so much and points to so many of the questions a modern social philosopher must ask. Social relativism, for instance, could surely do worse than adopt this identification of 'truth' with the majority vote even if the social relativist could not (at first) stomach the rest of the sentence. The alternative explanation of the majority vote — that which regards it as a procedural device for reaching a decision — does not concern us at the moment. If we choose a utility regulator for experience and if, furthermore, we see our 'good' *solely* as 'getting on with' our group, then it is difficult to see how we are to know what it is we are to get on with except by such devices as public opinion polls.

Some people feel themselves driven to this by the impossibility of what they privately regard as the only alternative, a concept of truth — *the* truth — as 'out there', outside all human dealings, absolute, unchanging, and, like the daylight at the end of a long tunnel or the sunlight outside Plato's cave, available to those who can reach 'it'. If they can no longer believe this (they seem to say), what alternative have they but to 'sound people out', get the consensus of opinion, seeing that day-to-day decisions have to be made with or without the help of the universe?

[1] For an introduction to the discussion of truth from the point of view taken by modern analytical philosophy the student may begin with J. O. Urmson, *Philosophical Analysis, its Development between the two World Wars* (Oxford, Clarendon Press, 1956); A. J. Ayer, *Language, Truth and Logic*, 2nd ed. (Gollancz, 1954). See also the bibliography in Urmson, op. cit.

[2] Oliver Wendell Holmes Jr, quoted in E. M. Burns, *Ideas in Conflict* (Methuen, 1963), p. 58, from M. Lerner's *The Mind and Faith of Justice Holmes* (1946), p. 306.

What is 'truth', after all, but a *word* — so they say with the help
of quasi-philosophy — as they land on their heads, so to speak,
after their fall from the heights of absolute truth. And what
is a word but a 'label' and what is a label but a device which
can be used how we like to suit the convenience of the changing
hour?

'Truth' *is* a word. We show we are talking about it as a word by
putting it inside quotation marks. Nor is the discovery quite so
trivial as it seems for there is a lot to be said for the view that *truth*
(that which the word 'truth' means) is a convention, or a group of
conventions, and words, too, are conventional signs. But to draw
attention to the verbal characteristics of a concept does not mean
we have disposed of the concept; and to call truth a convention is
not to deprive it of its significance. If we can show that the whole
point of the 'truth-conventions' is their ability to lift us above
whims and fancies, passing appearances, the customs and habits of
the time, to a more enduring reality both generally and particularly in human relations, then we may not have soothed the
anguish of the man who has lost his dream of 'absolutes' but
we may have put him on his way to answering the demand for
reality.

Truth, pins, and concepts

Men do not only 'have' sensations, they 'have' ideas. For
instance, if you stick a pin in me I shall wince and, possibly, make
noises signifying 'having sensation'. More — I shall keep an eye
on you in future: many animals would do as much. I not only feel
the pin, however, I *write* about it. (Writing about the *possibility* of
such an undignified incident is even more remarkable.) In writing
I use such words as 'pin' and 'pin' makes clear to millions of
people that you attacked me with an object of a certain sort. We
all have an idea of 'pin'. 'Pin' does not only mean the weapon
with which you attacked me but a countless number of similar
objects most of which I have never seen, most of which have still
to be made (unless we are, in future, to meet sartorial emergencies
with plastic adhesives). The same is true of other words used to
describe this possible incident — 'feel', 'stick', 'wince', are signs
which go well beyond one particular experience and give it
meaning by relating it to a 'universe' of comparable incidents,

with or without pins, but with something in common which the general or 'universal'[1] words call to mind.

'Pin' — the word — is dependent upon pins (the objects) for its meaning because the word would not have come into use but for the objects, though it might well go on being used for a generation or two (even longer 'in the literature') after pins become obsolete. 'Pin' is dependent on pins; but while there are pins all our commercial and domestic dealings with such objects require 'pin' and would become awkward if we passed a grammarian's law banning the use of the word or any other (*épingle? Stecknadel?*) to take its place.

Now 'truth' differs from 'pin'. We may use the word 'truth' *about* what we hear, see, or otherwise experience through sensations but there are no small, bright sharply pointed objects lying around which we can point to an say, 'See! A truth!' nor indeed any other objects in the ordinary sense of the word which can impinge on our senses and make us say, for instance, 'Ouch! A truth!' Or, as the logicians say, words like 'truth', 'freedom', 'justice', and so forth cannot be defined *ostensively*. Where 'pin' is the name for an idea which, nevertheless, points to objects 'out there', 'truth' has no immediate or obvious connexion with the senses. Nor has 'freedom' or the other concepts we discuss in this book.

Yet we can distinguish a more general idea called 'truth' from less general, more particular experiences in which we speak of 'truths', 'this truth', or 'a truth'. (This looks like the difference between 'pin', 'this pin', and so on.) Similarly, then, we might argue that there could be no more meaning in 'truth' (the name for the general concept) apart from 'truths' (the name for the particular experiences) than there could be meaning in 'pin' (the idea) apart from 'pins' (the objects).

But this will not do. We said we could not do without 'pin' while 'pins' were in use, but now try saying we cannot do without 'truth' while 'truths' are in use: it sounds odd, there is something

---

[1] Aristotle, *On Interpretation*: 'By the term "universal" I mean that which is of such a nature as to be predicated of many subjects, by "individual" that which is not thus predicated.' For an introduction to medieval and Greek thought about the logical (or ontological) status of universals the following may be consulted: Russsell, *HWP*, bk i, ch. 29; C. E. M. Joad, *A Guide to Philosophy*, part iii, chs 10–11; the earlier volumes of Copleston, *CH*, using references in the index of these volumes to such terms as 'realist', 'nominalist', 'conceptualist'.

wrong. To start with we do not *use* 'truths' — we ourselves declare them, pronounce them rather as a jury pronounces a verdict. We may 'find' them but whatever this means, 'true' is a *judgement*: our judgement. Then if our judgement is challenged and in order to sustain it, we are compelled *either* to relate what we have found to a 'whole' — a scheme of ideas or propositions or theories we believe to be acceptable — *or* to submit our judgement to the general rules of the logic appropriate to the situation. In both cases we have appealed from the particular situation to what may be called the content of a general concept of 'truth'.

To imagine a state of affairs without 'truths' is to imagine not a change in techniques but a change in the fundamentals of human intercourse. In order to explain *this* we must have recourse to a general concept, 'truth', not to a particular experience of 'truths'. To imagine such a state of affairs is to conceive of a radical change in the meaning of 'human'. Moreover, such a change is likely to provoke many people to resistance and resistance would take the form not of a campaign for 'more truths' (like 'We want more pins') but for more understanding and the further implementation of the general concept of truth.

It is necessary to say this since many people, deprived of belief in absolutes of some sort 'out there', slump into the view that truth, freedom, justice, are 'only words' (which is extremely disrespectful to words, to say the least). Now without doubt it makes for precision and dialectical finesse if we can put a belief into the kind of statement which can then be judged 'true' or 'false' either according to the rules of logic or by observation and experiment. But truth, the word, depends upon the concept 'truth', even as the recognition of such a concept may in its turn depend upon the word, while the experience of truth requires concrete situations.

The view taken in this book not only of truth but of other general concepts such as freedom, is that however these may be said to have 'begun' they are now parts of our real world, 'located' (if the metaphor may be excused) in the mental function of individuals but also in human relations. In fact, it may well be that it makes more sense to talk of these general concepts as 'in' society, 'in' the continuing modes of human relations which transcend particular groups and particular generations, than it does to call them 'abstractions' from particular, concrete experiences.

Objectivity and conventions

Recall now the trial of Galileo. He was denounced for 'holding as true the false doctrine that the Sun is the centre of the world and immoveable and that the Earth moves',[1] a judgement on the Copernican theory which Galileo presently accepted as his own.

Here is a level of experience where 'truth' is used to evaluate the relation between a belief and its object. Galileo Galilei before the trial holds one belief, after the trial he says he holds another; the first is said by the Church to be 'false', the second is now said by Galileo (and the Church) to be 'true'. It looks as if truth is indeed the 'majority vote' — or so it would seem if we confined our attention to the particular situation or even to special aspects of the situation.[2]

On the other hand, if 'truth' is the name we give to the truth which is 'out there' (in this case the solar *system*), the most we can say for 'truth' is that its relations with truth are dubious. One man — or a majority — may today call 'true' a belief which tomorrow is called 'false'. This makes sense of Protagoras' pragmatism; it explains his sceptical rejection of all 'knowledge'. But it does not make much sense of what we feel called upon to do every day — come to terms with our two worlds, of nature and of man.

Remember, we are talking of truth now on one particular level of experience — the level upon which we discuss relations between belief and object and evaluate the statements we make in such a discussion. Men not only give voice to their experience — articulate — they try to regulate both the experience and its expression in order to set up a community of experience, in order to reach agreement. 'Reliability' in a belief has to do not only with the 'real' world but also with a community of meaning, a consensus of opinion. There are tests for all this. Beliefs which satisfy them are 'true'; those which fail are 'false'.

---

[1] See the sentence in Koestler, *The Sleepwalkers*, pp. 602 f.

[2] Consider, on the other hand, this that Russell has to say about Einstein and relativity: 'if space is purely relative, the difference between the statements "the earth rotates" and "the heavens revolve" is purely verbal' (*Human Knowledge, its Scope and Limits*, p. 19).

These tests are *conventions*. They are agreements which may be more or less explicit, conscious, deliberate, depending upon a number of conditions. Prior to these conventions is the persistent demand for reliability in man's relations with his two worlds. This is how truth-conventions come into conflict with personal observations and personal convictions as well as with public prejudice. For the 'whole' (system of ideas, theories and so on) by which the meaning and truth of a belief are assessed may satisfy the primary demand for reliability where a belief which seems to some individual or small group acceptable may fail to fit into the whole. The modern astronomer, for instance, still has to *make an effort* if his calculations conflict with his observations or his experiments — he has to make an effort to leave the hitherto reliable 'whole' made up of a world-picture, a body of theories, and accept as 'true' a new belief which does not fit into them but which does satisfy other tests, other (and presumably superior) parts of the truth-convention. The source of the conflict is the primary demand for reliability on the one hand together with certain 'wholes' — theories, systems of theories — in which it has come to rest, and the truth-conventions on the other which, though they may include the 'whole' itself, have other tests which may come to conflict with this.

To call truth a 'convention' can only seem like cynicism if, at bottom, we lack respect for human effort or appreciation of the persistent demand to 'come to terms with reality' which has inspired scientist, philosopher, poet, and mystic throughout our history. In any case, we are not saying that truth *is* a convention but that judgements on the truth or falsity of beliefs in relation to their objects is a matter of referring such beliefs to certain prevailing 'wholes' and to certain tests and rules with the understanding that both the conceptual wholes and the tests arise through a genuine demand for 'reality'.

At the same time, the conventional basis of truth-judgements reminds us once more of our collective freedom. We cannot call in the universe to crush our opponents. The relevant part of the universe must first enter into our beliefs; these beliefs must justify themselves either within prevailing *systems* of belief or by general rules, or a logic which approves them, and by the same tokens criticizes the prevailing whole — all this being a matter of human discourse and human decision. The universe will not act against heretics or nonconformists. Men will only be judged by their peers — other men.

The Copernican theory did not fit instantly into the 'whole' of Catholic cosmology. Better therefore, some said, to call the beliefs it asked for *hypotheses*, instruments for handling the phenomena; and not ask for them to be judged 'true' or 'false' descriptions of the real world which was represented *by* the orthodox 'whole', the Christian cosmology. Galileo Galilei would not leave it at that. But neither did he pay overmuch respect to the general rules of rational discourse prevailing in his time.

I thought you could simply look through the telescope and convince yourselves.

Brecht's Galileo says impatiently to the Theologian and the Mathematician who wanted, first, a formal dispute on the theme: 'Can such planets exist?'[1] The Theologian and the Mathematician are appealing to the truth-conventions. Galileo wants them to 'believe in the telescope' as if all that was needed to dispense for ever with the mental habits of generations was a quick 'peek' through the lenses.

The Galileo of history may have had more sense, but he does not seem to have had much more patience with men's ways of judging 'truth' and 'falsehood'. It would be wrong to think of the trial either as 'the truth *v.* Galileo' or as 'the truth *v.* the Church'. If men are not to have some respect both for the 'wholes' of their meaningful collective experience and for the rules of discourse, then neither are they going to be able to make use of the truth-conventions in order to add to *reliable* knowledge of reality without rashly jettisoning their past.

Conventions and 'contract'

Social philosophers in the past used to talk about a 'social contract' as the origin of society. Men, they seemed to be saying, were 'naturally' non-social; but for one reason or another they came together and reached an agreement as a result of which a society was created. Today we would find such a view offensive — incompatible with the 'whole' of our social knowledge. Truth-conventions, nevertheless, along with other general concepts such

[1] Bertolt Brecht, *The Life of Galileo*.

as that of freedom, have a function not unlike that of the (fictional) social contract. They may be compared to the Constitution, written or unwritten, to which political communities as well as other associations may turn from time to time for the settlement of differences, for arbitration between opposing views.[1]

Several conditions are necessary if these general concepts are to do what is expected of them. Taking the situation in April 1633 as our model it seems that the conventions must allow for prevailing 'wholes' — the meaningful systems of ideas, theories, and so on — while making available general rules for discussion which tolerate the 'new', incompatible experience and expose even the prevailing wholes to criticism. A further condition is the readiness of parties to a dispute to submit their beliefs to the conventions and not to call for a change in these as soon as a 'new' belief fails to pass the test.[2]

This last condition is particularly important when we are discussing 'freedom'. What has been called 'the reconciliation of freedom with the compulsion of truth'[3] is a condition men put themselves under by their resolve to come to terms with reality. But they can refuse or neglect this condition and in doing so repudiate the unwritten constitution by which — as rational beings — experience can be regulated.

This is how our basic values, our fundamental conventions, interlock — the truth-convention in this instance requiring the support of such general concepts as freedom and responsibility. To make this clearer we turn to other levels of experience where 'truth' in some sense has meaning and we shall then be ready to give some account of such social values as freedom, justice, community.

QUESTIONS FOR DISCUSSION

1. Invent a sentence beginning 'It is true that . . .', then (a) see whether the sentence can be rewritten without the word 'true'

---

[1] This is a bit like what Hans Kelsen called the 'Grundnorm' (basic norm) but is meant to be here of wider application. See C. K. Allen, *Law in the Making*, pp. 49 ff., or Benn and Peters, *SP*, pp. 78–81 and 366.

[2] Epistemological questions are involved here. See the references on p. 88 above, and W. P. Montague, *The Ways of Knowing* (Allen & Unwin, 1925).

[3] A. N. Whitehead, *Adventures of Ideas* (C.U.P., 1933), part I, ch. iv, sec. 8.

while retaining its original meaning, and (*b*) whether what the sentence wants to say (in terms of 'true' and 'false') can be said without some reference to agreed standards or conventions.

2. Read Bertolt Brecht, *The Life of Galileo*, and A. Koestler, *The Sleepwalkers* (Hutchinson, 1959), part v, chs i and ii. What does Brecht have to say about the relations between Galileo and the Church? How does this agree (*a*) with Koestler's own account, and (*b*) with the documents he reproduces at the end of his book (especially on pp. 602 ff.)?

9

Truth and Morality

ONE fine spring day in the first year of the Ninety-Fifth Olympiad (339 B.C.)[1] an event took place in Athens as important to European morals as the trial of Galileo to our religion and our science. Five hundred and one citizens of blameless reputation sat in judgement on the philosopher Socrates, who was charged with impiety and the corruption of young people. They sentenced him to death and Socrates, in spite of attempts by his well-to-do friend, Crito, to persuade him to escape from prison, chose to drink the hemlock, and die.

This event illustrates two other uses of 'truth' and the connexion of these with objectivity — the use we have just been discussing. We cannot be sure exactly what happened in Athens at that time but we may at least use Plato's account of these events as we, earlier, used the biblical myth of the Fall of man as well as the myth of Protagoras — as a model of what men have thought about such matters: in this case, of 'truth' at various levels, of objectivity, inter-personal truth, and personal integrity.

When Socrates refused to accept Crito's offer of escape and death in exile he gave two reasons. The first was this: evading the penalty the laws decreed would undermine the authority of the laws and therefore threaten Athenian political life. The second reason had to do with Socrates' personal integrity: to go into

[1] From the year we call 776 B.C. onwards Greek historians dated events from the midsummer of every fourth year in which the Olympian Festival in honour of Zeus was held (at Olympia in Elis). The opening sentence of this paragraph is in part a quotation from T. Gomperz, *GT*, vol. II, ch. v (secs 2 ff. for the whole story). For Plato's account of the trial and its aftermath see his dialogues *Apology*, *Crito*, *Phaedo* published by Penguin together under the title *The Death of Socrates*. For another contemporary account see Xenophon, *Memorabilia*, ch. viii, and *Apology*. *DL* also has a record of these events (ii. 39 ff.).

exile meant to give up being a philosopher; Socrates without philosophy would be someone else, not Socrates at all. Mere survival was not worth that price, for what would it be that survived? If we take these two reasons as well as the connexion between them, we shall see how we use 'truth' about more experiences than those we call 'knowledge' yet how these various uses are related — the regulation of knowing has something to do with the regulation of conduct, the theory of knowledge with the philosophy of morals.

Truth, inter-personal

Objectivity — truth in our judgements on the universe or parts of it apart from our own feelings — is necessary if we are to have reliable knowledge about our world. Similarly, truthfulness between people aims at reliable personal relations. We can become reasonably sure of people we know well enough to trust them to keep their promises, to behave today and tomorrow more or less as they behaved yesterday. Where we do not know them, or, if we do, do not trust them, the laws and to some extent the customs and habits of our society give us some ground for expecting people to behave in one way rather than another. If they don't, provided the law is on our side, we can at least expect some kind of compensation for their failure. The regulation of behaviour falls to the positive laws on the one hand, to morals (and *mores*) on the other.

This brings us to the first of Socrates' reasons for accepting the death-penalty. The charges brought against him were nothing more nor less than a declaration that his fellow-citizens had not found him reliable. Neither he nor his followers, they argued, could be trusted in a crisis, but, on the contrary, had worked against the laws and customs of Athens. Galileo's theories were offensive to the 'whole' of orthodox cosmological theory. Socrates' methods were offensive to the *mores* of Athenian democracy, at war with non-democratic Sparta. Socrates was accused of 'impiety'. His way of asking questions and encouraging young people to question the 'experts', the self-proclaimed authorities — this was an offence to the sanctity of public life: it dispersed the awe and respect which otherwise might have regulated public conduct.

Yet Socrates did respect the community. He admitted, at least, that he owed a debt to Athens. His liberty to teach, to ask questions, was guaranteed by the laws and customs of the city. If, then, he has failed to create in others the trust upon which he has himself been able to rely, going about 'persuading you all . . . first and chiefly to care about the greatest improvement of the soul . . .',[1] he has now no alternative but to submit to the laws. For it is by the submission of others that he has been kept free and safe. Either morals or the laws may work to ensure inter-personal reliability. Socrates' failure to win the trust of his fellow-citizens without the intervention of the laws, however, has something to do with his own concern for objectivity and at the same time his relative disregard for the contemporary truth-conventions.

Plato, Socrates' most famous pupil, hypostatized 'truth'. He treated it, that is to say, as a substance, a thing 'out there' in spiritual (or logical) space, where all Plato's ideas were found. Whether this was Socrates' own view or not he argued that all claims to knowledge, all expertise, should submit to the test of his critical dialectic. This meant that the expert, the authority, might no longer rely upon his social *status* to win acceptance of his judgements and to vindicate his function; he must on the contrary submit all he said to a 'reasoning through' process based upon the rules of a logic seemingly inherent in the language.[2]

This method of casting doubt upon authoritative opinion, or in other words of shifting the basis of authority from status to logic, earned Socrates his reputation: you could not depend upon his or his students behaving in ways men could rely upon — not, at least, men who were used to the old mystical or pious ground of authority. Nor was this a laughing matter when the city was fighting for its survival. Had not the intellectuals proved poor patriots, cool towards the war effort, and to democracy, conspiring, like Critias, traitorous, like Alcibiades?

Inter-personal truth is a special concern of morals. If men are to trust each other there has to be rule-following, 'doing one's duty', fulfilling obligations. But it may also be necessary to break the rules if personal experience, 'private knowledge', conflict with

[1] Plato's *Apology*, in *The Four Socratic Dialogues of Plato*, trans. Jowett (Oxford, Clarendon Press, 1949), sec. xxx.
[2] For an example of the 'logic in the language' see Plato's *Apology* (ibid.) sec. xxvii: Socrates' question to Meletus on the charge of atheism.

them. In our own time we have come to call a man 'immoral' who keeps the rules when he 'ought' to break them even as our ancestors — more readily — called him 'immoral' for breaking them. Events such as the trial of Socrates encourage us to think in this way and so complicate the problems of social philosophy.

The conventions of objective truth require those whose beliefs are in conflict with them to make an effort. Suppose, then, that a man like Socrates finds himself at odds with his community, accused of unreliability, a failure at 'inter-personal truth'?

The method required by our truth-conventions is for a man to 'explain himself' — to put his private knowledge into public language, submit his beliefs to the tests of the prevailing logic. Socrates could claim to have done this, but then he was to a considerable extent the pioneer of explanation, of justifying beliefs by analysis of meaning and the processes of deduction; he was to a considerable extent a pioneer of what we have come to think of as rational discourse. What he failed to do was to appreciate the enormity of the effort required for most people to apply the truth-conventions in these ways. The new freedom his dialectic proposed from unquestioned authority was no sinecure — especially for the authorities. Most people were unprepared for it. Perhaps most people always are unprepared for it.

So the Athenians invoked that other regulator — the law. They brought the contentious philosopher before the positive laws of Athens in their democratic court. We shall say more about law when we discuss the value we call 'justice', but we have now to notice what Socrates said about the laws, for this has to do with truth, and the conventions of truth. He seems to have recognized that a 'city' is held together not only or mainly by its walls but also by those conventions we call 'laws' and still more by the people's *resolve* to sustain the laws. This would explain the first of his reasons for choosing to die when he could have escaped.

If I who have spent my life teaching men respect for truth now show disrespect for the laws either people will shut their minds to my truth or they will think that in accepting it they must consent to the betrayal of Athens.

This is 'reading into' what Socrates is supposed to have said, but this does seem to be what he meant. The 'new way' to objective truth must not be followed at the expense of inter-personal reliability. Truth on one level of experience cannot be permitted to do violence to another. Science (or philosophy) and morals have somehow to avoid conflict in the presence of those they are supposed to help. It seems that Socrates had more scruples in this respect than Galileo . . . or, perhaps, the Holy Office.

Integrity

Socrates' other objection to Crito's plan is closely related to the first — he objects to escape because the man who thus survived would not be Socrates.

'. . . is existence worth having on these terms?' he asks. On what terms? By 'running away' he argues, and 'turning your back upon the compacts and agreements which you made as a citizen',[1] one is involved in contradiction. He would save his skin 'having gone abroad that you may get a dinner . . .'[2] and for the purpose of displaying in foreign cities very little more than that — the skin of Socrates; for his survival, in exile, sworn not to do philosophy, would be the death of his 'self' and the survival of a caricature. This would render all his past life, his past self, meaningless.

'Meaningless' — why? Because a man's 'self' is a whole of his own making — it is that function of his person he has encouraged others to rely upon, to look to as real, by his professions, promises, undertakings, and even (in Socrates) by his rebellions, his criticisms and questionings. To say the opposite of all this or at least to *do* what seems to contradict it all with no chance of explanation is not only to make the self cease to 'exist' but to make it seem never to have been — as if the 'whole' professed by the person was and always had been a deceit, a pretence, a systematic untruth.

'Truth' is relevant to this inner world 'under the skin'. We speak of 'being ourselves' or of 'being true to' ourselves. Or when, for instance, an artist paints a picture which the critic suspects is not in accord with the artist's 'self' the critic will speak of the picture as 'false'. Thus Socrates complained to Crito of the 'ludicrous particulars of the manner in which' he would escape

---

[1] Plato's *Crito* (ibid.) sec. liii, from the address to the Laws. Plato personifies the Laws and puts into their mouth Socrates' reasons for rejecting Crito's offer.

[2] Ibid. sec. liii.

wrapped in a goatskin ... metamorphosed as the manner is of runaways'[1] and what he seems to be objecting to is a kind of deceit, a pretence, a requirement laid upon him if he chooses to escape to act as if he were not himself.

Much of this notion of the 'self' and its value has to do with the value of freedom, which is discussed in Part Two of this book. All we are trying to do now is to establish a connexion between the several levels of experience upon which men speak of 'truth' — a connexion not only in theory and for the purposes of analysis, but a practical connexion — one that is relevant, in other words, to the effort we make to achieve integrity and to work for a better arrangement of our relations with each other.

Now some of Socrates' contemporaries saw no such connexion.[2] Some took 'freedom' to mean that a man by himself could deal directly with 'nature' and, further, enlist 'nature' (*physis*) on his side against the conventions of society (the *nomoi*). Antiphon, for instance, quite clearly advocates the pursuit of 'self-interest' by systematic deceit. Socrates appears to reject this. Revolutionary as he was, a mystic, impious in his attitude to authority and custom, the *Apology* and the *Crito* at least show him as a man who acknowledges his need of the community and understands the task of self-making (or soul-care) as one that is inseparable from social obligation on the one hand, objectivity in learning on the other. Integrity, inter-personal truth or reliability, and objectivity are to some marked degree held together by his example if not at all times by his teaching.

Two faces of morality

'Truth', it seems, has to do with the regulation of knowledge and the regulation of conduct, with logic and method in evaluating experience, with morality both in self-knowledge and in human relations. But morality is two-faced. At the trial of Socrates the judges had to be 'good' men. They had to be men blameless under the conventions, having kept the law and done nothing to earn them a bad name. We often call a man 'immoral' because he has

[1] Ibid.
[2] For example, Antiphon 'the Seer'. His fragment *On Truth* can be studied in Freeman, *AP*, ch. lxxxvii. His antithesis of *physis* and *nomoi* is a prelude in Greek thought to natural law theory (see below, Chapter 12, etc.).

broken a rule or offended against a widely recognized convention. In this sense the judges were not immoral. On the other hand, Socrates is said by his accusers, by Meletus, Anytus, and the rest, to be immoral because he has broken the rules, though many Europeans since his time have regarded him not only as a good man but as an exceptionally good man, a moral expert, a secular saint.

For Socrates has won approval partly because, as we said, he was a pioneer in taking the stand he did for the objective truth. We would not now agree with his criteria for knowledge. Some would even cast doubt on the honesty of some of his arguments, but there still is general agreement that Socrates intended his methods to put objectivity above prejudice and unreflecting assumption even if this cost him his life. But then he took a view of 'the good' which most moral philosophers today would find hard to accept. Moral goodness, right conduct, depended upon a special kind of knowledge, a mystical, visionary experience of 'the good'. To this extent the ultimate test of right conduct was identical with the ends of all learning — the man who *knew* would inevitably be the man to do what was best. There could be no conflict between truth and goodness; the only important conflict was between knowledge and opinion (*doxa* — false knowledge) and in that conflict Socrates was prepared to lose his life. So he can be called a 'good man' even while we see why he was regarded as 'immoral'. When he submits to the laws (which are themselves based upon imperfect knowledge) this is either a kind of 'interim ethic'[1] such as Descartes recommended to those undertaking systematic doubt or a recognition that such submission was good in itself or an important part of good.

The notion that rule-following, doing one's duty by accepting obligations defined by conventions, has moral value has been developed most convincingly by Immanuel Kant. But Kant did

[1] That is, rules for regulating our behaviour in the interval before the dawn of the golden age. The early Christians probably thought about morals in this way as they waited for the Second Coming of Jesus Christ. This is the ethical problem of the 'good man in a bad society'. Compare it with that of the Communist Party member living in a capitalist society or that of the liberal in a totalitarian state. For Descartes's 'interim ethic' see his *Discourse on Method*, part iii. Descartes talks of building himself a temporary dwelling where he may lie while the house of intellect is being demolished and rebuilt.

not teach a blind submission to all rules whatsoever; he, like Socrates, had some concept of personal integrity — the integrity, as he saw it, of rational beings and of rationality as having to do with law — moral law. A rational being is unconditionally bound to conform to the 'categorical imperative' of reason. The dictates of reason must necessarily be addressed to all rational beings as such.

Act on a maxim which thou canst will to be law universal . . .

. . . act so as to treat humanity, in thyself or any other, as an end always, and never as a means only . . .[1]

Here the connexion between integrity and inter-personal reliability is explicit. The dictates of reason seek an end to restrictions upon the will by rational control of impulse or passion just as the laws and conventions of human society could create inter-personal reliability by securing universal recognition of universal laws. Whatever criticisms have to be made of Kant or of Socrates, both men take a position important to social philosophy: they insist that in the regulation of experience heed must be paid to 'truth' on three levels — truth in objective knowledge, truth between persons, and inner truthfulness or integrity.

Summary: The varieties of experience

We began Part One with the 'two worlds' which men, in common with all other animals, must come to terms with. In men we noted an *anxiety* in this quest. They were curious early on and continued to debate how they should think of the universe and how they should regulate their relations with each other. We noted the varieties of experience and in particular the various ways of knowing. We saw that the universe 'tolerated' all this (at least up till now) and that by various conventions men had put some order into their experience, putting it to the test in at least two distinct ways: the tests, that is, of utility on the one hand, reality or truth (in the objective sense) on the other.

During all this we had to recognize (for men at least) the

[1] For a relatively easy introduction to Kant see his *Fundamental Principles of the Metaphysic of Ethics* (*Grundlegung zur Metaphysik der Sitten*), 1st ed., 1785. A translation by T. K. Abbott is published in *Kant's Critique of Practical Reason and other works on the Theory of Ethics*, 6th ed. (Longmans, Green, 1909). Further comment on both Kant and the utilitarians will be found below.

significance of an inner world for our purposes. It was possible to speak of private knowledge and, in due course, of the 'self'. Recognition of these three principal levels of experience gives the scope of what faces us in discussing social values. Tension between these levels brought about by attempts to regulate experience on them was dramatized by the trials of Galileo and of Socrates. Such tensions may be increased or modified and the values we shall be discussing may be considered in this light.

'Freedom', 'justice', 'community', and other social values can be understood as parts of the conceptual arrangements used in making demands for social reconstruction, now in the interest of one and now in the interest of another level of experience. ('Freedom', for instance, is often primarily interested in the right to private knowledge or in maintaining the sheer variety of experience.) We shall attempt to show that such values stand or fall together and that in our time they are exposed to special risks which also threaten the connexion between the principal levels of experience either by increasing tension overmuch or by excessively reducing it.

QUESTIONS FOR DISCUSSION

1. Ought Crito and his friends to have compelled Socrates to escape? A dialogue might be constructed giving the arguments for and against such a course. (Is Rousseau's notion of 'forcing' a man to be 'free' relevant?)

2. Are the following combinations of qualities in persons (*a*) conceivable, (*b*) desirable?

(i) self-deception + trustworthiness; (ii) trustworthiness (or reliability) + ignorance; (iii) erudition + self-deception; (iv) wisdom + unreliability; (v) unreliability + self-knowledge; (vi) integrity + ignorance.

When discussing 'desirability' attempt a scale of preference for these particular combinations or, if they prove unsatisfactory, formulate others.

Part Two

FREEDOM

IO

Nature and Freedom

'IF all existing things turned to smoke the nose would be the discriminating organ.'[1] Heraclitus forgot to mention that on this hypothesis noses, too, would have gone up in smoke. 'It is not possible', he said elsewhere, 'to step twice into the same river.' No doubt he knew well enough that words like *potamos* ('river') are signs we use to signify the regularity, the permanence, we need and are able to impose even where nature may seem to provide nothing but flux, unchanging change, a formless, pointless, endless, purposeless stream — whether of 'consciousness' or other events. Change and rest, identity and difference, however, divided Greek thinkers as if on opposite sides in a contest, a war of ideas. Heraclitus was apparently on the side of change: if there was continuity anywhere in the universe as he saw it this was in fire.

... all things for Fire and Fire for all things, like goods for gold and gold for goods.[2]

Parmenides of Elea and others retaliated by trying to deny all change. Nor was the conflict merely about nature. Heraclitus most probably was driven to his views by the breakdown of old norms and traditions in Ephesus. On the other hand, thinkers who postulated changelessness in nature may well have done so as part of their resistance to social change, to increases in human freedom.[3]

[1] Heraclitus of Ephesus. See Freeman, *AP*, ch. xxii, fragments vii and xci, and with xci compare fragment xii: 'Those who step into the same river have different waters flowing ever upon them.'

[2] Ibid. fragment xc. On the thought of Heraclitus in relation to 'science' and, at the same time, as 'historicist' and anti-democratic, see K. Popper, *The Open Society and its Enemies*, vol. i, ch. ii, and other references.

[3] This is part of Karl Popper's case against both Plato and Heraclitus and as such it illustrates the possible relation between thought about nature and thought about human freedom.

Whether the universe cares about men or not, men who have cared about it and about society have found it very hard indeed to know what to think of the connexion between changes 'out there' (in the universe) and the demands for change within the city, between the order they need in the city and the 'laws' they think they can find in the elements.

Part One of this book presented the varieties of experience with the suggestion that these in themselves provided the conditions for freedom. That same diversity of opinion which led Protagoras[1] to turn in disgust from 'truth' to the pragmatic, social criterion for beliefs could be seen as evidence that at least the universe had not compressed us into uniformity but had left us free to make of it what we would. Life may be a university in which the examinations come before the lessons, but we have been able to choose our questions or even to make them up ourselves. The 'varieties of experience' were not the endless flux and formless change of Heraclitus; they were *experience* — and this always means, in some sense, 'putting to the test': whether the complex, sophisticated tests of science, of mathematics, of formal logic, or those less precise, less formal experiments by which such wholes as 'self' or 'society' seek to regulate experience and so give it meaning, 'within the whole'.

This is why we should hesitate to talk of 'natural liberty' unless we are going to mean by 'natural' all that is 'there' and 'given' for each new generation as the conditions of its freedom; and this would mean expanding 'natural' to include so much that is 'social' that there would be little left to justify the word.

For the varieties of experience have increased in range and diversity through processes which lie well within the domain of social order, enabling us today, for example, to pursue the study of such processes independently of physics, astronomy, geology. The distinction Protagoras made between *physis* (nature) and *nomoi* (conventions — social regulations as opposed to natural regularities) lies at the basis of our modern social studies and it leads us to this thought: if freedom is possible only within such conditions of variety, and if these conditions in their turn are increasingly dependent upon social regulation, would it not be as well to address our interest in freedom to what *men* can do and

[1] See above, Part One, Chapter 7.

have shown they can do about it; for by the same processes which have increased variety may it not be possible to *decrease* it and limit freedom? Education, that is, may at first 'widen the horizon' but it may subsequently cut down the approved and equipped levels of experience.

Regularity and regulation

'Man is born free,'[1] so Rousseau said. The 'Principles' of 1789,[2] echoing him, set themselves in the name of *liberté* to do something about the rest of his proposition:

> Man is born free, yet everywhere he is in chains.

Our point now is not that we cannot speak of 'natural liberty' but that in doing so we should begin with man's quest for regularity both in nature and in society. For some at least of the so-called 'problems of freedom' are traceable not to 'neutral' nature but to the need we have of regularity in nature and the regulations we impose upon ourselves in looking for it. This search for order, for regularity, may be itself evidence of our freedom in the universe. But there is something to be said for calling this 'collective freedom'; for so powerful is the need behind it that we seize upon an established pattern and defend it bitterly against 'nonconformists', 'deviationists', denying them liberty rather than exposing ourselves to the upsets and discomforts of having the picture spoilt. In such moods we keep our trust in nature's regularities by a harsh regulation of 'private knowledge', of other levels or varieties of experience.

Remember Socrates. Remember Galileo Galilei. Truth may not in our hearts be 'the majority vote of the nation that can lick all others',[3] but there is always a risk of interest vested in some model of order precious to a group, small or large, in its guarantee of distinction if not of survival, leading the members of the group to use or abuse the truth-conventions for their own ends and so do violence to the liberty of others. We ought not to take it for

[1] *Social Contract*, bk i, ch. i.
[2] That is, the *Declaration of Rights* preceding the first French Constitution of 1791. Article One reads: 'Men are born free and equal as regards their rights. Social distinctions can be based only on the common interest.' A translation of the *Declaration* can be found in G. de Ruggiero, *History of European Liberalism*, trans. R. G. Collingwood, 1st ed. (O.U.P., 1927; Boston, Beacon paperback, 1959), pp. 66 ff.
[3] Oliver Wendell Holmes jr (see above, Part One, Chapter 9).

granted that this cannot happen in our modern sciences. On the contrary, since far more careers depend today on the reputation of far more special studies than ever before, this alone might make us hesitate to assume that nature is on the side of every professional group which claims a monopoly in her regularities.[1]

What we are saying has nothing to do with the question whether the universe provides for human liberty. It *has* to do with the question whether we can trust what men say about nature to be neutral in respect of liberty. Lord Kelvin once said that he could understand any phenomenon if he could make a mechanical model of it. This is not to say that the 'real world' (whatever that may be) or even the phenomenal world *are* machines; it is to say that Lord Kelvin and others who think like him are satisfied with machine-like regularity: a model of the mind which resembled a telephone-exchange, for instance, would doubtless give them satisfaction. Others seeking to 'understand' human behaviour like to reduce it to homogeneous particles — to sensations, perhaps, or 'sense-data' — possibly, in the process, dissolving an original experience which baffled and teased them in order that they might be comfortable with 'elements' more familiar, less troublesome.[2] If we are in so much of a hurry to escape the complex, the mysterious, the unfamiliar, we may or we may not uncover viable 'regularities'; what we have to be prevented from doing is imposing our 'understanding' as a regulation upon other people's experience in such a way that they are denied what we could not endure, and we in our turn are deprived of challenge to further, more creative thought.

A *regularity* is an order of events we sometimes say we 'find' in nature. A *regulation* is an order we seek to impose upon events whether in experimenting with nature or in the arrangement of our human relations. Now the variety of experience suggests that the regularities we 'find' are also to some extent imposed;[3] that is, the 'flux' of Heraclitus' river is also 'there' to be found just as

[1] Psycho-analysis should provide some examples. For some evidence see W. Sargant, *Battle for the Mind, A Physiology of Conversion and Brain-Washing*, 1st ed. (Heinemann, 1957; revised ed., Pan, 1959), ch. iv.

[2] Note, for instance, the use made of Democritus's atomic theory by Epicurus and his followers. See C. Bailey, *The Greek Atomists and Epicurus* (O.U.P., 1928).

[3] For the way this might happen in 'reductionist' psychologies see a comment by F. V. Smith, *Explanation of Human Behaviour*, 2nd ed. (Constable, 1960), p. 55.

much as the constancy we might call 'riverness'. The regularities we formulate are, after all, our formulation. The dividing line, then, between 'finding' regularities and imposing regulation is not so sharp and clear as we sometimes think. For this reason great care is needed in seeking the aid of 'nature' either for or against the cause of human freedom. (Nature, like many neutrals, has her price and may be bought over for an exchange of ideas.) *Men* make rules and follow them: rules, that is, both of the 'primary' kind such as the truth-conventions, and of the sort we call 'moral' or 'positive'. By such rule-making and rule-following we manifest our freedom even as, from another point of view, we limit it. (This is like defining a term — you show what it is to mean by showing what it is not to mean.) In this chapter we shall see how ambiguous 'nature' can be as a term in rule-making, as an ally of freedom. In the following chapter we will turn to problems of freedom arising from the confusions we are discussing here and, in particular, the problem of 'free will'.

Nature and natural law

The advantages laid down by the laws are chains upon nature, but those laid down by nature are free.[1]

Fifth-century Sophists, like Antiphon, were so upset by the variety of social rules on the one hand, the conflict between them and a man's felt interests on the other, that they appealed to Nature (*physis*) as a source of regularity, unchanging, invariable, *and* amenable to human need. As a protest against social regulation this looks like a demand for liberty — liberty from the conventions (*nomoi*). When, however, we turn to find *what* it is Nature protects, so far as the records show Antiphon, for instance, has reduced human need to such animal necessities as eating and breathing. Antiphon was no anarchist; but his contempt for the conventions and his respect for Nature gave him no more exalted view of what freedom could mean than we found in models of human behaviour

---

[1] Antiphon the Seer. For references to Antiphon see above, Chapter 9, p. 102. The fragment quoted is in Freeman, *AP*, no. xliv and the argument seems to be that the *nomoi* (conventions) threaten survival, but at the end we read 'We all breathe into the air through mouth and nostrils and we all eat with hands'. On the other hand, note fragments lx, lxi, the first on the need for education, the second against anarchy and for obedience. Antiphon does not encourage rebellion. Prudent conformity is as necessary as private respect for *physis*.

which reduce men to the order of the machines they have made or the homogeneous particles they have observed or thought it possible to observe. Antiphon, for instance, had to go 'down' to the animal level of breathing and eating to establish that men were both equal and entitled to be free of the conventions.

'Back to nature!' is, none the less, a slogan used in demands for freedom. Sometimes it is obviously misleading. Leo Tolstoy's[1] attacks on corruption and artificiality in civilization, for example, may be traced to his own inner conflicts — to the conflict, for instance, between the spontaneous and unreflecting on the one hand, the reasonable and lawful on the other. But unless we are going to mean by 'natural' the same as we mean by 'spontaneous' Tolstoy's demands have much more to do with acquired freedom — with what we have to make of ourselves — than with a 'going back', a 'return to' nature. They are demands that society be not dissolved, but simplified. So with the teaching of Mohandas Karamchand Gandhi.[2] He identified himself with the poor; he said he was a politician trying to become a saint. *Satyagraha* — 'soul-force' or 'truth-force' — has nothing to do with a 'return' to animal nature. Gandhi questioned the uses to which we should put our science; he did not propose to unravel a scientific culture, return the wool to the skein, and try to live as if scientific man had never happened.

The Greek Cynics are better examples of the 'back to nature' way with human freedom. The very name 'cynic' — 'dog-like', 'houndish' — shows what was thought of them. They were no mere pleasure-seekers. Diogenes the Cynic embraced statues covered with snow 'using every means to inure himself to hardship'.[3] The Cynics abused etiquette, manners, good taste, showing contempt for the conventions and the conventional. What had (non-human) 'nature' to do with it? Diogenes 'claimed that to fortune he could oppose courage, to convention nature, to passion reason':[4] this was mistrust of social regulation, yet at the same time it was human art imposing upon men a regularity thought to be more in accordance with human reason.

---

[1] Leo Tolstoy (1828–1910). His *Confession* is an account of his religious conversion to a 'new Christianity'. See further *What I believe in* and *A short exposition of the Gospels*.

[2] M. K. Gandhi (the *Mahatma*), 1869–1948. He called his autobiography *The Story of my Experiments with Truth*.

[3] Diogenes the Cynic, as quoted in *DL*, vi, 23.   [4] Ibid. vi. 38.

The Stoics,[1] the Men of the Porch, put nature to new uses. Zeno of Citium (in Cyprus), their founder, was succeeded by Cleanthes of Assus — the man who tried to prosecute Aristarchus of Samos for saying that the earth moved round the sun, this being out of keeping with the Stoic model of the universe. Man, according to the Stoics, was one with nature but different from other animals because the creative *pneuma* takes in him the form of rational soul, situated in the heart and nourished by the blood. Zeno (it is said) was the first to say that the proper end for man was 'life according to nature'. But the differences in later Stoic beliefs are interesting. Chrysippus of Solsus, who followed Cleanthes, explicitly included the 'nature of man' in the 'nature' which should be the standard,[2] while Cleanthes seems to have taken 'nature' in its more limited sense. Again, it is easier to believe we are listening to men disputing about the good life or the good society than to genuine appeals *from* what man is *to* some non-human authority called 'nature'.

'Rational soul', to the Stoics, was on the one hand a distinctive form of Nature in men, on the other hand it was the basis for a new 'community of meaning'. All wise men were 'naturally' friends. In place of the familiar city — Athens, Rome — with its narrow territorial and inherited affinities, would come the Cosmopolis, the world city under nature's law — the law, that is, of reason.

So emerges the powerful European concept of natural law. Powerful, and ambiguous.

Nature could be used to consecrate the monarch as well as the people.[3]

[1] For the Stoics see E. Zeller, *Outlines of the History of Greek Philosophy* (Meridian, 1955), pp. 58 ff. For earlier comment here on natural law see above, Part One, Chapter 8.

[2] Even as Edmund Burke, opposing Rousseau, said: 'Art is man's nature' (*Appeal from New to Old Whigs*). Compare with this Sir Thomas Browne, *Religio Medici*, part i, sec. 16: 'Nature is not at variance with Art, nor Art with Nature . . . Art is the perfection of Nature . . .'.

[3] Sir Ernest Barker in his introduction to O. Gierke's *Natural Law and the Theory of Society* which he translated into English (C.U.P., 1950). The whole of this introduction is relevant. A good introduction to the subject (perhaps the best) has already been recommended in A. d'Entrèves's *Natural Law* (Hutchinson, 1916). For the Stoics and the place of natural law in European political thought see also Sabine, *HPT*, part ii, ch. 8, and for more detailed study, R. W. and A. J. Carlyle, *A History of Medieval Political Theory in the West* (Chapter 2, p. 35), vol. i, part i, chs 1 and 2.

One way of understanding what happened is by means of the notion of *alienation* developed by Ludwig A. Feuerbach[1] after some ideas of his master, Hegel. Writing of religious belief, Feuerbach said that the symbols of such belief were nothing but the 'essence' of man, the believer, projected outside himself, reified, personified. We may apply the same explanation to the Stoics and their natural law. Human reason and the human sense of justice — both at war so often with established usages — are projected outwards on to the panoramic screen of nature where they take on size, magnificence, authority enough to overawe some opposition — at least until the opposition to reason and justice works out ways and means of making use of them. For, once 'out there', detached from their proper, human sources, once given the stature and the abstraction of Nature, those more concerned for power than for reason or justice can invest themselves with the mysteries and so debase the very human activities natural law was 'meant' to exalt. Institutions sacred and secular, absolute monarchs and infallible popes are able to place their powers under the protective awning of these 'huge, cloudy symbols'[2] and to suggest that their authority is nothing more nor less than the authority of the universe incarnate.

Karl Marx took a great deal of interest in Feuerbach's explanation of religious symbols, but he criticized such Hegelians for not going on with their analysis of the causes giving rise to such alienation of human qualities. What they did instead, on his view, was to 'dissolve' man into nature by failing to take account of the social conflicts at the root of all this and calling for remedial action.

... the fact that the secular basis deserts its own sphere and establishes an independent realm in the clouds, can only be explained by the cleavage and self-contradictions within this secular basis ...[3]

[1] Ludwig Andreas Feuerbach (1804–72), son of a famous jurist and father of Anselm, the painter. Feuerbach shares the views of Spinoza on immortality as reabsorption into nature. His concept of alienation appears in *Das Wesen des Christenums* (1841), which was translated by George Ekiot. See H. B. Acton, *The Illusion of the Epoch* (Cohen & West, 1962), pp. 52 ff. and pp. 115 ff., and S. Hook, *From Hegel to Marx* (London, 1936).

[2] John Keats (1795–1821), from the sonnet 'When I have fears that I may cease to be' (1817).

[3] Karl Marx, *Theses on Feuerbach*. See Bottomore and Rubel, *Karl Marx: Selected Writings in Sociology and Social Philosophy*, hereafter referred to as 'Bottomore and Rubel' (Penguin, 1961), ch. ii.

In short, though 'history . . . is a real part of natural history, of the development of nature into man',[1] the understanding of the human condition must be sought not in the clouds or the elements but within human relations. One does not have to be a Marxist to accept this view.

Europe and natural law

'Natural law' in a variety of forms has had a large part to play in European political and social thought. Still, when there is need to defend human rights against the laws, policies, and prejudices of powerful communities, men may reach out for 'nature' and natural law as if to old and well-tried weapons. To resist arrogant nationalism, to condemn inhumanity and injustice, in order to defend faith in universal *human* standards, something like this concept is essential. We have to keep the need in mind through all our discussion of social values.

Let us now recall in order to see the difficulties in using 'nature' a comment made after the First World War by a German scholar troubled by the ideas he found at work in his own country. In an address to the German *Hochschule für Politik* in October 1922 Ernst Troeltsch said there was a common European tradition of natural law which he saw as a blending of Stoic theory with Christianity.[2] The intellectual tradition in Germany shared this general system of ideas and it persisted 'in the ranks of German Catholicism'. After the Reformation, however, came an 'excess of emphasis on original sin'[3] together with a comparable stress 'on mere authority': a connexion to which attention was drawn in this book when we discussed the myth of the Fall. Thus, according to Troeltsch, the old, humanitarian concept of natural law in Germany was reduced to a concept of 'enlightened despotism'.

Then, he said, the Romantic movement emerged in rebellion against much that was undesirable in European thought before and after the French Revolution. Ideas of equality and utility, the mechanistic interpretation of nature by the new science, all these were resisted by the mystical and poetical impulses they offended.

---

[1] Karl Marx, *Economic and Political Manuscripts*. See Bottomore and Rubel, p. 85.

[2] Troeltsch's address is published as an appendix to Otto Gierke's *Natural Law and the Theory of Society* (see p. 115 above).

[3] Original sin. See also above, Part One, Chapter 8.

The thought of Romanticism is directed to the particular, the positive: to what is eternally productive of new variety, constructive, spiritually organic...[1]

Troelstch by this argument supports the view that 'nature' and 'natural law' need more comprehensive concepts of freedom and other social values if they are to be useful. He also suggests that attempts to rationalize *all* experience with consequent injury to its variety may provoke rebellions which deal harshly not only with the evils which provoke them but, as the Romantic movement in German politics did, with institutions which protect human freedom.

'Natural selection'

The Social Darwinists[2] are among our more recent examples of those who appeal to 'nature' with harmful consequences. The laws of nature Charles Darwin was said to have formulated were the bases for ideologies which in some instances lent themselves to violent attacks on liberty and justice. We recall, for example, Houston Chamberlain's view that the 'Teutons' were those 'fittest to survive' and how this notion was used ultimately to justify the elimination of other races and less 'fit' persons. The antisemitism of Nazi policy was thus able to claim the authority of 'nature'.[3] It may help to recall what Darwin himself said about man's place in nature. Having spoken of natural, sexual selection, he takes note of intellectual and social qualities in man.

Important as the struggle for existence has been and even still is, yet as far as the highest part of man's nature is concerned there are other agencies more important. For the moral qualities are advanced ... more through ... habit ... reasoning, instruction, religion ... than through natural selections.[4]

---

[1] Troeltsch, op. cit., pp. 210 f.

[2] Social Darwinists: see above, Part One, Chapter 5.

[3] Houston Chamberlain and the National Socialists. In addition to previous references see A. Bullock, *Hitler: A Study in Tyranny* (Companion Book Club, 1954; originally by Odhams Press), p. 72. The author gives an account of Hitler's visit to *Haus Wahnfried*, home of the Wagner family in Bayreuth. Houston Stewart Chamberlain married one of Wagner's daughters. He was captivated by Hitler. 'At one stroke', he wrote to him, 'you have transformed the state of my soul.'

[4] Charles Darwin, *The Descent of Man*, part iii, ch. xxi.

QUESTIONS FOR DISCUSSION

1. Compare the fragments of Heraclitus on p. 109 with the opening clauses of the *Declaration of Rights* in the footnote to p. 111. Discuss the part that 'nature' plays in each in relation to the concept of human good. Additional reading: K. Popper, *The Open Society and its Enemies*, ch. ii.

2. 'Man is born free . . .' In what sense could this be (*a*) true, (*b*) false, (*c*) meaningless? (For the third possibility ask whether *man* is 'born' at all?) Have in mind also Burke's 'Art is man's nature'.

3. According to Feuerbach the objects of religious faith are nothing but the projections of human qualities on to nature. By the same tokens so might be Stoic natural law and Protagoras's social virtues. If Feuerbach was right what does this tell us (*a*) about man, (*b*) about nature, (*c*) about society? On the last point see the quotation from Marx on pp. 116 f.

I I

Nature, Will and Act

> I must have liberty
> Withal, as large a charter as the wind,
> To blow on whom I please . . .[1]

said the fool, Jaques. In Shakespeare's day and after, the kings of
Europe granted charters for trade and colonization, thus doing in
particular what we do generally when we call men 'free'. What
was a 'charter'?[2] If you mean what 'thing' was it, the answer is
little more than 'no thing'. A little paper. A bill. A page or two in
the records today. Such a thing in 'nature' would blow away
before a gentle puff of wind or pulp into mush after a shower or
two. Such a thing within the world men had made *enabled* them to
create new trade relations, make homes, build cities, and so set in
motion the new civilizations of America and the Antipodes, the
old and settled communities extending their kinds of order like an
invisible barrier around the creative activities of their sons.

The idea of freedom is like a general charter we exchange with
each other sometimes through the agency of our authorized
governments, sometimes despite them, often as a way of protecting
our human, creative work against our own hasty, passionate need
for order both in society and in nature. When in social philosophy
we try to arrange a general concept of freedom we may be said to
be mapping out the distinctively human, drafting a charter to
protect those experiences in which it is developed, and, like
diplomats, working to secure respect for it among all men.

[1] *As You Like It*, II, vii.
[2] There are, of course, many examples of charters issued in the period but one
easy of access is in Tawney and Power, *Tudor Economic Documents*, 3 vols (Longmans,
Green, 1924), vol. ii, no. 10, the *Charter to Merchants Trading to Andalusia, 1531*. The
conceptual basis of such a document is worth studying.

Here we are still concerned for the protection necessary against 'nature' — or, more particularly, the habits we get into through our study of nature, habits which may endanger human experience if we do not respect the 'charter'; in other words, take proper precautions to pursue our study without doing violence to its objects. We will take two of the most familiar difficulties people find in talking about freedom and see how these arise *partly* at least from misunderstandings which, in their turn, may be traceable to other ways of knowing than those called for in the study of human relations.

Free will

We may [said John Locke] as properly say that it is the singing faculty sings, and the dancing faculty dances, as that the will chooses ...[1]

The habit of supposing that for every name given to an activity it should be possible to find a distinct, specialist agent to which an appropriate title can be given no doubt has its roots in superstitions as primitive as animism. Something moves; so either someone moved it or it is self-moving. Refine the point of view and it becomes a special kind of movement, therefore a special mover whose whole-time job it is to carry out such movements. After all, we call one who sings a 'singer' and one who dances a 'dancer'; but since prior to dancing and singing we must suppose both the singer and the dancer *willing* to sing and dance, and since 'singing', 'dancing', and 'willing' all sound the same (all alike in English being participial forms of the verb), there must be a 'will' to do the 'willing' as there is a singer for the singing and so on.

'Faculty' psychology honoured this habit of thinking about men. To that master-agent of human, mental functions — the soul or psyche — others were added each with its special function. Reason did the reasoning. The appetites did the feeling. Willing was done by the will. It was easy then to slip into the habit of asking whether or not the will was 'free'; for this sounded every bit as reasonable as, for example, asking some human agent for his credentials, trying to find out whether he was his own master or the servant of another.

---

[1] Locke, *Essay*, II. 17. The whole chapter should be read. The *Essay* is regarded as the formal initiation of British empiricism in psychology.

'Is the will free?' is then a false question unless we persist in thinking of 'the will' as a name for a specific faculty. To say that a man is *willing* to sing or dance is to say, provided no hindrances are stipulated, that he sees himself as choosing to entertain himself or us in this way rather than pass his time in some other occupation. We add nothing to our account of the situation if we say, 'he is freely willing'. On the other hand, if the 'pub' has no licence for singing or dancing, if he has drunk too much to stand upright or articulate clearly, or if we simply cannot bear his performance, we can say, 'Despite his willingness he neither sang nor danced'. Or if he refuses in spite of our entreaties, 'He was not willing . . .' Alternatively we might say, 'He was free', or 'He was not free'. Nothing is gained save confusion by giving an account of this fascinating incident in terms of 'the will' and its freedom.

The trouble with this kind of verbal tidying up, however, is that we may be caught by another deceit: one to which we are exposed today in much the same way as Locke's predecessors were caught out by their 'faculty' way of thinking. This is the deceit of supposing that a problem which for centuries has been complicated by verbal misunderstandings ceases to be a problem at all once we have re-phrased it. So pleasant a thing is it to score off the ancients (who cannot answer back) by showing our dexterity with words, so delightful is it to silence a living opponent by using similar devices to make a fool out of him that in our conceit we sometimes imagine we have done much more. We mistake word-play for thought; we throw out precious babies with their dirty bath-water (a dastardly project which comes more easily to those with no love for the victims); when we have done our tidying up we fancy we have finished our philosophy.

The free will controversy in psychology, in ethics,[1] in law, and in theology was the form given for centuries to the task we have set ourselves here — that of marking out and defending the place man has made for himself in nature. We want to know how we are to treat ourselves and each other; whether we owe each other a special kind of respect; whether the conduct of our affairs requires

[1] For one statement of the problem in Ethics see H. Sidgwick, *The Methods of Ethics*, 7th ed. (Macmillan, 1907), bk i, ch. v, and compare A. J. Ayer, 'Freedom and Necessity' published in his *Philosophical Essays* (Macmillan, 1954). For a most useful introduction to the whole concept (or the concepts) of freedom see M. Cranston, *Freedom: A New Analysis* (Longmans, Green, 1953).

us to bestow on a man, simply because he is a man, a *status* enabling him to be what otherwise he would not be. Let us leave 'will', then, for the moment, and turn to another way of approaching the problem of freedom — the concept of an 'act'.

Movements and acts

Studies of man most satisfactory to those methods of science which have gained pride of place in our time are those which lead to measurement, to the quantification of variables.[1] In order to achieve these ends we are required to *analyse*, to concentrate on such features of an object as mass, motion, chemical constitution — features susceptible to measurement, to quantification. It is assumed that the features isolated by analysis will recur — we are looking for regularity — and it is hoped that the differences between specimens will be irrelevant, while those which are relevant can be expressed as quantitative values of the variables in the scientific law. Hence, in psychology, some of the procedures called 'Behaviourist'.[2] They call, in some cases, for language 'the same as that of an observer recording the movements of any physical object in the environment . . .', the language, as the same writer says, of 'things', of things, we would add, in relation to observers.

'Movements' is the neutral word suitable to the role of 'observer' in relation to 'things' suitable to measurement by analysis and the relative ignoring of differences in order to establish laws as the basis for prediction. To undertake to observe movements with such ends in view is by the same undertaking to 'bracket' such concepts as freedom — to set *them* aside as irrelevant, not specifically to undertake their refutation. For the aim is first to isolate the movement from possible 'wholes' *not* susceptible to the methods, then to relate it to chains or patterns of movements or events which *are* amenable and may lead to the desired results. It is to choose one way of knowing in preference to another.

Even so — even within the purposes chosen — there are, of course, acknowledged limitations. The psychological phenomena

[1] This is not to say that measurement is all that science is about or that an experience which is not quantifiable cannot be studied scientifically. On this see H. Margenau, *Ethics and Science* (Van Nostrand, 1964). This is, of course, partly a question of how we decide to use the word 'science'.

[2] 'Behaviourism': see F. V. Smith, *Explanation of Human Behaviour*, part iii.

which do not measure precisely might either be said not to exist or to have no significance: the first alternative leaves out much that is of most interest in human experience; the second may not be satisfactory, for instance, to the evolutionist. For he holds that states not useful to organisms will atrophy or vanish whereas in fact these human qualities increase in complication and diversity. Analysis, similarly, when applied to human character may require abstraction from the very 'whole' which is the object of interest. As for regularity, as for the hope that the behaviour of one man or one group of men will instruct us in the behaviour of others, it is possible that this will only be achieved by deliberately ignoring those prominent and significant qualities which lead us to talk about persons as 'unique'.

'Movements' in this neutral sense are in any case of little help to social service: they do not help us to mark out the territory of the distinctively human let alone to embark on the reconstruction of human relations. What we have to contend with is something quite different. Once we in our turn have set aside the ends and procedures of the physical sciences we find ourselves, in society, contending not just with movements but with *acts*.[1] Acts are movements given a new status under some such 'primary convention' as those we related to the uses of 'truth'. They are movements 'under the charter', with a difference.

There was once an oriental king who in the course of an attempted invasion of Europe had his plans upset by the currents of the Hellespont. The legend says he had the waters whipped for their *lèse-majesté*. If so, Xerxes bestowed on the movement of the waters the status of an act. This is an honour which, with time, we have come to bestow first on men only and then subsequently on some but not all human movements. On the other hand, arising no doubt from our now long-term habits of mutual respect, it has for a long time rested not with the courts alone nor even with public opinion to distinguish between movements which are and movements which are not acts. Men have claimed the 'right' or the 'dignity' to do this on their own behalf, 'accepting responsibility', as we say, even where public opinion is prepared to 'excuse' or in some other way, for a variety of reasons, to deny to their movements the status of action.

[1] On this use of 'act' see R. S. Peters, *The Concept of Motivation* (Routledge, 1958).

Our argument is that the concept of freedom is part and parcel of this 'charter' under which we agree to accept the possibility of a man's 'owning' his movements — whatever that may come to mean — and that all we have to say in our social philosophy about freedom in morals, politics, human relations generally, freedom circumstantial or acquired, can be said in terms of the *value* we put upon this practice, the demand we make either to be relieved of action or to have more of it.

'*The name of action*'[1]

'A man is free,' let us say, 'so far as he can make what he does his own action and what he achieves his own property.'[2] We have now to say in general what is implied by 'making what he does his own action'. The detail of this, together with what is implied by 'making what he does his own property' will occupy us in the following chapters.

Let us say for the moment that we are asking how movements can come to be a man's 'own actions', and let us mean by this first not 'by what processes could this come about' but 'what is necessary before we can speak in this way'. What seems to be necessary beyond all reasonable argument if we are to speak of movements as a 'man's own actions' is that we should be able to conceive of the man as in some sense and to some degree an independent 'whole'. This in its turn means a different kind of approach from the procedures we discussed just now — those which abstract a particular movement from any such possible whole in order to explain it quantitatively. On the contrary, we are now determining to 'respect' the act as belonging to such a whole whether or not there are good reasons to do otherwise. This is what the 'charter' requires of us. This is what we mean by the *mode* in which human relations are to be conducted.

Movements can be rated as actions by their being attributed to

[1] The quotation, of course, is from Prince Hamlet's soliloquy, *Hamlet*, III. i. He says that 'enterprises of great pith and moment . . . lose the name of action' under the enervating influence of thought and conscience.

[2] This is the form given to the general concept at the end of the first part of the massive work done by the Institute for Philosophical Research and published under the title *The Idea of Freedom*, ed. Mortimer J. Adler (New York, Doubleday, 1958). My use of the proposition should not be taken as commitment to the findings of this work or to its methods.

such conceptual wholes as 'the self', 'the person', or 'character'. We are now brought back by another route to the problem we agreed not to think of as that of 'free will'. For while we are equally committed not to talk of 'free acts' (though for reasons yet to be rehearsed), we are proposing to talk and behave as if 'selves' (or whatever) were in some sense 'independent'.

'Independent', however, need not give too much offence to our scientific conscience. We are not proposing to talk of the movements as the scientist studies them, or even of the parts of the organism or the personality as they may be 'scientifically' studied as unconditioned or 'indeterminate'. On the contrary, a man's movements can be said to be his 'own' if and only if he has determined them, or otherwise, in some way, determined that they or their consequences or both shall be treated as determined by him. So if, for instance, I bump into you 'accidentally' and knock a priceless heirloom out of your hands, quite apart from what the law may or may not say I might choose to 'assume responsibility' and by paying or helping to pay for the damage 'make the act my own', or, more strictly, turn the movement into my action.

The question about 'independence' is now shifted from a question about such isolatable characteristics as 'will' or 'movement' to what we have called the 'whole' — that is, the 'self' or 'the person'. Let us use 'person' in the broadest possible sense for all that 'I' am — the organism, its functions, the 'conscious', the 'unconscious', character, temperament, and so forth. Now let us use 'self' to mean[1] the person in respect of a special condition — as aware (in part) of itself and as struggling through awareness to integrity, to wholeness, to *self*-recognition.[1] And this is being done by laying claim to the whole person not by mere acceptance or shuddering away from what is unacceptable but by acceptance or rejection of elements in the person 'under rule' according to a pattern *and* (as part of the same process) by making one's movements so far as possible one's own acts.

Now clearly the person (as we are using the word) has an environment and many of his movements are as dependent upon his physical conditions as many of his functions are, equally

---

[1] 'Self' is to be used, for example, for the conscious 'inner circle' including the notion of what I prefer to be or become while 'person' is used for the whole of what the self must accept if it is to *become* progressively.

clearly, upon his social context. But this is not the same as to say that his movements are *wholly* determined by his environment. (Of how many objects of science would this be said today?) As for the 'self', we can liken this in some respects to an 'independence movement' within a nation ruled by a foreign power. As such a movement may rally more or less of the nation around it, as it can, by finally ejecting the foreigner, and become the government *de facto*, yet do all this within the limits imposed on 'independence' by the actualities of domestic and foreign relations, so may the 'self' in somewhat the same terms measure its success or its failure as the growing or diminishing freedom of the person.

We have to have some such notion if we are to speak of movements as becoming 'a man's own actions'. We can give the name of 'action' to movements seen as having meaningful relation to the agent's person; though perhaps it is only the person who can give us an account of their relation to the self, for he and he alone can *claim* movements as his own actions — a thought to which we shall return later when we discuss acquired freedom.

Now we will turn to the processes by which, conceivably, a man's movements may come to be regarded as his own actions.

Acts and 'society'

Whether the Persian king whipped the waters or (as another story goes) flung fetters into them to show his mastery he might have profited from the remark of his contemporary, Heraclitus, about never stepping into the same river twice. With time we have come to hold as responsible only those agents who can be said to be 'there' not only when the deed was done but after. Movements are converted to acts by virtue of the continuity of their agent and this in its turn is both recognized and *realized* not only in the institutions which punish and reward, not only in our habits of praise and blame, but in all co-operation. When we spoke of inter-personal truth, of the primary conventions arising from the need we have to rely upon each other, we related this in its turn to integrity — to inner truth, to the wholeness and reliability of what we were, just now, calling the 'self'. It would be hard to work with a man if you had a shrewd suspicion that his movements were the outworkings of post-hypnotic suggestion; impossible to *plan* to work with a man whom you could not rely upon to act in the same general way tomorrow as he has acted in the past. *Liability* — having to own movements as your own acts for the purpose of reward or punishment — is a special case of *reliability*. Both assume something like what we have called the 'self' and by their assumptions, by the institutions which regard men in this way, help to realize this.

That is why we cannot discuss freedom without at the same time discussing responsibility. And that is why in all criticism of contemporary social values we have to have in mind the hypothesis that any value which plays down responsibility or 'whittles it away'[1] may upon reflection also be shown to be inimical to freedom. Our ownership of our acts, as we said at the start, calls for a general agreement that we *shall* treat each other in this way, though the question to what extent a man is 'free' to do this even though his fellows try to deny him the right is an important question to which we shall return.

'A man is free', we said, 'so far as he can make what he does his own action and what he achieves his own property.' Our movements are made within a given area of the universe; they impinge upon that area and the people who share it. They utilize parts of the universe as tools or even people as means and when they are recognizable as acts they do all this for ends or purposes seen and pursued as such by the person who makes them. It seems reasonable, then, in discussing freedom to make a great deal of this property question; to argue, that is, that a man should have *room* to move and also — included in the 'freedom charter' — some special claim to the consequences of what his movements achieve — to the 'fruit of his labours' as Locke would say, to the enjoyment of his achievements, as we might more carefully frame it.

That this is what men have demanded in demanding freedom there can be no doubt. We shall consider such demands as we go. But what we shall also try to show is that a social philosophy must

---

[1] The phrase, 'whittling away of responsibility', can be traced, I think, to P. Fauconnet, *La Responsabilité, étude de sociologie* (Alcan, 1920), but that does not mean I am following this analysis. Fauconnet's views are discussed by J. Piaget, *The Moral Judgment of the Child* (Routledge, 1932), ch. iv, a writer whose conclusions are more in accord with what is maintained here. The phrase 'dispensing with responsibility' was used by B. Wootton in her *Social Science and Social Pathology* (Allen & Unwin, 1959). For a note on this see N. Haines, 'Dispensing with Responsibility', in *Philosophy*, vol. xxxviii, no. 143, pp. 69 f.

have a concept of freedom broader and deeper than this. If we call the demand for space and for rights enabling men to 'make what they achieve their property' 'circumstantial freedom' and all that is necessary for 'making their actions their own' 'acquired freedom' then the point we are making is that we need a general concept of freedom to include both the circumstantial and the acquired and that (we shall try to show) in the interests of both. For if there is little hope of becoming one's self without space and without resources, there *is* no self where all you have is a person moving about like others and having no distinctive qualities. So we have to discuss demands for circumstantial freedom (as in politics) side by side with their moral implications and what has been said independently of the qualities men need in order to be 'free'.

QUESTIONS FOR DISCUSSION

1. What does a charter *do*? Compare it with, for example, the *Declaration of Rights*. Is the function of a charter comparable to that of a chart? Compare the function of, say, Darwin's *Naturalist's Voyage round the World* with the American Declaration of Independence. Does this suggest anything about the relation of science to moral and social philosophy?

2. Does it help to stop talking of 'free will' and to start talking of 'a man willing'? Read M. Cranston, *Freedom: A New Analysis* (Longmans, Green, 1953), part iii.

3. What must I do in order to 'make what I do my own action'? Does it help, or hinder, to talk of my 'self'?

12

'Let Them Act, Let Them Go!'[1]

CAMPAIGNS for 'freedom from nature' are rare. By and large when someone strikes an attitude and says, like Margaret Witter Fuller, 'I accept the universe', we approve of Thomas Carlyle's reported reply: 'By Gad! you'd better!'[2] Campaigns for freedom have been directed against those 'set in authority over us'. The habit is a good one if only because power tends to corrupt and we wish to save our rulers from corruption. What we may have overlooked, of course, is that in gaining more freedom men may also by the same processes gain some power and therefore be themselves exposed a little to the same sources of corruption. It would need something like blind faith in the incorruptibility of the 'masses' to resist that suspicion. Our purpose here is to put the matter in this way: if demands for freedom are not to involve us in contradiction, we shall need a general concept of freedom by which to criticize each specific demand. Here, in this chapter, we will examine demands for circumstantial freedom, more particularly of the economic kind.

Demands for circumstantial freedom were described at the end of the last chapter: they are demands for 'room' to move, for the removal of restraints regarded as 'outside', external. Some demands of this sort simply kick against restrictions as such — anarchism,

---

[1] *Laissez faire, laissez aller*: coined by the French Physiocrats of the eighteenth century.

[2] There are several versions of this incident. A reading of Miss Fuller's *Dryad Song*, however, strengthens the probability that it was she who uttered the notorious declaration. Here is a sample:

> I am immortal! I know it! I feel it . . .
> Upwards I mount — faith is sight, life is feeling . . .

After such flights it seems likely that one may come down to accepting the universe.

for instance, and what we will discuss later on as 'permissiveness'. Then there are demands for circumstantial freedom which object to restrictions because they get in the way of some quite definite proposals, some specific activities. We can call these *enabling* demands. But we shall have to distinguish these from calls made upon the State not merely to get out of the way of those who have ends in view but to take action to redistribute wealth and so enable many more people to have ends of their own — we shall call this distributive Justice and so distinguish it from enabling demands for freedom.

Here we will discuss two kinds of enabling demands for freedom: the first we will call 'economic', the second, 'political'. What we have to do is see how both kinds of demand would be all the better for a fuller concept of freedom, and for this reason we recall the proposition introduced in the last chapter:

A man is free so far as he can make what he does his own action and what he achieves his own property.[1]

Labour and value
John Locke said:

Whatsoever [a man] removes out of the state that Nature hath provided . . . he hath mixed his labour with it . . . joined to it something that is his own, and thereby makes it his property.[2]

John Locke's 'labour theory of value' could now be made the starting-point for an economic demand logically more satisfactory than much that was said by the Liberals and Radicals of the nineteenth century. If we now work it out in this way, we can show, as we go, how the theorists diverged, and this may make clear the implications for our general concept of freedom.

That which the labourer 'mixed with' a part of nature was nothing less than the 'property' every man has (in Locke's words) 'in his own "person" '.[3] As this fundamental 'property' owed nothing, he said, to society, so the right to whatever it achieved by

[1] See above, p. 125.
[2] J. Locke, *The Second Treatise of Civil Government* (Oxford, Blackwell, 1948), ch. vi, para. 26. This was first published in 1690 as *An Essay Concerning the True Original, Extent and End of Civil Government*. For a general account of Locke's political and economic ideas see J. W. Gough, *John Locke's Political Philosophy* (Oxford, Clarendon Press, 1950), in which, for the purposes of this present chapter, see especially ch. iv.
[3] Locke, *Second Treatise*, para. 33.

labour was grounded in nature, not in positive law or social convention. Nor was the material used by labour provided by social institution but, again, by 'nature' — by pre-social, non-human providence. Given these conditions we can formulate a demand for circumstantial freedom to be addressed to the State and designed to enable labourers to make what they achieve their own property, as indeed it would be, anyway, but for interference. The State must use such powers as it has to see that nothing intervenes between the individual labourer and his enjoyment of what he achieves. On no account must the State itself come between a man and the fruits of his labour — this would be flagrant tyranny, a contravention of natural law, virtually blasphemy.

In order to do justice to such demands remember that in the 'person' as Locke saw him there was regulation arising from recognition of the law of nature. Men were able to understand that they ought not to appropriate more than they could use. Land was, indeed, 'given to the use of the industrious and rational', 'not to the fancy or covetousness of the quarrelsome and contentious'. So the intrusion of the State for any other reason but that of enabling the labourer to enjoy his achievements would be bad: it would cut down man's autonomy, his self-rule; it would inhibit his self-determination. On the other hand, if the State did *not* act firmly to put down all interference between labour and the enjoyment of its fruits, it would be falling down upon its chief if not its only proper function. Suppose, for instance, when Gerrard Winstanley wrote 'neither the earth, nor any fruits thereof, should be bought or sold by the inhabitants one among another ...',[1] communism of this sort had threatened to deprive the labourer of his property. The State (on the argument we are basing on Locke's theory) would be justified in doing as, in fact, Cromwell's officials did do to the 'Diggers' — it would be justified in suppressing them. (It is another question whether the Diggers might in their turn appeal to the labour theory of value against General Fairfax and Parson Pratt.)

[1] G. Winstanley, *Law of Freedom: True Magistracy Restored*, ch. i, in *Selections from the works of Gerrard Winstanley*, ed. L. Hamilton (Cresset Press, 1944). Winstanley was the only articulate representative of the Digger movement. See Gooch and Laski, *English Democratic Ideas in the Seventeenth Century* (Cambridge, 1927); P. Zagorin, *History of Political Thought in the English Revolution* (Routledge, 1954).

The French Physiocrats,[1] following Locke, coined the phrase *laissez faire, laissez aller* as a demand that the legislator should not interfere with 'natural' economic laws. François Quesnay, founder of this school, thought of property as land — the fixed parcel of nature which could be enclosed and readily be measured in terms of the wealth it would yield. Each man is the best judge of his own interests, according to the Physiocrats (and the Benthamites after them), and therefore the surest way to happiness is to reduce restrictions on individual effort. On the other hand, this does not necessarily require *political* liberty; an 'enlightened' despot would have satisfied the Physiocrats just as well.

Taking this as the simplest possible form of an economic demand, what criticisms could we make of it in the name of 'freedom'? Plainly it *is* a demand that a man should be able to make what he achieves his own property. But with this kind of property — in land and its produce — how many people out of a growing population in a more or less fixed territory may hope to be 'free'? No doubt 'in the beginning', as Locke said, when 'all the world was America'[2] a larger proportion, but whatever 'nature' has done for human freedom she has not expanded available land to keep pace with population.

Yet on our own view of freedom, as was said at the end of the last chapter, there must be an *area* a man can move in and affect. If his movements are to have meaning, they must have purpose and this in its turn must derive from the 'whole', the 'self', or at least the person. Now Locke seems to appreciate this up to a point. He speaks of the 'property in the person' and, of course, of putting this into the land and its produce. He may say all too little about the 'person' (outside his *Essay*, that is,[3]) but he is right about the 'area' of freedom and its need of materials.

The solution to the difficulty of an increasing population with no corresponding increase in land lies in making a new kind of 'area' supplying new sources of material or wealth for men to

[1] 'Physiocrat': note the implication about the rule of nature and see G. de Ruggiero, *History of European Liberalism*, trans. R. G. Collingwood (Boston, Beacon Press, 1959), various references; Sabine, *HPT*, ch. xxvii, on Helvetius and the Physiocrats; F. J. C. Hearnshaw, ed. *The Social and Political Ideas of Some Great French Thinkers of the Age of Reason*, 1st ed. (Harrap, 1931), lecture viii.

[2] Locke, *Second Treatise*, ch. v, para. xlix.

[3] Locke, *Essay*, could be said to be *about* the person.

'mix their labour with'. The Industrial Revolution is just such a contribution to freedom. For the machines make new 'goods' (note the word); and the techniques themselves provide new areas within which men can achieve. When we turn, however, to the ideas with which men seek to regulate these new levels of experience and in particular to the demands for circumstantial freedom in which such ideas participate, it is by no means clear that those who construct such ideas and make such demands have advanced further in their appreciation of human freedom than Locke or the Physiocrats.

The free market

The classical economists[1] give us a picture of society which seems to follow logically enough from the demand we simplified just now: the picture, that is, of society as a *market*. For if freedom means unrestricted enjoyment of what one produces, and if this leads inevitably to exchange of produce, then one thing at least is clear about the good society — it will not only provide but will in a sense *be* a freely competitive market where prices are fixed by supply and demand.

If we take this market-picture of human relations as an enlargement, so to speak, of the snapshot we have in Locke's labour theory of value, we shall see something Locke did not and presumably could not foresee — the *features* of the man who works in the market, making what he achieves his own by buying and selling. *Homo economicus* he is sometimes called — economic man, who in asking to be freed from external restraints is seeking to realize nothing more nor less than the interests signified by 'buying', 'selling', and 'consuming'.

It would be invidious, of course, to blame economists any more than specialists in any other field for doing their work properly by abstracting from the 'whole' those human movements which can best be arranged in sequences according to laws used as the bases for prediction. All we are doing now is to suggest an overriding need for a general concept of human freedom if the various special studies of man which from time to time do make such demands are not to do more harm than good. All we are doing is to select such features of such demands which underline this need. The

[1] i.e. Adam Smith and David Ricardo to J. S. Mill.

portrait of the 'person' which Locke called man's fundamental 'property' becomes in the economic demands of the nineteenth century an example.

For remember what we said about the Industrial Revolution a moment ago: it produced that new kind of space and material which the member of a multiplying race in a 'shrinking' habitat required. What we find in economic ideas and theories is, to start with, a dismal[1] spectacle of what such freedom is *for*.

Then again, the 'free market' is only one side of the picture that emerges. In such classical economic theories as David Ricardo's we have also a theory of distribution which drives out rosy illusions we might have based on a (tourist's) view of the market: a Lebanese *suk* or the colourful market-place in an Italian city. A free market may seem to provide for the interests of all who frequent it by a 'natural harmony of interests'; but Ricardo's picture is of a deadly (if decorous) brawl between the *classes* involved, the landlords opposing all others and generally gaining the advantage while contributing nothing to the increase of wealth.

Now the economic theory is not itself a demand for freedom; but it goes with such a demand and therefore its concept of the person and its concepts of human relations — of economic man and economic classes — are important: they belong to the general idea of freedom at that time.

The Liberal manufacturers and the Radical reformers tried to break the power of the landowners over the State. Whether or not they cared about political power for its own sake they had to have it: they had to use it to get what they wanted. This shows how so-called 'negative' demands for freedom from restriction not only enable people very often to get on with what they want to do (so having 'positive' consequences) but embroil them inevitably in power and its responsibilities whether they bargained for these or not.

The Manchester School[2] campaign for free trade in the eighteen thirties wanted to remove restrictions on the activities of the

---

[1] Thomas Carlyle once described political economy as a 'dismal science' but the word here refers not to the science but to *Homo economicus*. (Give me *Homo anxius* any day.)

[2] For one clear account of the Manchester School see Ruggiero, op. cit., I. i. 4.

commercial classes and, more particularly — through the Anti-Corn-Law League — they worked to get rid of the tariff which protected the agricultural interest. Cobden, Bright, and the rest were on the side of the manufacturers and the merchants. If the Industrial Revolution can be seen as a liberating movement, then, to the extent to which the interests of the industrialists and the merchants marched with these liberating tendencies, the Manchester School was on the side of the freedom it certainly thought it cared about. The success it had added to the numbers of those who had an area of freedom; it enlarged the area available and made it possible for more people to call what they achieved their own. After all, many merchants gained a stake in *empire*, no less. Then again, what today we call 'social mobility' was speeded up by the Industrial Revolution and, subsequently, by the progress of the commercial classes toward power and pride.

Our business, however, is with ideas and the ideas deployed in making these economic demands no longer please us. We turn now to some of their shortcomings.

Economics, utility, and 'the person'

The watchword 'Let them act! Let them go!' was created in days when men still looked to nature to ensure what they hoped for from men. To nature or, as we would say, to what they had projected of themselves on to nature. Even in the nineteenth century 'nature' was used to justify ideas favourable to economic demands. There could still be talk, for instance, of the 'natural harmony of interests'. But in place of nature and its supposed characteristics Helvetius[1] before this and Jeremy Bentham after him put 'pleasure' and 'pain'. Bentham, opposed as he was to old-style natural law, had still to doff his odd headgear to nature as he laid down his own principles:

Nature has placed mankind under the governance of two sovereign masters, pain and pleasure. It is for them alone to point out what we ought to do, as well as to determine what we shall do.[2]

This 'principle of utility' is so phrased that it is logically required

---

[1] Helvetius: his works are *De l'esprit* (1758), *De l'homme* (1773), *Du bonheur* (1773). See p. 133 above.

[2] Jeremy Bentham, *Principles of Morals and Legislation* (New York, Hafner, 1948; 1st ed., 1789), ch. i.

to take precedence over freedom or any other value which might conflict with it. (If 'pain' and 'pleasure' are *sovereign* masters you can hardly reasonably require men to pursue freedom where this ensures pain and cannot *guarantee* an ultimate surplus of pleasure.)

The advantages of the utility principle as a way of solving moral and legal puzzles are obvious. For one thing — as Bentham develops it — the principle can submit such problems to *measurement* and, since Isaac Newton at least, that is a very great advantage indeed. On the other hand, it fits in very well with an industrial civilization able to turn out more and more *goods* (note the common noun, note the plural number) and therefore to supply more and more customers, consumers. The utility principle has an uneasy relation with 'freedom', but it suits very well any demand for satisfaction by possessions (pleasures?) you can count.

It is true that Bentham's principle aimed to augment the 'happiness of the community' and was critical of economic demands which brought pleasures to few (even if this 'few' was greater than those who would have enjoyed themselves without the Industrial Revolution or free trade). Nevertheless, there is nothing in the principle itself to say what kind of 'community' is proposed. On the contrary, there is no reason why the principle should not support whole-heartedly economic demands for more and more goods for more and more people whether 'progress' of this sort favours their liberty, their dignity as free persons, or not. True, the Benthamites were committed to the view that in the last resort each man is the best judge of what constitutes his own happiness and this is indeed a 'liberal' idea. But when 'happiness' is so emphatically related to quantifiable pleasures and when there is no reason, as we said, to suppose that man *ought* ever to pursue freedom until it hurts we are at least entitled to treat such a principle with caution. We shall, in fact, find it necessary to return to it later on.[1]

To demand room for the person, to ask for the means to enable him to achieve property, is to demand freedom within the terms of our hypothesis,[2] but even the hypothesis calls for more. 'To make what he does his own action' may involve not only conditions

[1] On the history and ramifications of Utilitarianism see E. Halévy, *Le radicalisme philosophique* (Paris, Alcan, 1904), trans. Mary Morris and published as *The Growth of Philosophic Radicalism* (New York, 1928).

[2] See above, p. 131.

other than those appreciated by economic demands but also conditions which economic demands, aided and abetted by hedonistic utilitarianism, might disallow. Economic demands may divide class against class; they also may divide a man 'against himself' by throwing his own integrity into disorder and encouraging him to make too much of some interests, not enough of others.

In passing judgement on the ideas we have just briefly reviewed, in passing judgement on them, that is, by reference to the value of free men, it is helpful to reflect on the habits of social study which grew up at that time. There was, in the first place, a new academic distinction between economics and politics.[1] The academic advantages of this can no doubt be defended beyond much question, but we are not now discussing academic advantage. What such a division might well suggest to the layman is that the art or science of government is quite another thing from the art or science of 'housekeeping' just as, on the other hand, men who were not laymen in this matter were led to suppose that economics *was* government and ought to take the place of politics.[2] Of course, the social scientist is not to blame if lay people get into bad habits

---

[1] 'Economics': a twentieth-century word, by and large. In the nineteenth century 'political economy' suggested a reluctance to part with 'politics'. In the early seventeenth century 'political economy' appears for studies later to be styled 'mercantilist'. The Physiocrats called themselves '*les économistes*' but classical economics begins with Adam Smith's *Wealth of Nations* (1776), by which time the study of nationalistic economy (political economy in the old sense, with which compare *Kameralwissenschaft* in German) had been separated as mercantilism, and economic interest had shifted from the new moral and world view, more suitable to science. For readings from the earlier period see A. E. Monroe, ed., *Early Economic Thought* (Milford, 1924), S. H. Patterson, ed., *Readings in the History of Economic Thought* (McGraw-Hill, 1932).

[2] The kind of influence economics or political economy might have on thought about man is suggested in the following passage from B. de Jouvenel's *Power* (Hutchinson, 1948): 'What makes it possible for Political Economy to be a science at all is that it looks on social life, and all the activities . . . of human beings as the regular flow of one and the same energy . . . homogeneous and always measurable in units of value. But the very feature which makes a science of it makes it incapable of explaining the whole of social reality, or even of taking account of all the phenomena which occur within its proper sphere. . . . It is a valuable science but one grafted on to a false psychology which regards the race of men as a physical mass pin-pointed in place and acted upon only by the mechanical force of self-interest. Hence it is that the point of view of the economist is the worst of all for discerning social disharmonies: these must react on quantitative adaptations before they receive his attention.'

of thinking about 'community' on the one hand, 'economic interests' on the other; or 'economic interest' on the one hand, 'the good man' and 'the good society' on the other. But if academic interests do in any way, however inadvertently, encourage this kind of disorder in practice, in the making of day-to-day decisions and the constructing of 'the self', then it is up to someone in the academic world to do what can be done to correct such tendencies and that is what we are trying to do here.

A similar need was created at the same time by a sharpened academic division between morals on the one hand, law on the other. The work of the Benthamite J. L. Austin[1] firmly set aside the old concept of natural law by means of which positive law and moral judgement could come together under the principle of (supposedly) universal validity. The positivist approach to law discouraged any such liaison and this could be a source of difficulty in practical affairs. It makes it difficult, that is to say, to find a way of saying that an act can be both lawful (or legal) and *bad* (as for instance so many acts were under the Nazi régime in Germany).

To the extent, then, that economic demands belong to the early nineteenth-century passion for quantification, for the 'positive', for the 'useful', we are right to take care in the way we treat their apparent support for human freedom. And all this quite apart from the main attack on such slogans as *laissez faire* today — its *injustice*.

QUESTIONS FOR DISCUSSION

1. (*a*) Trace the uses to which Locke's labour theory of value was put or the forms it took, using Sabine, *HPT*, for Ricardo, Marx, etc.

(*b*) If labour 'creates value' what happens to value when automation reduces labour?

2. Was *laissez faire* wrong because it did not 'work' or for some

[1] J. L. Austin, *The Province of Jurisprudence Determined*. For some comment see C. K. Allen, *Law in the Making*, 6th ed. (O.U.P., 1958), Benn Peters, *SP*, pp. 74–78, 83–85, 364–5; H. L. A. Hart *The Concept of Law* (Oxford, 1961), ch. ii.

other reason? (What would 'work' mean here?) If Winstanley's communism could be made to 'work' what would 'work' mean here and how would it differ from the meaning in the first part of the question? (Winstanley, *Law of Freedom: True Magistracy Restored*, Cresset Press, 1944.)

3. Study the quotation from B. de Jouvenel on p. 138 n. What does it say (*a*) about the usefulness and (*b*) about the defects of political economy? Does it imply anything about other social sciences?

Political Liberty (I)

IF your hat is whipped off by a breeze, or a gale topples you over in the street, you may be irritated, scared, even badly injured; but you will probably show little resentment, make no complaint to the police, let alone pause to consider whether the time has come to appeal to the Ombudsman. If, however, I took the greatest possible care to produce precisely the same consequences with a barge-pole, the situation could well turn out very differently: there could be serious moral, legal, and social consequences the extent of which would, of course, depend partly upon our respective places in society.

The differences we make between our response to human interference and to nature's blows may be partly explained by the indifference a storm could be expected to show, for example, to the reading of the Riot Act. Then again, all struggle for identity among human beings is bipolar: first there has to be separation (from 'nature', 'society', parents, each other), then, and only then, can there be truly human relations. If in this history of human development it has mattered for us to 'think ourselves apart from' nature, it is understandable if it matters still more for each to think himself apart from others who so resemble him. But every interference, every trespass by one person upon the free area of another in such a way as to come between the person and his movements seems an outrage just because we *are* so like one another and stand, therefore, in such need of stressing our difference in order to establish our identity.

'Coercion' is one of many harsh words we use to resist this being 'shut up together'. The energy and passion with which we protest and fight against forcible restraint tells of a need we may well share with other animals but which we men alone seem to have systematized and given ideological expression. To check movements is to 'restrain'; to compel them is to 'constrain'; to do either without calling on the judgement or the choice of the 'mover' is to coerce — forcibly to check or direct. Threats of this kind — threats to freedom — come more readily from those who have both the authority and the necessary force at their disposal. The maximum of such force and authority in a community is organized in — or as — the State. This is why we get our best known and most thorough-going defences of freedom in political language and even think of freedom mainly in terms of political liberty.

In this chapter we shall talk about some leading ideas in political liberty. In the next chapter we shall consider a number of 'liberal' institutions and relate these to the concept of freedom.

Natural rights

The American colonists[1] in 1776 and the French revolutionaries in 1789 issued statements of a type and a content similar to each other and together creating a new kind of foundation for political relations between men: an explicit declaration of the rights of man[2] clearly intended to restrict State coercion of individuals.

Men are born and live free and equal as regards their rights . . .

began the *Principles* of 1789.

The end of every political association is the conservation of the natural and imprescriptible rights of man. These rights are liberty, property, security, and resistance to oppression.

By 'natural' rights we are to understand conditions which it is proper for a man to enjoy simply because he is a man and not by virtue of his citizenship. This is the difference between a right called 'natural' and one which is called 'legal'. By a legal right we

[1] Thomas Jefferson (1746–1826), third President of the United States, whose *A Summary of the Rights of America* influenced the *Declaration of Rights* which he drafted, is said to have regarded the American nation as an experiment which would lead to men being trusted to govern themselves without a master. See, for example, Nye and Morpurgo, *A History of the United States: The Birth of the U.S.A.* (Penguin, 1955), p. 213, and the same source for the part played by Tom Paine's *Common Sense* in the acceptance by the Americans of the *Declaration*. Paine's *The Rights of Man* was published later.

[2] *The Rights of Man* (see n. 1) was published in 1791–2 in answer to Edmund Burke's *Reflections on the Revolution in France*. For the French *Principles* of 1789 see Ruggiero, *The History of European Liberalism*, pp. 66 ff.

understand one that has been prescribed by the legislative act of a political community with the implication, more often than not, that this is a privilege created by the community and therefore able to be withdrawn or cancelled. A natural right, on the other hand, is 'imprescriptible'; it cannot be withdrawn for it does not derive from a legislative act, from the political community as such.

Natural rights may be thought of as requiring to be *implemented* by law and in this sense given the force of positive law. A European Social Security Code was opened for signature by members of the Council of Europe on 16 April 1964 following upon a Human Rights Convention. All the provisions in such conventions require implementation by political communities, but the language used, though the word 'nature' or 'natural' is dropped, is comparable to that of 1776 and 1789. 'All workers have the right to just conditions of work . . .',[1] and so on. This helps us to make clear the function of natural rights, and to dispose of a facile objection.

Earlier we spoke of the general concept of freedom as like a 'charter',[2] earlier still (in Part One) of certain primary conventions in human relations. It is true that in the eighteenth century men still spoke as if Nature in person were armed and at their side and this has made it easy for the enemies of natural rights to make nonsense of such declarations. But it seems clear enough that we have to deal here with a resolution, a determination, a primary convention, representing a recognition of what is involved in being a man which must be insisted upon, held over the heads of all holders of power until the political institutions which govern men have translated this into positive law and provision.

'Nature', as we said, is an ambiguous symbol; better, perhaps, if we can do without it. But if human relations are to be reconstructed again and again with a view to reducing coercion, there is need of a mustering point, a constructive concept to be used as a standard, a final, supreme authority to which even positive law is subordinated and this is what the framers of declarations have been at.

In the heart of social life itself the individual had now a sphere reserved for him which was itself immune from society . . .[3]

[1] Quoted from *Keesing's Contemporary Archives* (1964), 20158.
[2] See above, Chapter 11.
[3] Otto Gierke, *Natural Law and the Theory of Society*, xvi. 5. All Gierke's references to natural rights are important.

The figurative language in that sentence describes a situation created by men which is *conceptual* — it is made up of ideas; and as such it can be given concrete expression in institutions, laws, regularities which have themselves visible, tangible outworkings in social life. By such tokens, let us say, men create social *space* — no more, perhaps, at any given time or for any particular group or individual than the possibility of room to move, room to make one's acts one's own and what one achieves one's own property; but a possibility it is, and one at that which can lie like a weight on the conscience of a community which in respect of any of its members has neglected to realize it.

. . . *and their limitations*

Talk about 'rights' has, nevertheless, a disadvantage which can be seen even before the 'natural' right is transformed into a 'civil' right by legislation. The very word 'rights' (in the plural), helpful as it is when the need is to be positive and precise in order to meet the requirements of law-making, encourages a division and subdivision of the goods we are after which in its turn separates them from each other as if each were an end in itself. This is the first of the disadvantages to be considered. The other is not unrelated. The language of rights goes with a mood, a general attitude proper to men in arms against coercion but which may become a habit contrary to the needs of free human relations.

Article Two in the *Declaration of Rights* lists 'natural and imprescriptible rights' as those of 'liberty, property, security, and resistance to oppression'. The first objection is that 'property', for instance, is likely to be separated from 'liberty', so that the man who owns property may defend this as a 'natural right' irrespective of its bearing either upon the liberty of others or upon his own personal freedom. It is a valid criticism of John Locke's political ideas that they give this kind of prominence to one 'right' because of an inadequate development of concepts which are in the *Second Treatise of Civil Government*, but not worked out in such ways as to keep property in its place. Today it might well be the case that 'security' has been seized upon by many as a 'right' to the detriment both of freedom in general and of the dependence of freedom upon property (in some sense) in particular. The difficulty is that unless we particularize about rights we will be accused of abstraction and told, with some justice, that we are not providing proper defences against tyranny; if, on the other hand, we do particularize, there is this danger of fragmentation with (apparently) distinct rights losing much of their value in the process.

The mood that goes with stress upon rights was dramatized by the French Revolution, by the Third Estate, the burning of the Bastille, the trial and execution of aristocrats. Claims are presented. On the one side are the privileged keeping an iron grip on the money-bags; on the other, the impoverished fighting to loosen their hold. The mood is essentially unilateral, non-reciprocal. 'I've got my rights' may mean, at such times, 'You've got it to give and I'm here to take'. This mood is proper to 'resistance to oppression'; it is inadequate for co-operation, for community, for the full pursuit of freedom. Endeavour, on this argument, lies between the Bastille walls and one's own front doorstep. Liberty is something to be wrested from the hands of others with nothing thought or said about the sequel. Rights may go no further than 'property' in the sense of claiming a share in what someone else has; the notion of achievement on the one hand, making 'one's acts one's own' on the other, may be incomprehensible.

As checks upon coercion — take them no further — natural rights and their implementation may be said to be as successful as the arming of a national frontier is successful in achieving national prosperity. For as the whole work of the nation is necessary to its independence, so the whole activity of a person is necessary, in the end, to non-coercion.

Trust, toleration

In John Locke's political philosophy there are two concepts which have one thing at least in common: they occur in the arguments of a man who wants to reduce coercion and they suggest a manner of conducting political affairs difficult to put into institutions, not very satisfactory, perhaps, to the logic of political science, but providing, nevertheless, insight into the nature of freedom. The first is the notion of government as a *trust*,[1] the

---

[1] 'Trust': see Locke's *Second Treatise*, secs. 136, 139, and 149; J. W. Gough, *Locke's Political Philosophy*, study vii.

second, a recognition of the importance to liberty of toleration. Neither is without relevance today.

Trusteeship (in the legal sense) has to be contrasted here with contract. The legislature in Locke's theory is the trustee — the one trusted or entrusted — and as such incurs a unilateral obligation implying no rights for the trustee himself on his own behalf. This, says Otto Gierke, 'leaves no room for a "contract of subjection" '.[1] The sovereign or the legislature has no rights of its own; the people have not contracted to subject themselves to their government. Gierke says this concept pervaded English political thought in the eighteenth century and was applied not only internally, to the 'relations between the Public and the supreme legislature' but also (as, for instance, by Edmund Burke) to the relations between Great Britain and India: 'which is regarded as held in trust for the benefit of the people of India'. 'Trust' here conveys 'the suggestion of a duty, enforceable indeed, but rather as a matter of "good conscience" '.[2] Nor need we limit our appreciation of the word to legal usage, for law in its turn has drawn upon the vocabulary of human relations. 'Trust' shows inter-personal truth and reliability needing no coercion. That is why Locke's concept is important, more important, perhaps, than his lack of interest in democracy. For he reminds us that the only guarantee we have that coercion will diminish is that more men will serve us with less need of sanctions or, as we sometimes put it, that there will be an increased 'sense of responsibility'.

'Trust' implies a dignity, a status; it relies to some extent upon a moral capacity which, as we suggested in discussing the primary 'truth' conventions,[3] was the only alternative to law and sanctions, without, at least, a radical alteration of human characteristics. The concept today is of growing importance in proportion to the numbers of those 'social' and 'civil' servants who are, in fact, entrusted with vast areas of our social life often under no other guarantees than those they care to provide within their own professional associations. If trust is to persist, let alone increase, we ought to know a little more about the conditions which justify

[1] Gierke, op. cit., p. 299, n. 68 to sec. xvi of Gierke's text.
[2] H. Maitland, *Collected Papers*, quoted in Gough, op. cit., p. 136.
[3] See above, Chapters 8 and 9.

it and in these we would include an appreciation of human freedom and *its* conditions.

John Locke's *Letter on Toleration* was a tract for the times, but it handled a concept of lasting importance to political and social liberty, one which we tend to see in terms of 'positive rights' such as 'free speech', the right of publication, the right to worship, and so on. Here for the moment we will consider it more generally. Locke said that toleration was 'the chief characteristic mark of the true church'. You might think that where absolute truth is believed to be attainable and where this is believed to be identical with the absolute good — with man's ultimate destiny and eternal salvation — toleration would be as vicious as it would be false. The burning of heretics may have been imprudent, but the hatred of heresy was surely 'logical'[1] and it is at least arguable whether you could both hate heresy and tolerate the heretic to the point of permitting him to preach.

Locke's purpose, of course, was to exclude the 'civil magistrate' from religious debate. The value of his arguments, however, is the distinction he makes between 'outward force' and the 'inward persuasion of the mind' for here, whatever its significance for religious orthodoxy, Locke shows quite clearly his understanding of the general concept of freedom. First, he marks out an area — man's personal dealings with the universe — as outside the scope of political regulation.

... though the rigour of laws and the force of penalties were capable to convince and change men's minds, yet would not that help at all to the salvation of their souls.[2]

Second, he attaches value to the variety of experience with all this means for liberty.

... their very dissension unavoidably puts us upon a necessity of deliberating and, consequently, allows a liberty of choosing that which upon consideration we prefer.[3]

Force, Locke admits, can change men's minds. We do not have

[1] 'Logical', that is, in the sense of 'following upon' the beliefs indicated, but no doubt it could also be made logical in the strict, deductive sense, starting with the presumed premises about the nature of heresy.
[2] Locke, *Letter on Toleration*.   [3] Ibid.

to claim the burden of having originated 'brain-washing' and other methods of indoctrination in the twentieth century. What has been called the 'battle for the mind'[1] is a feature of ancient as well as modern attempts so to regulate individual experience as to dissolve difference in 'togetherness'.[2] Distinctions must be made, however. In our horror at what has been done by our contemporaries to the minds of their victims we sometimes talk as if all ways of getting people to change their beliefs and their attitudes were equally deplorable, but distinctions must be made, both for the variety of experience in general and for the understanding of teaching, leadership, guidance, in particular.

We must distinguish, for instance, between mass movements of the kind some psychologists attribute to the 'fear of freedom'[3] the outcome of which (temporarily at least) is loss of identity, and deliberate attempts by a few men with clear objectives to utilize mass hysteria for their own ends. This second alternative is plainly coercive. Similarly we may distinguish 'indoctrination' as a deliberate circumventing of a person's critical awareness or an overwhelming of it by fear from 'persuasion' of the sort that meets criticism on its own ground whatever appeals may otherwise be made to emotion provided these do not overwhelm criticism. Persuasion in this sense (whatever else may be said against it) is not coercive. Indoctrination violates the person by disrespect for the self. Persuasion may engage the person through the self without threatening integrity.

The variety of ways in which men confront reality — the varieties of reality this creates — 'puts us upon a necessity of deliberating and, consequently, allows a liberty of choosing . . .'. Therefore the preservation of variety is the preservation of liberty in some sense, as the use of coercion to reduce variety would undoubtedly be a reduction of liberty. Locke's own reservations are instructive. The first of these — against Roman Catholics —

---

[1] By W. Sargant in the book so named (see above, Chapter 10, p. 112).

[2] 'Ancient as well as modern': see R. Graves in Sargant, op. cit., ch. viii, and compare the account given of the Mysteries in J. Harrison, *Prolegomena to the Study of Greek Religion*.

[3] The title given to the work by E. Fromm (Routledge, 1942), originally published as *Escape from Freedom* (New York, 1941). With Fromm's thesis compare E. R. Dodds, *The Greeks and the Irrational* (California, 1956), ch. viii, and G. Murray, *Five Stages of Greek Religion* (New York, Doubleday, 1955), ch. iv.

confirms what we suggested earlier about his difficulties in associating toleration with the beliefs of the 'true Church', but Locke's approach is political. If we accept his premisses, it is also unexceptionable:

... any sect that teaches ... that men are not obliged to keep their promise; that princes may be dethroned by those that differ from them in religion ...

can beyond a certain point only be 'tolerated' at the risk of the very conditions within which toleration and human freedom itself is possible. For what Locke is saying is that human relations depend upon certain primary conventions prominent among which is this of trust in oaths and promises, reliability, inter-personal truth. Some degree of conformity to the primary conventions is essential for the enlargement and protection of all other goods. We do not have to accept Locke's insinuations about the Catholics of his time as wholly or even partly justified in order to follow his reasoning. For we have had in our own time a similar difficulty to face in the question of how far we ought to tolerate the 'secret' activities of International Communism. The difficulty, however, is not in agreeing that there have to be limits but in deciding where those limits should be placed and this is a question for another day.

Locke's other excepted class is, perhaps, more interesting.

... those are not at all to be tolerated who deny the being of a God. Promises, covenants, and oaths, which are the bonds of human society, can have no hold upon an atheist.[1]

The second sentence is meant, apparently, to be an empirical proposition or at least it is exposed, as it stands, to empirical tests. We could in this sense dispose of it by our experience of any number of atheists whose 'word is their bond' just as the cynics, no doubt, could produce any number of professing Christians who have shown precious little respect for inter-personal truth. But we will not trouble ourselves with John Locke's logic — there is not much of it at this point. The view he puts forward, however, is not without importance even to political liberty today and is certainly germane to our thought on human freedom.

Some philosophers today hold that to 'deny the being of' God

[1] Locke, *Letter on Toleration*.

is as nonsensical as to affirm it.[1] This they do on grounds we criticized when talking about the varieties of experience. They say that propositions about the existence of God are meaningless whether they claim that God exists or that He does not exist. Phenomenalists, for example, hold that since all we can call 'knowledge' must ultimately be derived from sense data and since the so-called knowledge of God is not so derived, it is not possible to make such statements meaningfully. Logical positivists used to say that there are two kinds of meaningful statement: tautologies, 'analytical' statements, such as definitions in a dictionary or propositions in a textbook of geometry; and 'synthetic' statements which are about our sensory experience and can be verified by experiment. Statements about God — theistic or atheistic — come in neither category.

But there are many things we want to say which do not fit into these two exclusive categories besides statements about God. The phenomenalist, the positivist, who would make both theism and atheism meaningless, are perhaps more to be feared than the atheist whom Locke opposed; because if we submit to their rulings not only religious belief but a whole range of human interests and activities including those by which we seek to construct conceptually our relations with each other might seem meaningless. Art, religion, morals, but also the whole business of putting values upon things and relations lie outside meaningful discourse — if these people were to be followed.

Now the man who says 'there is no God' is *logically* on common ground with the man who says 'there is a God'. There is the possibility of discourse between them. But the man who tries to dogmatize about meaning and truth to the extent that both are equally excluded deserves the suspicion which Locke, curiously, reserved for the atheist.

Speaking of 'truth' earlier we suggested a connexion between three areas of experience in which truth could be used — the area of inner truth or integrity, the area of inter-personal truth or

[1] See, for example, A. J. Ayer, *Language, Truth and Logic*, 2nd ed., revised (Gollancz, 1954), especially ch. i. Consider the view called 'Phenomenalism' — the doctrine that all statements about material objects can be analysed into statements about actual or possible sensations. For a contemporary comment on Phenomenalism of importance to social philosophy and with specific reference to Marxism see H. B. Acton, *The Illusion of the Epoch* (Cohen & West, 1962), pp. 22 ff.

reliability, the area of objective truth or objectivity. Locke's argument would throw this into confusion — we would have to say that men could be reliable in personal relations and in political life even if they lacked intellectual integrity, whereas an atheist who said what he took to be objective truth must not be trusted.

Of more importance to political liberty is the possibility that some who try to govern our affairs or reconstruct our relations have no respect for the varieties of human experience where these do not fit their formulas. In the last chapter we said that this was the danger in the concept of man as *Homo economicus*. A. D. Lindsay said that the scientific revival of the seventeenth century set in motion an attempt to *reduce* men as it had reduced the universe.

When men are regarded as objects of scientific inquiry so conceived, they are regarded as atomistic individuals, not as personalities. Society is regarded as analysable into a collection of independent, isolable, alike atoms. The doctrine of human equality when held as it is by Bentham, for example, means that men are regarded as for all practical purposes identical. They are like the replaceable parts of a machine . . .[1]

Perhaps Locke would have done better to be on the look-out for such views. We, at any rate, can see them as hostile to liberty. The mischief of it is that many who would call themselves the champions of freedom have favoured such estimates of their own kind.

QUESTIONS FOR DISCUSSION

1. Read G. de Ruggiero, *The History of European Liberalism* (O.U.P., 1927; Boston, Beacon Press, 1959), part II, ch. i. Discuss the possible abuses of such rights as freedom of association or

[1] A. D. Lindsay, *The Modern Democratic State*, vol. i, p. 77. Compare this quotation with that from Bertrand de Jouvenel, above, p. 138. This method of reduction in the study of man calls for careful study. Cicero spoke of 'minute philosophers', meaning those who deny the immortality of the soul. The title, however, would equally suit modern reductionists. Bishop Berkeley, referring to Cicero and 'minute philosophers', adds 'which name admirably suits them, they being a sort of sect which diminish all the most valuable things, the thoughts, views and hopes of men; all the knowledge, notions and theories of the mind they reduce to sense; human nature they contract and degrade to the narrow, low standard of animal life, and assign us only a small pittance of time instead of immortality' (Alciphron, *First Dialogue*, 10). Immortality apart, this book, too, has a bone to pick with such reductionists or 'minute philosophers'.

freedom or speech and publication today. How would such abuses be corrected (if at all) by a 'general concept of liberty'? That is, how might such a concept as Ruggiero is discussing *work* in such matters?

2. Can we be said to 'trust' our rulers today? Does the extension of bureaucracy increase or diminish trust? (What does 'bureaucracy' mean, anyway?)

3. Locke would not trust atheists. Why not? We have suggested (pp. 150 ff.) that there are others less to be trusted in government than atheists. Who are they and what reasons have been given? Criticize the position taken up in the book. See the quotation from A. D. Lindsay on p. 151.

4. Following on from Question 3, compare what is said about Phenomenalism on p. 150 with what is said in a footnote and the references given, especially H. B. Acton's comments in *The Illusion of the Epoch*, pp. 22 ff. Recall what was said about the varieties of experience in Part One and review now the relation between theories of knowledge and concepts of human freedom.

14

Political Liberty (II)

WHAT are political institutions? How do they work? What do people say they expect of them? Do they produce the desired results? If not, are people aware of this? Are they disappointed? Dissatisfied? If so, what can be done either to improve the institutions or to reduce dissatisfaction without institutional change? Such questions are proper to social (including political) science and to social technology (if this phrase seems tolerable).

Social (and political) philosophy wants to know what is desirable; what overall ends are conceivable for political institutions; not merely what men say they want but whether there may be some things they want that matter more than others and what kind of order can be brought into their interests by deliberation. Whatever obligation the scientist has to consider only what *is* the case, the philosopher has to go on trying to find ways and means of saying what *might* and what *ought* to be. We do this by reconstructing the concepts we find in the thought of our own society — concepts of the good life, the good man, the good community.

So in these two chapters we are not attempting so much as a summary of political ideas. Our purpose is to note some of the best known ideas used to instruct institutions in ways and means of reducing coercion, to suggest where these may mislead and to do so by reference to a general concept of freedom:

A man is free so far as he can make what he does his own action and what he achieves his own property.

Majority rule

If the majority of people in any group have the last word, then it is reasonable to say that the number of those who are coerced will be less than the number of those who coerce. If majority rule means no more than this, then, taken by itself, it may seem to offer a reduction of coercion provided you assume that (for instance) a monarchy (government by one) or an oligarchy (government by a few) would coerce more people more of the time than a majority would. This does not seem obvious to us.

We do not, of course, have to assume a fixed majority — that is, one composed of the same persons or the same groups of persons. Where majority rule means no more than a procedure for reaching decisions in committees (which is perhaps the only thing it ought to mean) it may very well happen that a man overruled one day is himself on the side of the majority the next. Besides, there is very little in such small groups that could be called coercion. On the other hand, in political communities with considerable racial, religious, or other ideological divisions, majority rule may very well come to mean not only the dominance over long periods of a few by the many, but dominance of a kind which could be called 'coercive'. The fate of the Turkish Cypriot or the Kurds of Iraq (to select examples of the kind not so well advertised in the West) may well seem to be of this order.

Sanctity is given to majority rule (or what is thought to be majority rule) by the franchise. Here surely (so the argument runs) is a movement which can be made by every citizen with the status of a governing *act*. 'The people of England,' sneered Rousseau, '. . . is free only during the election of members of parliament.'[1] But at least they are free then — the science of politics should be able to tell us what this voting act amounts to. Of the connexion between voting, representation, and government something will be said in a moment. Let us keep now to majorities, whether the universal franchise in a country like Britain gives the majority political power or not. The question is, 'Does the concept "majority rule" agree with the concept of freedom?'.

'Decision by majorities', according to the Liberal statesman W. E. Gladstone, 'is just as much an expedient as lighting by gas.'[2] Once importance is given, that is, to the variety of opinion (as freedom requires it should), once a show is made of giving to every member of a group equal weight in deliberation, a procedure has to be found for enabling people to get done and go home to

---

[1] *Social Contract* (Dent; Everyman's, 1913), bk iii, ch. xv.
[2] W. E. Gladstone (1809–98), speech in the House, 21 January 1858.

their beds. Unanimity would take too long — even if it were conceivable. A show of hands (discs, beans, ballot-papers, computer-readings) brings an end to deliberation and, momentarily, reduces issues baffling to the intellect and the passions alike to crude quantities.

As such a procedural device, 'majority rule' is an alternative to decision-making by one man or a few and a corrective to the temptations to which a few in authority are exposed. When to the procedural rule, however, is added concepts of majority rule such as those associated with utilitarianism on the one hand, the sovereignty of Parliament on the other, what was intended as a corrective to coercion may become a serious threat to human freedom.

The 'supreme test of a social doctrine', according to Harold J. Laski,[1] would be the 'number of those whose demands upon life' have been satisfied by its implementation. A test, perhaps; but the *supreme* test? A test, because it is better to have government sensitive and responsive to the felt interests of the many than one which ignores them in order to pursue its own notion of what is 'in the public interest'. But the meeting of majority demands, though it may prove the supreme test of a political party's programme, is hardly the final criterion for a 'social doctrine'. Taking 'social doctrine', that is, to include the attempt to appraise interests, resolve some conflicts between them, and above all prevent them from cancelling each other out, the supreme test of a social doctrine might well be its faithfulness to those primary conventions of objectivity, inter-personal truth and integrity which man, in his collective wisdom, has held on to in spite of his stupidities, in spite of crises and the passions of the moment.

'Holding on to' such primary conventions is an activity someone must undertake as a vocation and persuade others to undertake at least from time to time. Who if not the makers of 'social doctrine', and how are they to continue to do this if they yield to the crude formulas of 'public demand'?

This leads us to say something of representation and representatives.

[1] H. J. Laski, *The Rise of European Liberalism* (Allen & Unwin, 1936, Unwin Books ed., 1962), ch. i.

Representation[1]

By 'representative government' we ordinarily understand a form of government which includes provision for a legislature — a law-making or law-modifying body — the members of which are periodically called upon to face popular election. One could list a number of reasons why this procedure is preferable to forms of government which lack it, but our first question is the part such institutions might be thought to play in limiting coercion, our second, their relation to freedom more generally.

There is no reason on the face of it why representative government so understood should not behave as coercively toward some members of the community or some groups in the community as, say, a dictator might be expected to do. It is not our business to conduct an empirical inquiry into the question. Henry Sidgwick in the nineteenth century suggested that while in Imperial Russia nothing was done to prevent a man from getting as drunk as he pleased, the 'vigorous democracy of North America' had introduced severe prohibition of such pleasures.[2] Nevertheless, it is arguable that where a large number of legislators are dependent on the votes of a majority there is less likelihood that this majority will be exposed to the same degree of coercion as in governments where there is not the same kind of dependence.

That representative government so understood *ensures* the progressive reduction of coercion is another matter and in order to appreciate why it is another matter we have to dispose of the proposition that representation (in this sense) is in some way a method for increasing human freedom. Progress in freedom, as we understand it, means a growing area of action for persons whether by themselves or as members of groups with the possibility — through political community — of moments, decisions, rare experiences in which they 'touch the world', reaching out to participate in decisions which bring them into real relations with men outside their community. Representative government, on the other hand, does not exclude the possibility of concentrating power (once the brief moment of popular election has passed) not

[1] On the development of and variations in the idea of representation in England see C. S. Emden, *The People and the Constitution* (O.U.P., 1933).

[2] H. Sidgwick, *The Elements of Politics*, 3rd ed. (Macmillan, 1908), p. 196.

only in the members of the legislative assembly but in such minorities as the political party on the one hand, the Cabinet on the other, together with such other well-organized minorities in the community which can bring most pressure to bear upon them.

The word 'representative' helps us to forget these things. No doubt there are still people who suppose themselves represented in parliament (and therefore in government) in something like the way a national government is represented abroad by a paid civil servant (an ambassador), in something like the way a private citizen may be represented in court by his attorney. Precisely *how* the elector is represented the social scientist may care to tell us; all we can do is to suggest that 'to represent' is obviously a word with uses other than this. For on the one hand the elected representative is usually in the position to be elected because he belongs to a highly organized minority — the political party — whose policies and directives are the conceptual scheme within which he will have to fit whatever he might otherwise choose to regard as the interests of those who have elected him; and on the other hand governing acts will be well out of his reach (and therefore still further from that of his constituents) unless the organized minority (the party) to which he belongs has more members in the legislative assembly than any other party *and* can keep a significant hold upon the much smaller group — the Cabinet — which performs the governing act.

Sometimes an individual elector may succeed in getting his representative's support in high places and this certainly looks like more freedom, less coercion, than there would be without him. There is no reason why representative government should increase such incidents. Nor is there any reason why the individual member of the assembly should have a great deal more participation in governing acts than the individual non-member. For there is no reason why those who do the governing should desire this; it is not in *their* interest and since there may be no contrary view (since an official opposition hopes soon to be the government) they may spare no pains to convince an otherwise politically uneducated people that it would not be in *their* interest either.

Some other political concepts may be considered as attempts to improve upon this situation from the point of view we are taking up — that of human freedom.

The Constitution and 'sovereignty'

The written constitution is like a law above laws — above laws and, in our terms, below the primary conventions whether or not we conceive of these as natural law. The interest of the idea for our purposes is best illustrated by its relation to another political idea — that of 'sovereignty'.

> The English Constitution, in a word, is framed on the principle of choosing a single sovereign authority, and making it good; the American, upon the principle of having many sovereign authorities, and hoping that their multitude may atone for their inferiority.[1]

The 'unwritten' constitution of England to some extent illustrates that constructive function we are attributing to a number of concepts in social philosophy throughout this book. The (written) American constitution is a good example of what becomes of 'natural rights' when the attempt is made to filter them down through a hierarchy of laws into political and social practice. The point to concentrate on, however, is the notion of the constitution, written or unwritten, as it relates to the 'sovereign authority' or 'authorities' — that is, to the institutions which have 'conclusive power' in the State.

John Locke spoke of the majority as 'concluding the rest' but he did not mean much by it: not as much, for instance, as a universal franchise. On the other hand, while he gave legal sovereignty to parliament, he reserved a 'political' sovereignty to the people, and did at least allow for the possibility of its exercise. What is more to the point, he took for granted a certain distinction in his day between 'executive' and 'legislature' and therefore the possibility of their exercising checks upon each other. The question is whether we should continue to do this: continue, that is, to believe that there is sufficient provision in our 'constitution' against arbitrary power.

Let us suppose that a parliament is 'sovereign' in the legal sense: there is no higher court to which appeal may be made from its

---

[1] W. Bagehot, *The English Constitution*, 2nd ed. (Kegan Paul, 1872), no. vii. For the alleged account of the English Constitution given in (*a*) Locke's *Second Treatise* and (*b*) Montesquieu's *De l' Esprit des lois*, and the relative influence of both on the American constitution, see Gough, *Locke's Political Philosophy*, study v. For Locke's views on Parliament see the same authority, p. 115.

decisions. These decisions may, in their turn, relate to laws which parliament makes with no other to gainsay or correct. Let us then suppose that parliament itself has little or no power to resist the will of a tightly organized, party-controlled group — the Cabinet. Once the party has a majority in the assembly it may use its legal sovereignty as if it were politically sovereign. That is, it may use its powers to make laws irrespective of tradition, mandate, precedent, or constitutional hindrances. (Of course where it can however insecurely claim a 'mandate' this will give it still more 'right' in its own eyes to act as it pleases.) Given some rough, Benthamite principle its actions could speedily look much the same as those of any other arbitrary power. What assurances would the people now have that their 'representative' government would interest itself in *their* freedom, more particularly if a lot of people were now in the pay of government?[1]

Locke thought we ought to be able to rely on those in power. But trust presupposes certain moral qualities in the rulers as well as a readiness in the people to see that those qualities are there and an ability to provide men of the right quality from among their own number.

The *written* constitution guarded by a supreme court with power to judge the acts of legislatures is looked upon by a large number of political communities as a proper safeguard. A written constitution properly defended might be seen as that 'social wisdom' which Edmund Burke[2] found in the whole society (past as well as present). This social wisdom embodied in the written constitution enforced and interpreted by the courts might be able to reduce the danger from majorities in the assembly using their powers to reduce human liberty. Less need be taken 'on trust'; legal sovereignty could in its turn be subject to checks; an ebullient majority in the legislature could be prevented from

[1] In the eighteenth century the Wilkes affair gave rise to serious doubts about the limits of Parliamentary power. The Commons at that time claimed the right to debar the elected member (Wilkes) from re-election. Said Edmund Burke, 'The circumstances of having no appeal from their [the Commons'] jurisdiction is made to imply that they have no rule in the exercize of it' (*Present Discontents*).

[2] Burke said that the individual was foolish, the multitudes blunder at any given moment, but 'the species is wise, and, when time is given to it, as a species it almost always acts right' (*Present Discontents*). For an interesting summary of Burke's philosophy see L. Stephens, *English Thought in the Eighteenth Century* (Hart-Davis, 1962 (2 vols); 1st ed., 1876), ch. x, section 102.

destroying traditional safeguards by revolutionary enactments for a period during which those who had voted for them could be given the facility for understanding more fully what they were at.

The idea is to leave as little as possible to common sense, to take as little as possible on trust, to hedge 'supreme power' against the rainy day when the 'men of the moment' with their time-serving urgencies plunge all that the community has accumulated through centuries of social experience into the acid-bath of reform.

Yet the truth of the matter is that no formula, whether in writing or memorized in the oral tradition, is proof against the evil contrary to headlong reform — ossification — the hardening of 'rights' (for instance) into 'privileges'. An infinite regress of norms, super-norms, and super-super-norms, all codified and protected by higher courts, is no substitute for a defence much less precise and satisfying to the positivists — the defence that a people has in its profound, though possibly inarticulate, appreciation of what it means to be free.

To illustrate the ossification of rights and the nature of the corrective consider for a moment one or two of the 'positive' rights which the British and American peoples have come to regard as their surest protection against coercive inroads on freedom.

The property rights

The discussion of property rights calls for a discussion of justice as well as what has already been said about economic demands. But two comments are relevant here. What Burke called 'prescription'[1] — the uninterrupted use or possession of an estate whether from time immemorial or for a period fixed by law as giving a title or right — is undoubtedly a very important part indeed of a society's protection against arbitrary State power. To sweep all such rights away in order to make room for a 'massive' programme of redistribution, quite apart from the moral argument in favour of redistribution, which is another question, ensures that the community is at the mercy of future governments as it has never been before. However much the 'propertied class' may rouse the envy and the righteous anger of the dispossessed, however just may be the demand for equalization, a community

[1] That is, Burke's is the most notable use of this legal term in political philosophy see the references in the previous notes).

whose whole wealth is taken away from such a class, and therefore from all possible future private ownership, and concentrated in the hands of its civil servants has deprived itself of a major obstacle to despotism: it trusts too much to the civil servant.

On the other hand, a 'natural' right to property which has become formalized in a constitution or other legal instrument creates privilege and may restrict the moral development of the man who claims the privilege as it may most certainly deny room and opportunity to others. If, on the other hand, a community's 'property sense' is part of its appreciation of human freedom, the 'right' to property will always be subject to this understanding — to the owner's 'sense of responsibility', to the overall need of all men in the community for the conditions in which they can make their acts their own, what they achieve their own property. When the owners of machines and factory plant withhold fit conditions from their workers on the basis of the 'property right', such a right has lost its moral value: in a word, whatever force it has in law it is no longer 'right'. The State in correcting this may have to be coercive, but, provided it does so with the clear intent of enlarging the liberties of its subjects without depriving men of the property necessary to such liberty, coercion will seem 'just'.

So would it seem in a different situation as where, for instance, the 'right' granted to a workers' syndicate has similarly hardened into a 'privilege' permitting such an organization to withhold work and service from the community for no other cause than to enlarge the property of its members without respect to law and by all means short of violence. For in the exercise of such privilege a syndicate may well become coercive while, by pursuing 'property' (in the form of wages) without regard to the consequences either for its own members or for others, the moral basis justifying such a pursuit has been destroyed. Yet none would question the original contribution to human well-being such organizations made or the justice of their having been given in their time such rights as they may now exercise 'without right' and to the endangering of the community.

Free speech

One other illustration will suffice — the right to free speech. The force of this right is perhaps better expressed if we call it the right 'not to be forcibly prevented from speaking'. As such its check upon coercion is clear enough. This, too, is the justification for the collateral right to freedom of the Press.

as good almost kill a Man as kill a good Book; . . . he who destroys a good Book, kills reason itself . . .[1]

a position which, as John Milton himself recognized, meant either that you must have men good enough to say what is a good book and put the rest on the Index, or abolish all forms of censorship save that which public interest may indirectly impose without the aid of law.

Not that free speech need have much to do with political liberty in general. As the institution of the 'filibuster' can be used to inhibit action, so a government may well prefer to let its people talk rather than act: orators in Britain's Hyde Park, for instance, seldom saw their speeches implemented by the action of their audiences. Speech apart from political organization may be effective in an acute crisis when mass hysteria can be engaged, but it is by itself no guarantee of liberty — save only the liberty of not being silenced. The nations today where men are not free to speak their minds are plainly under coercive government; those where they are so free are not necessarily advancing in human freedom.

For not only can the exercise of this right fall into the hands of subversive groups, it may, along with other tendencies, bring the institution itself into contempt if too little is done to inform the opinion which claims expression, to discipline the critical ability, while at the same time people are encouraged to regard all opinions as equally valid provided only that they are *published*.

The first question in respect to any political institutions [according to Mill][2] is, how far they tend to foster in the members of the community the various desirable qualities . . .

[1] John Milton (1608–74). The *Areopagitica*: *a Speech of Mr. John Milton for the Liberty of Unlicensed Printing to the Parliament of England*, was published in 1644. (Now available in World's Classics edition of *Milton's Prose*, O.U.P., 1925.) The work was named after the Areopagus, the hill of Ares (Mars), near the Acropolis in Athens where the Upper Council met to deal with general supervision of political and religious matters. 'Give me the liberty to know, to utter, and to argue freely, according to conscience, above all liberties.' Milton's words are addressed to a Presbyterian-dominated government with strong leanings to strict puritanism.

[2] J. S. Mill, *On Representative Government* (Dent; Everyman's, 1910), ch. ii.

Our conclusions are: first, that this is a function which falls to the lot of many today — social and civil servants — who are not strictly the government, second, that in determining the 'desirable qualities' we must put freedom first among our principles or run all the ancient risks of moral despotism.

A government is to be judged by its action upon men, and by its action upon things; by what it makes of the citizens, and what it does with them; its tendency to improve or deteriorate the people themselves, and by means of them. Government is at once a great influence acting on the human mind, and a set of organized arrangements for public business . . .[1]

A people gets the government it deserves, but a government then retaliates by making the kind of people who deserve it. Social service is a complication of this relation, distributing it over much wider areas of the community. The social servant is an (unelected) representative. He may have little knowledge of 'public business' and even less interest; but there is a possibility that what he 'makes of the citizens', one way or the other, may come between them and their institutions and settle more decisively than parliaments or positive laws what kind of people they are to be. That is why we must explore both the values men have professed and those which are seeping into our public life more secretively through social service.

QUESTIONS FOR DISCUSSION

1. Note what Mr. Gladstone said in the House (p. 154). What part do majorities appear to play in law-making in a modern democracy? Majorities of *whom*? What value do we attach to a majority decision (*a*) if we are one of the majority, (*b*) if not? Read C. S. Emden, *The People and the Constitution*, 2nd ed. (O.U.P., 1959), pp. 22 ff. (in the paperback edition), and note (p. 53) the quotation from a speech by Charles Fox: 'I pay no regard whatever to the voice of the people'.

2. Study Harold J. Laski's 'supreme test of a social doctrine' (p. 155) and discuss the objection to it made in the text. Are we to

[1] Ibid.

follow such 'demands upon life' before social education has developed, after, or at some definable stage? Compare, for instance, the conditions dramatized in Golding's *Lord of the Flies* (Faber, 1954) and select the 'demands upon life' here for comparison with, say, those discussed by Plato in the *Republic* bk i.

3. Read J. S. Mill, *Representative Government*. Today who represents whom and in what situations, with respect to what needs or interests? Other reading: Rousseau, *Social Contract*, bk III, ch. xv; Pericles' Funeral Oration, in Thucydides, *History of the Peloponnesian War* (Everyman's ed.), bk II, ch. vi, especially sec. 57. (The speech may also be found in A. Zimmern, *The Greek Commonwealth*, 5th ed. (O.U.P., 1951), ch. viii.) See also C. S. Emden, op. cit. (Question 1 above), ch. II, sec. iii; ch. VIII, sec. iv; ch. XII, sec. v.

4. Read first these three quotations from John Milton's *Areopagitica*:

Give me the liberty to know, to utter and to argue freely, according to conscience, above all liberties.

... he who is made judge to sit upon the birth, or death of books ... had need to be a man above the common measure, both studious, learned and judicious.

Banish all objects of lust, shut up all youth into the severest discipline that can be exercized in any hermitage, ye cannot make them chaste that came not hither so ... were I the chooser, a dram of well-doing should be preferred before many times as much the forcible hindrance of evil-doing.

Then discuss censorship of books, films, scripts, in terms of (*a*) the aims of censorship, (*b*) the qualifications required by those who perform it.

Finally, turn to Plato's *Republic* and read (i) ii. 376–iii. 400; (ii) x. 595–608.

15

Permissiveness

'FREEDOM' (the word) is under suspicion today. We use it less in our talk of personal or social good. Philosophy has taught us to doubt its logical status; in politics other words pay better — lend themselves more readily to powerful interests and cause less blushes among the intelligentsia. Ordinary morality never has liked the word: 'liberal' can also mean 'loose'; 'free thinking', 'free love', and 'making free' are all phrases of no reputation. Wars have been fought for 'freedom'; but the weapons our science has provided have so scared us that we would rather forget about (other people's) freedom than risk a war by talking about it.

Yet if 'freedom' means the removal of restraints whether or not this is intended to enable the free man to pursue certain specified ends, it could be argued that many of us care more for freedom today than ever before, though we use other words to show it. Of all the words we use to show our respect for freedom the word 'permissive' is the most interesting. It shows up a range of human relations on the one hand, a battery of ideas on the other, which together throw light on present-day thinking about man and society and (in the process) they may show what we mean by the need for a general concept of freedom.

'Permissiveness' does not belong to any one academic discipline nor has moral philosophy taken much notice of it, as yet. Its usefulness is that it seems to characterize much thought about human relations among people who know enough about ideas or at least have enough phraseology to deploy in defence or explanation of their conduct, but who may never be able to trace their ideas critically to an academic source or even have been given a hint in their education that this ought to be done. Therefore we will talk first of 'permissive relations' irrespective of the ways in which these might appeal to the various social sciences, and then consider the type of argument used in defence of such relations, so that we can appraise both the qualities and the arguments in relation to freedom.

'Permissive' relations

Doctors and patients, gaolers and prisoners, employers and employees or, alternatively, trade unions and employers, these and a whole range of other relations are subject to conventions which, more often than not, it is the responsibility of one partner, not the other, to insist upon. The same could be said of teachers and students or indeed of any group in which one person or one group of persons is regarded as having a certain authority recognized by the conventions and based upon special 'qualifications'. Where, in such circumstances, all those concerned, or in particular the authorized persons, permit the removal of conventional restraints, we may speak of a 'permissive' relation.

Now since 'conventions' represent the society beyond and 'above' the persons involved in a particular, concrete situation, permissiveness anywhere in such relations is interesting for what it shows of the conventions — their strength or their weakness — for what it shows of relations between the social 'whole' and its parts. No relation can be of greater interest than that between parents and their children or, in some measure, any adults and children for whom they are responsible. By means of such relations the social 'whole' preserves itself as an identity in difference; but also by such relations adult men and women show most about their objectives, their appreciation of human relations, the values by which they direct their own lives.

Let us take as our model a parent who exercises no recognizable systematic restriction of a child's conduct — not because this is the 'type' of the permissive relation, but because in arguing for and against such a relation we are more likely to clear the ground and see what permissiveness could mean both in terms of scientific justification and as a social value.

Now the point of our model is not that the parent *never* restrains a child, never compels him to do what he does not choose to do. We can permit the mother, for instance, occasional uprushes of fear or anxiety, we can allow the father his paddies and to both of

them appropriate measures to 'put a stop to' whatever their
offspring is doing to upset them. The important feature of the
model is that none of this is done 'to rule', and for the most part
the child's conduct is left free of adult regulation at least so far as
his parents are to be reckoned with. Arbitrary coercion is not
regularity.

We cannot predict the consequences of such a relation, first,
because they may very well vary from child to child, second,
because that is the work of the scientist — it is beyond our
competence. In any case, it is not what interests us. We are not
asking about the empirical effects of types of relations; we are
asking about concepts of relations and to do this we need only
take into account *possible* consequences and ask whether these are
to be included in any subsequent argument for permissiveness.

Among the possible consequences of the crude model with
which we have begun we may distinguish two sorts: those which
affect other people directly, whether immediately or subsequently;
those which affect the child. We may call the first 'social'; the
second, 'private'. A child who is never systematically restrained,
or who is restrained hardly at all save perhaps where he arouses
sudden anger or fear in his parents, may conceivably injure other
people outside the family in some way as well as the members of
his own family: some social consequences of permissiveness may
be harmful.[1] The personal consequences, quite apart from those
following upon the harm done to others, 'bouncing back' as it
were upon the perpetrator, can include at least one sort: the
child's estimate of his place in the world among his fellows. It is
conceivable that where no regular restraint is exercised the child

[1] An example of what may reasonably be considered the kind of consequences:
a train in the United Kingdom was derailed, two people killed and a number of
others injured as a result of 'hooliganism', to wit, vicious action by young persons
who placed obstacles on the permanent way. This was one of a long series of such
incidents. *The Times* in a leading editorial said: 'It is an unattractive feature of the
permissive society in which we now live that more regard is apt to be paid to the
psychological well-being of the children who are allowed by their parents to do these
things, than to the danger of injury to innocent persons — until a catastrophe
actually occurs, when hands are thrown up in horror' (*The Times*, 10 April 1965).

No doubt social scientists would want to dispute the causal connection between
'permissive society' and these acts of destruction. The least we can say is that the
leader-writer is aware of a more dangerous confusion — that between 'psychological well-being' (so-called), ensured by permissiveness, and the general well-
being of members of the society.

will expect the connexion between any and every want or impulse to be direct and positive or, in plain language, to have what 'he' wants.

Ignoring the possible social consequences for the moment, we have to take notice of the way this personal consequence was worded: to have what 'he' wants. This only makes sense if we can be assured that the sources of the 'self', of the child's integrity, lie wholly within the child or at least can be relied upon to work without external restraint and orderly guidance.

Some such argument may come to the defence of permissiveness under the general title 'self-realization'.

Self-realization

Talking of action, we said earlier that if we are to speak of a man's movements being 'his own actions' we must be able in some way to conceive of the man as a whole.[1] We then agreed to use 'person' in the broadest sense for the whole organism and its functions, but to keep 'self' for the person in a special sense — as aware and as 'struggling through awareness to integrity, to wholeness, to self-recognition'. The 'self' was likened to an independence movement in a nation ruled by a foreign power. What we are now listening to in the name of permissiveness is argument that this 'independence movement', the self, can best succeed or be realized by the removal of all circumstantial restrictions *not* from the adult who might presumably have advanced somewhat toward self-recognition but from the child at the earliest age. It is of 'self-realization' solely in this context that we are now speaking.

Permissiveness in this connexion *either* proposes that the 'realization of the self' is a good that should take precedence over all else (including the interests, the feelings, and so forth of other 'selves') *or* that there is an inner source of regulation in every child to replace the traditional external restraints. In both cases it assumes that the rule-making, rule-following habits are at best unnecessary, at worst injurious. Permissiveness in social values resembles anarchy in politics.

What can be meant by saying that self-realization should take precedence over all other interests? It looks as if we were meant to

---

[1] See above, Chapter 12.

understand that the realization of the child's self should take precedence over any such process in adults. Perhaps we are meant to assume that adults either have 'realized' their selves or have no right to more time for the process once they reach a certain age. If, for example, you have a school in which children are under no restraints, while their teachers continue to find themselves ruled by innumerable restrictions on their behaviour, this is surely what we are asked to understand by permissiveness — a child-centred association in which all else must be set aside for the realization of the child self.

But this is evidently a different notion of 'self' from the one we arrived at before when talking about acts and movements. We said then that movements are converted to acts 'by virtue of the continuity of their agent' (the self) and this 'in its turn is both recognized and *realized*' through such institutions as liability on the one hand, co-operation on the other. The permissive view we are now considering proposes to realize the self by reducing liability to a minimum (denying it educational utility). What about co-operation? There can surely be no co-operation when the interest of one is given priority over all others as the 'child-centred' interpretation of permissiveness suggests.

We have, then, a different view of the self — the permissive view of something to be realized not even partly through rule-making and rule-following, but only in spite of these or, for preference, without them. What kind of object do we expect to emerge from such conditions of freedom? To what shall we liken the self if it is thought of as realizable in such ways?

Either the self is thought of as a distinct entity, a thing along with other things, or it is not. If it is, then to talk of 'realizing' the self is odd; for while we do talk of 'realizing things are there' — taking notice of them, putting them to some use — we do not talk of things 'being realized' in the sense of coming to be; we speak rather of 'making them' or of their 'growing' (perhaps with our help). Friedrich Froebel's[1] word, 'kindergarten', seems to suggest the second alternative, but Froebel in likening education

---

[1] Friedrich Froebel (1782–1852), a disciple, together with Johann Friedrich Herbart (1776–1834), of Jean Henri Pestalozzi (1746–1827), who, together with Rousseau and Comenius, also used the plant analogy. English students may consult Curtis and Boultwood, *History of Educational Ideas*, 3rd ed. (University Tutorial Press, 1961), chs xiii and xiv.

to the cultivation of plants does not deal in 'self-things' and their realization.

Each person, as a small, essential portion, contributes to God's purpose in so far as he performs his part as a smoothly functioning, balanced unity.[1]

This requires two things: contributing to the efficiency and integrity of the social group but also mobilizing his own powers 'into an integrated whole'. This resembles the view of 'self' taken in this book but not what we have so far understood of the 'self-realization' aimed at by permissiveness.

Rousseau, on the other hand, is sometimes thought to take some such view in his *Émile*. But there are two things to be said about this. The first is that if 'permissiveness' means the removal of all restrictions upon a child's behaviour then Émile's tutor had no such clear intention.

Sometimes I say children are incapable of reasoning. Sometimes I say they reason cleverly. I must admit that my words are often contradictory, but I do not think there is any contradiction in my ideas.[2]

But his aim with Émile is clear enough: 'Well-regulated liberty',[3] and this is very different from what, so far, we have understood by permissiveness. The second comment on Rousseau is this: in 'regulating' the liberty of Émile as in all his social and political philosophy he believed himself to be living in a corrupt society whose institutions would necessarily corrupt any child compelled at too early an age to conform to them. This makes sense of what otherwise would be contradictory in his writings: the determination to exclude traditional regulation but at the same time the recognition, as in the phrase just quoted, that regulation of some kind is essential.

Rousseau provides no excuse for permissiveness, not, at least, until we have taken up his position with respect to our own social institutions — and these are, to say the least, different from those in Rousseau's time. On the contrary, each time we approve our institutions we commit ourselves to ways of educating children which will sustain and perpetuate those institutions. Permissiveness as the absence of all restraints may not easily be shown to do this.

---

[1] Curtis and Boultwood, op. cit. p. 376.
[2] Rousseau's *Émile* (Everyman's), p. 72 n.   [3] Ibid., p. 56.

Reasonableness

'Reasoning' as an alternative to coercion, however, must surely fit the bill. For as permissiveness (whatever its intrinsic values) is best seen in the light of contrast with the nineteenth-century horrors depicted by Charles Dickens and others, so 'reasoning' might well be taken as the enlightened, democratic, Western alternative to totalitarianism, force, and coercion. Nevertheless, though this may be what many people intend by relations which they would call permissive or which resemble the crude model with which we began, the more we think about 'reasoning' the less suitable may 'permissive' be as a name for a reasonable relation.

'Reasoning with' a child may, of course, mean no more than arguing with him in order to get him to do what his guardian wants without respect to what we called the primary truth-conventions. If this is permissiveness, it may scarcely be preferable to coercion, for it is a deceit: it is a confusion of decision with discussion. Decision is the adult's responsibility in many situations and reasoning of this order may be little more than an adult attempt to ease himself of the discomforts of responsibility. The error is not in making a decision — often this has to be done — but in pretending that it is not being made. The moral fault we are discussing is not what is sometimes (misleadingly) called adult 'selfishness' in choosing one of several alternatives, more particularly when there is no way in which a child could be said to have those alternatives, but in pretending that these are the child's alternatives, that the choice is his when it is not and probably cannot be.

A useful distinction here is between 'reasoning with' and 'giving reasons'. If I know the dietary arguments for not sucking sweets in bed (at least without tooth-cleaning after), I have to decide that sweets are not to be sucked. I give my reasons. But if 'reasoning with' means trying to get the child to make the decision and not merely to accept my decision as 'reasonable', then I am not going to 'reason with' him. Whether he is convinced of my reasonableness or not sweets will not be sucked. The other alternative is what one would expect from the 'permissive' relation: reasons are given, reasoning with is done, but then the child is free to ruin his teeth or not. In this case the parent observes the truth-conventions in part — his 'reasons' respect objective truth and the giving of them inter-personal truth, but there is doubt about his *integrity*: there is some doubt whether his failure to decide is 'respect for the child's self' (whatever that could mean in this situation) or simply a yielding to his dislike of decision, at least where unpleasant feelings may be involved.

In short permissiveness, where this is taken to mean reasoning in place of coercion and where reasoning in turn means discussion substituted for decision, may well be not a demand for the 'freedom' of the child but a device for reducing the responsibility of the adult. If, on the other hand, 'reasoning' means the giving of reasons in a situation where one is to decide but wishes the other to co-operate, then this kind of relation does not benefit by the title 'permissive'. It is, on the contrary, the type of all relations where one person is authorized to make decisions affecting others but is anxious to reduce so far as possible the coercive aspects of such relations.

Indifference?

The danger in the word 'permissiveness' is that it can come to associate freedom with a number of attitudes and ideas, some of which may be positively hostile to freedom as well as to other social values. We note, for instance, the difficulty there is in distinguishing between permissiveness and indifference. This is increased by the ease with which the opposite of indifference — concern — can be seen as *unwarranted* concern, interference, trespass, possessiveness. But such difficulties are scarcely new. They are as old as the demand for personal liberty. Many of the rules, the conventions, the manners, morals, laws, and habits of civilization have arisen in the search for ways and means of protecting liberty while at the same time sustaining community and co-operation. Justice is in some senses the 'middle term'. General permissiveness, on the other hand, attacks this fabric of social interchange, neglecting ways of distinguishing proper from improper concern. This could deprive us of both reliable freedom and reliable co-operation.

To keep ourselves apart without depriving ourselves of community is the aim of freedom as a social value. We have two devices (among others) which we use for this end. First there is the device of 'authority' — authorized interference; second, there are 'manners' — formal ways of acknowledging each other's identity and so maintaining distinction and communication at the same time. In the situation we have been considering parents have authority to care for their children and this (given certain qualities in the parents) could make sure that the community's interest in the children was protected; at the same time parental authority might keep others from interfering and so save the child from being drawn too soon into too wide a social circle. This could help him to become 'himself' by keeping him effectively a member of a small, compact group. To have authority means at least to take on behalf of children decisions which they cannot be expected to take for themselves. There is a possibility that permissiveness is an abdication of such authority, which may present itself to a child as the community's indifference to his fate or his personal significance.

But further. Suppose that permissiveness then intends to do nothing about the manners and morals of the society in which the child is born. A child may, for example, be in the habit of receiving gifts from adult relations and friends, but with nothing in his permissive upbringing requiring him to reciprocate, whether with gifts in return or merely with formal expressions of gratitude. He continues to be treated as a 'receiving thing' from whom nothing is expected in return. Perhaps he constructs his picture of human relations on this model. For plainly people are indifferent to what he *does*; all that matters is that he *receives*. Since, moreover, he is never required to go through the forms of acknowledging the status or even the existence of others, who is to speak of a 'relation' between him and them and how are we to distinguish between his non-response and indifference?

'By his feelings', we are sometimes told. A child ought not to be required to give formal thanks or perform any other courteous gesture 'unless he feels it'. Whatever the current view in psychology of the causal relation between feelings and movements,[1] this

[1] William James (1842–1910), American psychologist and philosopher, and C. G. Lange, the Danish philosopher, independently proposed in 1884 and 1885 that emotions are the conscious awareness of the bodily changes which occur as direct responses to emotion-provoking situations. Thus we feel sorry because we cry, we are afraid because we run away. Walter Cannon and Philip Bard revised this theory with special attention to the function of the hypothalamus. James and still more

quasi-romantic permissiveness is plainly anarchic in respect of all social forms. Perhaps it is based on faith in original virtue and expects that the child will without teaching or promotion perform the required acts. Or perhaps action is not rated very high: it is the *feeling* (real or supposed) which matters.

The first alternative is self-contradictory. It proposes that *conventional* forms will be adopted and agreed to 'by the light of nature'; unless, of course, someone taking this view supposes that centuries of civilization have somehow 'built into' the child an awareness of the appropriateness of forms, in which case it is odd that he does not follow them, does not know 'intuitively' the 'right thing' to say or do. Certainly it is not unknown for the same person at short intervals to complain of ill-manners in children *and* about parents who take care to teach good ones to their offspring.

The other view is typically romantic and, like all romantic comment on society it has to be examined with some care. For if 'what matters' is feeling and if we are not to require right action unless it springs from feeling, then not only manners and morals, not only positive law, but the whole fundament of primary conventions — the truth-conventions at least — is to be abandoned. This may sound like nothing less than the abandonment of civilization; it would certainly represent an entirely new concept of civilization,[1] one in which feeling would have to be engineered to suit the requirements of order or order disastrously abandoned to suit the requirements of feeling. In either case freedom would lose its meaning, for in the first alternative the social engineers would have got rid of the possibility of a self to be free and in the second there would be no longer a clear demarcation between

---

John Dewey (1859–1952) represent *functionalism* in psychology or what has been called the 'Is — for' school, the psychology of how to be successful whether as an animal struggling for bare survival or, presumably, a nineteenth-century American struggling for social and economic success. The James–Lange theory was in a measure anticipated by René Descartes. In article xxi of *The Passions of the Soul* he says there is a small gland in the brain in which the soul exercises its functions more particularly than in other parts. In article xxxvi he describes the process by which an exciting image prepares the body for flight or defence and in the process 'sends to the brain the spirits which are adapted for the maintenance and strengthening of the passion of fear'. (See vol. i of the Dover ed., pp. 329 ff.)

[1] A 'new concept of civilization': here it is interesting to have in mind Aldous Huxley's *Brave New World*.

areas of freedom, and such chaos is the same as no freedom at all.
(For you would never know what was going to happen and never
be able to plan.)

We conclude that the word 'permissive' may well indicate
modifications of coercion in some kinds of relation; but 'permissiveness' as a total concept of the good relation is far too
ambiguous and misleading at its best, possibly wholly destructive
of social values at its worst. If freedom is to be protected against
such conceptual abuses, we shall have to pass from demands for
circumstantial freedom, enabling demands (like the economic)
and permissive demands of the kind we have been considering, to
what men have meant by freedom as the name for personal
qualities, for something which must happen within men as well as
for those changes called for without.[1]

QUESTIONS FOR DISCUSSION

1. Does 'permissive' sound *approving*? Discuss experiences of
permissive relations and note how they differ from examples given
in the text. Go back to Chapter 11, Question 3. Discuss the
connexion between permissiveness in parents and the experience
of 'self'.

2. Read the opening chapters of Aldous Huxley's *Brave New
World* and discuss the connexion between permissiveness and
social engineering. Then relate this to the suggestion made by
Felix Greene and mentioned in a footnote below. Finally do
some research into contemporary psychology for arguments for
and against his suggestion.

3. Would you call Pestalozzi and his disciples 'permissive' in
their attitudes to education? (See the references in a footnote on
p. 169.)

[1] On the relation between extreme permissiveness and political freedom an interesting observation has been made by Felix Greene in *The Wall has two Sides*, following
upon his experiences in China. Permissiveness in childhood, he argues, leads to
docility in adults. 'Total belonging' in childhood (that is, with every child indulged
by every adult) makes the idea of *not* belonging intolerable once the child has grown
up. A monolithic society may very successfully be built on such a foundation. On
the other hand, Greene admits another factor: China may never have passed through
our own post-Renaissance stress on individuality.

16

Free Men

'EVERY man,' [says Thomas Hobbes], 'hath more or less liberty, as he hath more or less space in which he employs himself: as he hath more liberty who is in a large, than he who is kept in a close prison.'[1] It sounds as if a man becomes more free as he gets a bigger cell in his gaol. On the other hand, Father Zossima (in Dostoevsky's *Brothers Karamazov*) said something rather different.

I know of one 'champion of freedom' who told me himself that, when he was deprived of tobacco in prison, he was so wretched ... that he almost went and betrayed his cause for the sake of getting tobacco again.

No wonder, the priest added, 'that instead of gaining freedom [such people] have sunk into slavery'. This suggests that space alone or freedom from constraint will not make men 'free'. In addition they need certain personal, inner qualities.

Laissez faire, 'majority rule', 'no taxation without representation' —all such slogans are aimed at circumstantial freedom. They are aimed, that is, at getting more space, ending restrictions, and, for the most part, enabling men to get on with what they want to do. This (say many thinkers) is all we ought to mean by 'freedom'. Better still if we make a list of all the restrictions we want removed, get rid of them, and say no more about freedom. If we go on to ask questions about the 'inner man', we may find ourselves making absurd *indeterminist* statements: saying, in short, that some human movements are 'free' in the sense that they are not caused. This would be nonsense. All movements are related to preceding events

[1] Thomas Hobbes (1588–1679), *Philosophical Rudiments*, in *English Works*, vol. ii, pp. 120 f.

as their effects, even as they are related to subsequent events as their cause or part of their cause. That does not prevent our distinguishing, however, between movements caused by uncontrolled impulse and those which derive their meaning from purpose as the purpose of the movement is derived from an organization called the 'self'. In other words a man's movements can become in some sense his own to the extent that he achieves integrity and recognition. If he fails to do this, then no amount of space around him, no degree of liberation from restriction, will make it possible for us to say with truth: 'This man is free'.

Oddly enough, we make less of inner freedom at the very time when the psychologists and those who are influenced by them lend most weight to the argument that freedom, to be meaningful, must be enjoyed by a person who is in possession of certain qualities, dispossessed of others. We are all very willing to agree that a wide range of mental conditions can deprive a man of responsibility for his movements, but the obverse of this is that a man who is responsible for his movements has not such conditions. It is true we are more interested in using the theories of psychology to deny responsibility than we are to affirm it, but it makes no difference to the logic: a man freed from restrictions is to that extent the 'owner' of his movements, liable (under the conventions) to answer for them, bound to care for himself and therefore — according to the moral law — for others affected by what he does. If for any reason we now say that he is unable to behave in this way, that despite the free area he cannot be master of his movements and that therefore he ought not to have to answer for them or be relied upon to consider others, then not only are we calling this man 'non-responsible' but by the same tokens we are calling him 'not free'.

Moralists as well as mystics and poets have been clear enough about this. Some have gone so far as to hold that circumstances do not matter at all — what matters is not the world but the way a man deals with it within himself. Others have taken the view that the whole point of circumstantial freedom is to make free men — that is, in this inward sense; while others again have simply held — as Father Zossima seemed to hold — that no matter how wide the space a man is given in which to move he will not be free if he is at the mercy of his own unorganized feelings, appetites, or passions.

The second and third of these views are obviously compatible, though they call for different emphases. The first might be; but then again it could be wholly detached from interest in external freedom. So we will begin with this view and return to the others when we are clearer about its implications.

'Live hidden'

'Live hidden'[1] is supposed to have been the favourite maxim of Epicurus (341–270 B.C.) whose ethical teaching was continued by his followers for some four centuries or more after his death, but whose influence is more far-reaching. This way of dealing with the demand for freedom is typical of others who could by no means be called 'Epicurean'. Epicurus,[2] like Pythagoras,[3] subordinated interest in science to overall concern for human well-being. The physical theories of the Greek atomists[4] which he accepted are much more 'modern' than those of many who followed him. On the other hand there is little doubt that he followed Democritus only so far as his version of atomic theory suited Epicurus' ethical aims. These were to find 'a place for men in the order and course of nature' and to subdue the passions. 'The way to freedom of mind and liberation from all fear,'[5] lay in 'the soul's freedom from disturbance'.[6]

This living 'hidden' in order to avoid upsets may not look like a demand for freedom, but if we interpret it as a systematic attempt to be independent of circumstance the point will be clear enough. We must keep in mind, however, what was probably the starting point in Epicurus' thinking — the view that *pleasure* is the sole ultimate good and pain the sole evil. This *hedonism*,[7] as it is called in ethical theory, became in the Epicurean view the ideal of

[1] Quoted by E. Zeller, *Outlines of the History of Greek Philosophy* (Meridian, 1955), p. 258.

[2] For one account of Epicurus' ethical theory see H. Sidgwick, *History of Ethics*, 6th ed. (Macmillan, 1931), ch. ii, sec. xvii.

[3] On Pythagoras see also above, Chapter 1.

[4] Democritus held that the atoms had an infinite variety of shapes and a rotary motion, whereas Epicurus preferred the view that there was a limited variety (not determinable) and a falling motion in empty space. It was important for him to be able to show that without any external cause atoms deviate to an infinitesimal degree from the perpendicular thus colliding, becoming entangled with one another and partly forced upwards, leading to the creation of worlds. See Burnet, *EGP*, ch. ix, and *DL*, x.

[5] E. Zeller, op. cit., p. 296.   [6] Ibid., p. 295.   [7] From *hedone*, 'pleasure'.

katastematikē hedonē — the 'pleasure of stable condition'.[1] This high point of achievement is reached by the mere removal of pain or disturbance. Dread of death, fear of the gods — these were serious sources of disturbance which could only be removed by a true theory of the physical universe and man's place in it. The principal virtues, the moral qualities by means of which men would sustain their achievement of bliss, were temperance and fortitude. They must avoid excess, including the excesses of intimate, intense emotional relations such as those of the family and of political embroilment; if pain was unavoidable, they must avoid complaint and fruitless protest. Such cultivated habits were necessary if one was to remain undisturbed by the world. Similarly, one would be well advised to keep the laws, little as they might deserve respect; for to be discovered in law-breaking would be painful and the dread of discovery, too, would be a serious disturbance.

'I don't want no trouble' is a saying sufficiently familiar today for this part of Epicurean teaching to be understood. If ordinary morality uses such an explanation in refusing to aid the police or to resist unjust government, this makes little difference to the basic agreement with Epicurus on this point: the avoidance of disturbing conflicts is recommended by both. Then again, though Epicurus may have settled for the 'pleasure of stable condition', he is far from being an ascetic and therefore wholly in sympathy with a society different from his own in which it is possible to enjoy an increasing variety of pleasures without their producing painful consequences.

It is possible to go still further and see how 'being free' must come to mean some of the things it meant in Epicurus' teaching. If a man cannot at some point detach himself from susceptibility to public demand, popular tastes, group excitements and values; if he is wholly unable to enjoy private knowledge and keep himself for a season undisturbed by the opinions, judgements, and interests of society, then it is hard to see how one can distinguish between such a man and other men sufficiently to speak of him (significantly) as 'free' at all. Or, in the language we have used earlier, if he cannot so separate himself in some way we shall find

[1] Epicurus, *Letter to Monoeceus* in *Stoic and Epicurean Philosophers*, ed. Oates (Random House, 1940).

G

it impossible to speak of his 'self'. A wholly 'public' man is in this sense no man at all.

Then again, if there is little or nothing that can be done to change external circumstances, to overthrow an unjust government and reform the laws, *not* to take up some such ethical principles as these would mean that one could be free in no sense, but be wholly defeated. For Socrates at the end to 'live hidden' was a contradiction; but this is not necessarily the case for all men. On the contrary, even in more 'open' societies to be free may very well mean for many if not for most to be *private* and it may be that for this reason many more people would be more free if they would acquire those habits which make for detachment, for independence rather than for gregariousness, conviviality, being 'in the swim'.

But this is unsatisfactory as a *social* philosophy. It is true that the Epicureans, the men of the Garden, were friendly people and enjoyed other society than their own; but any ethical view which makes non-disturbance not one of its aims but its *chief* aim, and which in pursuit of that aim recommends withdrawal from public life, holds out little hope for a constructive concept of the good society save (perhaps) as a protective federation between small associations busily pursuing peace of mind behind their garden walls, a federation for the protection of closed orders.

Messianism[1]

Epicurus sought happiness now and for individual men. By cultivating proper mental habits, by detaching themselves as far as possible from contemporary society, there could be the minimum of disturbance. The link with what we may for the moment call 'messianism' lies in the notion of *detachment* from the institutions of contemporary society; the difference between Epicureanism and messianism lies in the comparative indifference of messianism to immediate happiness.

But messianic views differ among themselves. The ancient Hebrew, for instance, was often urged by his prophets to detach himself from the policies of his kings and the occupations of surrounding society and to practise instead certain moral qualities

[1] For 'messianism' as a key to the political and social thought of Europe in the nineteenth century see J. L. Talmon, *Political Messianism: the Romantic Phase* (Secker & Warburg, 1960).

appropriate to a Coming Age, the age of the Messiah. His present
happiness did not matter so much as the future salvation of his
people. Nevertheless, this in its turn called for inner, personal
qualities, increasing emphasis upon which is typical of the later
Hebrew moralists, just as they come to speak more and more of
personal rather than corporate salvation as the work of the
coming Messiah. The personal Messiah in such thought occupies
something of the place that natural law takes in later European
thought — an 'alienation'[1] (perhaps) of the qualities which the
moralists advocate.

... this is the covenant I will make ... saith the Lord: I will put my
law in their inward parts, and in their heart I will write it ...[2]

Among the Christians who develop this tradition there is
considerable difference of opinion about the nature and extent of
the detachment from secular life which their salvation requires,
but some agreement about the inner qualities necessary *and* about
these as the conditions of freedom. When orthodox Jews were
told by Christ that 'the truth' would make them free they protested
that as the 'children of Abraham' they never had been slaves. The
reply was: 'Everyone that committeth sin is the bondservant of
sin.'[3] The Apostle Paul[4] has a great deal to say about spiritual
freedom, which he contrasts, after his conversion, with the
condition he was in when he was a scrupulous observer of Hebrew
law. We get the impression of a present, immediate satisfaction
called 'freedom' though Paul attributes this, of course, to the
Messiah and shares the hope of a new order.

'Quietism'[5] is a useful name for the extremes to which attention
to inner qualities of the person can go in detachment from what we
have so far called the conditions of freedom. The less 'sense of

[1] On alienation see above, Chapter 10, and references to Feuerbach.
[2] Jeremiah, xxxi. 33.   [3] John viii. 31 ff.
[4] For Saint Paul's teaching see Romans vi; 1 Corinthians vii. 21 f., ix. 1 and 19;
Galatians iii. 28, v. 1, and compare with Acts of the Apostles xxii. 28, where the
freedom of Roman citizenship is discussed.
[5] Quietism was a seventeenth-century movement in France, Italy, and Spain;
de Molinos was a Spaniard resident in Rome; Fénelon was censured by the Pope in
1699. On the place of Quietism in religious thought see W. R. Inge, *Christian
Mysticism*. For a classical comment on the psychology of such experiences see W.
James, *The Varieties of Religious Experience* (Longmans, Green, 1905), lectures
xi–xvii.

proprietorship' a man had in his own actions, the more they came from a source outside himself, the surer he might be that they were divine. These were the views of Miguel de Molinos, Fénelon, and Madame Jeanne Marie Guyon with whom the name 'quietist' is usually associated. They prefer divine inspiration and reject one of the conditions we have laid down for liberty — the 'sense of proprietorship' a man has in his own actions. Quietism in this original sense has a 'dangerous "double character" of passivity and beatitude'. Evelyn Underhill asks us to see Madame Guyon, 'basking like a pious tabby cat in the beams of the Uncreated Light'.[1] Another mystic quoted by the same authority leads Miss Underhill to distinguish the 'true and healthy mystic state of "Quiet" from the morbid perversion of "Quietism" ':

the difference between the tense stillness of the athlete and the limp passivity of the sluggard, who is really lazy though he looks resigned.[2]

It is as well she does so, for this helps us to keep a necessary balance between interest in the private and the public aspects of freedom. Quietism of the more extreme sorts, on the other hand, would seem to justify some of the criticism which religion, along with other sources of interest in the 'private sector', has received from such energetic concern with the public aspect as Karl Marx and his followers represent.

Yet Marxism, too, in some sense, is 'messianic'. Contemptuous as the Marxist is for religion as an 'opiate', he, too, detaches himself from the existing institutions of a (non-Marxist) society and while the individual, in his view, must be saved with the group or not at all, the Marxist is encouraged to *feel* his separateness from capitalist or *bourgeois* society and to *feel* his togetherness with the proletariat. He has to be educated or reeducated.[3] He has to come to see things in a certain way and to do all this not indeed

---

[1] E. Underhill, *Mysticism*, 12th ed. (Meridian, 1955), p. 247.

[2] Ibid., p. 321. The author suggests that Quietism in its extreme form existed long before Guyon and the seventeenth century; see her chapter on *Introversion, Recollection and Quiet*.

[3] For instance the former British Communist, Douglas Hyde, in his book, *I Believed* (Heinemann, 1950), talks of the need for hatred in the good Party member, the hatred that membership encourages (ch. xiii). That is not to say that the Marxist has to be a person of strong feelings — see, for instance, Hyde's account of Palme Dutt. What is meant is that the member's feelings must be arranged around a particular set of objects by processes suitable to his temperament and experience.

for his personal freedom so much as for the ultimate freedom of the workers.

The difficulty with all messianic treatments of the personal qualities necessary to freedom is that in following them one has to detach oneself from the concrete, proximate social situation, from concrete obligations and, to some extent, from all those institutions which service the primary truth-conventions. This is the *revolutionary* approach to morals, politics, and social values of which men in the nineteenth century made a religion in itself, provoked to do so in many cases by flagrant injustice and a general failure of social institutions to cope with the Industrial Revolution and its aftermath.

Revolutionary messianism in any form, however, calls either for systematic and lifelong detachment from man's attempt to work out his own salvation communally through what he has inherited as well as through his own ingenuity — either for this or for equally systematic *subversion* of all those institutions, for habits of interpersonal untruth, unreliability, for large assumptions in the realms of objective truth going well beyond what the conventions of reasonable discourse can justify, and for the risk of personal integrity by such subversive contempt for 'society' with all too little knowable about the consequences both for oneself or others. These are large objections to messianism as a form for social philosophy. And there are others.

Marxist messianism, however, unlike some other forms, explicitly takes the view that it is the purpose of free institutions to make free men, with the implication that men will then be free not only because of changed institutions but because they will differ in quality.

Only in association with others has each individual the means of cultivating his talents in all directions. Only in a community, therefore, is personal freedom possible ... In a genuine community individuals gain their freedom in and through their association.[1]

It is possible to take such a view without the 'messianic' context and objectives. We will consider one attempt in this direction now before working out the implications in more detail in the next chapter.

[1] Karl Marx, *German Ideology*.

Individuality

'The absolute and essential importance of human development in its richest diversity'[1] was the end to which John Stuart Mill dedicated his essay *On Liberty*. The interest of this essay at the moment, however, is the way in which individuality is used to draw attention to those personal qualities which on the one hand give liberty its *value* and on the other constitute the proper end or aim of institutions in a free society. He argued for 'different experiments in living'; for 'free scope' to be given to 'varieties of character'. But this is no mere permissiveness.

He who lets the world, or his own portion of it, choose his plan of life for him, has no need of any other faculty than the ape-like one of imitation. He who chooses a plan for himself, employs all his faculties.[2]

By making responsible men the proper objective of social institutions Mill repudiates explicitly what he believes to be certain assessments of human capacity dominating nineteenth-century thought in England. The model of human nature as a machine was one such; conformity of a kind which maims 'by compression, like a Chinese lady's foot, every part of human nature which stands out prominently' represented another. Above all it was the tyranny of mediocrity he feared: 'collective mediocrity', as he called it, was the enemy of freedom. It could destroy individuality.

Education is very important to Mill's ends. He is quite ready for it to be compulsory 'up to a certain standard' but State education should be strictly limited, 'one among many competing experiments'.

The worth of the State in the long run, is the worth of the individuals composing it . . . A State which dwarfs its men in order that they may be more docile instruments in its hands, even for beneficial purposes —

---

[1] W. von Humboldt, quoted by Mill on the title page of his essay. In 1792 Humboldt wrote *An Essay on the Limits of the Action of the State*, a 'masterpiece of political individualism in the romantic period' according to Guidode Ruggiero. Humboldt was influenced by revolutionary writers such as Mirabeau (*Education politique*). Ruggiero suggests that romantics changed their attitudes — to the French Revolution among other things — partly because liberal individualism is only a part of the romantic outlook. See also H. S. Reiss, *Political Thought of the German Romantics* (Oxford, Blackwell, 1955), ch. ii and compare the quotation from Troeltsch on p. 118, above.

[2] J. S. Mill, *On Liberty*, ch. iii. Note Mill's reference to Alexis de Tocqueville.

will find that with small men no great thing can be really accomplished . . .[1]

At the time when Mill was writing two great changes were coming about in England, both of them important to freedom. The movement toward a universal franchise was an advance in external, public, circumstantial freedom. The movement toward universal State-sponsored education might well be taken as a complementary attempt to look after the qualities of the individual thought necessary to freedom. But now consider how these were regarded by contemporary thought closest to government, having in mind John Stuart Mill's proposed objectives for free government.

The Reform Act of 1867 — Disraeli's 'leap into the dark' — extended the franchise to a large number of artisans. Forster's Elementary Education Bill was introduced in 1870. It was in the period between these two events that a Vice-President of the Education Department, Robert Lowe, remarked that it was necessary now 'to compel our future masters to learn their letters'. It is the contrast between this as an aim for the State and what John Stuart Mill desired for a free society which should be taken into account.

Literacy[2] (in the minimal sense) is widely accepted as the chief 'quality' which a liberalizing State should create in preparation for democracy. We now have some reason to doubt whether there is any necessary connexion between reading, writing, and being 'free men'. Literacy was thought to be an insurance against exploitation, a means to self-determination. With no other intellectual equipment it can just as surely be an increased susceptibility to mass opinion or indeed to all forms of propaganda. Robert Lowe spoke of 'compelling our future masters' but not of 'compelling' or otherwise inducing them to any special facility for 'mastery' — other than minimal literacy. Mill, on the other hand, thought that a government concerned for 'Permanence as well as

---

[1] Ibid., ch. v.

[2] R. Hoggart, *The Uses of Literacy* (Chatto & Windus, 1957), is an interesting study of literacy and its influence on the working classes in England. Bertrand de Jouvenel has this to say: 'The spread of education, which was designed to counteract the consequences of universal suffrage by providing the citizens with the minimum of knowledge necessary to enable them to form sensible opinions, has in fact furnished the purveyors of cheap emotion with an inexhaustible reservoir of consumers' (*Power*, p. 314).

Progress' must encourage 'activity, energy, courage, originality . . .',[1] that the 'first element of good government' was 'the virtue and intelligence of the human beings composing the community', and that

The first question in respect to any political institutions is, how far they tend to foster in the members of the community, the various desirable qualities, moral and intellectual . . .[2]

If 'individuality', in Mill's sense, signifies such qualities, then we may say that in his view a government could only be called 'free' if it could be shown to be in earnest about encouraging individuality and therefore perpetuating its own free institutions. This, at any rate, carries more conviction than a reliance upon mere literacy. It also exemplifies a mode of thought about society which, without overthrowing all concrete institutions, allows for their creative reconstruction not primarily 'from the top' as in many messianic concepts, but 'from below' *through* the 'top' (so to speak) rather than toward a fixed goal, according to an overall plan.

Epicurus offers sound advice for private lives, especially in a society both 'bad' and impossible to change. Some 'messianists' turn their backs on society and may easily be using their long-term hopes as an evasion of short-term obligations; others will not work with what they find, but — with or without appeal to extra-human agencies — want to pull the whole house down and start again. Liberals like Mill recognized the interdependence of State and personal qualities and thought these last could be created partly at least by the educational influence of social institutions. All alike agree in some sense that 'free men' are men of a certain kind as well as men having the advantage of certain conditions in their environment. In the next chapter we will discuss what some of those qualities are without which it is hard to speak of a man as 'free'.

QUESTIONS FOR DISCUSSION

1. On p. 176 are two quotations, one from Hobbes, the other from Dostoevsky. Do these give two different meanings of

---

[1] J. S. Mill, *Representative Government*, ch. xi.   [2] Ibid.

'freedom'? However we answer this question are we prepared to say that the 'demand for' external liberty in some sense necessitates freedom in the sense that Father Zossima meant? What does our answer imply for the relations between morals and politics?

2. Put up a case for the moral aim, 'Live Hidden'. Compare this with Quietism (see references on p. 181). How would a modern quietist justify his 'social' philosophy (or, if you will, his not-social philosophy)? Have in mind here J.-P. Sartre's propositions: (i) 'Man is responsible for what he is.' (ii) '. . . he is responsible for all men'. Read Sartre's essay, 'Existentialism' (e.g. in Kaufmann's *Existentialism from Dostoevsky to Sartre*, Meridian, 1956).

3. What kind of knowledge or what theory of knowledge would appear to justify the Marxist-messianic ideology in its polemic against existing (non-Communist) society? Before discussing, read F. Hayek, *The Constitution of Liberty*, ch. ii, Bottomore and Rubel, *Karl Marx: Selected Writings in Sociology and Social Philosophy* (Penguin, 1963), pp. 93–5, 236–41. Further reading: H. B. Acton, *The Illusion of the Epoch* (Cohen & West, 1962).

17

Responsibility

How is it possible to declare men 'free' and yet at the same time, by one means or another, take steps to educate them for society? The answer lies partly in the logic of freedom itself. Having agreed about the possibility of showing where the facts of social life correspond to the logic, we can then go on making plans for social reconstruction without doing violence to liberty. If the argument is sound, we may conclude that we cannot be serious about human freedom *unless* we undertake some kind of moral, social education.

. . . and the logic of freedom

Whenever we use the word 'free' we imply the absence of certain restraints. If we speak of movements, human movements, as 'free', we mean that to all intents and purposes they begin in the person who moves, not in someone else. 'You didn't have to do that; you are a free agent' means (among other things) 'what you did proceeded from you, not from me or some other'. If, on the other hand, the person we are criticizing protests that he could not 'help himself', he was the victim of passion, impulse, or some mental disorder, then he has denied his freedom; he has rejected a dignity we were prepared to give him — perhaps because he does not like the cost: he does not want to answer for his movements as if they were his own acts. If we were to say, for instance, 'No, you could not help it' we would at the same time be saying both that he was not free and that he was not responsible. The two go together. Whatever 'free' and 'not free' mean used about things, when used about people they imply the presence or the absence of a condition or a relation called 'responsibility'.[1]

[1] See also below, Chapter 23.

A man who is free in some respects shows his freedom in movements we call 'action'. In human discourse, by the rules of human communication, if called upon such a man must admit he *owns* such movements. He must 'own up to' his acts. Otherwise we cannot 'do business with' him. The acts he performed are left unattached, meaningless. It is a condition of his freedom on the other hand that he should not leave them so. It is all 'there' — in the 'charter'.

Nor does 'being responsible' apply only to acts liable to punishment. It may be true even today, as Bradley said it was in the nineteenth century,[1] that many people think of the courts and of punishment whenever the word 'responsible' is used. It may also be true that we have been taught our concept of responsibility by our legal institutions. But it is also true that 'responsible' (like 'free') has applications well beyond the range of the laws. Whenever I am freed from restraints imposed by others I am by the same tokens invited to become the owner of my own movements so that in future, whenever questions arise about such movements, I either have to answer for them or deny my freedom. And such 'answering' does not require the intervention of the courts; it can be called for among friends with no question of 'punishment' and it can be called for in my own reflections. True, we can by figures of speech talk of the 'court of public opinion' or the 'tribunal of conscience' (as Bradley does); but this is to miss an important point. The point is that we can come to do without — or 'grow out of' — legal institutions as moral agents. By whatever process (introception, empathy)[2] we develop equipment for self-criticism and by means of this we see ourselves as free and responsible in new ways. The psychologist, the social psychologist, may be able to show us how this comes to be. Social philosophy has to say that it is so and upon what conditions we can agree to regard each other as free agents; and the logic of freedom requires that in so far as a man makes his acts his own thus far within the scheme of human relations he, and he alone, is answerable for them.

[1] F. H. Bradley, *Ethical Studies* (O.U.P., 1876), essay 1.

[2] 'Introception': 'the adoption by an individual, into his own system, of motives or standards set by the social group' — the definition given by J. Drever, *A Dictionary of Psychology* (Penguin, 1952). According to the same source 'empathy' is 'feeling oneself into and losing one's indentity in a work of art'.

and 'free men'

The 'champions of freedom' have not, on the whole, made much of this. On the one hand, political demands and economic demands for freedom have, as we noticed, called only for the removal of restrictions, the reduction of coercion; on the other hand, even those who have understood that free men have to acquire certain qualities have been more concerned to avoid disturbance or to have their souls saved by extra-human agents than to make plain what was involved in being free.

Yet the demands for circumstantial freedom were *enabling* demands: that is, *laissez faire* Liberals, for instance, asked for restrictions to be removed from their movements and for right to be given to their achievements. Such demands mean that one can no longer refer one's movements to a higher authority; they mean a readiness to assume responsibility. Demands for political liberty on the other hand have had suspiciously little to say about what the majority would *do*, about the movements they would henceforth be encouraged to call their own, and next to nothing about ways of preparing people to enjoy such freedom.

On reading about the movement toward democracy in Britain, for instance, the impression is of radical reformers enjoying increased freedom of movement while they recommend for the majority increased pleasure, less pain, with no great care to show that there may be a contradiction between the utilitarian ideal and the enjoyment of freedom. John Stuart Mill was an exception, but his express preference for men who choose their plans for themselves and so employ all their faculties is not very good utilitarianism nor does it go far enough in appreciating the connexion between freedom and responsibility.

The difficulty is this: in demanding external freedom men have, of course, seen themselves as in opposition to contemporary institutions and more particularly to the *laws*. But there is no way of pursuing human objectives in society, no way of enjoying freedom except under *law*. This led Rousseau to frame the problem as one of finding 'a form of association which will defend and protect with the whole common force the person and goods of each associate'[1] while leaving men to obey themselves alone and

[1] *Social Contract*, bk i, ch. vi.

remain as free as before. An impossibility since, on the one hand, there is no 'free as before' — no 'original condition' preceding association to use as a criterion and, on the other, freedom is conceivable only within the 'general charter' according to the terms of which a man becomes answerable in proportion to the freedom he is given to make his movements his own acts. In short there is no way of thinking about human freedom without taking a full account of the demand for regularity in human relations. The 'laws' can retreat only as those relieved of them come under 'law' of another sort. Inter-personal truth, reliability, has to be constructed either by making men accountable to the courts or by their integrity, their appreciation of the moral law. The only alternative is an abandonment of the 'charter' and a conspiracy to achieve some ends of society by denying others and in particular that of free men.

'Everything in nature works according to laws,' said Immanuel Kant.

Rational beings alone have the faculty of acting according to the conception of laws, that is, according to principles, i.e. have a will.[1]

Kant more than most has understood what is involved in being free. We do not need to be offended by his use of such words as 'faculty' and 'will'; it is clear enough what he means: men are able to govern themselves because they are able to explain to themselves and to each other the value of an end and the relation of end to means. We know, too, how drastically they can disagree in all these respects, but the possibility of agreement is there and once it has been achieved it is possible for them to work together (or alone) for common or private ends 'under law', but in the sense that calls for no coercion, since the law, the regulation, understood by those who observe it, is no longer an interference but on the contrary an aid to selected ends. We can consider this further by reflecting on the common phrase, a 'sense of responsibility'.

The sense of responsibility

A frightened little man who always does what the man with the loudest voice or the strongest arm tells him to do often earns our contempt, but he is not what we mean by a man with a 'sense of

[1] *Fundamental Principles of the Metaphysic of Ethics*, para. 36.

responsibility'. On the contrary, in any day-to-day situation the kind of person meant is one who is likely on the one hand to do better when least coerced, least supervised, least threatened; and on the other in any contractual situation may well do more work and do it much better than a contract could require. Such a person may conceivably have come to his state of mind through an early fear of authority and a desire to put himself well beyond the necessary reach of official criticism; that is not, for the moment, of importance. What is important is to see in this quality a model of the free man.

Now this can be abused. It could be taken to mean that any man is free who can learn to wear his chains comfortably, so that we have to take some care in indicating what we understand by a 'sense of responsibility'. We do not mean an uncritical submission to what others impose, but a *critical* survey of demands that are made upon us with a view to assessing their value both to ourselves and to others. We would have very little difficulty, in fact, in illustrating this by the example of behaviour on the roads. It is possible to compare the behaviour of the driver who observes the regulations (the Highway Code) only when he thinks he might be punished if he broke them and the driver who observes them because he has a sensible appreciation of the need they meet to protect himself and others against injury and sudden death. If we are being driven by a friend we would probably feel more able to rely on the second driver than on the first. Let us say that the man who relates the rules to ends of value to all as well as himself has a 'sense of responsibility' quite apart from any personal fear he may have either of injuring himself or of offending the laws.

To understand the importance of such a concept in social philosophy compare this example with that of the worker in an industry where labour relations are governed by employers' and workers' federations. The difficulty now is to know how a worker would be said to have a 'sense of responsibility'. Would it be in respect of the ends to which the factory 'as such' is devoted, or would it be with reference to those represented on the one hand by the employers' federation and on the other hand by one or more of the trades unions engaged? Does a man who helps to produce a well-made object by working rather harder or more carefully than he need or perhaps for longer hours have a sense of responsibility, or does the man who botches his work in order to meet the requirements of the restrictive practices laid down by the union?

We might think we have got rid of this difficulty by adding modifying clauses; by saying that he can be said to have a 'sense of responsibility to' his fellow workers, or 'to' his employers; but that neglects some of the requirements. For merely to do what is demanded by one or the other in such a situation is not what we mean by having a 'sense of responsibility'. What is needed, on the contrary, is a critical appreciation of the ends involved and of the values attached to them. The question is not only whether the worker has such an appreciation as would make him 'responsible', but has he been given the chance to have it, undeterred by the various special interests involved. If he has, and if he has acted upon what he has seen and understood, then he is at any rate more free than before. He is more free if he no longer acts simply because the 'rule' directs him and he is more free because he has to some extent made the ends of the group his own, taken them as the purpose of his own movements and thereby earned for his movements the status of action. The task of a 'free society' would be at least to see that no impediments to that kind of understanding — impediments such as coercion by a union or an employer — lay in the way of such understanding.

A responsible person

The connexion between responsibility and freedom may be still clearer if we go back now to the notion of permissiveness. Put into practice, permissiveness does not mean that no one accepts responsibility for what a child does; it means more often than not that where the social institutions require someone to answer for undesirable movements the parent will have to answer for what the child has done. This will happen anyway, whether the parent thinks of herself as permissive or not. The difference is that if her relation with the child is permissive she is proposing an unreality for him — a freedom to move that she will not teach him to treat as ownership of acts. She is suggesting to the child that this is both possible and desirable. In short she is proposing to prepare her child for a new kind of relation with men, one in which his movements are 'free' until they conflict with those of other men; then he may disown them, leaving others to answer for them or attributing them to parts of his person over which he has no control: a relation, in short, where the benefits of freedom are to be enjoyed but with none of the corresponding obligations which constitute a system of human relations. It is quite conceivable that we could organize society like this; we could, that is, plan and provide for a community of feckless, non-responsible, impulse-following, grown-up children though this would require very careful thought about the guardians. Our purpose is to draw out the possibilities in such concepts and then say whether, after all, this was what was intended or whether we prefer the kind of arrangements suggested by the charter of freedom.

Of course it is open to psychologists to tell us that the permissive way is the most efficient method for turning children into respon-sible adults, but we must be quite sure that we are both talking about the same thing — whether it is 'permissive' we are discussing or 'responsible'. Jean Piaget, for instance, asks what will 'best prepare the child for its future task of citizenship'.

Is it the habit of external discipline gained under the influence of unilateral respect and of adult constraint, or is it the habit of internal discipline, of mutual respect and of 'self-government'?[1]

There is, of course, as he adds, the possibility that 'only those who have gone through the external discipline imposed by a master will be capable later of any inner discipline'. But we may very well object that words are being used here to suggest a lack of other alternatives. When does discipline cease to be 'external' and become 'internal'? The use of the word 'master' confuses the issue: it suggests only one kind of relation, one capable only of constraint. 'Master' is a title which signifies such a relation and quite clearly leaves out the love between parent and child by means of which the 'external' and the 'internal' restraints may be indistinguishable. Piaget also suggests (intentionally or not) that 'respect' between parent (or adult) and child may become 'mutual' merely through the ending of external restraint. We suggest that, on the contrary, a parent who does not regularly restrain a child may be said to show as little respect for him as a child and a growing person as was shown, say, by the fictional Wackford

[1] J. Piaget, *The Moral Judgment of the Child*, trans. M. Gabain (Routledge, 1932), p. 266.

Squeers of Dotheboys Hall,[1] who admittedly paid his respects to a limited area of the child's person only.

We shall try to say now what is meant by a 'responsible person' for this will summarize much that has been said in this second part of the book.

A responsible person is not simply one who is 'able to respond' — this would be more like one possible definition of an animate object, of life: we could say that a living thing was one which could respond to stimuli.[2] 'Responsible' has more to do with being able to *answer* and that means to give an account of one's movements which in its turn means to make them meaningful, worthy of the name of action, by referring them to the purposes which derive their significance from the person as 'self'. To be responsible is certainly to do all this if called before the courts of law, but to do it anyway by co-operation in society and by reflective self-criticism.

A responsible person has to have a degree of freedom, first, by having an area within which he can move to utilize things and people according to his own aims, second, by being prepared to accept his movements as his own acts. This second condition is important both to his self-mastery and to inter-personal reliability: if he owns up to his acts others can make sense and order of their dealings with him; they can rely upon him, for better or for worse, as a continuing part of their reality, as the source of movements and of chains of consequences which have, he admits, begun within his person, according to his meaning.

A responsible person may go further than his society requires and this *exceeding* of liabilities is an increase of freedom. By doing more and better than can be required in any general, formal contract he is free even of contractual restrictions. In taking an affirmative view of his whole person (saying 'Yes', that is, to the question, 'Do you accept responsibility for what you are?') he guards against attempts to deprive him of his person by attributing his movements to agencies 'not himself'. We have not now to discuss the desirable limits of this either as a moral ideal or according to standards of mental health, though limits there must be. Nor do we mean by 'more and better' what would seem so only in accordance with the standards of the group. All we have

---

[1] Charles Dickens in *Nicholas Nickleby*.
[2] A 'behaviourist' definition at any rate.

now to do is to give some definition to the notion of 'responsible person' in order to make the point which will particularly interest us in the next chapter — the point that, whatever the value of this as a concept of man, there can be little doubt that society finds means these days to encourage men to abandon it by regarding less and less of their movements as their own.

If we demand freedom, however, we also accept responsibility. The difficulty is that such acceptance may be reluctant, grudging, even unrecognized. We may assume that at one and the same time we can have the advantage of freedom and the benefits of non-freedom; the advantage of moving where we will and at the same time holding others answerable for what we do. It would hardly surprise the skilled observer of human behaviour to discover that we have devised ways and means of enjoying 'freedom' and concealing from ourselves and others what this entails. In this book we take up the following two positions and they must be appreciated if the reader is to avoid being misled by them. First, the primary truth-conventions alone (quite apart, that is, from any prognoses based upon psychological hypotheses) warn us of danger in such deceptions. As inter-personal truth requires personal integrity and both rely to some degree on objectivity, a 'pursuit' of freedom which is at the same time a 'flight from' its consequences and conditions would require a revision of the primary conventions so drastic as to call for such language as a 'change in human nature' or a 'revolutionary concept of man'. If men want to enjoy the feeling of freedom without the discomforts of having to answer for their movements or to accept them as their own, then the whole foundation of human relations is being shifted and we must enquire into the consequences.

Nor is this an academic enquiry for the social servant. 'Man is responsible for what he is', and by the same tokens 'he is responsible for all men.'[1] The social conflict, for them at least, is also a personal crisis: no general positions can be assumed which are not at the same time necessarily particular and personal resolves.

The second position taken up is this: this general concept of man as free and responsible is the only conceptual alternative not indeed to that of an unhappy or suffering society, but to a

---

[1] J.-P. Sartre, 'Existentialism', trans. Kaufmann in *Existentialism from Dostoevsky to Sartre* (Meridian, 1957), ch. ii.

totalitarian, collectivist, or 'closed' society. It may seem that in requiring men to accept the conditions of freedom we, too, impose upon them a 'pattern', an 'order' every bit as comprehensive as that called for by the totalitarian, the 'holist'. But that is like refusing to make a distinction between the prison governor who insists on prisoners taking their parole however reluctant the 'old lags' may be and the dictator who hustles all his political opponents *into* gaol. Yet the difference is clear enough: one gathers in, confines, and submits the whole life of his victims to a regimen which, however benevolent, is detailed and particular, leaving little or nothing to the reasoned choice or whim of the prisoners; the other sends out and away from the centre into an area where control is drastically reduced and what there is of it is general, formal, inapplicable to detail, leaving all, or virtually all, the detail to the free man. All we are insisting upon is that provision be made to ensure that 'parole' is extended and its conditions understood in time and in doing so we are following the only possible alternative to making the whole of human society a kind of enlightened 'good-conduct', 'open prison'.

The principal objection we shall meet with before the end of the book is that we are *too* general, not detailed or precise enough, that we fail to give the kind of guidance to free, responsible living the rail time-table gives to travellers, the 'Good Book' (supposedly) to believers. Quite so. For while we will in a moment turn from freedom to other social values we would be involved in naïve self-contradiction if on the basis of the freedom-value we proceeded to lay down in any detail how men are to live the good life.[1]

---

[1] The concept of responsibility will be discussed from other points of view later in the book. The literature is considerable. The following may serve as an introduction suitable to the problems raised in this book: Benn and Peters, *SP*, ch. ix; P. Nowell-Smith, *Ethics* (Penguin, 1954), chs xix, xx; Bradley, *Ethical Studies* essay 1; H. L. Hart, 'The Ascription of Responsibility and Rights' in *Essays on Logic and Language*, 1st series, ed. Flew (Oxford, Blackwell, 1951); W. D. Lamont, *The Principles of Moral Judgment* (Oxford, Clarendon Press, 1946), ch. viii, and S. Zink, *The Concepts of Ethics* (Macmillan, 1962), ch. vi.

QUESTIONS FOR DISCUSSION

1. Read F. H. Bradley's essay, 'The Vulgar Notion of Responsibility', in *Ethical Studies* (O.U.P., 1876; 2nd ed. 1927, now available in paperback). Would his account of ordinary usage be adequate today? (See additional references in a footnote to p. 197.)

2. In his essay *On Liberty*, ch. iii, Mill says: 'He who lets the world, or his own portion of it, choose his plan of life for him, has no need of any other faculty than the ape-like one of imitation. He who chooses his plan for himself, employs all his faculties.' If, however, we make the maximization of pleasure and the minimization of pain the *chief* good, as Mill seems to in his essay *Utilitarianism*, might it not be *better* to stick to conformity and imitation? See Mill's *Utilitarianism*, especially chs i and ii; *On Liberty*, ch. iii, and G. E. Moore, *Ethics* (O.U.P., 1912), chs i and ii.

3. What is the connexion in practice between inter-personal reliability and freedom? (Reread Chapters 9 and 10 above, especially what is said about 'truth conventions', and turn back to Chapter 13, Discussion, Question 2, for what is said about Locke and 'trust'.)

4. Read J. Piaget, the *Moral Judgment of the Child* (Routledge, 1932), ch. iv, and discuss the question he asks which is quoted above on p. 194.

18

Freedom and Health

MANY people today earn their living doing social service; others earn their reputation by writing about social service. If we were to arrange the different kinds of social service in a series to show the status of each kind judged by their popularity ratings, we would probably find that physicians, surgeons, and nurses came at or close to the top of the series. If we were to ask, 'Why?', the answers we would get would probably for the most part use the word 'health'. In the status vocabularies of social service 'health' — the word — has a prominent place: it exerts the kind of influence on the language of all social service that the Court exercised on the aspirations of 'society' in nineteenth-century Europe.

'Health' — the word, the concept — has wide professional appeal. 'Freedom' has little or none except, perhaps, to professional rabble-rousers. In examining this difference we are not only illustrating conflicts between social values, we are discussing the most important contemporary conflict in social philosophy as this manifests itself in social service and throughout Western — European and American — values.

Values
In this book we have spent little time on the ethical, meta-ethical, and epistemological problems of philosophy. The reason is that we wish to engage far more people in criticism of social aims and values than could conceivably give time and effort to the training of the professional philosopher; a great deal of such critical activity, moreover, is possible without exploring all the meticulous work in philosophical theory that has been done over the centuries. Nevertheless, we are now at a point where it is

necessary to say what we mean when we speak of 'values' otherwise it will make little sense to talk of a 'conflict of values'.[1]

If we use the verb 'to value' and not the noun 'value', it is fairly easy to see what is meant by 'valuing' this or that. 'I value my spare time' means that I enjoy my spare time and that under some circumstances I would take action to avoid losing any of it or even to increase it. 'To value' is (among other things) to make a 'statement of intent'. We are hardly likely to talk about valuing unless a situation is envisaged calling for a decision involving the objects valued. If you sell your household effects, for instance, you may not be able to get what you want for objects of 'sentimental value' but you do have to make decisions. You do have to 'put a value on' your possessions.

Valuing is an activity of a special kind; it belongs to the life-process we call 'coming to terms with reality'; it is what we do in exercising our freedom within the area given us to instruct our own choices, to help us strike a bargain with others, to bring some order into the conduct of our lives, and, more particularly, to create some order within our own wishes, fears, longings, needs: valuing is a part of self-making.

It is when we shift our attention from the valuing of things in relation to ourselves to the valuing of conditions and relations, not things, or of things as means to conditions or relations that we approach the kind of questions we are considering here. Put to it, I may say 'I value my time because I want to write, paint, or compose a symphony'. This is simple enough. It becomes markedly less simple when I begin to talk of such desirable activities as 'having value' or 'being values', when I start to talk, for instance, of 'beauty' as 'a value', and so with 'truth', 'freedom', 'health', and so on.

So at the start of this book we talked about freedom as a condition which men were in, rather as Erich Fromm does when he says: '. . . human existence and freedom are from the beginning inseparable'.[2] In saying this we were not *valuing* freedom: that only

---

[1] 'Value' has an interesting derivation — from Latin *valere*, 'to be strong and vigorous', 'to be healthy' etc.

[2] E. Fromm, *The Fear of Freedom*, p. 26. He explains this as follows: 'Human existence begins when the lack of fixation of action by instincts exceeds a certain point; when the adaptation to nature loses its coercive character, when the way to act is no longer fixed by hereditarily given mechanisms'.

becomes necessary when there is a question of 'more or less' and this in its turn only arises within the human order. We then begin to call the condition or the conditions named 'freedom' *values*. This is a statement of intent. We mean that in situations where we decide that men are likely to be deprived of freedom we propose to resist and to justify our decision by such reasons as have been given for considering freedom 'good'.

We put 'a value' upon the condition or the relation we consider 'good'. This is rather like putting a price on a thing, with the difference, however, that we do not always say that the 'value' is so much 'and no more'. (This is what we have to say now in relating health and freedom.) But 'freedom' is not the name of a *thing*. The value we attach to it may call for a certain arrangement of things (to give room to persons, to allow them a property in their own achievements and so on) but freedom is not a thing. A 'free man' may be one who enjoys a certain relation not simply of things or only of things in relation to his self and to other persons; but obviously such arrangements must vary from person to person and the arrangements of things which would make me feel free might make another man feel the opposite. Freedom is a concept; so for that matter is 'man'; but where it is possible (though not necessarily satisfactory) to explain 'man' by 'men' as, earlier, we said you could explain 'pin' by 'pins',[1] you cannot in the same way explain 'freedom' by a lot of local 'freedoms'. For in calling any particular situation between a man and his world a 'freedom' you have to explain *this* by reference to the general concept.

'Freedom', like 'truth', is a constructive concept.[2] That is to say

[1] See above, Chapter 8.

[2] 'Natural law', in part at least, represents constructive concepts of the same sort. One criticism is that such concepts 'evade the necessity of adducing empirical proof for . . . categorical asseverations, as indeed [they are] designed to do' (M. Birnbach, *Neo-Freudian Social Philosophy*). We would question whether this is a valid objection to such concepts as natural law viewed as constructive; certainly it is debatable whether such concepts are in most cases *designed* to evade the demand for empirical proof. On the other hand we would ourselves prefer to use such concepts as 'freedom', 'responsibility' and the like in such manner as to make no such evasion necessary. On the contrary the kind of things we are saying in this book about the connexion between freedom and responsibility could not be said at all without tacit recognition at least of propositions underlying the argument which are themselves open to empirical verification or falsification. For instance, the proposition that to free a man from coercion is to make him answerable for his acts can be both a tautology and a 'synthetic' proposition open to verification by the social sciences and

it is to be understood in terms of what it leads us to propose, to attempt, to make out of ourselves and our society. And when we speak here of 'values' we mean not things-valued but constructive concepts, general ideas subject, no doubt, to considerable variation, which are 'constructive' in two senses. First, men have 'made' them not as they make things — out of their physical environment — but as they make poems or the creative ideas of science: out of other ideas, other concepts. Second, they are constructive (as descriptive or explanatory concepts in the sciences do not need to be) in their function: they have to do with the future, with possibilities, with the making of facts, with human decision and choice — that 'leap in the dark',[1] as Kierkegaard called it, which the accumulated facts of the sciences cannot make for us.

Conflicts of values

The things we value may be many and various. When we come to sort them out, to 'grade them',[2] however, we find it possible to arrange them in a series or in several different series in accordance with relatively few 'values'. This is what happens when we make 'value judgements'. Or this is what happens when we try to explain and justify our value judgements and it is then that we can become aware of a conflict of values.

What we called earlier 'primary conventions' are ways men have used to simplify this by indicating that priority should be given, not indeed to precise values, but to certain kinds of value rather than to others. So, in learning, the value we attach to prestige is supposed to yield to the superior value of objectivity, for this is intrinsic to learning where reputation is extraneous and

psychology. Further, in the Kantian sense that all conception is a deliberate combination of a manifold into a whole, all conception might be said to be constructive; but what is being stressed here is the *practical* sense of this word, i.e. that such concepts as those indicated by 'freedom' and 'responsibility' have the function of changing or seeking to change behaviour, attitudes, institutions. A. D. Lindsay, in *The Modern Democratic State*, speaks in this way of what he calls 'operative ideals'. On the other hand, compare this with the concept of the myth in George Sorel's *Reflections on Violence*.

[1] Sören Kierkegaard (1813–55). In such writings as *Euten/Eller* (*Either/Or*) he taught the absolute dualism of faith and knowledge, thought and reality. Decision, for example, is a 'leap into the dark' and cannot be confused with the mere accumulation of facts.

[2] For the notion of valuing as grading see J. O. Urmson in *Mind*, vol. lix (1950).

likely to defeat the end of learning. Similarly, in conducting our relations with each other the value we attach to admiration or approval is expected to yield to the superior value of inter-personal reliability, irrespective of whether or not being honest will in the end win other rewards.

Ethical thinking has very often attempted a further organization of constructive concepts by determining an answer to the question 'What is the highest good?' 'What is that "end" of so great value that all other values should yield right of way to it and all human activity, if it is rational, be directed toward it?' The Benthamites, for instance, said that happiness was 'the good' in this sense. Are we in this book saying that freedom is the highest good and complaining now that health is competing with it?

No. On the contrary, by valuing freedom as we do we are saying a good deal less about 'the end' in any definite, precise fashion than the Benthamite tried to do when talking of the sum of pleasures, the maximization of pleasure, the minimization of pain. We are in a sense allowing for any number of 'greatest goods', perhaps an infinite variety. We are certainly saying that we propose to construct human relations so that men will be more free, and we are equally clearly suggesting that no society 'is good' which has not some such intention. But we are altogether rejecting the possibility of prescribing a 'highest good' for 'man as man' (whatever that could mean) and therefore of prescribing in any detail the institutions and social forms which would serve such an end as means. The importance of such a standpoint is rather in what it rejects than in any detailed proposals and this brings us to 'health'.

'Health', as we shall now see, is not in competition with 'freedom' as one highest good with another; rather we object to it when, and only when, it begins to take on the shape and character of a 'highest good' at the expense of other values and, by reason of its attempts at precision, its professionalism, to threaten that general concept of the good life and the good society which the 'charter of freedom' has defended. This, we shall show, it may do not only by direct attack on the concept of freedom but also by a 'war of attrition' on that concept of responsibility which we have shown to be necessary to freedom as a value.

Health, 'nature', and the 'norm'[1]

There is nothing 'natural' about health if by 'natural' we mean proper and inevitable in the physical world apart from man's intervention. If we take the regularities of nature as our guide, disease is as natural as health, even as death is as natural as life (in so far as such distinctions have an objective reference at all). No doubt the word 'health' can be used to mean the *normal* state of an organism, with the word 'disease' to indicate departures or deviations from the norm, and in this sense it could be said that health is the concept of normality in organisms. This however is like saying that freedom is a primitive, human condition — we are using 'health' as we are using 'freedom', to give an account of the facts as we see them, but not to instruct decisions; we are using neither as a constructive concept.

Any attempt to point to what is 'given' in nature as a norm or standard for human good takes us back to all the difficulties and contradictions we were warned of earlier, arising from the use of 'nature'. We may add to what has been said before a further difficulty — one that belongs especially to all discussions of the 'good'. To give an account of what is normal in nature, of natural regularities, is not the same as to say what ought or even what might be. It may be normal for animals to prey upon each other, but it does not follow that we call this 'good'. On the contrary we may disapprove of the normal and take steps to change things within the human order.

If, on the other hand, by 'natural' we intend also everything that man has done or can do, then we are back where we belong — within the human order with no non-human 'nature' to lay down norms for us. This is where we belong because we are to some extent free of nature. Where 'health' is an attempt to deny that freedom by recalling us to dependence upon nature it is obviously at variance with what we conceive to be our human situation.

But 'health' as a human standard — as it seems to be when we talk of 'proper standards of health' — represents what we like to think of as an improvement on nature, and the reason for the high reputation of the 'health services' is that they can claim a record of

[1] For the point of view taken in this section see G. E. Moore, *Principia Ethica* (C.U.P., 1903), ch. ii, secs. 27 ff.

such positive improvements as prolonged life and the defeat of many once-fatal illnesses. Few would question that 'standards of health' in this sense are good things to have; few would deny that the demand for health in this sense is virtually universal with a claim to a high place in the scale of values.

Where 'health', that is, represents the absence of specific diseases[1] or, more generally, the well-being of the organism over a longer span of years, there is no disputing the value. On the contrary, there is every reason for the social servant to take pride in having public health as his aim; for while it is true that other values may be enjoyed where disease persists, while it is also true that it is worth risking health for the sake of some aims, it is nevertheless true that by and large and for most people most of the time a certain minimum standard of health is an essential protection of their elementary freedom. One has only to reflect on what it must be like for a man who has made something of himself to be condemned toward the end of his life through disease to be shut up in an institution where he is treated like a child or a lunatic to see what dangerous nonsense it would be to make light of health in the interests of freedom.

Our difficulties begin, however, when the word 'health' extends its meaning and this it begins drastically to do through the work of Sigmund Freud.

Mental health

Recall what was said of Freud's work earlier;[2] in particular how he 'considered mental health and individual freedom as well-nigh identical' and the claim then made about a 'Freudian revolution' by which the 'hitherto clear distinction between the healthy and the neurotic' was eradicated.[3] For our purposes two implications of 'health' in this sense have to be borne in mind: first, what our authority called the end of clear demarcation between the 'healthy' and the 'sick'; second, the possible extension to 'mental sickness' — by analogy at least — of the kinds of relations between men which 'health' and 'sickness' in their earlier, narrower connotations created.

---

[1] The concept of 'specific diseases' is unsatisfactory, too. See H. Cohen, 'The Evolution of the Concept of Disease', published in *Proceedings of the Royal Society of Medicine*, vol. xlviii, pp. 155–60, and a comment on this by R. Brock, *Philosophy*, vol. xxxix, pp. 63 ff.

[2] On Freud see above, Chapter 5.   [3] Ibid.

'They that are whole', said Jesus of Nazareth, 'have no need of a physician'; but if concepts are introduced into social service which allow of no sharp line between the whole and the sick it is open to all kinds of 'physicians' to lay claim to all kinds of 'patients'. The concept 'health' and its implied opposite, 'sickness', has, in fact, come to be of such wide application that many now call 'sickness' what once would have been called 'wrongdoing'. This may be done for a variety of reasons which we will now briefly summarize. There is first some encouragement here to *excuse* — a man who has used his freedom to perform acts which could get him into trouble may seize the chance to 'deny ownership' by attributing his wrongdoing to a 'sickness of the mind'. This is a denial of the self, a deliberate giving up of freedom, an abandonment of responsibility. Then we may excuse others for their unlikeable actions in the same way to avoid trouble for ourselves. We gave an example of this earlier[1] in the case of the American Negro whose protest in the Senate took him (rightly or wrongly) not into the law-courts but into hospital for 'mental observation'. We shall return to the effect of this specifically on legal responsibility in Part Three.

Finally, there is just the chance that because of the high status attached to the concept of health social servants remote from medicine in the old, limited sense may welcome the chance to designate as 'sickness' many more peculiarities of their fellows because they want the kind of relation with their 'clients' that this calls for. Before we say something about these relations, however, let us see the dangers of so loose a concept as 'mental health' as this stands today. Here is a 'definition' of mental health.

... it is the same for all men in all ages[2] and all cultures ... [it] is characterized by the ability to love and create, by the emergence from incestuous ties to clan and soil, by a sense of identity based on one's experience of self as subject and agent of one's powers, by the grasp of reality inside and outside of ourselves, that is, by the development of objectivity and reason.

As characteristics of the 'good man' we may find nothing to quarrel with in that statement, though no doubt the mixture of characteristics may strike us as odd. This is, in fact, part of the

[1] See above, Chapter 7.
[2] E. Fromm, *The Sane Society* (Routledge, 1956), ch. iv.

difficulty: to call all desirable qualities alike by the same name, 'health', may lead to our imagining necessary connections where there are none and — which is more to the point — associating with each distinctive quality the techniques, the methods, the characteristic relations implied by 'health' in its more limited sense, whereas, in fact, much that is said here about the 'self' can be more satisfactorily pursued with the aid of such concepts as freedom and responsibility and with these explicitly *not* identified with the notion of 'health'. If 'one's experience of self' and so on means what we have meant by 'making one's acts one's own', then it would be better to say so and not to imply (however unwillingly) a different way of living — the way commonly associated with sickness, the role of patient, and the *protective* role of the healer.

But to come now to these relations, and first to the suggestion that social workers might welcome the extension of the health concept for its professional advantage.

The case work idea is now, however, fortunately no longer circumscribed by the practices of relief giving, but may be utilized wherever people have impaired capacity to organize affairs of life, or lack satisfaction in their ordinary social relationships.[1]

This illustrates the social servant's need to expand his interests. What has been called the 'Rehabilitation School' of thought on social work regards social service as a part of the 'health service' while the same authority says that the 'Public Health' school represents ideas developed 'to satisfy frustration of the public health workers'.[2] The danger is that the social servant will carry over into his work what he supposes to be the relation proper to that between the 'sick' and the 'healer' and this is a danger so long as he has no proper notion of what the 'whole' condition would be. We suggest that for this and for a proper conceptual defence against such dangers he needs the concept of responsibility as it has been introduced so far here.

Each is the proper guardian of his own health, whether bodily, or mental and spiritual.[3]

[1] G. Hamilton, *Theory and Practice of Social Case Work*, quoted in the Younghusband Report on *Social Workers in the Local Authority Health and Welfare Services*, para. 335.
[2] S. Leff, *Social Medicine: A Survey of Human Biology* (Routledge, 1953).
[3] J. S. Mill, *On Liberty*, Introductory.

John Stuart Mill said that long before the concept of 'mental health' had assumed the proportions it has today. 'Casework,' says a social servant, 'seeks to help the client to come to terms with reality . . .',[1] and he goes on to show he is well aware of the dangers we are talking about, calling for efforts to prevent 'undermining the client's right to self-determination'. Yet he says: 'in order to do that the worker must first come to terms with the reality of the client's life as it is, not as it might become'. In seeking to encourage a man to 'self-determination', however, one must also have some notion of what he might become.

'Wholeness'

The more 'health' comes to mean 'wholeness', the nearer it *could* come to the general concept of a free man. But if a whole man must be in some sense free, and if freedom involves specifically *not* letting others be responsible for us, then there must be a point at which we distinguish very clearly indeed between what used at least to be thought the proper relation of patient and healer and that of the autonomous self. Freud saw himself as *restoring* men to such a position. All social service may intend this. The position would be much clearer if the aims of social service were defined more precisely in terms of what it means for a man to be 'responsibly free'.

A genuine intention to make 'wholeness' an aim could in any case go wrong for reasons we have already mentioned. If, that is, by a 'whole man' you meant one who 'fitted the bill', satisfied a whole battery of norms, resembled the blue-print of your particular professional requirements, then by converse argument all irregularity, all idiosyncratic behaviour, all nonconformity and failure to fit into the system of classification would be treated as a sickness or (to use another popular word) a maladjustment. As there are specialists in medicine who tend to think of health solely in terms of the particular organ or piece of tissue which interests them (with the odd possibility of discovering such health in a corpse), so on the other end are those who in social service will find it hard to think of any person as 'whole' who does not respond to their methods or satisfy the norms of their professional training. Since

[1] Martin Darwin of the Berkshire Probation Service, in *New Society*, 18 June 1964, pp. 13 ff.

the kinds of social service will multiply and since each kind is always likely to be aggressive in the search for its own significance, we could end up with as many concepts of a whole man as there are professional associations of social servants.

The goal of increasing freedom, involving increasing responsibility, does not lend itself quite so readily to professionalism. There, latent in the very notion of a free man, is always the threat of *difference*, of obdurate refusal to adjust. Here, if anywhere, there may be something to be said for 'permissiveness' — in so far, that is, as the aim of social service could be called the *self-determination* of those who benefit by it. (Self-determination in two senses: the aim of getting people to selfhood, and the aim of doing this by encouraging them to determine their own movements, their own decisions.) A social worker may, of course, think she is aiming at self-determination when all she means is that she wants to get a 'client' 'off her books'. On the other hand one critic of social work has pointed out that in getting rid of the concept of responsibility we may be committed to the 'unquestionable authority' of the doctor.[1] In short, some social workers may have no interest at all in the independence of their clients. We are suggesting that all methods in social service should, on the contrary, have self-determination as their explicit aim. It is not aim enough but without it all other aims in social service may lose their value by tending toward a debasement of human relations, an increase of protection, giving satisfaction to some, encouraging the 'flight from freedom' of the rest.

QUESTIONS FOR DISCUSSION

1. G. E. Moore, *Principia Ethica* (Cambridge, 1903), ch. ii, pp. 27 f., uses the health-value as an example of naturalistic ethics. Discuss his argument. How, if we accept his conclusions, ought 'health' to be used? Should it be a *primary* value (i.e. one to which *all* others are subordinated)?

[1] B. Wootton, *Social Science and Social Pathology* (Allen & Unwin, 1959), ch. viii. A book by Paul Halmos, *The Faith of the Counsellors* (Constable, 1965), has appeared since this chapter was written. Both Halmos's argument and his sources add considerably to the kind of material introduced here. His book would repay careful study by all social servants (among whom are Halmos's 'Counsellors').

2. Read the extract from E. Fromm's *The Sane Society* on p. 206 above. What kind of arguments are necessary in order to make valid judgements about 'all men in all ages'? That is, do such judgements rest upon empirical propositions and the evidence these formulate or upon some other kind of propositions? (Note, in the quotation, the uses of such words as 'reality' and 'self'. Is there a fallacy in his use of 'incestuous'?)

3. Read B. Wootton's *Social Science and Social Pathology* (Allen & Unwin, 1959), part II, ch. vii, and discuss the various concepts of mental health referred to. Then read ch. viii of the same work and discuss whether her 'getting rid of' the concept of responsibility is useful in terms of the ethics of social work.

4. 'Each is the proper guardian of his own health whether bodily, or mental or spiritual' (Mill, *On Liberty*). Would we want to modify Mill's proposition? If so, in what respects and upon what criteria?

Part Three

JUSTICE

19

The Sense of Justice

On the banks of a famous river 'east of Suez' stands a huge, white-walled, modern house. It has some twenty rooms, most of them large enough, high enough, to contain a small English bungalow; there is garage-room for three of the largest American cars; a fine terraced garden overlooking the famous river and a spacious paved courtyard where the servants work behind high protective walls. The rooms are air-conditioned; the expensive furnishings have been imported from Europe; it is hard to believe that the rich people who live there as they move from their cool rooms to their air-cooled cars ever feel the sub-tropical sun or catch a whiff of the famous city's famous smells.

There are several such houses on the river's bank and elsewhere around the city, and against the high, windowless wall on one side of them rests a house of another sort made of mud and palm fronds. These houses, it is true, do not allow a man to stand upright; they have only one room and instead of large cars their owners have to make do with a tethered mule. On the other hand, they can be put up overnight, and if they get too hot there is always the possibility that a tropical storm will wash them away; nor do they need more furnishing than a packing-case or a petrol-can thrown out by the servants of the rich man.

Nevertheless, when the foreign tourist sees these picturesque mud hovels cheek by jowl with the rich man's villa he may very well feel shame and indignation. It is true that in his own country it may be possible to find people enjoying — or enduring — similar extremes of wealth and poverty, but where he comes from this is not done openly; his people do not flaunt their contrasts. So far from huddling up against the rich man's house the poor man lives as far away as possible so that to *sense* the contrast efforts must be made, the intellect engaged, the more or less learned periodicals be read, research must be done, and in the end, perhaps, the passions must be appealed to by no stimulus more provocative than tabulated statistics.

We *may* have to go abroad, in short, to prove that we have what Protagoras[1] thought to be essential to the citizen — a sense of fair play, a capacity for shame.

Yet Protagoras's social virtues were meant, presumably, not to make the rich ashamed, the poor rebellious, or others indignant on their behalf. *Dikē* and *aidos*, however we translate them, were the human qualities by which, it was hoped, men would avoid strife and respect the laws. All the same, the Sophists and others of Protagoras's and Plato's contemporaries were well aware that respect for the laws was not the whole of justice. If the laws appeared to protect the interests of all alike, well and good; if, on the other hand, as Thrasymachus and others said, what passed for 'justice' was nothing but the interest of the stronger, then submission to the laws was tempered by resentment if not by rebellion. Justice, as old Cephalus said, quoting the poets before he slipped away to honour the gods, was 'to pay every man what is appropriate'.[2] The few Athenians who talked about these things, it seems, had feelings about their relations with each other which could not adequately be reduced to respect for the laws, whether of Athens or any other city, nor to the shame they might feel if they broke the laws and got found out. The laws, on the contrary, could cause offence; they might not give a man what was due to him.

In our own reflections on justice we will take account of two distinct social values: the value of order or regularity, and the

---

[1] On Protagoras see above, Chapter 7.

[2] Plato, *Republic*, i. 332. The poet whom Cephalus quoted was Simonides of Ceos (c. 556–468 B.C.), said to have been the first of the Greek poets to write to order and for payment. Thrasymachus of Chalcedon was a teacher of rhetoric: see ibid. 336 f. for his lively contribution to the debate on justice, and compare with his views those of Antiphon the Seer already introduced above in Chapter 9. Plato's *Republic* sets out to be a discussion about justice but in this context what we are to understand by the word is very much what we would mean by 'morality'. The literature on the *Republic* is, of course, limitless. For the purposes of this book students might use E. Barker, *The Political Thought of Plato and Aristotle* (Methuen, 1906), or the radical revision of that work, *Greek Political Thought: Plato and his Predecessors*, 3rd ed. (Methuen, 1947). Criticisms of Plato such as the first volume of K. Popper's *The Open Society and its Enemies* are more profitable if read *after* a study of the *Republic* itself.

value of 'fair shares' — which may or may not be served by the laws. We shall see, too, how these criteria stand in relation to freedom. But first, in this chapter, there is something to be said about the 'sense' — or the sentiment — for justice.

Morals and sentiments

'The moral sentiments', said William McDougall, 'are formed in early youth under the influence of admired personalities.'[1] Then he went on to talk of correcting or adjusting them, and of 'setting the moral qualities in their true places in our scale of values'.[2] Elsewhere the same writer makes a diagram to illustrate how the character of one, John Doe, is made up.[3] In this diagram a sentiment for 'justice', together with one for 'generosity', is incorporated within the dominant 'self-regarding' sentiment. The sentiment for justice is a 'cognitive disposition' derived from two 'conative-emotional cores' of the 'instinctive dispositions' called 'submission' or 'self-abasement' on the one hand, 'curiosity' on the other.

We are, it seems, thanks to our modern psychology, better equipped as moral educators than Protagoras could have been with nothing more to go upon than *aidos* (shame) and *dikē* (justice). Yet if, as McDougall says, the 'process of character-formation' is 'the essential work of reason',[4] it would seem we have still to do as the Sophists and others did when confronted with problems in human relations: engage reason in the task of arranging a 'scale of values' within which the moral qualities can assume their 'true place'. For giving names to the sentiments, describing them, and suggesting their relations with each other and with their emotional 'roots' will not by itself solve the difficulties we have with their objects nor will it do anything like enough to provide for their control.

The psycho-analysts have been engaged in the task of controlling the sentiments. J. C. Flugel says:

[1] W. McDougall, *Character and the Conduct of Life* (Methuen, 1927), pp. 116 f. For a comment on his place in contemporary psychological theory see F. V. Smith, *Explanation of Human Behaviour*, 2nd ed. (Constable, 1960), part ii, ch. vi.
[2] McDougall, op. cit., p. 117.
[3] McDougall, *An Introduction to Social Psychology*, 24th ed. (Methuen, 1942). The diagram referred to faces p. 440 of this edition.
[4] McDougall, *Character and the Conduct of Life*, p. 117.

The notions of punishment and justice are, it is now obvious, very deeply seated in the mind of man, which in its moral endeavours seeks to establish and maintain a kind of equilibrium between suffering and satisfaction.[1]

Flugel's 'Polycrates complex' relates a need for punishment to an ancient fear of good fortune, a recognition to be met with among the Greeks (for instance) that a man should expect so much and no more of the universe otherwise he will be exposing himself to the wrath of the gods. He suggests a variety of ways in which guilt-feelings may be assuaged without recourse to punishment, but while the analyst must undoubtedly have his preferences he would not claim to impose these authoritatively upon us nor indeed is his therapeutic control available except to the man who for one reason or another has admitted failure in self-control — whether through an excess or a deficiency.

In his study of moral judgement in children Jean Piaget concludes that a child's behaviour toward other people 'shows signs from the first of those sympathetic tendencies and effective reactions in which one can easily see the raw material of all subsequent moral behaviour'.[2] But he agrees that such impulses can only be called 'moral' 'from the moment that certain norms impress a given structure and rules of equilibrium upon this material'. Morality is to the affective, emotional life what the 'sum-total' of logical rules of control is to the intelligence. Piaget finds in the 'very functioning of sensori-motor operations a search for coherence and organization'. There is an 'ideal equilibrium' implied in such functions, but it is necessary for the mind to 'extract norms' from this equilibrium. This it does, he says, by becoming conscious of the search 'and of the laws governing it', 'thus translating into structure what till then had been function and nothing more'. Reason, logical and moral, is a collective product. The individual left to himself 'remains egocentric'; this affects his logic as well as his morals. (Piaget here would seem to be saying what we said earlier about the relation between 'objective' and 'inner' truth.)[3] The lack of society also affects morality — a child's feelings are given value without their being 'submitted to some ulterior evaluation'.

[1] J. C. Flugel, *Man, Morals and Society* (1st ed., 1945; Penguin, 1955), p. 201.
[2] J. Piaget, *The Moral Judgment of the Child*, p. 405.   [3] See above, Chapter 9.

It is only through contact with the judgements and evaluations of others that this intellectual and affective anomy [lawlessness] will gradually yield to the pressure of collective logical and moral laws.

The whole of Piaget's argument in this chapter may be taken in support of what we have just been discussing under the heading of 'responsible freedom', but for the moment what interests us is the psychologist's recognition of the need the moral sentiments have on the one hand of social norms and on the other of such co-operative development as we attempt through critical discussion. The sentiment for justice, no less than any other feeling or complex of feelings cannot be left to look after itself or be expected to act unaided as a guide to decision.

Mixed feelings

Perhaps we never supposed it could; but in order to see how some people may think otherwise and what is involved in opposing them we will take some account of other strong feelings which sometimes earn the name of 'moral'. At the same time we may discover that some of these are easily mistaken for or associated with the sentiment for justice.

'Conscience'[1] has in the past been the name given to feelings rather like those Protagoras must have meant by *aidos*. People were said to have 'pangs' or 'twinges' of conscience when they had done what they knew they should not have done or left undone what they believed they ought to have done. Difficulties were created by the belief that conscience was yet one more special faculty and a faculty, at that, which was infallible — always to be relied upon as a guide to right action and therefore to be obeyed by the good man, come what may.

By giving some account of how men come to think con-

---

[1] Flugel, op. cit., ch. ii, for some typical Freudian analysis. For McDougall's 'hormic' treatment see the index to his *Introduction to Social Psychology*. From Freud's own work read *Totem and Taboo*, especially ch. ii. In sec. 4 of this chapter he writes: 'Conscience is the inner perception of objections to definite wish impulses that exist in us' and, later, '[it] originates on the basis of an ambivalent feeling from quite definite human relations which contain this ambivalence'. It is interesting to read, later in this same paragraph, that 'if the origin of guilty conscience could not be discovered through impulsive neurotic patients there would be no prospect of ever discovering it'. The layman might wonder precisely what it is corresponding to his own experience of conscience that could be 'discovered' only under such conditions. The quotations are from Freud, *BW*, pp. 859 ff.

scientiously, psychology cast grave doubt on the belief in a distinct, let alone an infallible faculty. The moral difficulties psychology is sometimes blamed for, however, were partly due to the need men seem to have felt to believe in 'a conscience' rather than in their own considered judgement. 'Conscience' — sometimes, though not always — could be a substitute for thought and a powerful alternative to discussion. If, that is, the appeal to conscience came at the beginning and not at the end of reasonable debate, it was very hard indeed to distinguish between the man of conscience and the man of unthinking, unreasoning prejudice. On the other hand, nothing psychologists have said about the origins and functions of conscience deprives us of the obligation to accept the implications of moral argument; getting rid of reliance upon a distinct, infallible 'guide', on the contrary, increases rather than diminishes our responsibility for moral judgement and moral decision. It is still just to give men 'freedom of conscience' provided this means also an obligation to inform one's decisions and attempt to explain them, but if the 'sentiment for justice' should ever be identified with the blind and thoughtless pursuit of uncriticized prejudice it is hard to see it as a social value.

'Envy', again, is a name for a feeling easy to recognize when we encounter it, whether in ourselves or others. Easy to recognize, perhaps, but also easy to dignify beyond recognition by associating it with justice. As 'mortification and ill-will occasioned by the contemplation of another's superior advantages'[1] envy is not usually thought of as a desirable feeling. The laws indeed have had a great deal to do with the control of envy in the past but it has also been open to many so to complain against the 'superior advantages' of the few as to invoke the aid of the laws — often in the name of 'equality' — to bring an end to such painful disparity. Only when those who take such action are themselves enjoying such 'superior advantages' can we be quite sure that the 'sentiment for justice' is not another name for envy.

'Anger', 'resentment', 'indignation' — there are a number of names which would fit the feelings already suggested at the

---

[1] *Oxford English Dictionary*. See F. Hayek, *The Constitution of Liberty* (Routledge, 1960), ch. vi. Hayek begins with a quotation from Oliver Wendell Holmes jr which is worth repeating here: 'I have no respect for the passion for equality, which seems to me merely idealizing envy.'

beginning of this chapter as likely to be aroused by gross and obvious disparity between the excessively rich and the excessively poor. 'Anger' in a special sense, however, may be felt when a man has suffered an injury at the hands of another who has subsequently made no reparation, expressed no contrition, and himself suffered not at all but perhaps, on the contrary, profited by the wrong he has done. What used once to be called a 'demand for satisfaction' might now be considered in our western society indecent. For many of us have a curious benevolence toward wrongdoers and this often goes with indifference to those they have harmed.

Now we do not need to be told that positive laws enforced by a political authority have it as part of their function to punish offenders who otherwise might find themselves directly at the mercy of those they have hurt: later we will discuss punishment in more detail. Yet at a time when on the one hand we are less and less inclined to punish and on the other hand more and more permissive toward men's feelings, it is odd that little or no attention is paid to the feeling of anger or the demand for satisfaction at least in the speech and writings of those who talk most about justice, punishment, and the reconstruction of society.

'Benevolence', 'sympathy', 'kindly feeling' toward others are, no doubt, the emotions or sentiments to which we would like to refer our more typical attitudes to justice today. 'Paying a man what is due to him' — Cephalus' or Simonides' account of justice — *could* include punishment on the one hand, satisfaction on the other. We prefer a *warmer* approach. Our explanations of what is just fall most easily into the Benthamite formula: an act is just when it adds to the sum total of pleasures, or, 'what comes to the same thing',[1] when it diminishes the sum total of pains. No one, surely, can find fault with that.

On the contrary, we can insist that the taking for granted of *any* sentiment as adequate guide to our decisions is to be deplored. By 'taking for granted' we mean, that is, supposing that a man has only to act upon certain feelings and his conduct will be right; that a law, for instance, has only to satisfy certain feelings for it to be just, and both such conclusions to be reached without examina-

---

[1] J. Bentham, *Principles of Morals and Legislation* (New York, Hafner, 1948), ch. i, sec. 4. This work was first published in 1789.

tion of the feelings in relation to each other and their criticism upon a scale of values, without consideration of the criticism which is provided by a comprehensive study of consequences. So if, for instance, kindly-feeling is taken as sufficient 'argument' for an act, public or private, a man's kindness toward one man or one group of men may well entail consequences for others which would look better if they proceeded from malevolence. A mother out of 'kindly feeling' may destroy her child's capacity for independence. A law made out of kindly feeling toward felons might encourage the criminal at the expense of the law-abiding citizen and so on. Both morals and legislation have it as a large part of their function not to implement feeling but to correct and control feeling, and to implement reasonableness.[1]

Sense and 'good sense'

Unless we make men free from the will of others we cannot ask them to be 'good' neither can we reasonably regard them as 'bad'; so that a society in which most men were coerced most of the time would be one in which it would only make sense to pass moral judgements on the few who did the coercing. On the other hand, 'freedom' does not make men or societies 'good': it makes goodness possible by providing large numbers of persons with the wherewithal to 'act justly' and thereby to make theirs a just society. As a society could hardly be called 'free' unless the overwhelming majority of its members had sufficient freedom, so it will only be called 'just' to the extent that its members act justly toward each other. All this means we have yet to see. One thing we have made clear: the justice of an act cannot be proved solely by reference to the commendable feelings of the actor even when we are agreed that such feelings are commendable. More, far more, is needed; and to meet such needs has been the function both of morals and legislation.

[1] For an ethical theory which keeps benevolence in its place see Joseph Butler's work. Butler lived from 1692 to 1752. His ethical teaching is found in the *Sermons* and in a dissertation, 'Of the Nature of Virtue', *The Analogy of Religion Natural and Revealed* (Everyman's). In the dissertation he writes: 'benevolence, and the want of it, singly considered, are in no sort the whole of virtue and vice'. Otherwise, he argues, if benevolence were all we would not discriminate between persons nor speak of justice or falsehood at all, except as these satisfied the primary need for benevolence. See further C. D. Broad, *Five Types of Ethical Theory* (Routledge, 1930), H. Sidgwick, *History of Ethics*, iv. 7.

The difficulty is to distinguish between and yet hold together in close relation three ideas: the idea of certain feelings (sometimes called by analogy 'senses'), some of which from time to time we value more highly than others; the idea of rules of many kinds which both regulate the expression of feelings and provide for such expression; the idea of reasoning both about our feelings and about the rules to the end that we may make a moral judgement and reach a decision.

Some moral philosophers have attached overwhelming importance to the *feelings*. The third Lord Shaftesbury,[1] for instance, says:

To love and to be kind ... is itself original joy, depending on no preceding pain or uneasiness, and producing nothing but satisfaction thereby.[2]

Shaftesbury held that every rational creature was capable of a 'moral sense':

a love of goodness for its own sake and on account of its own natural beauty and worth, and aversion to its opposite.

'Cultivate your taste' was Shaftesbury's last word, according to his critic, Leslie Stephen.[3]

In Germany, where sentimentalism is more congenial to the national temperament, he found a warmer reception than amongst his own countrymen.

Yet it was in Germany that Immanuel Kant gave his account of the moral life with its emphasis not upon feelings but, on the contrary, upon reason, upon the moral law in opposition to feeling. Only the 'good will' is good 'without qualification'. This is a notion, he says,

[1] The Earl of Shaftesbury (1671–1713), that is, the third Earl, grandson of the first Earl, who was John Locke's friend. Locke was made responsible for the (future) third Earl's education when the boy was three years old and this he did according to the principles of his *Thoughts Concerning Education*. Most of the third Earl's writings are in *Characteristics of Men, Manners, Opinions, Times*, ed. J. M. Robertson (1900). See H. Sidgwick, op. cit., iv. 6. For a rather different account see L. Stephen, *English Thought in the Eighteenth Century*, paperback in 2 vols (Hart-Davis, 1962), II. ix. 3.

[2] Shaftesbury, *Inquiry Concerning Virtue and Merit*. See also his *Sensus Communis: an Essay on the Freedom of Wit and Humour*.

[3] L. Stephen, op. cit., ix. 32, 34.

which exists already in the sound natural understanding requiring rather to be cleared up than to be taught.[1]

The good will is found in the action done from duty and its goodness lies 'in nothing else but the conception of law itself, which certainly is only possible in a rational being', it lies in this conception so far as this and not the expected effect of the act determines the will.

In social philosophy, however, our field of interest is wider than that of traditional moral philosophy. For one thing we have to take account of 'rules' of the political as well as of the moral sort and of the relation between these. But this does not exclude our interest in moral sentiments as it might if we were limited to political thought. The truth is that we cannot let go of any of the three ideas just mentioned but must look at positive law in reference to moral feeling both as that which the sentiment of justice is about and as that which, in its turn, creates or modifies moral feelings. We must also at all times hopefully persist in looking to critical, rational discourse as a way of both regulating and implementing the feelings and of helping us to decide how to arrange them in the scale of values with whatever this may imply for institutions and social services which can be said to engage in moral, social education.

'Law' in its various uses may be a good place at which to begin an appraisal of the various elements in the concept of justice.

QUESTIONS FOR DISCUSSION

1. Does the 'explanation' of moral sentiments diminish our confidence in them? Take Flugel's Polycrates Complex as an example and compare with the graph of John Doe's character in McDougall's *Introduction to Social Psychology*. (See J. C. Flugel, *Man, Morals and Society* (Penguin, 1955), ch. xi. For McDougall see p. 215, footnotes.) Lord Devlin, the British jurist, recently complained of a weakening of the 'sense of guilt' and anticipated a

[1] Kant, *Fundamental Principles of the Metaphysic of Ethics*, trans. Abbott, 6th ed. (Longmans, 1909), pp. 12, 16 f., and in Rosenkranz and Schubert's edition, vol. viii, pp. 16 and 20.

time when the psycho-analyst might be called in 'to condition the community into a sense of guilt' about anti-social acts. In discussion recall the social virtues of Protagoras and refer back to Chapter 7, above.

2. Do some personal analysis into the part envy plays when commenting on wealth at home or abroad, or upon education — particularly in the United Kingdom. Read F. Hayek, *The Constitution of Liberty*, ch. vi.

3. Read Bishop Butler, *On the Nature of Virtue* (see above p. 220, footnote), and discuss the place given to 'kindly feeling' in contemporary value-judgements.

20

Law (I)

'ORDER must be maintained.'[1] Order in some sense is not only necessary to life, it *is* life: the difference between the living and the dead is partly a matter of order — that is, of regularity in the succession of events; to say that social life 'needs' order is misleading if it makes us forget that social life *is* order. Order, that is, in the regularity of our conduct toward each other as well as order with some relation to function. When order has to 'be maintained', however, questions of value arise. For while order of some sort is inseparable from all social values, as a value itself, as an end to be pursued against obstacles, we are bound to distinguish between 'order' and 'good order'. Man is 'free', we suggested, not only by his ability to perceive — or to construct — natural regularities, but (collectively at least) by his ability to impose regulations on his own kind. When the regulations oppress some, those oppressed are likely to demand freedom from them or complain of their injustice. Without good order, on the other hand, they are deprived of community. Order is a value attendant upon all others — the enjoyment of beauty no less than the pursuit of truth has been called by a master, 'a matter of size and order'.[2] How to 'take over' the ordering of events and make it

[1] A misquotation. 'It's my old girl that advises. She has the head. But I never own to it before her. Discipline must be maintained' (Dickens, *Bleak House*, ch. xxvii). An interesting comment on the desirable relation between intelligence and authority possibly applicable outside the domestic circle to the relations, say, between scientists and politicians? Or is that an abuse of 'intelligence'? Compare Plato's philosopher kings.

[2] Aristotle. In the *Metaphysics* he says that beauty is a matter of order, symmetry, and limitation and, in the *Poetics*, a 'middle magnitude which is equally removed from the diminutive and the inordinately large'. What is said in the opening paragraph in this chapter may be compared with R. G. Collingwood, *The Idea of Nature* (Oxford, Clarendon Press, 1945), part iii, ch. ii.

serve other values without doing irreparable damage to this general factotum of the values — that is one way of looking at the practical problems of social philosophy.

Law has been the major instrument of this endeavour. Law is also a useful focus for attention when reflecting upon the problems of good order. The value of justice may oppose the laws or appeal to them. But 'law', the word, has many uses arising from our interest in a just order and in these uses we aim to see some of the obstacles — the 'scandals' in the Greek sense of 'stumbling blocks' — which men have made out of 'law' either wilfully or out of confusion.

Regularity, regulation

To *detect* regularity in the sequence of events is one thing; to impose a regulation in an attempt to *secure* such a regularity is another. The use of 'law' for both kinds of activity — for the end-product of detection (as in science) and for the means or instrument of regularizing must confuse.

In Part One, recalling the varieties of experience, we saw how this could happen as men seek to come to terms with their universe.[1] If your city is well-ordered but you lack an adequate account of the weather, the stars, the biological sequences of life and death, you may use the vocabulary of political and social order in an attempt to make sense of nature. Or if, on the other hand, men trouble you with their fickleness and caprice, you may turn for comfort, reassurance, and vindication to the mighty regularities of sunrise and leaf-fall, the ebb and flow of the tides, to seed-time and harvest, summer and winter.

Nor can we make the distinction we are talking about always so sharp and precise as we would like. We may be convinced that our expanding (or contracting) universe has no personal interest in how we behave, but we are not likely to forget that nature, of which we are a part, is a matter of order, an order within which we have our human identity *because* of our limitations, that there are necessities and that these regulate our human affairs. Any man in doubt of this has only to leap off a cliff, build himself a villa on Stromboli, or behave after the legendary example of Canute to cast doubt upon his doubt. Yet these are observed regularities —

[1] See above, Chapters 2 and 5.

the effect on a man of a fall from a high point, the unsuitability of a volcanic mountain for human residence, the implacability of the tides. The 'laws of nature', as the layman calls them, have to do with what has often or usually happened in the past and most probably will happen again in the future. The formulas in which we give an account of such probabilities are man-made; we have good reason to suppose that the sequences such formulas depict are not.

Yet when some men spoke of natural law they clearly believed that it was possible to discover in the universe *directives* of the same order as those we put on the statute books. Over and above the regularities of nature — those which interest the scientist and which he may call 'laws of nature' — were laws in the other sense: directives, imperatives, requirements that men behave in one way rather than another or suffer the consequences. Of course it is true of all 'laws of nature' that we can, like Dostoevsky, cry,

Merciful Heavens! but what do I care for the laws of nature and arithmetic, when for some reason, I dislike those laws and the fact that twice two makes four?[1]

for many laws of nature are irrelevant to much of individual life — that is, it makes little difference whether we know about them or not, and in many cases the possibility of ignoring them, let alone defying them and taking the consequences, never comes our way. But now we are considering two notions of what could be called 'law', both of which might be called 'natural law', and both of which have to be clearly distinguished first from each other, then from other uses of 'law'.

Divine and moral law
The distinction between these uses depends on the account we give of the ground on which the supposed law rests. Some men

[1] Dostoevsky, *Notes from Underground*, part i. The author had, of course, good reason to dislike the other sort of laws as well — those, that is, which condemned him to death and, after a last-minute reprieve before his executioners, packed him off to Siberia. Dostoevsky's views on nihilism are relevant to this comment on laws. *The Possessed*, together with the character of Raskolnikov (the 'split asunder') in *Crime and Punishment*, is the chief source for Dostoevsky's portrayal of nihilism. For a study of nihilism with numerous useful references see R. Payne, *Zero: the Story of Terrorism* (London and New York, Wingate, 1950) and especially the *Revolutionary Catechism* of Sergei G. Nechayev (pp. 7 ff.).

(whether they speak of natural law or not) have believed that by the right methods it is possible to elicit from the universe directives like those Moses is supposed to have brought down from Mount Sinai and many other ancient civilizations to have received at the hands of such renowned, superhuman law-givers as Lycurgus, Solon, and Hammurabi.[1] Thought of in this way, the distinction between 'laws of nature' in our modern sense of 'observed regularities' and natural (or divine) law is obscured. We have on the one hand natural regularities and now on the other the Decalogue or some such code, but all alike have proceeded from the same source — the will of a divine person. This leaves us with some directives which do not require obedience but rather impose themselves by necessity, and others which can be virtually ignored provided we are prepared to risk the 'threats of hell' or the loss of the 'prophet's paradise to come'.[2]

The difficulty from our point of view is that this use of 'law' to signify divine directives (whatever its origins or authenticity) inclines us to think of all law similarly — that is, as a matter of will and command on the one hand, submission and obedience on the other. The ultimate criterion, the final test for human action,

[1] Lycurgus was the legendary legislator for Sparta. Plutarch's *Life* is an interesting example of a form of political writing to which further reference will be found in Part Four of this book. Solon (*c.* 640–558 B.C.) was named Archon of Athens in 594 and he introduced the constitution for which he is famed. He was also a poet. Plutarch also has a life of Solon. The comparison between Spartan and Athenian law is instructive. For a brief comment see A. Zimmern, *The Greek Commonwealth*, 5th ed. (O.U.P., 1931), part ii, ch. 5, and especially p. 132, where Zimmern says of Sparta: 'She had not the courage to extend her new code of justice to all who lived within her borders', and traces Sparta's 'peculiar and ferocious asceticism' to her failure in this respect. Hammurabi, King of the Amoritic dynasty in Babylonia, reigned from 2067 to 2025 B.C. A text of the Code found at Susa and inscribed on horizontal columns has a bas-relief of the king standing in an attitude of prayer before Shamash, the sun god, who delivers the law to him. We are reminded of the story told in Exodus xxxi. 18 of the tablets inscribed by Yahweh and given to Moses on Mount Sinai. Some excerpts from the Code of Hammurabi with comment may be seen in L. T. Hobhouse, *Morals in Evolution* (Chapman & Hall, 1915; revised ed. now available). Moses may have had hardly more to do with the Hebrew codes than one called 'Lycurgus' with the Spartan. The importance of the legend lies in the reverence with which those who perpetuate it regard the law and its originators.

[2] From that somewhat dubious 'prophet' Omar Khayyám, whose cheerful scepticism wins him no easy acceptance among those who prize bigotry, narrowness, austerity. Omar was a mathematician of renown who died somewhere about the year A.D. 1122 (A.H. 517). His *ruba'is* or quatrains have been memorably translated into English by Edward FitzGerald.

personal and public, is to be located not in man himself and his deliberations, but outside him in the sense that while he may find it reasonable to submit to the laws his reason could never be engaged in formulating them or assessing their value. The difficulty is not one of belief or unbelief in a divine, personal creator; it is a difficulty in so thinking about law as to make order compatible with freedom.

When, on the other hand, we speak of 'moral law' we are not bound to signify personal directives, the imposing of a will not our own; nor for that matter are we bound to abandon belief in an interested universe, a divine Providence. There are many ways in which 'moral law' can be used, just as some ways of speaking of 'divine law' need not be open to the objections we have just made. But it is possible to speak of 'moral law' in the sense of an abstract from human experience, having to personal conduct and to other laws something of the same relation as, say, the *Highway Code* has to the activity of driving. That is, the *Highway Code* is a formularization of conditions without which life on the road would be extremely hazardous if not in the end impossible, even before it is a threat of sanctions for those who ignore its provisions. So the moral law may be thought of as a recognition of at least the more general conditions upon which human relations are possible, personal wholeness realizable, even before we attempt to implement the moral law by positive laws in political communities or in the ethical codes of smaller associations.

So we may conclude that men should be treated 'as ends in themselves and not as means only'[1] after reflection on human experience, even as we may act toward men in this way before we have heard of such a formula, without any idea that we must do so because we have been *ordered* by another. On the contrary, it may well seem that to accept and act upon such a principle for any other reason that that we ourselves thought it good irrespective of what the universe may have to say about it would involve us in a contradiction — we would be letting ourselves be used as a 'means only' in the fulfilment of a divine purpose which by such means could never reach its end. A divine person who willed that all men should be 'ends in themselves' would, presumably, have

[1] Kant, *Fundamental Principles of the Metaphysic of Ethics*, pp. 51 f., of Abbott's translation, and in Rosenkranz and Schubert's edition, vol. viii, pp. 62 f.

to create them capable of coming to appreciate such a moral law and this could only be done if they were *also* capable of ignoring it.

By 'moral law', then, men may mean what they take to be a reading of a divine, non-human will. But it is also possible to mean something different whether or not they would say it 'comes to the same in the end': that is, it may be taken to mean rather what we meant in Part One by 'primary conventions' — those abstracts from human experience offering directives with the widest possible generality and therefore having their direct source not 'out there' (if that is what 'nature' means) but within the peculiarities of human structure and human function. Nor does it follow that this is the same as to say,

One day we will understand human nature in the same way as we understand other natural processes and will be able to manage it as, for instance, we manage electricity.

Human nature is what human nature does; and it is characteristic of our nature always to be striving to act according to laws of our own devising — in other words to be attempting to reconcile freedom with order, or, in other words again, to be responsibly free. We may, of course, come to act in different ways and to reduce these characteristics; but that will not be an 'understanding of human nature' or a basis for 'managing it'; it will be a change, a fundamental change, and it is our task to evaluate such a change.

Commands

The habit of relating moral law to divine commands may account for two other assumptions: first, that morality 'depends upon' specific theological or religious beliefs; second, that the 'proper' meaning of 'law' is 'a command'. The first of these assumptions need not concern us now. The second is directly relevant to our thinking about justice.

J. L. Austin's 'command theory of law' was, strictly, an attempt to bring order to the study of jurisprudence and if we could leave it at that it might not be of great interest to us. But the theory has wider applications. 'Laws or rules, properly so called', wrote Austin, 'are a species of commands.'[1] This proposition calls for a

[1] J. L. Austin, *The Province of Jurisprudence Determined*. See also T. H. Green, *The Principles of Political Obligation* (London, 1911), pp. 80–85.

conclusion of fundamental importance to social philosophy — a conclusion about the use of 'law' and also about the ground of obligation to obey — and poses an old question with new emphasis: the question about who is to command. The second question, the question about the 'sovereign', need only be important in a discussion about legal procedure. So far as the organization of law goes the legal processes obviously require that there should be an end to appeals against judgements in the courts. There must be a final court of appeal, otherwise we could never get a decision. Similarly, there must be some person or some group of persons in a political community (what Austin calls a 'determinate' person or body of persons) either to make a new law or to settle what the law is. If this is what 'legal sovereignty' means it is a procedural matter very important to jurisprudence, but not by itself of great interest to social philosophy.

The difficulty lies both in the notion of 'command' as identical with 'law' and in the connexion of this with a concept of sovereignty which goes beyond matters of legal procedure. For on the one hand 'command' suggests (intentionally or not) the *will* of the commander as the source of law and on the other hand, if the commander is thought of as 'sovereign' in more than a narrowly legal sense, he may also be thought of as himself 'above the law'. We will try to see why each of these possibilities is not only interesting to the social philosopher but relevant to the concept of justice in our own time.

A command, according to Austin, was a 'signification of desire' together with the likelihood that the person who refused to obey would suffer pain at the hands of the commander. It has been said that Austin's 'command theory' is the reverse of that held by the earlier jurist, Blackstone;[1] for where Blackstone had said that the king was not the *spring* of the laws but their reservoir Austin was saying the reverse. The sovereign (whether king, parliament,

---

[1] Sir William Blackstone (1723–80), the most famous English jurist and Bentham's rival in this field. His most important work is the *Commentaries*. He so relates the various meanings of 'law' which we have distinguished that he considers it possible to proceed from the law of nature (the revealed or inferred will of God) to municipal law, which commands what is right and prohibits what is wrong. Both gravitation and the laws of England are rules imposed by a superior. Blackstone's defence of the *status quo* made him a proper target for Bentham's radicalism. Blackstone has had considerable influence on jurisprudence in the United States.

president, congress) was the source of the laws in the same way as, during battle, a commanding officer is the source of an attack or a retreat.

This illustration is instructive. An officer in the field, according to his rank, issues orders of varying generality. 'Command', in fact, is most suitable to such orders as 'Fire!' 'Advance!' 'March!' 'Halt!' — that is, to directives having to do with immediate action. The officer's authority for such commands is derived from a 'chain of command' leading backwards or upwards toward the places where directives of ever-wider generality, in tactics and strategy, are issued, and the whole series, both the hierarchy of command and the place in it of various ranks is itself governed by Army Regulations (or their equivalent) and the authority of these regulations as well rests upon laws of still wider generality. 'Command' seems more appropriate at the bottom end (so to speak), and even here the 'signification of desire' is more like the carrying out of a pre-ordained function according to one's place in a series, a conventional order.

Of course it is possible to think of a political community as resembling an army just as some Christians think of the Church and its Commander. If, however, this is taken to mean that the 'sovereign's' 'will is law', and if the sovereign in a particular community is a 'determinate person or body of persons', what you are doing is to deprive all except the sovereign of any virtue except obedience and the sovereign himself of responsibility except, perhaps, as King James I[1] or Marshal Pétain of Vichy[2] might have said, 'to God'. There is a simplicity, a restfulness, about such a concept, which has undoubted appeal provided you can agree on the identity of the sovereign and provided the group within which this principle is accepted does not come into conflict with other groups (whether or not they adopt a similar principle

[1] King James I, *Trew Law of Free Monarchies* (1598), held that kings are 'breathing images of God upon earth', the 'authors and makers of the laws'. See Sabine, *HPT*, ch. xix.

[2] Philippe Pétain, Maréchal de France, was head of government at Vichy from 1940. As such he considered himself responsible to none but 'God' and 'History'. Roger Bonnard wrote of the Vichy State: 'The value, authority and legitimacy of this power has not been delegated to him by the people, it emerges from the person of the Chief himself.' (Quoted by Alexander Werth, *France, 1940–1955*, Robert Hale, 1956.) Werth himself says that Vichy's *Travail-Famille-Patrie* ideology 'is by no means alien to the thinking of Charles de Gaulle' (op. cit., part ii).

as the source of their laws). Austin's 'command theory' did not, of course, intend such developments, but it is up to us to see how such theories can support and contain such possibilities. We have, on the other hand, to construct or reconstruct ways of thinking about laws which will protect us against such possibilities.[1]

Laws, moral and positive

'Positive' laws, to Austin and others, are so called to distinguish them favourably from moral rules, what some have called natural law, but not (in Austin's case) from the laws of God — for these are commands. By calling all legislation together with the whole body of laws in a political community 'positive' there is an implication not only that these and these alone can be applied in the courts (which may be true) but that they have a degree of objectivity and certainty that other so-called laws have not and also that they are subject to no higher tests. Against such implications we put forward the following points.

We begin with the ancient dispute about whether positive laws are 'made' or 'found'. This may be partly a matter of words — that is, of how we agree to use the word 'law' — but we have seen several times that this kind of dispute is never about 'mere' words: the decisions reached, the conventions established, are themselves activities of extensive significance. So the decision to call only those 'laws' which can be said to have been *made* is more amenable to the view that law 'is imposed upon society by a sovereign will'; whereas the decision not to limit 'law' in this way at least allows for the notion that law 'develops within society of its own vitality'.[2] There is no reason why we should confine the word to the one or the other, though we may prefer to say that no custom or convention becomes legally relevant until it has been 'found' and formalized by recognized authorities. Yet when we have said this we have, of course, drawn attention to the decisive activity of the 'authorities' and so to the need for evaluating what they have done, and therefore of clarifying criteria — ways of saying that their law-making or law-ratifying activities are justified.

Unless we are prepared to abdicate all responsibility for what is

[1] On laws and commands, see further, F. Hayek, *The Constitution of Liberty*, ch. x.
[2] C. K. Allen, *Law in the Making*, p. 1.

done to us, for us, on our behalf by legislators we are, therefore, bound to repudiate legal positivism if this asks us to accept the laws without question and to abandon our right to criticize them as moral agents.

Hans Kelsen's[1] theory of Pure Law starts from a point in Kant's system of Pure Reason and with the clear distinction (as he sees it) between *Sein* (the Is) and *Sollen* (the Shall Be). Law 'exists solely in the world of Sollen'.

It depends upon a certain initial assumption which does not arise out of the necessities of nature but is laid down by an operation of human will and reason.[2]

Norms, laws, are 'the elaborated rules of what human will and reason say "shall be" '. We would today prefer not to make so clear a distinction between the *Sein* and the *Sollen* at least not in respect of the bearing of this upon the differences between the natural and the moral sciences. Kelsen also shares with Austin an emphasis on the imperative nature of law which calls for considerable modification. But there are two aspects of his theory we should note. The first is his insistence that law is a distinct activity, or the instrument of a distinct activity, which we may describe as the attempt to regulate human conduct by enforcing certain regularities. The other is his substitution of what he calls a *Grundnorm* — a 'grand, indispensable postulate to which all the roads of the law lead, by however devious routes'. We in social philosophy are concerned with all kinds of activity deliberately seeking to control future action for ends regarded as values and therefore with law as one of these. We, too, have found it useful to speak of 'primary conventions', resembling in some ways Kelsen's *Grundnorm*, but with this important difference. The *Grundnorm* 'has no necessary connexion with order, or justice,'[3] but is the 'will of that . . . or those . . . who have the power to express their will and to impose it on the community'. This may be a written constitution — otherwise Kelsen is not quite sure what it is. Our view would be that whatever person or persons have the power to express their will and impose it on the community it is possible for them,

---

[1] H. Kelsen. Professor Kelsen was leader of the so-called 'Viennese School' of jurisprudence.
[2] C. K. Allen, op. cit., p. 49.   [3] Ibid., p. 51.

and for us, to appeal beyond the laws, beyond their wills, to constructive concepts crudely summarized as 'justice' but having their life in the past through notions of natural law, bearing some relation to what Protagoras had in mind when he spoke of 'shame' and a 'feeling for justice' and possibly at the root of what Kant meant when he said,

Act on maxims which can at the same time have for their object themselves as universal laws of nature.[1]

For this reason we cannot, like the legalist, enjoy the precision and clarity of separating 'positive' laws from morals as a field of study and leaving it at that. We are aware that the kind of order we maintain in every human association is a kind of life; that what we 'are' is partly what we determine we shall be; therefore that both in the naming of laws and in administering them, in the keeping of laws as well as in breaking with them, we have to acquire awareness of ourselves and our relations, beginning, perhaps, with the relation between law and order on the one hand, inter-personal reliability and personal integrity on the other. A definition of 'law' which discourages this connexion will be inadequate.

QUESTIONS FOR DISCUSSION

1. 'I think we should do much better if we repealed the whole of the criminal legislation and went back to the Ten Commandments, perhaps slightly enlarged to deal with modern situations, such as motor cars and so on' (Mr. Justice Stable, in an address to new magistrates of Shropshire, *The Times*, 16 September 1965). Read the Ten Commandments (Exodus xx. 1–17). Consider what is said in the text about Austin's command theory of the law, and discuss the possibility of presenting the Ten Commandments in a form suitable to those who reject Austin's theory.

2. 'Do unto others as you would have them do unto you' is often called the 'Golden rule'. What makes it a 'rule'? Is it possible to discuss whether it is a 'good' (let alone a 'golden') rule?

[1] Kant, *Fundamental Principles of the Metaphysic of Ethics*, Abbott's translation, p. 56, Rosenkranz and Schubert's edition, vol. viii, p. 68.

If so, do we begin by asking 'does it work'? Read the first section of Kant, *Fundamental Principles of the Metaphysic of Ethics*; G. E. Moore, *Ethics*, ch. v; P. Nowell-Smith, *Ethics*, iii. 16; Benn and Peters, *SP*, ch. ii. (Publication details of these books appear in footnotes to the text.)

21

Law (II)

JUSTICE between just men requires no law. To work for a just society, therefore, must mean to work for an increase in just actions. Our purpose in social philosophy is to construct concepts which may help men in their turn to make rules for their conduct which will lessen the sum of injustice. Law by reason of the very qualities which make good law may impede this task or assist it, but cannot do it for us. We will reflect upon certain characteristics of law in order to make this clearer, showing as we can where the characteristics we are discussing belong both to morals and to other kinds of law and where they apply only to positive law.

Laws as 'abstract'

'Command', we said, is a word more appropriate to concrete situations where a specific wish is implemented and a specific action or sequence of actions is performed. Commanders may arise in a crisis — when a house is on fire, at an accident, in a national emergency — but even so their authority is very often derived from laws which subsume the needs of a crisis under conditions of wider generality. So a government may claim emergency powers at the outbreak of war, but the nature, the limitations, and the procedure for such powers may all be laid down in a constitution or in precedent without reference to the kind of situation which has arisen. The larger the community, the longer its history, the wider and deeper its experience, the likelier it will be to have laws of the widest possible generality, *abstracts* from experience far removed from anything we normally mean by 'commands'.

This abstraction and generality of laws — positive laws — no doubt accounts for the saying of Justice Holmes that 'general propositions do not decide concrete cases' and for the so-called 'realist' precept:

The prophecies of what the law will do in fact, and nothing more pretentious are what I mean by the law.[1]

Some have taken this to mean that the eminent judge was saying that there was no constancy in law, but only a series of fortuitous decisions.[2] Others think this is a strange and inexcusable misinterpretation. Aside from this dispute, however, it is possible to hear people argue that the very generality and abstraction of the laws entitles us to *disregard* them in particular cases and to make judgements on concrete cases on principles other than the laws provide. Let us be quite clear what attitude it is we are criticising.

Suppose the laws in a particular community require a member of the public to go to the aid of a policeman who is being attacked. Such a law, we will suppose, is as general as we have made it and abstracts from all such concrete and individual characteristics as the nature of the attack or the physical condition of the passing citizen. If the citizen reasons, 'The attacker is armed', or 'I am not very strong', or both, and (not in so many words, of course) 'Therefore the law did not mean *me* in *this* situation', he will be thrown back entirely on his sentiments of which his personal (and understandable) timidity may come uppermost. He may make his own escape and do nothing. Should he *respect* the law, however, he may appreciate that it could not take account of his personal

---

[1] Oliver Wendell Holmes jr (1841–1935), leading American jurist, son of the poet and essayist. In 1881 Holmes published a general view of the common law in a book entitled *The Common Law*. For comment on his philosophy of law see C. K. Allen, op. cit., pp. 42 ff., etc. The quotation in the text is from *The Path of the Law*, an address by Holmes quoted by Allen, op. cit., p. 42.

[2] Hayek seems to take the 'low' view of Holmes's intentions. Hayek is making the point that by 'rule of law' we mean that the rules must apply to those who lay them down and those who apply them, whereas he regards the 'law' that is a specific command as the 'chief instrument of oppression'. He seems to regard Holmes as one of those jurists responsible for the 'loss of belief that laws can rule' and he quotes Chief Justice John Marshall's words ('Courts are mere instruments of law, and can will nothing') approvingly against Holmes's view that 'general propositions do not decide concrete cases'. See *Constitution of Liberty*, part ii, ch. x, sec. 5. Allen, on the other hand (op. cit., p. 42), thinks the realists are to blame for misinterpreting Holmes. Whereas Holmes held that to master the law meant 'to look straight through all the dramatic incidents and to discern the true basis of prophecy' (i.e. of what the courts would do) the realists concentrated too much attention on the 'dramatic incidents'.

difficulties, let alone of this particular situation, and consider it his duty to do *something* — if only to find the nearest call-box and summon help. The possibilities, however, are not the point; it is the argument which proceeds from the inevitable abstractness of law to the conclusion that *therefore* it can be ignored 'in my case' that has to be faced.

For the peculiar features of the individual instance are not a sufficient ground for disregarding the law; on the contrary, it is of the very nature of law that there should be this 'gap' between the general and the particular. What would happen if it were otherwise? Laws (if we called them such and not, more appropriately, 'commands') would have to be made to suit all possible instances and all possible individual peculiarities; pushed to its logical limits this would subject every individual to detailed ordering of his will and reason, for he would have to be anticipated and provided for with nothing left to his ingenuity and decision. What is much more likely is that laws would lose their usefulness as guarantors (in part) of inter-personal reliability. Since you could only have some trust in a stranger's behaviour if you could be sure he had been accounted for in the detailed instructions, and since you could never be sure of this, then there could be no expectation that he would behave co-operatively. On the contrary, there would be every reason to expect that he would behave in totally unexpected ways, since this would be what the rules required.

One has only to put such a case to see how absurdly opposed to the whole purpose of law this would be. The law deals with abstract classes of individuals and situations. The courts render the laws concrete by applying them to cases. Unless the citizen respects laws for their general end and while they remain such even if meanwhile he struggles to convince the community of the need for change, the laws, as Socrates put it in the *Crito*,[1] would be destroyed and with them the city.

A moral law similarly abstracts from individual persons and concrete situations. 'Thou shalt love they neighbour as thyself' not only does not mean, for instance, 'provided his skin is of the right colour or his income adequate', but intends deliberately to reject all such exceptions. We may, and, indeed, we must, have

[1] Socrates. See also above, Chapter 9.

'rules' of some sort arranged, perhaps, in a hierarchy under such general laws, but if they are to be *rules* they have to abstract from the particular just as the rules of a game must ensure that the game will be more or less the same wherever it is played and by whatever players. As the rules are the game so are moral rules morality.

Laws as 'universal'

Every rational being must so act as if he were by his maxims in every case a legislating member in the universal kingdom of ends.[1]

Leaving Kant's moral aims for the moment we may agree that the laws of a community are intended to be universally applicable within the community.

The rule of 'leges' is the original meaning of the Latin word for laws — 'leges' that is, as opposed to 'privi-leges'.[2]

Their universality distinguishes positive laws from commands for if a positive law is truly universal (within a given community) *all* members will be subordinated to it including the so-called 'rulers'. This, Professor Hayek argues, does not get rid of coercion by government. Nevertheless,

If all that is prohibited and enjoined is prohibited and enjoined for all without exception (unless such exception follows from another general rule) and if even authority has no special powers except that of enforcing law, little that anybody may reasonably wish to do is likely to be prohibited.[3]

Let us say, not that all we actually call 'law' is of this character but that the concept of justice requires that this should be so.

Hayek allows for 'exceptions' to an otherwise universal law where this 'follows from another general rule'. To make the requirements of justice clear we must illustrate an exception of this kind. A law requiring all young men to register for military service provides such an example. If the law excepted, say, all with parents whose incomes were over (or under?) two thousand pounds a year there would be a great deal of argument and at the end of such argument many people would be left not merely disliking the law (that is another matter) but persuaded that it was

---

[1] Kant, op. cit.   [2] Hayek, op. cit.   [3] Ibid.

unjust, not strictly universal. If on the other hand a clause in the law allows for the possibility of conscientious objection to military service, provided the objector can satisfy a tribunal that his objections are genuinely moral ones, there may still be objections but they will probably have much less force and are certainly less likely to manifest a sense of injustice. The difference between the two kinds of exception is instructive. Put simply, it is one of *relevance*: a man's income, the social status of his family is not relevant to laws about military service; a man's convictions about taking life *are* relevant: whether we share them or not we would not call a law 'just' if it required a man to do what he felt so strongly to be morally wrong. It may also be that the logic of the objection has some force: if enough men of the right kind or in the right place felt as the objector does, then the need for military service of all kinds would come to an end. Therefore a law presumed to be made in the name of justice which did not take what steps it could both to protect a free community and to allow for moral development such that this kind of protection would no longer be necessary would be an inadequate law.

Positive law differs from moral rules in the use it can make of coercion (a characteristic to be considered later). Undoubtedly, an extension of moral agreement would, therefore, lessen the need for coercion and reduce the authority of positive law, provided 'agreement' could include performance. In the meantime, the law would fail of its purpose if it had no force to call upon and the organization of force in the form of the 'State' constitutes the boundaries of political community and at the same time the limits of law's 'universality'. In brief, a just law in England does not have to be universally applicable to the citizens of France; a law made in Paris is just if it applies without exception to all Frenchmen, whether or not it has application to some Englishmen.

By 'moral law', on the other hand, we mean a regulation of human conduct capable of true universality simply because it *cannot* be enforced, does not depend upon the State or any other coercive organization, may indeed have the 'sanction' of public opinion, but cannot be said to be recognized at all save in the individual's moral experience, in his personal judgement and his willing movements, or acts. Yet moral law is law by reason of its generality and universality. That is why no man can both claim to be a moral agent *and* talk of an act as being 'right for him' when this simply means he is doing as he chooses without thought for the universal significance of his act. Law appeals to rationality; positive law prepares for the limits of rationality; moral law is an attempt to push back those limits even where the positive law itself forms part of them. We have to go on trying or else permit such an extension of positive law (or some other regulating method) as would drastically reduce the capacity of future generations for moral freedom.

Law as coercion

I consider I have been coerced if my movements (including my not-movements) not only were not what I would choose to have made, but were made within an area of choice drastically reduced by others, and at the promptings of feelings in myself which others caused to be so powerful that I could not exercise my normal self-control, and if both conditions (whether occurring together or not) were brought about deliberately by other people with the intention of so determining my movements. So a rioting or hysterical mob may sweep me off my feet and leave me with no chance to extricate myself from a lawless situation, but this would not constitute *coercion*, though no doubt it would amount in law to what is called 'diminished responsibility'. On the other hand, if a man shuts me up in a confined space without arousing strong fear or any other powerful emotion, but requires me to put my signature to some document before he lets me out, I would call that coercion just as much as if he had threatened me with death. In fact, where violence carries one off bodily, unconscious perhaps but certainly wholly incapable of movement (though not of being moved), it would probably be better to call this simply 'violence' and leave 'coercion' for situations where I can at least make some kind of choice between movements, though with the consequences so heavily loaded against me that I cannot exercise anything like my normal self-control.

Suppose, that is, that I hardly ever do exercise much self-control — being a wayward person giving way to every powerful impulse, or being mentally sick and not, as we sometimes say, 'in possession of myself', it may still make sense to talk of my being used 'violently' (as in being thrust into a strait-jacket and taken off to hospital), but rather less sense to talk of my being 'coerced', if all that happens is that someone appeals to one of my several 'weaknesses' and simply, for his own sake, gets me to do what I might well have done anyway to my own detriment on another day and all alone.

The point to be made is that the relation we call 'coercive' is relative to the personality and character of the person whose movements are under consideration. Thus the analyst may say that 'among the readiest victims of brain-washing and religious conversion may be the simple, healthy extrovert'.[1] Passing over, for the moment, the question-begging word 'healthy', our point would be that you do not have to call 'brain-washing' or 'religious conversion' 'coercive' in such cases in order to regard them as, perhaps, equally evil. To do so may be to miss the point — the inadequacy of the 'simple, healthy extrovert' as a model for the moral agent. 'Coercion' may, perhaps, be a more useful word if we use it more sparingly.

Law, for instance, is usually said to be coercive and *therefore* is sometimes held to be inimical to a free society. For many other reasons which ought by now to be reasonably clear we reject the opposition between law and freedom. Now in particular we suggest that in many instances law is not properly coercive at all (though that is to say nothing about its justice in any given instance, only about its liberal effects). So the police may arrest me and confine me in a small space and this in some cases, if not all, they may be said to do for ends I do not approve and to do so deliberately. They have coerced me, though when I begin to ask what movements I make which have been coerced it may be that I shall find this to be a question of what movements I *cannot* now make — in gaol. Now the law could be said to be coercive inasmuch as it authorizes the police to act in this way, but as soon as I admit that they are acting according to the law, provided I do not feel that this particular law is unjust, my readiness to call their acts coercive may be lessened. For this is not so much a matter of one (or several) doing with me what they will, but of their doing what the law requires, as indeed they might do with one of their own number if he infringed the same law.

It is possible to modify coerciveness by making laws general and

[1] W. Sargant, *Battle for the Mind* (Pan, 1959), p. 70.

abstract without getting involved in extreme concepts such as that of Rousseau's 'general will'. And this is possible only so long as we insist upon keeping positive law in its place and criticizing it in accordance with such values as 'justice'.

If, in fact, law is felt to be coercive to an extent which goes beyond what has been suggested, this may be for one of two reasons. The law in question may be in fact unjust — for instance, it may not be truly universal, it may make irrelevant exceptions, or, to quote another requirement of justice of which we have said nothing so far, it may not have been known to be law for long enough.[1] These are the first kind of conditions which can add to the coercive effect of law — conditions inherent in the law itself. On the other hand, there are conditions, as we have already seen, inherent in the person whom the law arrests and punishes. We do not accept the all-embracing category, 'mentally sick', for those who break laws: to do so would be to neglect all important distinctions and this would be as harmful to the truly 'sick' as to the not-sick and to men in general. Men can choose to be regarded as sick, of course; that is the mischief of it. But they can make other choices with respect to the law. They can elect to see themselves as having some kind of 'right' not to live under law. They can attempt to 'contract out' of the community (though 'contract' here has little meaning). Not that this would sustain a right to protest if the law subsequently does not protect their interests, but this is not a sufficient argument against their position. Indeed, in a sense there is no such argument for they are on their way to putting themselves beyond the frontiers of reason. Law, for all its weaknesses, is *arguable*; the claim to exemption is not — except on the law's terms.

The possibility of coercion is included in all making and administering of laws in a political community. To see how it can remain only a possibility in an increasing area of the communal life we turn finally to some other characteristics of just law.

Just laws

Just laws must be universal and to be this they have to abstract from specific conditions and concrete cases. Impartiality, on the

[1] The principle of *known* laws has to do with what we earlier called 'inter-personal reliability'. (See above, Chapter 9.)

I

other hand, is a quality of judges and juries rather than the laws themselves. In other words, strictly speaking, for impartial justice we must have just men and, while the codes and rules of procedure — as for instance about the interrogation of prisoners and the manipulation of evidence — can do much to protect the accused against partiality, we can never dispense with the personal qualities of the men who administer the law.

In considering 'impartiality' as in discussing 'exceptions' to universal laws the principle of relevance is important. Thus in some communities a man's past misdeeds are not considered relevant to a judgement on the offence under review, yet a 'good character' also acquired in the past may be relevant to the mitigation of his offence. Most, but by no means all, communities agree that race and skin pigmentation are seldom relevant in passing judgement, but there are communities where political opinions may weigh with a judge even in cases where such opinions could hardly be considered relevant. So if there is a political movement actively and explicitly dedicated to the overthrow of a government by violence, the political opinions of a person suspected of complicity in such a plot are relevant (though that is not to say that such persons are morally wrong or the laws which try them just). If, on the other hand, a man is accused of theft, rape, or forgery and it is counted against him that he has political opinions disapproved by his judges, then this would lead to a partial judgement and we would call it unjust.

On the other hand, laws which are made for the specific purpose of suppressing a racial, religious, or political group are unjust because they are not truly universal. That is, those who administer them may argue, plausibly, that they too, should they become members of the party (or change the colour of their skin?) would be subject to the laws, but no one ever supposes they will make such a choice; on the contrary, the laws have been made to sustain a party or class or sectarian interest against opposition, and not to sustain the 'equilibrium' of interests as a just law should.

Known laws, laws which have been *there* and recognized by all reasonably literate or otherwise informed persons for a long time, can (if they are not markedly unjust) have much less coercive effects than new laws or secret laws, or laws which cannot be understood before an offence occurs. For men do not usually start something which they know will break regulations they have known all their lives, not at least without first attempting to *remove* the inhibition. Nor do known laws irk and frustrate as laws will if they are innovations.

The single, most important condition by which the coercive function of the laws can be transformed, however, is by our ensuring that laws are more and more co-operative. We have, that is, both to rely on capacity for co-operation between men within the political community and between such communities and also to take steps to increase it. Laws which spring from co-operation instead of being imposed by a few men dazzled by an idea become more and more like the rules of a game, the procedural rules of a free association, less and less like the 'commands' of a superior. In this sense law gains significance not in accordance with the concept of justice, only, but also as the pursuit of community. Law *makes* community: it does this by its coercive function, but more satisfyingly by inducing, requiring, and guiding co-operative enterprise. To suppose that even such laws can do away with all offence is to suppose that men will cease to be free and therefore to some extent unpredictable. But just as co-operation differs from collectivism in tolerating the rebel, so the concept of a free society requires overall co-operation and can only hope to progress as an increasing number of persons feel able to turn law to the ends and purposes of free co-operation.[1]

QUESTIONS FOR DISCUSSION

1. A 'Race Relations' Bill published in England in April 1965 purposes to prohibit discrimination on racial grounds in places of public resort. It would make it an offence 'to incite racial hatred in a public meeting or public place by spoken or written words' (*The Times*, 8 April 1965). Discuss the proposed legislation (i) in

---

[1] So though in war-time laws intrude into private life far more than in peacetime (in our society) it does not follow that the people feel more coerced and *therefore* less free. In some cases they felt more sense of 'belonging', enjoyed co-operation and were therefore able to see the laws as providing for what they regarded as *their* purpose, their own purpose. Whatever this says about war it illustrates the noncoercive possibilities of law in a free society.

terms of possible effects on human freedom, (ii) in particular for the check it could put on freedom of speech and publication. What is the *good* which is thought to justify such proposals in spite of such objections? Is the justification adequate?

2. What constitutes rule of law as distinct from rule of magistrates? See footnotes to p. 237 and read F. Hayek, *The Constitution of Liberty*, chs x and xi.

3. Suppose the law says that you, the private citizen, should aid the police if you see them in need, what moral rules would you think might justify your breaking such a law?

4. 'When legislation grows weak, morality degenerates' (Rousseau, *Social Contract*, bk IV, ch. vii). How can legislation 'grow weak'? By the multiplication of laws with inadequate enforcement? (Discuss the part played in such a process by the roads and the enormous increase in traffic.) By the granting of unlimited power to certain 'free' associations and the corresponding reduction of State power? (Discuss whether this could be the case with trade unions.)

22

Morals and Law

'JUSTICE' leads to talk of morals where 'freedom' is just as likely to discourage such talk. Yet the concepts belonging to the three can be brought into agreement provided we take care not to do the job hurriedly and to the detriment of one or the other. In this chapter we shall be mainly concerned with morals and law as these relate to the concept of justice; but this question can be approached from the other — that about morals and freedom.

Morals and mores
According to W. G. Sumner,[1]

All the life of human beings . . . is primarily controlled by a vast mass of folkways handed down from the earliest existence of the race, having the nature of the ways of other animals, only the topmost layers of which are subject to change and control, and have been somewhat modified by human philosophy, ethics, and religion, or by other acts of intelligent reflection.

'Intelligent reflection' reveals these folkways as 'regulators', or *mores*. Hardly surprising, then, if men who rebel against restraints should also come to regard the folkways as hindrances and demand to be freed from them. However the sociologist may speak of the 'topmost layers' as the limit of reflective change,

[1] W. G. Sumner, *Folkways* (Boston, 1907). Sumner was a Social Darwinist but his ideology is said to have given way somewhat as he developed to a 'sense of empirical responsibility'. See D. Martindale, *Nature and Types of Sociological Theory*, part iii, ch. 8. Social Darwinists, according to Martindale, held 'the notion that captains of modern industry represented the fittest members of society' and assumed that 'social welfare activities, in aiding the socially underprivileged, were destroying the biological potential of the race' (op. cit., p. 174). On Sumner and his Folkways see McIver and Page, *Society: An Introductory Analysis* (Macmillan, 1950), p. 19, from whence the quotation used here is taken.

attempts have been made from time to time to throw off all customary modes of behaviour in order to pursue an end, a good which the folkways denied.[1] Here is an important source of the distinction between the *mores* which the sociologist describes and the 'morals' which interest the reflecting moralist.

In the first place, a demand for freedom from the *mores* in order to seek a good, whether for oneself or for others, is as clearly a moral demand as it will (by conventional judgements) be considered 'immoral'. The conflict is not between freedom and morals but between two notions of what constitutes a moral person[2] — is he, that is, one who simply conforms to the *mores* perhaps without reflection, or is he someone who has some perception of good and determines to pursue it even in the teeth of established custom?

But then, in the second place, many have come to mean by 'morality' an achievement,[3] a way of living inconceivable without freedom. A coerced movement on such an argument, is non-moral simply because it is coerced. To have moral value the movement must have the status of an action and this is not possible if the agent is under restraint. So far, then, from freedom and morality being opposites on this argument the first is the necessary condition of the second. That is not to say, of course, that the moralist regards a breach of the conventions as endowed with superior quality simply because it is a breach of the conventions. The superior value is not derived from the quality of

---

[1] For such attempts to reject social habits consider (*a*) the Cynics of ancient Greece. See A. K. Rogers, *A Student's History of Philosophy* (New York, Macmillan, 1932), i. 9; H. Sidgwick, *History of Ethics*, ch. ii; T. Gomperz, *GT*, vol. ii, pp. 139 ff; *DL*, Antisthenes and Diogenes in vol. II, bk vi; (*b*) such Hebrew prophets as Amos and John the Baptist.

[2] In ordinary discourse both uses are common. On the 'good' see here G.E. Moore, *Principia Ethica*. Moore is sometimes called an 'ideal' Utilitarian. He will not have that there is one characteristic in virtue of which something is good (such as 'pleasure') but rather that there is 'an immense variety of different things, all of which are intrinsically good'. See also the same writer's *Ethics* (Oxford: Home University Library, 1912), pp. 152 f., which may be a better introduction than the first-mentioned work. With this compare W. D. Ross, *The Right and the Good* (O.U.P., 1930), who takes *right*, not *good*, as the basic ethical term.

[3] This is clear, for instance, in F. H. Bradley's ethical work. See his essay 'Ideal Morality' in *Ethical Studies*, 2nd ed. (Oxford: Clarendon Press, 1927). It is of course true of Kant (see his *Fundamental Principles*) and of most moral philosophers since it is dissatisfaction with the prevailing habits, by and large, which provokes them to philosophy. On the other hand, political philosophers may be much more concerned with the preservation of order and inclined to discourage moral achievement.

rule-breaking but from justifying rule-breaking by appeal to an end of greater value than keeping the rule.

On the other hand, willing conformity to a rule has been said by some moralists to *be* freedom,[1] since by willingly conforming the rule is deprived of its coercive power. This is a different emphasis and could easily lead to deceit: it is one thing to come to some such conclusion about one's own self-management, quite another to insist, as Rousseau was inclined to do, that others should 'willingly conform' to rules which one approves oneself. Other moralists have contrasted willing conformity favourably with unwitting conformity:[2] as we have seen, some degree of awareness is taken to be essential to morality, though here nothing need be implied about the relation between freedom and morals. Others again have favourably contrasted willing obedience to rules with impulsive or passionate disobedience and still others, more remarkably, have preferred rational, willing obedience to a conformity in response to impulse or desire — so that Kant leaves us with the impression that there is more virtue (for instance) in housing an aged relation out of a 'sense of duty' than because of affection.

It is undoubtedly the moralist's typical preference for obedience to a rule as opposed to impulsive disobedience which creates real conflict between freedom and morals. As we have seen, it is as false to claim that all acts of rebellion are morally superior just because some may be as to say that conformity as such is superior. We now discuss the notion of a moral rule in relation to the concept of justice.

The 'right' and the 'good'

If for the time being we take 'right' to mean 'in accordance with the rule' it will be possible to see how the 'right' and the 'good'

[1] A great deal depends upon our analysis of motives. (Fear may inspire 'willing' conformity.) Compare the views of J. S. Mill on individuality in his essay *On Liberty* with Rousseau's concept of a general will in his *Social Contract*.

[2] Compare Kant, *Fundamental Principles of the Metaphysic of Ethics*, and Ross, op. cit., with H. A. Prichard's 'Does Moral Philosophy rest on a Mistake?' (*Mind*, 1910; available now in Sellars and Hospers, *Readings in Ethical Theory*, New York, Appleton-Century-Crofts, 1952). Ethical theory of the utilitarian sort, whether 'ideal' or 'hedonistic', is called 'teleological' to distinguish it from theories which concentrate on the rightness of acts as duties or obligations and which are called 'deontological' (*telos*: an end accomplished; *deon*: that which is binding, right, or proper).

can come into conflict. For while it may always be 'right' to respect the rules of an association it will very often seem 'good' to break one. That is, it may be easy to see that some desirable end is impeded by the rules — an end desirable for others as well as ourselves as when, for instance, a physician is tempted to give an incurable an overdose of sleeping-pills. This is a very old problem which moral philosophers have debated at length. Here all we do is to consider rule-following and rule-making as these affect our concept of justice.

So soon as rules are made or heard about a need to *justify* breaking them arises. It is this, together with the deceits involved in justification, which will concern us here. Let us say it is a moral rule that a man should keep his promises. No doubt we could say (if we knew what we were at) that this arises from the need for inter-personal reliability in the conduct of day-to-day affairs and this would also lead us to say that such a 'need' never changes; that the rule about promise-keeping is in this sense permanent. Some people think that by creating fictional situations in which the keeping of a promise brings disaster they have proved there 'is no such rule'. But this is rather like saying there is no State railway service simply because there are departures from the time-table during floods, earthquakes, wars, or electricity failures.

When we do break a promise we feel obliged to justify what we have done to ourselves as well as to those we have disappointed. 'Justification' may take one of two forms: we appeal to some other rule — temporarily or even permanently recognized as of 'higher order' — such as, for instance, a contractual obligation to work later and therefore to set aside a promise to keep a 'date', or we insist on a 'good', an interest demanding attention without immediately relating this to any rule. (As, for instance, 'I simply had to wash my hair', or in the words of an infamous promise-breaker: 'Can't get away to marry you today: My wife won't let me'.)

The difference between the two forms of excuse — direct appeal to higher rule and the plea of more pressing interest — may be merely one of varying degrees of reflection. The gentleman in the song just quoted, for instance, may upon sober reflection have made some reference to the law of bigamy, though not, one fancies, to moral obligations to his legal wife. But it is none the less important. For where a rule is recognized and offered in justification two things become possible: first, agreement about a balance of interests involving far more than the two parties involved in promise-making and promise-breaking; second, a possibility of sustaining the rule about promise-keeping by explicit recognition that it *is* a rule, that it is part of a system of rules, and therefore cannot be treated lightly or disregarded.

If, on the other hand, a breach of promise is excused without reference to a rule either immediately or upon reflection, there is a strong possibility of deceit. The notion of an 'overriding interest' is of course useful but it is no easy matter to distinguish between a justifiable instance and one which is indistinguishable from any impulsive, careless disregard for the balance of interests. The danger lies in such words as 'good'. Almost any interest may be called 'good' by the person who has it and by such a title seem to have a kind of priority over rules whose concern is a balance of interests — a balance not only between one man's and another's but also between the many interests of the same man. (Money offered as a bribe may seem so 'good' to the footballer that he will agree to break the basic rules of the game and help his team to lose.)

For morality is a constructive and systematic attempt to regulate whole and parts without coercion so that no one may be sacrificed to the rest. It is concerned not with the instant only but with the period, and the instant as part of the period; not with the individual but with the individual as an end in himself and as part of a 'kingdom of ends'. Therefore morality not only uses the conditions of freedom to create rules different from those of positive law in being non-coercive, it also doubts the value of freedom without such rules. This is why morality and justice can at times seem identical.[1] But we will now examine both in the problem of their relations with positive law.

Obligation

Demands for freedom give rise to talk of 'rights'. Some say these are ordained by 'nature' and are 'imprescriptable'; others say there are no 'rights' except as the law decrees. What seems clear is that the 'ends' or 'goods' which the demand for rights defends

[1] As in Plato's *Republic*.

cannot be enjoyed except at a price. Nor does it follow that the persons who enjoy a right pay that price themselves, though they may be called upon to pay for rights which others enjoy. There is no necessary, precise, symmetrical relation between the rights I enjoy and the obligations I am required to fulfil — by positive law. So, for instance, I may demand the right to personal security against foreign attack or felonious intent. As it happens I have enjoyed such security for almost half a century. I may also demand a right to enjoy free speech, freedom from arbitrary arrest and, again, I have as it happens enjoyed such rights throughout my life. But while I have been obliged to contribute something in taxation to the cost of war and the upkeep of the police and judicial institutions, others have borne much heavier obligations both in the amount of tax paid and (in many more cases) the expenditure of health and life as members of the armed services. Thousands of men have died while fulfilling their obligations; thousands more have lost their health; many thousands more have lost their chief interest in life through the death of relations in battle. This is how the laws securing my rights have worked and this, in practice, is what 'justice' as order has meant in my generation.

Now I could slip away from the discomforts of such reflection by such observations as,

'I did not ask for this to be done.'

'It was not my fault that Europe went to war.'

'If someone is hanged in preventing the spread of crime that is not my doing . . . I am against hanging. . .'

but such observations are irrelevant. For law, as we have seen, is bound to be abstract, general, and universal in its applications. Justice is as blind to my uneasy enjoyment of rights as it would be to my unwilling fulfilment of obligations. There is no other way of working toward a balance of interests in the political community save through universal and impartial laws which take as little account of the individual's hurt pride as of his losses and injuries in the course of 'paying for' the rights of others.

Whatever moral criticism does it has no interest in denying that one man's rights are another's obligations and certainly none in mitigating the 'moral' logic of such a proposition as this: 'My enjoyment of rights commits me to a proper fulfilment of obligations'. Moral criticism might be much happier drawing attention to such aspects of this proposition as need emphasis at different times — as, for instance, the obligation of those who have been educated at public expense to return some service to the community which has paid for them. Then again, where a century ago men needed reminding that criminals were paying excessively for public order it is just possible that some humanitarians today need reminding that they must needs bear with their part in punishing criminals if order is to be maintained.

Moral criticism of the laws, of legal rights and obligations, is an endless effort to construct a concept of justice which will lessen the inequality between rights and obligations. The aim, too, is to widen areas within which we can co-operate freely with no one being required to contribute a great deal more than another and none being impelled into obligation against his will and reason. We do not normally need to be nudged into claiming our rights; so the moralist is better employed criticizing such claims and pointing up the obligations involved — not a popular role and one which accounts for the so-called conflict between morals and the good life. This is why we said at the beginning of Part Three that in talking about justice we have to take great care over sentiments this concept might dignify. Envy, for example, is not likely to heed the obligations others will be called upon to fulfil in order that the demands of the envious may be met.

In the past the question about 'political obligation' was very often one about the authority of the rulers. This question has its place today in political science. Some men said in the past that we were obliged to obey the laws because they rested upon the authority of the king, who in his turn received his authority from God. Others spoke with comparable reverence about the popular legislative assembly. Others again supported several different types of government by appeals to a 'social contract', the terms of which required the citizens to render obedience as a kind of payment in return for the benefits of government. Then the Benthamites intruded the utilitarian principle into the criticism of law and some people took this to mean — what Bentham could not have intended — not merely that a law was to be judged as 'good' or 'bad' according to its pleasure-making capacity but that our obligations under the law could be similarly assessed. On this argument, of course, there would be virtually no law since each man would claim to be judge in his own right of what made for his or other men's maximum pleasure.

The questions about 'authority' do not seem so important in communities which no longer look upon government as 'Them' but rather regard the State and the whole political community as a co-operative organization devoted to the many ends of the good life. In such a view it is no longer a question of my exacting from other men what they would not grant me except under pressure, but of joint effort to achieve a balance of rights and obligations for the pursuit of personal or public good. Here is possible moral progress. For when those who take part in a social enterprise see for themselves what is necessary if like or common ends are to be reached, when they make their own assessments, help in writing their own procedural rules, and find no coercive obstacles in the way of their work, they are both free of coercion and bent upon a common good to which they can devote their whole energies. Positive law, by contrast, can only require a low average performance if it is not to be disastrously coercive or 'more honoured in the breach than the observance'. (To substantiate this we might look into such records as there are of what has been done in modern Russia and China to increase production in the factories, comparing attempts at coercion with other methods.) When, on the other hand, the worker is subject to two conflicting accounts of his obligations, neither of which succeeds in engaging his own judgement, his potential as a moral agent, the prospect for moral progress would, presumably, be poor. Consider, again, the worker who has on the one hand a contract with his employer and on the other membership of a trade union — he is hard put to it to come to a clear thought about his obligations; the chances are he will give up trying, if indeed in such a situation it ever occurs to him to start.

For while conflict of obligations is moral experience, there is no moral conflict where there is no real choice. A society which allows large numbers of its members to pass the bulk of their 'social' time in such situations is a society wasting the greater part of its moral capacity.

Reason

The making of laws is our distinctive, human way of ordering our own affairs. By laws of all kinds we aim to reduce the imponderable, avert threats to our existence, guide co-operation over a wide area in complex operations, give to our common life a formal unity and a degree of security within which we may enjoy both privacy and fellowship. All these functions of laws are part of what we mean by 'reason' — part, but not all. The 'reasonableness' of law, which the concept of justice requires, lies in laws which can be both understood and criticized — made available, that is, to ordinary reason.

Whenever a law is 'made' we may assume that those who make it 'have their reasons' — that is, their aims, their motives, the interests to which the law is a means. This is involved in our being rational creatures and we may assume that, in this sense, all makers of laws are rational. But this is not a sufficient account of what is required of laws by the criterion of reasonableness. We want also the possibility that all who are subject to a law should be able to find 'good reasons' why they should be. It is this quality in a law which makes it good law, in our view.

Other people have regarded laws as 'reasonable' to the extent that they are not seen to be made but have been 'there' from time immemorial.[1] There is an element of this in the writing of Edmund Burke[2] and there is this much to be said for it: law would not be the servant it is if it did not have the characteristic of resisting change, exercising some sort of control over change. Burke's 'conservatism' ought to be appreciated thus far. But if a law is reasonable (in our sense) it must be exposed to the possibility of change simply because it is available to criticism. Positive law and moral law have this in common — both act rather like a rope by which a man may sling himself, hand over hand, across a deep and very troubled river. These laws, that is, give us something to hold on to in the midst of numerous and conflicting currents of opinion and impulse: we can hang, if we like, by one hand and ponder the matter while the stream pushes us about, but once we let go we may never reach a point where we *can* stand on our own feet, let alone change the position of the rope or replace it. This is why it is not only nonsense but dangerous nonsense both in law and

[1] See above, Chapter 20, and especially the notes on the myths which have given expression to this, and compare K. Popper, *The Open Society and its Enemies*, ch. v, 'Change and Rest'.

[2] See above, Chapter 14, and particularly the notes on Edmund Burke.

morals to say not 'the rules were made for man, not man for the rules' (which is true) but 'the rules were made for *me* and therefore I can drop them as it suits me' for this is like letting go of the rope when you are faint or the water is particularly rough.

The middle way between undue reverence for the rules and the chaos of lawlessness lies in our interpretation of 'reason'. Justice requires that all rules be understood (or understandable) and open to criticism; but by the same tokens it obliges us to have good reasons for breaking the rule and this in its turn requires that our reasons be subject to the same methods of criticism we require for the laws themselves. Reason (in this sense) is another name for 'communication'; but this is 'communication' of a special kind, of a kind, that is, which ignores every distinction between men save one — their willingness to seek through discussion a law which will relate the interests of one to the interests of all.

Always so choose that the same volition shall comprehend the maxims of our choice as a universal law.[1]

This is what Kant calls the 'principle of autonomy' or self-rule. We can put it this way. If men would reduce the area of coercive law and yet live in community under justice, they must deliberately widen the area of rational, critical intercourse, translating their purposes into suitable rules. There is no way of doing this by fiat, by Act of Parliament. We have to find ways and means of living 'justly' ourselves, both in the management of personal life and in our free associations. The way to progress in human relations lies primarily through moral progress. But this does not settle the moral problem of how we are to deal with those who either have no interest in such progress or claim to pursue it outside the 'reasonableness of the law'. In other words, we must now consider the problem of crime and punishment.

QUESTIONS FOR DISCUSSION

1. Can it ever be *right* to break the conventions? In addition to references given in footnotes on pp. 248 f. read R. M. Hare, *The Language of Morals* Oxford, Clarendon Press, 1952), ii. 5, 9; iii. 10.

[1] Kant, op. cit. (Abbott's translation), p. 59.

2. Is free education a right? If so, what obligations does it create? Suppose a society which pays for practically every undergraduate's education does not insist upon a return for its endowments, is such a society 'good' because 'free' (in the permissive sense of the word)? Or is it not good because it neglects to relate rights to duties effectively? On rights see Benn and Peters, *SP*, ch. iv.

3. The rights a worker enjoys as member of a trade union give rise to obligations — to the union. Discuss these obligations in terms of (*a*) the values called 'community' and 'justice', (*b*) personal morality. Read E. F. Carritt, *Ethical and Political Thinking* (O.U.P.; Clarendon Press, 1947), ch. ix, sec. A, ch. xiv, sec. i; and, by the same author, *The Theory of Morals*, viii and xi.

23

Punishment

'If it isn't useful, throw it away.' You might call this a good, sound rule for 'spring-cleaners'. We have been doing some 'spring-cleaning' of concepts and institutions in the past century; laws, positive and moral, have been put to the same test: the test of utility. But the test itself in its crude, common-sense form has its drawbacks. To start with, 'useful' does not explain itself; we have to ask, 'useful for what?' No doubt answers can always be found, but some of them, at least, when they are put into words, pose far more problems than they solve. Turning out an attic at home may be an operation in which it is easy to say what is 'useful', at least until you come across a relic of the past which counts for something in the coinage of feeling; but the reform of law and, still more, the criticism of morals is not so simple. For one thing — it is very likely that the 'usefulness' of some human institutions is lost as soon as we start treating them as 'means to ends'.

This seems clear enough when we are talking about what were called in Part One 'primary conventions'. As soon, for instance, as you begin to ask what truth-seeking or truth-speaking is useful *for*, the question, though it has its place, may well prove disastrous, since the kinds of answer we would be most likely to give would turn objectivity, honesty, trustworthiness — the qualities such primary conventions require — into something very different. 'Honesty is the best policy', for instance, seems to mean that you should be honest because it 'pays'. But in some cases it may 'pay' you to lie or to deceive; if you accept this you will be not an honest man but a plausible rogue. To rely upon people we do not have to expect them always to speak 'the truth, the whole truth and nothing but the truth', even supposing they could; but we do have to be sure they will not deliberately falsify the facts and we cannot be sure once they have made it clear that to them honesty is a matter of policy, not a quality valued for 'its own sake'. That does not take away the usefulness of honesty; it does show why the rule, 'If it isn't useful, throw it away', has important limitations.

This is the doubt to have in our minds when we are reflecting on positive law and punishment: a doubt, that is, whether the ultimate 'usefulness' of such institutions might not be lost if we take too far the 'spring-cleaning principle', if we expect too much of the question, 'Is it useful?' without first examining very carefully the implications of such a test.

Accountability

To make this clear we will now recall what was said in Part Two[1] about the 'logic of freedom'. If men are to be free from coercion, we said, it was necessary to our human discourse, to communication — we may now add: to community — that they should 'own up to' the movements they freely make, not leave them 'unattached' and therefore meaningless. Freedom was conceivable, we said, only within what we called the 'general charter' according to which a man has the more to answer for as he has more freedom from constraint. To call men 'free' we have also to treat them as 'accountable' but this in its turn implies both personal qualities and a type of human relations: in order to be 'accountable' men must be of a certain quality which is only manifested as they account to each other for their movements. Treating men as accountable is part of the condition for treating them as free and equal. Here the requirements of justice coincide with those of freedom; and legal institutions may be seen as 'useful' to both, but only if, in some sense, we see the 'rendering of accounts' as an end in itself. For if, for instance, we start asking whether such relations as legal accounting are 'useful', and if we mean by this (as well we might) 'useful for human happiness' it will be easy to slip into the conclusion that since accounting is often painful *therefore* we should have less of it; overlooking what this may lead to both in personal qualities and human relations.

'Accountability' is a matter of *status* and what we are arguing

[1] Above, Chapter 17. For a discussion about responsibility which is based primarily on legal concepts see W. D. Lamont, *Principles of Moral Judgment* (Oxford; Clarendon Press, 1946), ch. viii.

here is the risk to such status from overmuch concern for personal comfort. This may be the result of concentrating upon the 'usefulness' of institutions. It is, of course, undeniable that some men are wholly unable to account for any of their movements and therefore must be wholly denied the status of accountability. Failure to recognize such conditions in the past led to great cruelty to the insane and we are rightly pleased at our greater humanity. It is also true that many more people may for one reason or another be unable to account for specific movements and it is recognition of this which needs much more careful thought. For while none of us wants to be punished and we all shrink from accounting for unpopular or offensive acts, the risks of extending the category of unaccountable movements are considerable. Each time you treat a movement as unaccountable you treat the mover as less than free. Each time we excuse a man — out of kindness — from rendering an account it is as if we agreed to reduce his standing among men, to deprive him of status in order to save him, and ourselves, from pain. This would follow from an application to law and the courts of the principle, 'If it isn't useful, throw it away', when the object to be thrown away was accountability, and the test of usefulness, for instance, was pain-saving.

That is to say nothing about the justification for doing this; only to make the implication a little clearer. 'Legal responsibility' is sometimes spoken of as a subject fit only for lawyers or students of jurisprudence. Our point is that what is done in the courts about accountability is not only done partly under the pressure of more general social appreciations, but is likely to affect our overall concept of desirable human relations at the point where freedom and justice meet: in the status of men who treat each other as free and responsible.

For a man to be 'held accountable' it is necessary to set up certain kinds of human relations. Cases where this is not possible are easy to specify, but we point to such cases with regret; we regard them as disasters both for the persons held not responsible and for the society which has helped to produce them.[1] We agree readily enough that it is unjust to punish the insane as if he were a criminal, accountable for his acts; we do not agree so readily that

[1] On the role of 'patient' see above, Chapter 18.

it would be not only unjust but *inhuman* to deprive a man of his status as free because accountable in order to avoid the harsh requirements of punishment. The cause lies partly in too hasty an application to law and punishment of the principle of usefulness. For this favours concepts of punishment inadequate to the values of freedom and justice. We turn to the concept of punishment which is least acceptable today.

Retribution

'To pay for' what you have done wrong would have a simple enough meaning if it could be taken literally. If, that is, you had done damage which could be repaired by your work or your wealth this would be *reparation* and it would strike most people as just. Moreover, in making reparation the offender would be 'making his' offending 'acts his own'; he would be behaving as a responsible person; he would be safeguarding his status among his fellows. But suppose that the damage cannot be repaired (as when a man has been killed) or it can be repaired but without any cost to the offender comparable to the shock and dismay caused to the offended: this seems less than just. If 'reparation' in this sense was all that 'punishment' meant it would lead to some curious situations: we would have a murderer going free because there was nothing he could do about it while a poor man who had damaged another's property might spend the rest of his life paying for it.

'Retribution', on the other hand, can be used to mean much more than simple reparation. By 'retribution' we mean not literally 'paying for' the damage done but also and more often suffering *simply because* a law has been broken. Sometimes we call this 'satisfaction' and it may look like a civilized, sophisticated 'alienation' of (primitive) vengeance.[1] We still use such a word as 'retribution' quite happily about the *natural* consequences of wrongdoing: when, for instance, a joker busily laughing at a friend's slip on the ice falls flat on his face himself. But many people refuse to discuss law and punishment as retribution. They think it a more suitable approach to punishment to ask, 'What

[1] Compare a well-known saying of Francis Bacon's: 'Revenge is a kind of wild justice; which the more a man's nature runs to, the more ought the law to weed it out' ('Of Revenge': Essay IV in the Everyman's edition of 1906).

good does it do?', though such a question may, in fact, commit fallacy by assuming that punishment was meant to do good.

Retribution as 'satisfaction for the law' may, on the contrary, be the only *just* account of punishment and the only account, at that, which respects the concept of freedom. As to what such 'satisfaction for the law' implies we will speak in a moment; but first consider two other words which are used about punishment and see how these imply conclusions contrary to the requirements of justice and freedom.

Punishment as a 'deterrent' means using an offender as an instrument to protect us against other possible offenders. If punishment has such an effect — and we would be obliged to prove that it had — then those who use this argument would feel justified in punishing; but on this argument there is no sufficient reason why they should make any particular individual suffer if deterrence and only deterrence is their aim. All that matters is the effect, the end. We need not be over-scrupulous about the means unless the argument is sophisticated to show that would-be criminals are more readily deterred by accuracy in police investigation and fairness in the courts. On the other hand, it is open to us to say that to use one man as a means to deter others is not justice at all: at least not unless his punishment means more than this, unless punishment itself so far as the criminal himself is concerned has some other meaning.

Punishment as 'reform' (to take the second alternative) means using the offender as a means to more general social ends — those defined by the norms and conventions of contemporary society. We may argue that in reforming a criminal we are concerned for his good; but until we have got him to agree, we are treating him as non-accountable, as a 'patient', and we are taking for granted (as well we may in many cases) that our ways are better and that he ought to have no alternative but to conform. What we need to say about this view at the moment is that even in terms of its own ends it may be involved in contradiction; for suppose that 'reform' meant 'making a man fit for freedom' and suppose *this* meant 'making him responsible' it would be a little odd to set out on such a quest by ignoring a man's own judgement and choice about what was good for him by taking for granted that in time he would come around to our point of view.

This is to say nothing *either* about the possibility of reform *or* its methods. It is simply a comment on the logic of such concepts of punishment. Our view would be that you may or may not deter others by what happens to an offender; you may or may not succeed in bringing a one-time criminal to 'go straight'; what you may not do in the name of such values as justice and freedom is to confuse three quite distinct aims — that of reforming, that of deterring, and that of punishing.

Punishing, whatever its connexion with these other tasks, is a thing apart and that 'thing' can best be depicted as retribution. To be clear about punishment — whether we want to get rid of the concept or not — we have to consider it apart from other social activities however admirable these may be. For punishment is an integral part of that complex arrangement of our human relations by means of which we are able to treat each other as free. No one need question the desirability of reducing the need for punishment, but we would do well to question the ends for which this is done and the means by which such reduction is achieved. For these may well involve exchanging a painful arrangement for one less painful but worse.

Law, as we have seen, is capable of becoming an instrument by means of which men may regulate their relations with each other and yet not coerce each other, not make each other instruments of their ends or purposes without at the same time treating each other as ends. 'Law', however, is the name for an abstraction (abstraction being a proper quality of law) which only becomes concrete when an offence appears to have been committed. It becomes concrete by means of liability and punishment. My liability to answer for acts contrary to law is part of my status as a free man; it is also a proof of the law whether or not I am guilty and subsequently punished. If I am guilty and go unpunished, then it is as if the law was *only* an abstraction and all that society was meant to be in the law similarly is reduced and debilitated.

For when we speak of the law's being 'satisfied' we might also speak of the society's being satisfied. 'Society', too, is an abstraction and it, too, becomes concrete in such situations as those in which an offender confronts his judges. It is a sufficient account of punishment to say that at times when a man breaks a rule the reality both of society and the law (or of society through the law) depends upon what happens to him: if he is hurt in some way (whatever else happens) and the hurt follows upon a decision of the courts, then the law is realized, or made concrete. So is the society. Otherwise not.[1]

In everyday talk about punishment there are two objections (among others) which we must notice now for the light they throw on ordinary debate on such matters: first, the objection that we ought not to punish because 'society is guilty'; second, a rather more vague objection in the name of such virtues as 'forgiveness' and 'toleration'.

Social guilt

Even without much social science most of us today are able to see that the criminal, like other men, is a social animal and this must mean that the deeds of crime like the deeds of genius or charity have a social context. If a man breaks a law, it is hardly surprising if we can find in his environment conditions or influences which made such an offence possible — the same could be said of any act of any man, however base or exalted. But to pass from this to a view which abolishes distinctions between, say a work of art and a cleverly devised robbery, or useful public service and homicide, on the ground that all alike could be 'explained' in terms of their sociological antecedents, would serve no purpose except in academic work.

Yet this is what talk of 'social guilt' inclines to. For while few people would forgo their own just reward for meritorious acts or even deny it to others on the ground that it was 'society', not the performer, who was responsible, they will try to elude the unpleasantness of punishment with similar reasons. It is not the thief, the killer, the rapist, or the forger who should be punished, they say, but society. If all they mean is that we have all some responsibility for the conditions within which crime occurs, this would be both true and suggestive — there is a proper incentive here to social reform. But if they truly intend to deny the justice of punishment for breaches of the law on these grounds, then we have to take exception.

For society breaks no laws, neither does it keep them. Laws are respected or dishonoured by men. To suppose otherwise may be

[1] Compare with the discussion on permissiveness, above, Chapter 15.

to do no more than get out of a situation we don't like by a dangerous piece of self-deception. (And it is the business of philosophy to protect us at least from that.) As there is no 'social thing' which breaks the laws, so there is no social *guilt* for breaking the laws; on the contrary, the laws are society or at least one of the most tangible forms of society. Nor does it follow that because I (very properly) feel some responsibility for the conditions making crime possible therefore *I* am guilty of the criminal's offence in the same way as he is guilty. On the contrary *he* has committed the offence; I have not. To make 'society' in general or lots of us in particular bear *his* guilt would be to deprive his movements of status by depriving them of an agent. We need not suppose that he would complain, but we are bound to see that this is yet another way of depriving persons of their self-hood by pretending that their movements are not their own acts.

When Rousseau talked about 'forcing men to be free' he could have meant this: if men are held accountable for what they do even if these include their liability to punishment, they are at least treated as if they are capable of the freedom they have abused. If, on the other hand, immediately they offend we rush in and try to attach the offence to other (and especially nebulous, abstract) 'agents', then we are acting as if a man were only capable of freedom when his actions pleased us, otherwise not.

Forgiveness

To 'live and let live' is a principle which resembles toleration[1] but which lends itself to broader categories and looser thinking. Others who take their moral life more seriously will sometimes introduce into talk about crime and punishment the notion of such virtues as 'charity' and 'forgiveness'. For the sake of the concept of justice but also to protect what is valuable in such everyday notions of virtue it is necessary to make a few distinctions here.

To 'live and let live' is no doubt an admirable principle when it means enduring the foibles of your own neighbours, putting up with ways and tastes which are not only different but distasteful. Even so, there may be times when a rearrangement would be better especially if you are doing all the enduring while your

[1] For John Locke's discussion of toleration see above, Chapter 13.

neighbours remain oblivious and cannot even enjoy your virtue. But when the phrase, 'to live and let live', is used about people and offences which are more remote, which do not, at least for the moment, impinge upon our comfort, we may be hard put to it to distinguish between this so-called principle and indifference, inertia, insensitiveness. This is a similar objection to the one raised earlier against 'permissiveness' as a so-called interpretation of freedom. Lines have to be drawn. How do we distinguish, for instance, between the international virtue of 'co-existence' and a nervous, isolationist indifference to the fate of people in oppressed communities? Similarly, we have to be clear that in 'tolerating' the criminal we are not conniving at the offence in order to evade social, engagement, responsibility.

'Forgiveness' and 'charitableness' on the other hand ought not to be confused with the easy slogan, 'to live and let live'. But neither are they particularly relevant to the question of crime and punishment. That is, 'mercy' and 'charitableness' may be possible for judge and jury provided they respect the law; they may on the other hand inspire law-reform and those ancillaries to punishment whose aim is to help an offender return as soon as possible to full enjoyment of his citizenship. But 'forgiveness' is a rare and difficult accomplishment often confused with lesser ones and only permissible in the person who has been injured. This touches crime mostly in our attitudes to the former criminal and with him we may be less successful than might be expected after our talk about toleration and social guilt. For if we can take it that to 'forgive' means to restore a person to the place in one's esteem he had before the offence or to treat him as if the offence had never occurred, then it is doubtful whether many ex-prisoners would claim to have found much forgiveness once their punishment had been completed.

To insert 'forgiveness' between the crime and the punishment, on the other hand, is another matter altogether. Remember, we are talking of crime or civil offence — acts against the laws of the community — not of personal relations. Where there are no laws, between friends and members of a family, the alternatives to forgiveness are for the most part tragic. Where there are laws, on the other hand, no forgiveness is possible until trial and punishment are complete, for there is none who can come between the offence and its consequence without threatening the function of the laws. If the 'rule of law' means that all alike subject themselves to the law, then it also means that for some to take to themselves the power to 'forgive' an offender except through due process of law would be an injustice. For justice can only be said to be done when it can be seen to be done and no private arrangement can take its place.

'Punishment', in our view, should be given a strict and limited meaning — that of 'retribution' as this has been explained. This is necessary to the rule of law, just as the rule of law, in its turn, is essential to our concepts of justice and freedom. But there is nothing in this view to discourage every rational attempt to reform laws or carry out social reconstruction with the aim of reducing the incidence of crime while maintaining good order. On the contrary, if the retributive consequences of crime are as clearly understood by would-be reformers as they are endured by the offender, we might be a good deal clearer about the direction of reform and more impressed by its necessity. For justice calls for sound reasons *and* good sentiments. 'Sentimentality' is a friend to neither.

QUESTIONS FOR DISCUSSION

One or more of the following should be studied before discussing any of the questions which follow: E. F. Carritt, *Ethical and Political Thinking*, part i, ch. v; *Theory of Morals*, ch. xii; Benn and Peters, *SP*, ch. viii; W. D. Lamont, *The Principles of Moral Judgment*, (O.U.P.; Clarendon Press, 1946) ch. viii, paras 165–77; F. H. Bradley, *Ethical Studies*, essay 1; S. Zink, *The Concepts of Ethics*, ch. vi.

1. When does 'punishment' become 'treatment'? Which is preferable (from whose point of view and upon what criteria)?

2. Suppose it could be shown that punishment neither deters nor reforms, what would we propose to do with law-breakers and upon what grounds?

3. What objections could we have to a society in which crime was impossible? (In answering this question we have first to suggest the conditions, or the various kinds of condition, which would make this feasible.)

24

Distribution

'THE sense of justice', we said,[1] is more easily excited when we see the very rich living cheek by jowl with the very poor. Most talk of 'justice' in this century has this as its background. The law has been favoured mostly as a useful instrument for distribution. Distribution rather than retribution is what many people mean by justice. Not that this is a new or even a different 'kind of' justice. No doubt there have been centuries of subordination, habitual, unconscious, mystical, during which few asked why the laws were kept or the rulers obeyed. But with awareness and criticism those who had possessions took very little time to discover how important law and order were if they were to keep them, while those who had none might favour revolution and disorder until their position improved, but once enriched their politics tend to change and they become as conservative as the rest.

In short the connexion between maintenance of order and enjoyment of possessions is permanent. All that changes is the number and identity of those who *own* and therefore take more interest in order than in change.

Possession

To 'possess' means to have at your disposal some part of the universe outside your own skin-frontier. We must have some ideas about possession before we can discuss the notion of distributive justice let alone the notion of the State as the instrument of distributive justice.

Life in the elementary, biological, sense cannot go on without consumption — the organism's taking into itself part of its environment. The point need not be made in a small tribe or a

[1] See above, Chapter 19.

family: everyone 'knows' it and the group moreover is collectively engaged in 'coming to terms with' reality by keeping itself fed. When groups are large enough for some members not even to meet others, when it is possible for some to spend their lives elsewhere than at the coal-face or in the furrow, when wealth can be accumulated, food stored, and differences develop not only in function but also in resources, then a point has to be made if some are not to die of starvation while others eat to excess.

Consumption is not the same as possession. On the contrary: every time you eat a bit of the universe you cease to possess it for it has become part of you. Your interest in possessing a larder full of food is an interest in eating, not in possessing. But if the food is not lifted straight from the ground — your ground — if, on the contrary, you have little hope of getting it at all *without* possessions, then the demand for justice merely as a demand for survival will fix upon other things than food and will take in, for instance, such matters as a '*just wage*' or a '*proper standard* of *living*'.

What we intend by the 'standard of living' moves with the times. In these times we intend a lot more than the bare necessities of survival. There are whole communities today who might justly lift up their voices to other communities as once classes or minorities or impoverished majorities lifted up theirs to their own rulers — in demands for survival. The relations between nations and groups of nations today is in some respects comparable to that between, say, serfs and masters, peasants and owners, within any given nation a few generations ago. We do well, then, to be impressed with justice in this sense, for it is in all probability the main issue between nations today: the issue between the well fed (or overfed) and the starving.

Yet, as we said, 'standard of living' within our western nations at any rate no longer has this simple connotation. When we use it we are not talking about bare subsistence or indeed about consumption as distinct from possession at all. What we are talking about, very often, *is* possession as distinct from consumption. We not only want a lot more to eat than is necessary or even 'good',[1] we want many more things and require that these shall be available to the greatest possible number.

Now things possessed, as distinct from food consumed, still

---

[1] 'Good', that is, on the criterion of *health*.

belong to the 'outside' and therefore constitute real relations both
with the universe in general and with the men who make,
provide, and protect our enjoyment of them in particular. Here is
a man who inherits a house and its nineteenth-century furnishings
— a houseful. Having no home 'of his own' he could of course sell
the lot and make one, but he hesitates: he never has been quite
clear about himself and so he hesitates long enough to sink into
one of the chairs he *wants* to loathe and discover the convenience
of not selling things which have no joy for him. In some sense his
inheritance 'takes over' and makes the man (or prevents his
achieving self-hood?). This is obvious enough in such an extreme
case, but the same may be true of many possessions: once we
begin to want we begin to enter certain relations and to modify
others. Mass-produced goods cunningly advertised induce wants
in a large number of people without distinction and create
relations — and 'selves' — accordingly. The 'need' created has
less chance of a meaning in terms of an integrated 'self' or 'whole'
— the demands to have such needs met are not then necessarily
parts of the demand for 'freedom' as we interpreted this value.
There is therefore no need to assume that a community responsive
to such demands even if it couches them in the name of 'justice' is
by its success more free than it was before.

It has been known for a poorer nation to refuse food supplies
where the distribution of these by richer nations tied it economi-
cally or politically. If the governments of such nations had the
motives they appeared to have then this would be some recognition
of the relation between possessions and social values, a recognition
which was once simply put, in these words:

What shall it profit a man if he gain the whole world and lose his soul?
or what will a man give in exchange for his soul?

To be what he can be a man needs room in the world to make his
movements his own acts but of how much room and what kind of
space he should be made free are difficult questions. Further, in
talking of freedom, we mentioned not only the free area but the
legal title a man should be given to 'make what he achieves his
own property'. The ethics of distribution might, no doubt, start
from here.

Property and power

As soon as a man is released from restraint he has 'in the terms of the charter' to be answerable for his movements in so far as these are to be given the status of acts. Now the range and variety of such movements depends both on the area within which a man is free of restraints and on two other factors. These are, first, his own qualities including what we mean by his 'abilities'; second, the 'furnishings' (so to speak) of his free area — that is, all the materials available as instruments and as direct, immediate satisfactions. (A piece of land may bring immediate satisfaction quite apart from its use as 'means'; so may books in a library, but pictures in a gallery may bring *only* immediate satisfaction.)

Does the concept of freedom as we set it out commit us to the justice of distribution beyond the requirements of bare survival? The answer usually given today would be 'yes' both in respect of 'abilities' (through education) and in respect of 'furnishings' — through public services, the 'standard of living' and so on. If we hesitate it is because some of the reasons given are not unequivocal in their respect for freedom. You may find people arguing the justice of distribution (in the broader sense of the term)[1] who either seem to have no idea of what freedom is about or else explicitly play it down, make it of less importance. And this seems to be the case not only with statists — those who see no harm in vastly increasing the power of the State provided this is used for distributive purposes — but with others more liberal in their politics who nevertheless give overwhelming importance to *secondary* distribution with no corresponding exposition of freedom.

Of statism more will be said in the next chapter. Here we will consider an example of the second kind — where distributive justice is made into the primary social value at some risk to freedom.

There is a principle which says that the acid test for all laws (and indeed for all moral rules) is the advantage they bring to the great

[1] 'Distribution in the broader sense': let us call this 'secondary' to distinguish it from 'primary' distribution of what are thought to be basic necessities. Compare the treatment of justice as distribution with Aristotle's method in book v of his *Ethics* where he distinguishes between (*a*) what is lawful and (*b*) what is fair and equal.

majority. Put like that we could hardly quarrel with utilitarianism[1]
unless it were taken to mean that each man had to decide this for
himself — that is, without respect for law, and that was certainly
not what Jeremy Bentham and the other utilitarians meant. But
put like that this would not be a very helpful principle. It is, of
course, important to remind law-makers and administrators that
their business is with the advantage of the *whole* community, not
with that of the government or its members alone. But on the one
hand the utilitarians do not say the 'whole community' (perhaps
they could not); and on the other they use language in order to
explain 'advantage' which makes it the business of law and
distribution to interfere in those areas in which the individual has
to be free if he is to be responsible.

For by 'advantages' the Benthamites meant specifically 'pleasures' and by 'disadvantages', 'pains'. The end moreover which
they set before government was that of 'happiness'. Now we do
not need to discuss any more the psychological basis of utilitarianism, but as moralists we have this to say: that while it would
be quite proper to insist that government meet the demands of the
people in distribution, or even say that this is what government
must do, it is a different matter altogether for *government* to concern
itself directly with pleasures and pains; another matter again, well
beyond its jurisdiction, for it to try to determine our happiness.
Once the makers of law see themselves as determiners of happiness
and see law-making as the manipulation of pleasurable and painful
sensations, all the finely interwoven but none the less distinct and
distinctive areas of personal autonomy are likely to be blown away
like dandelion-clocks and every man exposed to the dangers of
State benevolence.

A man is not robbed of his freedom simply by the bad intentions
of those who coerce him. On the contrary, where people squeeze
him until it hurts he is much more likely to fight back and get free.
Yet it is none the less coercion when the squeeze is called a 'hug' —
if you can't loosen an embrace when you feel you've had enough,

---

[1] 'Utilitarianism' in the general sense of utility as 'advantage'. Most of the objections raised in this book have been to hedonistic utilitarianism. J. S. Mill's essay
Utilitarianism (Dent, Everyman's, 1910; 1st ed. 1863) is the best-known exposition of
the English utilitarian school. G. E. Moore in his *Ethics* gives a critical account of
the theory but Moore himself is a utilitarian of the non-hedonistic kind. (See above,
pp. 248 f.)

then you are restrained and when the processes of restraint are such that they can claim with some show of plausibility to be doing for you what in fact you can only do for yourself — providing for your happiness — the danger is immensely greater.

But let us be quite clear where. Oscar Wilde once asked what the State is to do if it is not to govern and he gave as his answer:

The State is to be a voluntary manufacturer and distributor of necessary commodities.[1]

Need the utilitarians[2] have said more to achieve the positive aims of reform? Yes; for they needed also to justify the repeal of old laws regarded as burdensome and perhaps to answer such questions as, 'Why should the State undertake distribution?' Our objection is not that they took up such objectives — and indeed they were not all convinced statists — but that in order to do so they attempted a total morality as well as a political and social philosophy. This they did by using language of such extravagance and at the same time of such looseness that still today it is difficult to disentangle the web they wove and keep distinct what ought to be distinct.

Now we may say, for instance, that all men in order to be what they might must have food — the means to bare subsistence. But this is not very satisfactory for a civilized nation. We certainly want to say that a man ought to be given such opportunity to develop his own abilities as he has when taught certain skills and made free of certain information. Where do we go from there? Are we agreed that men ought to be free to make their movements their own acts? But if 'happiness' is to be determined from above by a clearly defined formula drawn up by administrators and abstracted from individual peculiarities (as indeed it must be to

[1] Oscar Wilde (1854–1900), 'The Soul of Man under Socialism'. Wilde has the distinction of being in this essay both an ardent individualist and a socialist though he is not alone, of course, in professing to combine these interests. He saw the socialist State as freeing us from responsibility for the needy and so enabling us to be ourselves. But the State (under socialism) 'must give up all idea of government'; 'there is such a thing as leaving mankind alone; there is no such thing as governing mankind'. Democracy, according to Wilde, is 'bludgeoning of the people by the people for the people'. (The essay was published in the collected edition of Wilde's works in 1908 but it appeared first in the *Fortnightly Review*, Feb. 1890.)

[2] 'Utilitarian' again means the Benthamite, hedonistic kind.

suit the utilitarian hypothesis) then it may well be the case that such freedom is ruled out as so likely to make pain for many as to be properly denied to all. If, on the other hand, happiness is agreed to be a man's own affair, then the State, the civil servant, and the social servant may quite properly give such services as they are asked to give, but certainly not deprive a man of assuming, if he wishes, responsibility for his own acts.

The same goes for that other facet of freedom — being able to make what one achieves one's own property. There are of course pretty strict limits to what can be done in this direction without giving rise to injustice. But it would be equally unjust if this aspect of freedom were altogether ignored, as well it might be if administration were trusted with something called the 'happiness of the greatest number'.[1] For as it is true that 'greatest number' might easily become the 'majority of those who voted for me', the majority of the ruling party's supporters (whether or not these were so much as a bare majority of the political community), so it is also true that where 'happiness' is an objective for overall administration this somewhat vacuous concept is speedily filled with more practical considerations such as administrative efficiency, the needs of economy in administration, the programming of computers, and so on.

A free society, on the other hand, may see itself as distributing under law the means by which more people rather than fewer will be able to behave more rather than less responsibly. To distribute 'ability' in this broad sense is *not* to remove coercion, but, provided other proper steps have been taken to see that people are not coerced, such distribution enables them to live so that as persons and as community they remain free. It is difficult to make this clear without more attention to detail. This we will now give by some further thought about what 'goods' there are for the laws to distribute and how these may bear upon our social values.

'Goods'

What have educational 'goods', for example, to do first with freedom, second with justice? We postulate a community where there is a system for education and institutions paid for out of public funds. Justice demands that places be made available on

[1] As in the Benthamite formula.

some principle of relevance and satisfactory to the general principle: 'a place for each and everyone in his place'. Is this at the same time a provision for freedom? How can we be sure, in fact, that it is a provision of any value at all save the somewhat limited sense of justice as 'equal shares' (of anything available, good or bad)?

Let us first make clear why such provisions need have little or nothing to do with the increase of freedom. As the system is financed by the national exchequer, it may be directed by policies devised at governmental levels and these, in their turn (since we are supposing a nation state), will suit the ends of economic competition with other nation states. All this may be a very good thing, but that is not, now, the point.[1]

The point is that under such conditions there is no necessary reason why what is done in class-rooms from post-primary level at any rate should not be done to achieve ends which have little or nothing to do with personal liberty and autonomy. On the contrary, the Ministry of Industry and Employment working with the Ministry of Education might organize the whole scheme for the sole purpose of keeping the labour-force up to strength, with each batch of new graduates, for example, 'prefabricated' for needs foreseen a decade before and every step taken to ensure that their choices were rigidly limited by the requirements of the Ten-Year Plan.

Education could mean such an organization. As such the government could defend it by some such principle as Bentham's. It would have little or no interest in personal freedom, but, on the contrary, would take good care (for example) to see that young people did not become scientists when technologists were needed or waste the nation's time on the arts when scientists were called for in the endless economic struggle.

Principles meant to give more form to the concept of justice and at the same time relate it positively to freedom have had just such situations in mind. For instance, 'From each according to his capacity, to each according to his need'. But these have no precise, reliable application to such goods as education. On the contrary,

---

[1] There is a point here for the discussion of social values: the effect of the nation-state as subject of values upon them. But as this belongs more to thought about community we will leave it for the next part of the book.

K

some people today — in Britain, for example — are inclined to recoil from all attempts at selection for education and to regard these as unjust, thus setting aside means which have been devised for deciding such questions as what constitutes a child's capacity. Still vaguer principles such as 'equality of opportunity' are put in their place and we shall have time to look at these below in the chapter on equality.

All we seek to do at the moment is to establish that distribution of goods, as such, is no guarantee of the value of those goods nor, more precisely, of their relation to such general social values as freedom. On the other hand, where it seems just that goods should be distributed equally without regard to their value it may seem that this is a poor concept of justice.

Other goods may not seem to create the same doubts. Take the goods distributed by the Health Service and other public services. If through these services the community is distributing the materials necessary for a man to make full use of his 'free area', justice and freedom surely go hand in hand. One conceptual difficulty has already been discussed — that which comes from talking not only as if health were being distributed (a troublesome enough idea) but as if this same 'health' were a name for all possible goods including for those we would once have called 'moral'. This may be no more than slipshod speech, but it could lead to confused thought and misleading social action.

We are surely on safer ground when we think of such services as *enabling* and safer still if we are quite clear, as social servants, that what we aim to do is to enable people to stand on their own feet in possession of critical ability and able to make decisions. But to be sure of this it is necessary to repeat that in distributing the goods proposed by such services there is no necessary reason why we should also have distributed the qualities which enable men to live in one way, rather than another. If, for instance, we were to suppose that as social servants we are distributing *happiness*, we would have gone a long way off the mark, for we would then be saying that this happiness is a quality of such uniform texture and pattern that it can be cut like cloth from the bolts we keep at headquarters and distributed in equal shares to all subscribers without further ado.

Most of what people today call 'goods', however, are distributed not directly by the State or by the social services but by the distributive trades in league with industry. There need be no doubt that if many people are able to buy a lot of such goods with the least effort at regular and frequent intervals they will enjoy themselves and not care too much about their 'mortal souls'. We could go further and agree with the cynics that if the majority most of their lives could go on buying most of what they wanted provided they did not run out of wants, less and less talk would be heard of *any* social values and that this may well be the way things are going. We could agree with this for it would make no difference to the proposition we are putting: that 'goods' in these senses might best be called irrelevant to the social values and their distribution, therefore, no sort of guarantee that men would become what the values demand; at worst we might argue that, on the contrary, and as the argument shows, the more, beyond a certain point, we distribute the less likely is it that men will trouble themselves to *become*.

Up to a point, then, justice and distribution are virtually the same — so far, that is, as primary distribution goes. Beyond that point the connexion tends to get looser until beyond a further point — one we reach, perhaps, when all great extremes of poverty and wealth are reduced — the demand for further distribution or redistribution may have little more of human and social value in it than, say, the dispersal among a class of overfed children of a pound of sweets to be consumed at their leisure. The proportions, that is, may be subject to criteria acceptable to the class but the 'goods' serve rather to depress than to elevate capacity or enable fulfilment.

QUESTIONS FOR DISCUSSION

1. What makes possession good? Read Carritt, *Ethical and Political Thinking*, ch. xi; Moore, *Ethics*, ch. vii; Kant, *Fundamental Principles*, sec. i.

2. Discuss the account of justice given by Aristotle in his *Nicomachean Ethics*, bk v. Distinguish what he means by 'distributive' justice from the meaning given to the term here. (Note:

the *Ethics of Aristotle*, trans. J. A. K. Thomson, is available in Penguin Books, Penguin Classics Series, 1953.)

3. 'From each according to his capacity, to each according to his need.' Does this help at all in discussing the possibility of a just wage? Read Benn and Peters, *SP*, ch. vi; Hayek, *The Constitution of Liberty*, ch. vi.

25

The State and 'Welfare'

OUGHT the State to be the principal distributor of goods?

To put this question in a form which would give it point here some variations of emphasis should be tried. For instance: 'Ought the State to distribute *goods* to *all*?' makes a very different question from: 'Ought the *State* to distribute goods . . . ?' Imagine, for instance, asking the first of these two variations on the original question in the kind of city we depicted at the beginning of Chapter 19. Where many struggle to survive while a few live in luxury the question, put like that, seems morally offensive and politically superfluous. (That is to assume nothing about the economics of so-called 'redistribution'.)[1] But then in saying this we are also taking for granted that the goods are those needed for bare survival and the distribution, therefore, what we called in the last chapter primary distribution. Making the question mean this — that is, a question about the duty of the State in protecting the lives of the people — is to make it one hardly worth debating in a book of this kind. For the only alternative in a community where plainly no free association of just men is taking care of the poor is a State which concerns itself only with the well-to-do and ignores the interests of a majority. Here at least we agreed with the utilitarians — that the State ought in justice to care for the many as well as for the few.

But when we ask, 'Ought the *State* to distribute goods . . .' and when in addition we take into account what we meant just now by secondary distribution — going well beyond subsistence, that is, toward equality — then this is a different matter. That it *is* a

---

[1] See Hayek, *The Constitution of Liberty*, part ii, ch. 15 and part iii, and, by the same writer, *The Road to Serfdom* (Routledge, 1944); but compare C. A. R. Crosland, *The Future of Socialism* (London, 1956), and R. H. Tawney, *Equality* (London, 1931).

different matter is clear enough, but the difference is easily
obscured by making the State responsible for such vague and
essentially personal matters as happiness. Here we shall take up
two aspects of Statism, meaning by 'Statism' here the political
philosophy which regards the State as the best agent for all or
nearly all social goods. The first of these aspects will be the
primarily political question about the implications for State power
of its welfare functions; the second will be a broader, social
question about the place the State might be said to occupy in the
construction of a 'just society'.

Welfare and power

... the greed of the State finds justification in the failure of the
intermediate bodies either to do well what they used to do well, or to
find functions in the modern world to replace those which were once
their justification.[1]

If the power of the State is criticized, in other words, it may today
claim that it has acquired this power simply in order to do what
men, freely, have failed to do. The quotation also helps us to make
clear a distinction often neglected by classical social philosophy —
the distinction between the State and 'other bodies' and therefore
the distinction between the State, a community such as the nation
(too often identified with the State), and the 'society' which may
be thought of as wider than the community the State governs.

But the important, distinguishing characteristic of the State for
our purposes is the power it organizes and deploys. For it is the
relation between this power and the modern, welfare functions of
the State which must be constantly examined. In the Preface to
this book it was suggested that in some sense social service
represents a contemporary — and perhaps temporary — distribution of social power so that the business of constructing human
relations and managing social affairs is shared among a large
number of bodies other than those of the Civil Service. This is true
and to reflect on this is a necessary discipline for people who need
to be reminded of their responsibilities as social servants. It is a
truth, however, which now calls for some modification.

In the first place, the power of the social services despite
powerful professional associations (such as teachers' unions,

[1] D. W. Brogan, preface to Bertrand de Jouvenel's *Power* (Hutchinson, 1948).

medical boards,[1] and the like) has to be assessed with an eye to their subordination to central government. Just what this amounts to it is not for us to say, but where funds for the services are provided by the central exchequer, where the social servant is on the pay roll of the State, let alone where there is a direct hierarchical relation between the responsible officers in the service and the Civil Service, it would be wrong to take for granted that we have in the social services 'other bodies' than the State and therefore efficient checks to its power.

In the second place salutary as it is to cure ourselves of thinking of a government as 'Them', so evading responsibility for government in a democratic society, it would be disastrous if we forgot that the State is *power* of a sort which distinguishes it from any other body within its regime. A British Cabinet, for instance, can propose legislation with very little fear of contradiction; the Exchequer can make or withdraw funds and so set up and break down any number of enterprises. The government and the Civil Service can enlist the ambitions and personal interests of men who will find it hard to question policy or criticize decision at the risk of their careers. No modern Western government is likely to provoke a rebellion requiring the use of armed force to put it down; but that is partly because no such government needs to — its power is much greater and much more subtly deployed than in the days when such needs did arise.

State power of this kind owes a great deal to the role of the State in welfare. Not only are the social services more and more instruments of the State, less and less the function of churches and other bodies; dependence upon the State's services increases with every extension. While it is true that we have to depend on each other if we are to make the most of our possibilities, it is also true that where so many depend upon one central body (the powerful State) we cannot take for granted that the State will continue to respect personal liberty, personal dignity if this is not insisted upon by its subjects.

Bertrand de Jouvenel notes that the growth in State power is accompanied by growth in the scale of war, in the numbers of those mustered for war.

---

[1] 'Medical boards' is meant as a covering term for all medical professional organizations.

It follows that, in the very act of handing over more of ourselves to the State, no matter how benevolent a face it wears today, we may be fostering tomorrow's war and ensuring that it will be to the last one as was the last one to the wars of the Revolution.[1]

This raises the question of the State as a concept of community and to this we shall return in Part Four. We do not have to accept de Jouvenel's prognosis; but we may agree that the State's welfare service does entail 'handing over more of ourselves to this powerful, central bureaucracy'. Such an increase in the power of the State does mean that one day we may find ourselves at the mercy of men whose mastery of its institutions leaves us with no way of repudiating policies repugnant to us.

Welfare and socialism

Socialism need not mean the same as 'Statism'. We may note, however, the way in which Socialism dealt with one constructive attempt to check the growing power of the State in the name of socialist principles: the attempt, that is, of guild socialism to plan for what was thought a more just society through co-operative effort and decentralized direction without increasing the power of the State. G. D. H. Cole, prime mover in the guild socialist movement, once wrote as follows:

I am neither a Communist nor a Social Democrat because I regard both as creeds of centralization and bureaucracy, whereas I feel sure that a Socialist society that is to be true to its equalitarian principles of human brotherhood must rest on the widest possible diffusion of power and responsibility, so as to enlist the active participation of as many as possible of its citizens in the tasks of democratic self-government.[2]

Within the socialist movement Cole represented what was called 'political pluralism' against the collectivism which finally

[1] B. de Jouvenel, op. cit., p. 23.
[2] G. D. H. Cole, 'Socialism and Fascism', in *A History of Socialist Thought*, vol. v. For a general survey of socialist thought see Alexander Gray, *The Socialist Tradition* (Longmans, Green, 1946). Here is a select list of works on guild socialism: A. J. Penty, *Restoration of the Guild System* (1906); Hobson and Orage, *National Guilds* (1912); G. D. H. Cole, *Self Government in Industry*; R. H. Tawney, *The Acquisitive Society*; G. C. Field, *Guild Socialism*; N. Carpenter, *Guild Socialism*. The movement has been compared with industrial unionism in the U.S.A., and with Syndicalism in France. See Alexander Gray, op. cit. ch. xvi, and H. J. Laski, *Grammar of Politics*, 4th ed. (Allen & Unwin, 1941), part i, ch. 2.

triumphed in the British Labour Party. The issue was that of the supremacy of the political machine. Industries were to be owned by the whole community, but more immediately by the 'workers by hand and brain'. The pluralists wanted to replace the State by a federation of guilds. Democracy, it was argued, could only be real if it was functional and by this was meant that government should be specifically related to the main activities of society not concentrated in a central bureaucratic organization.

We cannot now conduct a proper examination of the arguments involved in this issue but we may take note of the question raised and of the possibilities alluded to. For socialists more than most have magnified the power of the State, asking us to accept their preference for State ownership, State management, State direction, and State distribution of goods and services. No doubt men born in a class kept out of political power for generations can be excused for not wanting to deprive the central authority of power once they had grasped it. On the contrary they want to increase it. And this is still easier to understand when we recall the innocent self-trust of some earlier working-class movements. Fostered very often by benevolent — or guilty — middle-class leaders the mood of many early socialists was that of an innocence, a purity which could be trusted with the powers of the State not only as these had been in the bad old days but greatly enlarged to suit the noble aims and purposes of good men. In Britain socialism owed much to Nonconformist Christianity and there was a time when rousing Christian hymns, puritanical discipline, and evangelical enthusiasm spilled over from the chalice of religion into the earthenware of the working-class movement.[1]

> I will not cease from mental fight
> Nor shall my sword sleep in my hand,
> Till we have built Jerusalem
> In England's green and pleasant land.[2]

It was hard, then, to disentangle the sought-after power of a socialist State from the coming of the Kingdom of God on earth.

[1] For a fascinating fictional impression of the working-class movement in Britain see the novel by Howard Spring entitled *Fame is the Spur* (Collins, 1940).

[2] William Blake (1757–1827); 'Jerusalem' (from which the quotation is taken) is said to be an exposition of Blake's theory of imagination, 'the real and eternal world of which the Vegetable Universe is but a faint shadow'.

The passion for justice aroused by the evils of those times could not be expected to pause and reflect before storming the defences of the State — not to destroy but to possess and expand its powers.[1]

Yet it was the function of the State to protect the people and the Socialists were right to claim that throughout our Western civilization this function was being neglected. The 'failure of the intermediate bodies' to deal justly with the people was the occasion for the State's extension of power. Moreover, there is no reason why such 'intermediate bodies' (churches, trades unions, industrial organizations) should not pose as great a threat to personal liberty as the State itself and one of the functions of the State is precisely to prevent such threats. But both arguments point back to a question which it is our business here to ask again and again — the question of what kind of people in what kind of society can limit the power of the State not only by institutional checks and the reign of law but by progressively rendering its coercive power and its social interference unnecessary.

The 'just society'

For the major objection we have to statism is that its advocates encourage people to expect the State to do for them what can in fact only be done by the people, freely, in the way they conduct their affairs in personal relations and in free association. We will make this point now by reflection on the notion of a just society.

Wages, profits, pensions, the distribution of the national wealth — these are things we usually have in mind today when talking about justice in society. 'Secondary distribution' has to do

[1] For one account of reasons why the power of the state should be limited see J. S. Mill, *On Liberty*, ch. v. Note also the following quotation from *Our Partnership* by Beatrice Webb, herself an ardent socialist, passionately concerned to end destitution. '. . . the fact that sick and unemployed persons were entitled [under Lloyd George's reforms of 1908–11] to money incomes without any corresponding obligation to get well and keep well, or to seek to keep employment, seemed to us likely to encourage malingering and a disinclination to work for their livelihood.' For an account of Beatrice Webb which makes her social concern clear see Margaret Cole, *Beatrice Webb* (Longmans, Green, 1945), chs ix and x, and note John Burns's interesting comment that Lloyd George's schemes (borrowed from Bismarck's Prussia) had 'dished the Webbs' (ibid., p. 106). On the other side it can be argued that the State broadens responsibility by the machinery it provides for meeting human need. This, however, must surely depend on the amount of actual participation it provides as compared with such nominal, so-called participation as is made available for the majority through income-tax and insurance contributions.

primarily with such things: not with goods as such but with the means of exchange, the currency with which we can purchase the things we want, or can be persuaded to want. But if we try to debate such a question as 'the just wage', we run into insuperable difficulties. We run into such difficulties, that is, as soon as we attempt to reach a decision by weighing the value of one job against another whether by saying what it is worth to the community or by what it has cost the worker to qualify or by estimating the amount of effort the worker has to put into his work, or the 'responsibilities' he carries.

How, for instance, do you rate the value of a signalman to the community against that of a physician? How assess the worth of a pop-singer by comparison with a poet? What 'actually happens' is not our business; we are concerned with what ought to happen and little progress can be made by this line of argument. But suppose we try to measure the efforts a vocation costs the worker? A production graph would help in factories and farms, but 'payment by results' for teaching has been tried and found wanting while sheer quantity in novel-writing or any other forms of art will not do at all. Besides, someone will always point out that some of the work which calls for most effort also brings the most satisfaction and therefore (they might argue) 'needs' less monetary reward.

This is not, by the way, a very good argument, for the satisfaction a man has from his work is a private concern and has nothing to do with what I ought to pay him for enjoying the result.

The question remains very troublesome because it seems to many that some workers stand virtually above or outside the law because through powerful organizations they can force their will upon the rest, while others may have no such organization and a professional ethic, at that, which deters them from taking coercive action. There is no justice in it when workers in a public utility can force the public to increase their wages while nurses in hospitals are unlikely to leave their posts, however unsuitable their conditions.

But the difficulty becomes greater, not less, the more we grow used to demanding State action to bring ease to such injustices. The State would be fulfilling its proper function if it took steps to bring an end to coercive acts by workers or employers designed to force an increase in income by depriving the public of services. But if asked to remove all felt inequalities of income by general laws, *who knows* what the State, by such laws, would also be removing? Yet this is what men seem ready to demand when exasperated by their inability to see a way 'through' the so-called injustices of wage differentials. 'Better', they seem to say, 'to get rid of all the "infinite variety" than that I should continue to be teased by my neighbour's bigger house, larger car, and better dressed wife.' If this is indeed what lies behind much talk of a 'just society', then we may be in danger of sacrificing all values for one — that of not being envious, and there are cheaper ways of achieving that end.

A 'just society' is probably a mirage unless it means a 'society of just men', but let us consider the possibilities.

Each of us, partly by his own choice, takes his place in a profession which places him on a level in the wage-structure agreed upon as appropriate to his age, qualifications, and experience. If the rules relating to salary and other conditions are observed and if the rules were known when he contracted to enter the profession, a measure of justice will be seen to be done. We may note in passing, however, that it is not so easy to define the worker's *obligations* as it is to make clear his rights. The *quality* of his work at any rate is a difficult subject to bring within the scope of a contract of employment. But when the State tries to insist upon this — as presumably during certain critical phases in the modern history of Soviet Russia and Communist China — there is a drastic curtailment of individual liberty, a fearful increase in coercion. In a word, the quality of work must in the last analysis rest with the worker yet it is upon this quality as well as — in some cases — upon quantity that we must rely for the communal wealth which the 'just society' is expected to distribute. This is one instance of how appeals to the State can mislead: we cannot ask the State to distribute what poor quality or inadequate effort has failed to produce. The State, for example, may provide places in an educational institution; but only teachers and students can determine the quality of the work done and therefore the value of what is distributed.

Within the profession, the occupational group, nevertheless, justice of a sort may be done as each takes his place in the series. Between the professions, however, or between any one of them and the community apart from them, what can mitigate the injustice of sheer force on the one hand, the prejudice and ignorance of 'supply and demand' on the other? State action can check coercion but only up to a point: when, for instance, the members of a union call for the dismissal of a fellow worker who does not wish to join their union it is very difficult for the State to intervene without being accused of 'infringement of rights'. If the workers have no 'sense of justice' sufficient to correct such abuses themselves, the society in which they work will be that much less than just. As for the 'prejudice and ignorance' of 'supply and demand' — that 'principle', we mean, which will permit some wholly worthwhile activities to go virtually unrewarded while the less worthy but better publicized gain high prizes — any State action to correct this would lead to devastating incursions into private liberties and such an assumption of power to dictate or direct 'tastes' as could hardly be accepted in a free society.

In short, the removal of all injustices by State action is a chimaera, but the attempt to do this leads to swollen State powers, invasions of liberty, and, perhaps, to new injustices.[1]

Yet this does not mean that we must leave things as they are. It means, rather, that we must give more time and thought and effort to moral action and to this as the criterion of State interference.

Justice is a quality not of social arrangements, but of the human will.[2]

Surely of both, but primarily of the first.

... what we should be concerned with is that the whole ceaseless process of change should be increasingly permeated by the quality of

[1] See further B. de Jouvenel, *Sovereignty* (*De la souveraineté*, Paris, 1955), ch. ix. On the 'closed shop' and the role of the State consider, for example, the recent case of Rookes *v*. Barnard in the United Kingdom in which the employee sued the union officials successfully in the High Court for loss of employment which he suffered through their action when he refused to join the union. Subsequently the Labour Government of 1964 undertook legislation to see that the union officials could not be brought to court again in such a way. (The Queen's Speech, Nov. 1964, promised legislation 'to give workers and their representatives the protection necessary for freedom of industrial negotiation', but it did *not* undertake to protect workers from repressive policies such as those which gave rise to this case.)

[2] De Jouvenel, op. cit., p. 165 of the English translation.

justice in our individual wills. Every immediate field of choice open to us, in either our private or public capacity, offers us opportunity for the exercise of justice. Whenever we miss this opportunity we feed the sum of social injustice — a sum which it is comfortable but untrue to regard as the product of some single institution or mode of arrangement.[1]

The difficulty is both to press for social action and for political reform and at the same time remember not only that all this is useless without morality but that in making such efforts we more than anyone else have been committed to being moral. The hard fact is that we cannot delegate justice-making to political representatives or public corporations, any more than we can escape the obligation to see that such persons and bodies act justly. Justice *is* primarily moral action and moral action is nothing more nor less than the willing pursuit of the general good.

Even so, to be satisfactory, and to persist in its unending development, moral action has to be informed, and obstacles to its development have to be removed. Very few people indeed can become self-forgetting saints; but many many more are capable of much more willing co-operation with others than we get at the moment if the right kind of social action is taken both for their education and for their freedom. To increase the sum of justice we have to increase the number of just men or the number of their just actions; but in addition to our personal moral activity we can do this by concerted, systematic efforts to relate private to public good and by using the power of the State not to increase reliance upon it but, on the contrary, to turn every available institution and organization, including the social services, into *enabling* rather than protective agencies.

QUESTIONS FOR DISCUSSION

1. Assemble arguments for and against the State's role as distributor of goods. (Study the references in the text and footnotes which bear upon this.)
2. Study the quotation from G. D. H. Cole on p. 282 and

[1] Ibid.

discuss this as a comment on the educational function of political institutions. (See also the quotation from Beatrice Webb in a footnote to p. 284.)

3. Discuss the Rookes *v*. Barnard case referred to in a footnote on p. 287 in terms of (*a*) the liberty of the individual, (*b*) justice.

26

Equality

THE figure of Justice on top of the Central Criminal Court in London is blindfolded; she has a sword in one hand, a pair of scales in the other. These symbols of coercion on the one hand, assessment and selection on the other, have little popular appeal today. If this is 'justice' no wonder that since the French Revolution we have preferred in the trinity of social values to name 'equality' instead. How would we, today, symbolize equality? How replace the figure on the Central Criminal Court? A man of medium height, perhaps, of sallow skin, bespectacled, in a dun-coloured suit or mechanic's denims, a clinical thermometer in one hand, a Rorschach test in the other? Equality would have nothing to do with swords (or laws) and its single aim would be to create a society in which all placed in the scales would weigh the same and (by the abolition of awkward measures) none be found wanting.

Both freedom and justice are in some sense demands for equality. What we have to do is distinguish between uses of 'equality' which agree with these other values and those that do not. We expect to find — as in the discussion on freedom — certain 'positive equalities' but also a general concept of equality; but we also expect this will lead us to conclude that the relation between the particular and the general here is an undesirable one. On the contrary, the positive equalities derive their value from freedom or from justice and lose it if they are drawn up into some general egalitarian ideal.

Isonomy
'Equality before the law' is a misleading phrase inasmuch as it is difficult to know precisely what it means. The ancient Greek concept of *isonomia*, however, is easier to define and

is probably what 'equality before the law' ought to say. As Professor Hayek shows,[1] we can turn to Aristotle's *Politics*, where in the Third Book, Aristotle contrasts all forms of government which depend on the *will* of a ruler (whether it is a monarchy or a democracy which entrusts administration to one person) with those where the government is regarded as 'guardians, and servants of the laws . . .'

. . . and it is more proper that law should govern than any one of the citizens.[2]

Elsewhere Aristotle relates this rule of law to democracy.

The most pure democracy is that which is so called principally from that equality which prevails in it: for this is what the law in that state directs; that the poor shall be in no greater subjection than the rich; nor that the supreme power shall be lodged with either of these, but that both shall share it.[3]

But when everything is determined by a majority of votes and 'not by a law', there democracy is not, on Aristotle's argument, good government at all.[4]

Isonomy, the rule of laws and not of men, or the subordination of all alike to known laws, seems to us necessary both for freedom and for justice. If men, on the ground that the majority have elected them to a legislative assembly of representatives, make what laws they please without regarding themselves as under a necessity to treat long-standing, known laws with respect, then by whatever name such a State is called here is a decline in justice and a threat to liberty. In this sense 'equality' is implied by the social values.

The opposite of isonomy is arbitrary rule — rule, that is, by will or pleasure. If one's life is governed by the caprice, the whims, the ambitions of others whether close relations, dictators, or a dominant party in the legislative assembly, freedom is curtailed; one is subject to coercion; 'for who could be free when every other man's humour might domineer over him?'[5] Such a situation is comparable to what happens in personal life at the mercy of uncontrolled impulses or unconscious drives; this is why classical

---

[1] Hayek, *The Constitution of Liberty*, pp. 164 f.
[2] Aristotle, *Politics*, bk iii, 1287*a*.   [3] Ibid. 1291*b*.
[4] Ibid. 1292*a*.   [5] John Locke, *Second Treatise on Civil Government*, sec. 57.

social philosophers are so fond of discussing moral experience side by side with politics: in both it makes sense to talk of the 'rule of law' as a good.

When we turn, however, from isonomy, from the 'rule of law' in politics and in every association to other uses of 'equality' it is not so easy to see what values are served and still harder to see why the aims in view are called 'equalities'.

Equal opportunity

The difficulty is to set up here such a principle without asking 'opportunity for what?'. Immediately we do this we come face to face either with objectives too general and vague to mean much or with others more precise but hardly proper to egalitarians. Thus if you say 'opportunity for happiness' this sounds very pleasant if one does not enquire too closely into its meaning or ask in what particular field of action it is expected to be useful. If, on the other hand, you make it more explicit and say 'opportunity to make money, achieve a position, acquire status', then you are likely to offend egalitarians as well as to raise all sorts of questions about merit in relation to function, justice in distribution of wealth, and so forth.

No doubt the best field in which to employ such a principle is that of education. The best form to give it is, 'opportunity to develop skills, capacities', and so on. Even here there are difficulties. Let us suppose we play safe and aim at 'equalizing' opportunities — aiming, that is, at removing obvious and severe inequalities rather than at a dead level called 'equality'. We may find it much *easier* to employ our principle by removing the superior advantages some enjoy than we find it to raise the general level of educational opportunity. Suppose we decide that a child whose parents are more articulate and who talk to him give him an advantage over children whose parents hardly ever talk to him or have much less to talk about. We may apply the principle of equal opportunity by making quite sure that the first child is not given the chance to do better than others in school, or we may try to provide facilities which will give to other children some of the advantage his parents have given him. Very likely we will take the first course because it most readily suggests itself and seems 'just'.

Such a course, however, also illustrates what happens when interests of this sort are planned 'from above' with no reference to such social values as that of responsible freedom: those most able and willing to share a quality of life are not *forbidden* but are shown that they must not expect any advantage from this or even that in doing so they have tried to 'steal a march on' others whether those others may be regarded as less fortunate, less able, or merely less willing to try.

Of course the criteria we employ in education are man-made and therefore adaptable to our shifting scales of value. There is every reason why we should review them in order to make sure that they do not discriminate against some by offering opportunities on conditions which may seem irrelevant or inappropriate to the overall aims of education. If, however, we find ourselves lowering standards for no better reason than that higher standards prove selective and make a number of people feel (quite rightly) that they are not in some respects as good as others, then it is time to ask what the equal opportunities we are providing in education are opportunities *for*. If in the name of equality I invite a hundred guests to a feast meant for ten, it is likely that the ninety will feel less aggrieved — until they find there is not enough to eat.

Learning, it is true, differs from eating in that the 'food' is inexhaustible and has not to be shared out, like the loaves and the fishes, in hope that a miracle will make it go round. But national education is not simply distributing 'learning': what has to be shared out is space, equipment, teaching-time, and teachers. It may be that one teacher is as good as another once he has his diploma. It may be that much teaching can be done by automata. All we are asking is that a principle, such as equal opportunity, should not be bandied about as if its intentions were self-evident and its alliance with freedom and justice unquestionable.

This principle makes much more sense when we amplify it and use it against the injustice of *irrelevant* principles of selection or privilege. If it were known, for instance, that success in the Diplomatic Service depended not on intelligence, intellectual qualifications, integrity, good work primarily or alone but also upon, say, a private income and 'friends in the right quarter', then you might decide that these last were irrelevant to the needs of the Service. The principle of equal opportunity could be invoked against them. So with all nepotism, all place-making: the best argument against such things is that they commit injustice by imposing irrelevant bars to ambition. Yet even here the matter is not always so straightforward as those frustrated in their ambitions might choose to think. Who would say, for example, that — all other things being equal — in a choice between two well qualified candidates for a post it is always 'wrong' to select the one you know; for your personal knowledge may be of qualities wholly relevant, knowledge, none the less, which you could not have of an unknown. In any case, what constitutes or does not constitute relevant conditions is an important question in all more detailed discussion of justice and not one to be brushed aside with a naïve reference to 'equality', let alone a reliance upon such menacing sentiments as envy, or such ambiguous guides as fear.

Parity of esteem

One of the most telling phrases coined in the fight for equality in British education was that which in the years following the Second World War demanded 'parity of esteem' for all schools in the State system. The phrase is useful not so much for its inane possibilities (never intended by those who used it, of course) but for what it reveals of the demand for justice.

Everyone wants his mead of respect for his fellows. Still more surely none of us will suffer contempt a moment longer than we can help. It does not occur to most of us, however, even in our moods of deepest negative self-feeling, to go about the world requiring people to respect us. Respect, esteem, to say nothing of admiration, cannot be freely accorded save perhaps in such polite rituals as hand-clapping or the presentation of parting gifts to life-long servants. As feelings or attitudes, that is, respect, esteem, and admiration are aroused by what those who feel or manifest them regard as merit. Therefore the use of this phrase in educational polemics must be taken to mean a demand that all schools do meritorious work, however varied, and no one could quarrel with that.

Yet, schools apart for the moment, it is possible that what certain critics of democracy once prophesied is coming to pass and we are including in our concept of justice a right to equal respect; and to equal respect not as men, as 'ends in the kingdom of ends', but in the sense of not permitting some to be respected or esteemed more than others.

Alexis de Tocqueville found that the passion for equality increased with the growth of equal conditions. He saw the advantages to which this passion could lead but warned men also of the dangers.

... the more complete is ... uniformity, the more insupportable does the sight of ... difference become. ... This never-dying, ever-kindling hatred, which sets a democratic people against the smallest privileges, is peculiarly favourable to the gradual concentration of all political rights in the hands of ... the State alone.[1]

In order to escape intolerable distinctions the democracy, he argues, would far rather hand over its freedom to a tyrannical state which would at least deprive all equally of distinction. Already in America, he claimed:

Every individual is ... supposed to be as well informed, as virtuous, and as strong as any of his fellow-citizens ...[2]

... although the capacities of men are widely different ... they are submitted to the same method of treatment ...[3]

He found what he called a 'manly and lawful passion for equality' which tended to 'elevate the humble to the rank of the great'; but there was also a 'depraved taste for equality',

which impels the weak to attempt to lower the powerful to their own level, and reduces men to prefer equality in slavery to inequality with freedom.[4]

No doubt de Tocqueville believed there was a connexion between this and a characteristic of American education at the time — 'primary instruction', he admitted, was 'within the reach of everybody' but 'superior instruction is scarcely to be obtained by any'. On the facts of the matter we can hardly adjudicate but it is the passion we recognize — the passion to admit no superiority

---

[1] Alexis de Tocqueville, *Democracy in America*, trans. Henry Reeves (World's Classics, abridged, 1946), p. 555. See chs xxiv and xxix of the same work.

[2] Ibid., p. 61.   [3] Ibid., pp. 48 f.

[4] Ibid., p. 46. It may be interesting to compare some of de Tocqueville's comments with a contemporary view of what equality of opportunity could mean in the United States. See J. Barzun, *The House of Intellect* (Secker & Warburg, 1959), pp. 21 f.

rather than feel oneself in some respects inferior. Elsewhere de Tocqueville argues that equal conditions put an end to simple faith in the judgement of superior men but bring about excessive trust in public opinion together with a loss of confidence in one's individual judgement.[1] John Stuart Mill, influenced by de Tocqueville, wrote of a growing need 'for protection against the tyranny of prevailing opinion and feeling'.[2]

... even in what people do for pleasure, conformity is the first thing thought of; they like in crowds; they exercise choice only among things commonly done...[3]

which is, of course, one sure way to 'parity of esteem'.

The general average of mankind are not only moderate in intellect, but also moderate in inclinations: they have no tastes or wishes strong enough to incline them to do anything unusual, and they consequently do not understand those who have.[4]

Writing more recently and of countries other than Britain or the United States, the Spanish philosopher Ortega y Gasset speaks of the 'mass' which 'does not wish to share life with those who are not of it' but 'has a deadly hatred of all that is not itself'.[5] He distinguishes this 'mass man' from the 'excellent man' by saying that the excellent man 'makes great demands on himself' but the mass man 'makes no demands on himself, but contents himself with what he is and is delighted with himself'.[6] Whether or not this writer and the other critics of equality overstate their case we do well to have in mind the likelihood that in demanding 'parity of esteem', explicitly or indirectly, we are dignifying with such names as 'justice' nothing more valuable than the wish to enjoy without effort, not indeed the respect of our fellows, but the pain of being forced to recognize that some men are worth more than we are whether we have the grace to admit it or not.

General equality?

Equal burdens, equal rights — another way, perhaps, of putting 'equality before the law' — is not the way in which we usually

[1] De Tocqueville, op. cit., p. 297.

[2] J. S. Mill, *On Liberty* (Everyman's edition, under the title 'Utilitarianism'), p. 68.

[3] Ibid., p. 119.   [4] Ibid., p. 126.

[5] Ortega y Gasset, *The Revolt of the Masses* (Unwin Books, paperback edition 1961; first published in Spain 1930), p. 58.

[6] Ibid., p. 47.

hear an 'egalitarian' society depicted today. Wages, as we saw, may increase not in accordance with the quantity or quality of work done but under coercion: a situation as unjust as one in which a man is made wealthy at birth by inheritance. The very mood in which vague demands for general equality are framed is one which favours relief from obligations together with extension of rights. 'Distributive justice' is more a cry for distribution than for justice. All these are reasons why it is difficult to see just what a general concept of equality could intend as a social value coequal with freedom, justice, and community. Let us consider one or two possibilities.

First, 'social equality'. By this we are to understand the removal of distinctions within a community between different sectors. It is easy to see at once how this can be a viable principle if it is part of what we have said already about justice as the 'rule of law'. But put like that, simply as the 'removal of distinctions', 'social equality' can be meaningless if not positively harmful. We have no difficulty, for example, in agreeing that distinctions between groups in the same community based upon skin pigmentation, race, or religion *can* be unjust, but this depends, surely, upon the nature of the distinction made, or, more precisely, upon the field of social life in which it is made and the consequences for those distinguished *against*.

Thus Jews distinguish themselves from Christians by going to the synagogue on Saturday and not to church on Sunday. Is this unjust? On the contrary we would consider it unjust not to permit such distinctions and illiberal, inasmuch as this would diminish the varieties of experience and deny to such groups freedom to make their acts their own. But if in a Christian community Jews are denied the protection of the law because they are Jews, or are called upon to bear a heavier burden of taxation, military service or other public obligation, again because they are Jews, then this is unjust. In short it is not a distinction between groups which is unjust, but a distinction which the groups themselves do not will but which is imposed upon them at the will of others.

What of 'class distinctions'? 'Social equality' is particularly bitter about these. Now a class may distinguish itself primarily by its wealth or primarily by its cultural interests, its manners, its morals, and its general habits of life. Leaving aside for the moment the dust-raising distinction of wealth, we may agree that this is not necessarily the primary distinction and the others may even be insisted upon more violently by an impoverished gentry. Is this unjust? Would it not, on the contrary, be unjust to deny such a class the right to distinguish itself in these ways if it chooses?

It would be a different matter, of course, if the distinguishing characteristics of a group or class were insisted upon in such a way that they intruded seriously upon the enjoyment by others of *their* distinction; but it is surely not reasonable to say that this is the case when all we have is one group envying or grudging or even aping the habits of another.

Where extreme wealth goes with other class distinctions and more particularly where this leads to a monopoly of high office or political power this is another matter, but it has to do directly with justice and freedom and is misrepresented if we attack it in the language of 'social equality'.

This brings us, secondly, to 'economic equality', though most of what needs to be said on this has been said before. In view of all that was said earlier about distribution and the difficulties of determining just rewards we may confine ourselves here to two possibilities: either a demand for *less inequality* or in all seriousness a demand for total and absolute removal of all economic distinctions between men.

The first of these alternatives suits the concept of justice as we introduced it at the beginning of Part Three. But there are grave problems none the less. Economists have to ask whether it makes sense to talk at all of the 'redistribution of wealth'.[1] Many western nations since the beginning of this century have seen what appears to be widespread and immensely beneficial economic equalizing as between the various classes in their societies. It would be odd none the less if such levelling did not also have consequences both unforeseen and undesired, since this is the nature of all political and social reform.

The idea of an absolute economic equality is not precisely unthinkable. The seventeenth-century Diggers in England, among others, had it in mind if their spokesman, Winstanley, is any

[1] 'Redistribution'. See F. Hayek, *The Constitution of Liberty*, ch. xx and references in footnotes.

guide.[1] The only question one wants to ask in a book on social values is why this should be thought desirable. And since the least unconvincing of the answers often takes the form of 'Communism' with implications about the value of community, it would probably be better to say more about this in Part Four when 'community' is the theme.

Rousseau held[2] — or seemed to hold — that men were born equal or that at least their natural inequalities were complicated and added to by social conventions instead of society doing as it ought to have done — mitigating the inequalities of nature. As an approach to the discussion of inequality this may make more sense than the arguments that some naturists put forward to show that men were 'naturally equal'; for the truth is that when we try to conceive of men as naturally equal, equal, that is, quite apart from what society may do or not do, we seldom get much further than Antiphon the Seer.[3] He seems to have got no further in his concept of man than the need for eating and breathing.

Here is the danger of all excessive insistence upon equality — it is a *reducing* concept, not so much a value as a catalyst of values; it requires men to shed their distinctions or dissemble them in order to find, perhaps, a bald and naked animal condition of 'togetherness'. Justice, on the other hand, provides for the free pursuit of a variety of objectives and therefore of levels of attainment, seeking only to maintain an equilibrium, not to remove the very distinctions which it is its function to preserve. Uniformity lends itself to totalitarian rule; but justice favours equality in the sense of the rule of law. Justice, it is true, can be motivated by resentment or even vengeance but equality can easily be inspired by envy and envy (whatever its effects upon the envious) is not usually tolerant and therefore not amenable to freedom. Equality has its place in the scale of social values, but not at the top and only under the careful scrutiny of superior values such as responsible freedom and justice. As for its place with regard to 'community' this will concern us in the following chapters.

[1] On Winstanley see above, Chapter 12, p. 132.

[2] See the introduction to Rousseau's *Social Contract* and also his *Discourse on the Origin of Inequality*.

[3] Antiphon: this is far from adequate as a commentary on this Sophist's views. See M. Untersteiner, *The Sophists*, trans. K. Freeman (Oxford, Blackwell, 1954), ch. xiii and especially p. 252.

QUESTIONS FOR DISCUSSION

1. Read the references to Isonomy in the footnotes on p. 291.
Go back to Chapter 21, Question 2. How might majority rule
cease to be the rule of law?

2. What constitutes equal opportunity? (If we add 'for what?'
does this suggest a way of equalizing by reducing the variety of
possibilities?) Read J. Barzun, *The House of Intellect* (Secker &
Warburg, 1959), chs ii, iii.

3. When would demands for equality be likely to conflict with
liberty? Read Alexis de Tocqueville, *Democracy in America*,
ed. H. S. Commager, abridged ed. (O.U.P., World's Classics 496,
1946), chs xxiv, xxix; Mill, *On Liberty*, ch. iii.

Part Four

COMMUNITY

27

Social Animals

'Freedom' can be made to sound like an attempt to escape our relations; 'justice' like making use of them. In our own analysis we have tried to show that neither concept will take us far if we do not make use of moral language to show that both values *implicate* us in human relations. Freedom from coercion, for instance, not only leaves us to make our own decisions and make them our own, but all lessening of coercive rule is made possible only by an increase in willing, reasonable co-operation.[1] Justice, similarly: as a system of rights or demands upon the community it ceases to make sense without a system of obligations just as repeated withdrawals from a bank account would cease to make sense if no fresh deposits were made. In these ways the two values we have been discussing not only imply a certain kind of society, a certain arrangement of our relations, they also require a positive and willing approach to community.

Yet this could still mean no more than the setting up of social machinery for the achievement of personal ends and this has seemed to many people an inadequate account of what society should mean. Quite apart from the doubt whether individualism makes false assumptions about the nature of society, there are many who feel the need to think of the community as a reality

[1] The jurisprudence of L. Duguit early in the century forms an interesting link with the discussion on law in Part Three. Duguit postulated a natural law of interdependence. He dismissed the traditional doctrine of sovereignty and all theories which personified the state and argued that the true state is an agency for the performance of public service. Because of the growing number and complexity of the public services these can only be carried out by decentralization and federal syndicalism. This interest in the future of the public services should be compared with the point of view taken in the Introduction to this book. For an outline of Duguit's theories see C. K. Allen, *Law in the Making*, pp. 574 ff.

with value in itself in addition to or apart from the services it renders to individuals. The writings of Rousseau, Edmund Burke, some work of poets like Wordsworth and Coleridge, in a different way the work of historians like Herder and Lessing together with the Romantics who were influenced by them may all be said to have had an interest in common: the community as the subject of values. The German Romantics, for instance, objected to social contract theory on the ground that it

failed to describe social relations adequately because, in their view, it rested on one of two false assumptions, viz. either that society and the state were not identical or that society was created by human artifice. Either view, if adopted, would weaken the power of authority and eventually promote chaos.[1]

Now the fact that demands for community have sometimes been made in *deliberate* opposition to theories serving the other two social values we have discussed shows the dangers we face here. Some of these will be described later when we talk about 'models of community'. Here we raise a difficulty peculiar to our times — that which has been created by general acceptance of what sociology is often taken to mean by human 'sociality'.

The difficulty is that generalizations about sociality *because* they are often used to oppose individualism, may be confused with value-judgements about community and we have to show now how this can happen and why it matters.

[1] H. S. Reiss, *The Political Thought of the German Romantics, 1793–1815* (Oxford, Blackwell, 1955), p. 4. For Coleridge and Wordsworth in relation to Burke see A. Cobban, *Edmund Burke and the Revolt against the Eighteenth Century* (Allen & Unwin, 1960). Johann G. von Herder (1744–1803), the German philosopher who inspired the literary revolution known as *Sturm und Drang*, listened to Kant's lectures. He undertook the study of all human history as a basis for directing future development. The dominating feature of his work is the genetic or historical idea. He is regarded as a primary source of German nationalism but not of the aggressive sort. Following Benjamin Franklin he advocated a 'league of humanity'. In the *Sturm und Drang* emotion is given priority over reason, but Herder stressed the moral value of literature and parted company with Goethe and Schiller on this. Gotthold E. Lessing (1729–81) was a German critic and dramatist. His work *Laokoon* is regarded as a classic in aesthetics. In his more theological work he held that no dogmatic creed is final but that every historical religion has its share in the development of mankind. Like Herder, he held that history reveals a law of progress. It is this re-creation of community through history and, in both cases, the concept of 'humanity', not to be confined to religious sects or even to the nation, which make the thought of these men relevant here.

Dependence

Let us begin with a textbook statement about sociality.

Man is dependent on society for protection, comfort, nurture, education, equipment, opportunity, and the multitude of definite services which society provides. . . . His birth in society brings with it the absolute need of society itself.[1]

There is no doubt about the authors' intentions here: in the following paragraph they refer to the 'claims of "independence" we may hear from some persons' and they then deal roundly with hermits (who are either 'mad' when they begin their careers or become so 'in the end') and they conclude:

For normal humanity must have social relationships to make life livable.[2]

As it stands this section of the book, under the heading 'man as a social animal', has put what it has to say about sociality in the form of a statement of a relation between two entities. The entities are 'man' and 'society'; the relation is one of the dependence of the first upon the second. This is what logicians would call an 'asymmetrical relation' — you cannot invert the terms of the relation: that is, the dependence of man is on society but not only is society *not* (in these lines) made dependent on man, nothing is said here about society's dependence upon anything else, though we will be able to show in a moment that all this is modified elsewhere.

There is another noticeable feature of this statement: the two entities involved in the relation are abstract forms — 'man' on the one hand, 'society' on the other. Now the beauty of such forms is that they are not pestered with concrete, empirical tests. When you speak largely of 'man' or 'society' the terms you are using are wide open and it is up to you to make of them what you will. So in this case there is nothing to stop a moderately careless reader from using 'man' to mean all those qualities he can abstract from his experience of particular men which are obviously and indubitably 'dependent' on relations with others or on social institutions, forgetting any qualities of any particular men which do not fit so easily into the argument. It is equally easy to use 'society' to mean

[1] McIver and Page, *Society: An Introductory Analysis* (Macmillan, 1962), p. 8.
[2] Ibid.

just those conditions, those relations and institutions which would seem on the face of it at any rate to cause the qualities you now mean by 'man', so that your statement — 'man is dependent on society for this and that' — will be indisputable because tautologous: not adding, that is, anything at all to our knowledge of human science but simply defining, dictionary-wise, what you are going to mean by 'man' on the one hand, 'society' on the other, and the relation of dependence presupposed in between.

Abstract forms are, of course, necessary in all human discourse and we have no reason at all to say that these authors have abused them; we are thinking now of the use to which such statements are put by others than we are of the authors' intentions. For it is one thing to say, largely, that 'man' is 'dependent on' 'society' and quite another to try saying how each Tom, Dick, or Harry of your acquaintance can be said to be dependent in specific respects upon concrete social conditions and then to say that this gives a satisfactory account of these men's behaviour.

Our quarrel here, however, is with the kind of relation such an account of sociality might suggest — one of absolute dependence of 'man' on 'society'. If you turn back a page or two in the same text, however, there is a different kind of statement.

Social beings, men, express their nature by creating and re-creating an organization which guides and controls their behaviour in myriad ways . . .[1]

Is this the same relation we were led to expect a moment ago? Surely not. To start with, we now have concretes, not abstracts: 'men', not 'man'; and 'organization', surely rather more concrete than 'society'. To go on with we have men 'creating' and 're-creating' where before they were dependent. Not that they have got away, but they are now called 'social beings' instead of beings dependent on society and we have the curious picture of creatures said elsewhere to be wholly dependent now making and remaking that which they are dependent upon but doing so by virtue of a quality which, presumably, is intrinsic to them and not itself dependent upon 'society'.

Furthermore, the 'society' we heard of in the simpler statement of dependence is now depicted as a 'system of usages and

[1] Ibid., p. 5.

procedures ever-changing ... the web of social relationships. And it is always changing'.[1] Yes. And we know who changes it: men; the same men, presumably, as those who in their abstract representation as 'man' were said to be dependent upon society, the 'society' which then seemed so definite and reliable but is now, like Heraclitean fire, ever-changing, always changing — a very difficult object indeed for the scientist to observe.

We do not quarrel, of course, with the suggestion that men both create organizations and are dependent upon them. The objection we have is to the abstract statement of an asymmetrical relation of dependence and still more to the use of this as a basis for the criticism or disparagement of eccentricity. Who is to say what is called for if men are to 'create and re-create' the organization which 'guides and controls their behaviour'? No doubt the sociologist is wholly entitled to set up standards which permit him to speak of 'normal' or 'abnormal' behaviour; but few social scientists, surely, would say with like assurance that 'society' owes nothing to those who have preferred as large a degree of independence as possible, nothing at all to the prophets (even if they were 'mad in the end'), artists, rebels, nonconformists, who have chosen to withdraw as far as possible both from 'man' and from 'society'?

'Independence' is here spoken of disparagingly. Social service is likely to follow the lead of the social scientist here and discourage people from being 'too independent' and they have some right on their side. But only some. The difficulty with this kind of statement about sociality is that it appears to discredit all attempts at even relative independence let alone the supreme efforts which have been made by moral and spiritual genius to inspire the re-creation of society by their own withdrawal.

Sociality and morals

But the difficulty we are discussing may be much more serious than we have made it seem. It may be a difficulty arising from a misunderstanding about what social science can do. If in the past we suffered from moral and social philosophers who used concepts and made statements which trespassed upon the realms of scientific inquiry, it is likely that today we are more in danger from assumptions about science which trespass upon the territory

[1] Ibid.

of moral effort and moral vision. In the past individualists and social contract theories were really calling for special kinds of effort even when they appeared to be making statements of fact about the origins of human society. But today people listen to and repeat statements about sociality, scientific statements, and imagine these to be much more reliable (not to say less exacting) substitutes for the effort which has to be made toward good living and the good society. This is the more important reason why before we begin to comment upon the value of community we have to get our thoughts clear about social science.

Of course this question has come up before. Our worries over the concept of mental health,[1] for instance, were caused by the suspicion that people were now being taught to expect social service to do for them what they can only do for themselves or not have done at all. And the same applies in a more general way to popular ideas about social science. By accepting a general dogma about sociality on the one hand (whether this is understood or not), by listening to talk of 'social engineering', 'adjustment', 'adaptation', and so forth on the other, two conclusions are arrived at, which we have now to examine. The first is that a good thing called 'society' is already *there* and calls only for our fitting into it — certainly not for critical inquiry; the second is that all who behave as if this were not the case are in need of being 'adjusted' and that there are social engineers as qualified for this as other kinds of engineers are qualified to put right a fault in household or factory equipment. This kind of thinking makes impossible any creative thought about the value of community.[2]

The first notion — of a society already 'there' and not only there but satisfactory because it is there — is encouraged by the careless repetition of such statements as the one we looked at just now. This together with the misinterpretation of what a scientific statement about sociality signifies are the two sources of error we have now to examine. 'Society' very often means a more or less precise and actual system of relations and customs, an organization we can locate, perhaps, in a given territory or even in a certain part of the town. Therefore to talk of dependence on 'society' may

[1] On mental health see above, Chapter 18.
[2] For comment on the public attitude to the social sciences as 'superstitious' see G. R. G. Mure, *Retreat from Truth* (Oxford, Blackwell, 1958), ch. ii.

well seem to some people to mean a kind of relation with prevailing customs, classes, codes, and institutions; whereas one would assume that all the social scientist would want to say was that men were dependent upon relations with each other, or interdependent, partly dependent upon such specific organizations, but also able to change them, repudiate them, re-create them.

A scientific statement about sociality cannot in any case take the place of critical decision about the way relations are to be managed, organized, reconstructed. Either a scientific statement is empirical or it is not. If it is then it must be testable by experiments which expose it to falsification by observable facts. If it is not empirical it must be a statement of the same order as, for instance, a moral judgement, an aesthetic appreciation or else, a logical appraisal and it must submit to the rules of these kinds of discourse. We take it that the statement, 'man is a social animal', is intended to be empirical, though it may not be easy to describe the kinds of experimental test to which it has been or will be submitted. But if it is empirical — if, for instance, the case of the renowned Kaspar Hauser is regarded as a proper test for such a statement[1] — then it cannot itself have anything to do with the processes of creating or re-creating social organization. For when men make or remake they do something different from describing or explaining and they have to call to their aid such notions as 'right' and 'good' and with these empirical science — as it has been at pains to insist for centuries — can have no dealings.

It is an error, then, to treat a scientific statement about sociality as an answer to questions about the value of community. It is misleading to think of 'society' as an entity which is there waiting for the 'maladjusted' to 'adjust' to 'it'.

That does not, of course, dispose of such concepts as 'adjustment' or any other that may seem proper to what is sometimes (horribly) called 'social engineering'. To start with the social engineer may think in terms of concrete groups or associations such as the family or the work group and mean these when he speaks of 'society'. To go on with he will probably agree that 'adjustment' is a two-way operation to be described not in terms

---

[1] A radio lecture recently told of the work done by Professor H. Harlow and his wife at the University of Wisconsin Regional Primate Research Center to show the effects of varying degrees of social deprivation. See *The Listener*, vol. lxxiii, no. 1872.

of an asymmetrical relation of 'dependence' but rather as one of 'interdependence' so that he can use whatever tools he uses not only on the maladjusted individual but also on the group which has also in some sense failed in the business of adjustment.

Perhaps it is the language alone to which we are objecting; but then again, is language ever 'mere words'? When you use an analogy like that of engineering in order to talk about human relations are you not asking for trouble? John Stuart Mill insisted a century ago, 'Human nature is not a machine to be built after a model, and set to do exactly the work prescribed for it'.[1] Since 'society' on the sociologist's own showing is integral to human nature we may make a similar protest on behalf of *both* partners in the so-called 'adjusting' process. The objection is not trivial. Whatever machines may now be made to do they are still machines. Men have made them for men's purposes; the most intricate of them are programmed by men and set to work within the prescribed limits of human ends. 'Adjustment' of the parts of a machine calls for no independent reflection, judgement, decision, choice, by the adjusted part or its fellows.[2] All such qualities lie in the engineer and in him alone. The parts are his 'things'. And these are concepts which ought never to have been taken over for the discussion of human relations.

For on the one hand, as the sociologist said, the 'machine' is simply not there in any permanent, unchanging form long enough to be thought of as such. And on the other hand 'it' itself is but men in the process of living together. 'Sociality' is an important concept partly at any rate because it makes clear beyond all doubt what the individualist and the contractarian tended to obscure — that there is no 'society' on the one hand (the machine) and 'men' on the other (the parts to be adjusted). Rather have we only men and their ever-changing organizations, their rules, their 'conceptual skin' and because it is change alone that is unchanging all use of images which suggest the continuous social machine and the carefully oiled and adjusted individual parts is deplorable.[3]

[1] Mill, *On Liberty*, ch. iii.

[2] But not to overlook a much closer resemblance between modern machines and human beings see W. Sluckin, *Minds and Machines* (Penguin, 1960).

[3] On the broad view of the importance of concepts and conceptual analysis to the understanding of human relations see also P. Winch, *The Idea of a Social Science and its Relation to Philosophy* (Routledge, 1958), especially ch. v.

It is deplorable for several reasons, but above all for the illusion it cherishes of 'experts' and their 'expertise'.[1] There are several possibilities here. For instance, there is the possibility that 'social engineers' themselves will so misconceive their role and the extent of their 'knowledge' as to attempt to deal with society as if it were indeed a machine to be dismantled, overhauled, re-assembled, or adjusted at will. Of this more will be said later. Then there is the way in which such expertise, however modestly conceived, can be used for such divergent and even opposed ends. By maintaining, first, that as a scientist he is neutral in respect of values, second, that he can as a 'technologist' manipulate people and organizations in somewhat the same manner as an engineer can manipulate machines the social servant may find his skills utilized for ends he deplores once he understands them, but which he has done much to assist, if only by encouraging the view that values were not to be thought about or he himself not to be committed to them.

Those 'responsible for the training of teachers and social workers' according to one of them 'are concerned to equip students with the skill required to change prevailing moral attitudes and standards'.[2] They therefore, he added, need guidance in the matter of the standards involved in changing standards. This is the point we are making here: that bare affirmations about sociality are no substitute for a *value* of community, any more than they would be for the other values we have been discussing. Social science does not and cannot relieve us of the need to review again and again the ancient question about the good society.

Animals and men

Among the ancients it was Aristotle who once said something the sociologists we quoted at the beginning noted with approval. 'Man', he said, 'is a political animal.' The sociologists translated this 'social animal' and it is true that the English translators of Aristotle several times use the word 'social' (a Latin derivation) though the sentence which comes closest to what the sociologists

[1] Hayek, *Constitution of Liberty*, part i, ch. 2. The author speaks of those 'intoxicated by the advance of knowledge' as 'becoming the enemies of freedom'.

[2] A. E. Teale, 'Ethics and Psychology', in *Sociological Review Monograph no.* 3, ed. P. Halmos (Keele, University College of North Staffordshire, 1960).

want to say is this: '. . . a city is a a natural production . . . man is naturally a political animal'. The point is not unimportant — Aristotle and his contemporaries did their ethical and political thinking in more concrete terms than we do and for them the city, the *polis*, was necessary both to the preservation of life and to the circle of their being; whereas 'society', as we often use the word, means nothing so definite except, perhaps, the family or friends or public opinion.

But the more important contrast to make between Aristotle and the sociologists lies in the meaning he gave to such phrases as 'political animal' and 'natural production'. For these are more than the sociologists' empirical statements about sociality. When Aristotle calls the State 'natural' he does not mean merely that 'it is there' and must therefore be described but that it is the 'conclusion of a process of human development . . . in which each step is necessary and natural, the outcome not of human purpose but of human instinct [*hormē*] struggling toward its goal. . . .[1] Men are to be explained not only in terms of how they have come to be but of what they are becoming and this it is that distinguishes them from other animals.

Man is a 'political creature', in a higher sense than bees or other society-forming animals. For Nature, which does nothing in vain, has given to man, over and above a voice expressive of pleasure and pain, language which enables him to distinguish between the useful and the hurtful, and between right and wrong.[2]

It is the distinctively human which is to be developed in the State. To give an account of this Aristotle has to include a system of ethics as part of his politics. In considering the value of community we cannot be satisfied merely with an account of man's sociality. We have to ask what a good society would be like; we have to understand the 'distinctively human' by doing such distinctively human things as reasoning and valuing. All this would, in fact, seem to be involved in 'creating and re-creating an organization' which then 'guides and controls' behaviour which, by such means, will be 'distinctively human'.

[1] E. Barker, *The Political Thought of Plato and Aristotle* (Methuen, 1906), p. 269.

[2] Gomperz, *GT*, vol. IV, bk. vi, ch. 26; also H. Arendt, *The Human Condition* (New York, Doubleday, 1959), part ii.

QUESTIONS FOR DISCUSSION

1. Duguit's theory of the decentralization of State power (p. 303 n.) could lead to the parcelling out of such power among a number of more or less autonomous professional organizations or social and civil services. What are the more obvious risks in such a process?

2. What do we expect social science to do 'for us'? Recall above, Chapter 8, but distinguish between what is expected of social work and what we (including social workers) expect of social science.

3. 'Man is a social animal.' What kind of statement is this? For instance, does it give an account of certain facts *or* require us to behave in certain approved ways *or* affect to be the one but attempt the other?

4. Discuss the machine as a model for human nature. Read W. Sluckin, *Minds and Machines* (Penguin, 1960), and then turn again to the quotation from J. S. Mill on p. 310.

28

Love

To get away from people who make us do what they want whether we want it or not is to be free. Then there is the time of life when it seems there is no bliss in heaven or on earth like doing only what some other wants us to do. We say we are 'in love'. No doubt there are still parents who marvel that these two experiences can come so close together in the lives of their children. Yet though it is commonplace to want to be free of parents in order not to be free of others but to be in love, the two words, 'freedom' and 'love' may seem to belong to interests so different that it is perverse to discuss them together or even curious to talk at all of love in a book on social philosophy.

For men can demand freedom of their rulers, and make arrangements to ensure it among themselves both for themselves and for their children. No doubt the psychologists could talk quite happily of our demanding love, too; but their kind of 'demanding' is not what we mean in political and social action. They *interpret* conduct which to plain men seems remote from love as a demand. What they call the 'need for love' is very often a diagnostic explanation of unfriendly or even malicious behaviour. This is very different from the demands for freedom which we have been discussing, for these have been explicit, more or less rational demands which philosophers, among others, have been able to debate according to their logic.

To demand love by some such means as those used by the Americans and the French when they demanded freedom in the eighteenth century would be a strange, even perhaps an hilarious thing to watch. A social psychologist might keep a straight face when he tells us that Fascist Germany in attacking and destroying so much of Europe in 1940 was 'demanding to be loved'; but I doubt if we could do the same if grown men stood up in public assembly and with solemn voice and mien issued a Declaration of Rights beginning with the Right to be Loved. The fun lies in the incongruity. It would be like demanding 'parity of esteem'. If 'love' is the name for a sentiment or a whole complex of feelings then it can no doubt be won, earned, excited, aroused, provoked; but it cannot be demanded, commanded, coerced, or required by law or provided for under the terms of a contract.

Nevertheless, we must — as the poets have said before now — 'speak of love'. And this for the following reasons. In the first place, much analysis of human relations in recent years has been in terms of love rather than logic or reason and, on the other hand, it is true that some social philosophy by expecting too much of reason has abused our humanity. In the second place, and quite apart from expert analysis, idealists of one sort or another have often spoken as if all talk of justice and indeed all the problems of human relations could be disposed of if only men 'loved one another' and this truism can lead to unfortunate consequences. Then, in the third place, there are a variety of social feelings which need to be distinguished in the interests of the social values.[1]

Reason and the irrational[2]

A principal cause of complaint against the kind of political and social reasoning which went on in Europe during the seventeenth and early eighteenth century was that Descartes and those who followed him made too much of reason while neglecting the powerful and all-important forces of unreason. Edmund Burke's fears about the French Revolution had some of this in them. 'Is every land-mark of the country to be done away in favour of a geometrical and arithmetical constitution?'[3] he asked. For the revolutionaries, despising experience, had 'wrought under ground a mine that will blow up, at one grand explosion, all examples of antiquity, all precedents, charters, and acts of parliament',[4] and this all by way of rationalizing society. Later we will discuss in

[1] See above, Chapter 19.
[2] See also G. Wallas, *Human Nature in Politics*, 4th ed. (Constable, 1948).
[3] Edmund Burke, *Reflections on the Revolution in France* (O.U.P., World's Classics 1907), p. 61.
[4] Ibid., p. 62.

L2

particular the way in which the contract theory of human relations deserves this sort of criticism.

'Intellectuals' are sometimes lumped together as a class of men who have done violence to human nature by trying to force it into rational, intellectually satisfying moulds, at best in discussion, at worst in their concepts of the good society, their community-value. This is the kind of thing said today about Plato,[1] though it would be as well to note the obvious — that it is the intellectual who says this kind of thing about him. We remember that it was intellectual Romantics like Rousseau in his day and Nietzsche in his who made notable protests against the excesses of reason. The Romantic movement in every area of learning was, of course, a movement partly if not mainly of the intellect. To make a general charge against a so-called 'intellectual class' instead of against specific errors in reasoning or specific failures in discipline is not only an error itself but a dangerous error. For 'intellect' as distinct from 'intelligence' is a matter of effort and discipline and a facile criticism of 'the intellectuals' may be no more than a disguise for the critics' own indolence.

The mistakes of excessive rationalism in discussing human relations should be made clear. Some people confuse the issue by attacking theoretical error and (real or alleged) practical intentions without making a clear distinction. If Plato, for example, was wrong to suppose that men could be classified according to their inner qualities and then governed adequately in the light of a truth available to one class only, then it is enough to show that he was wrong in theory without at the same time hinting at sinister, 'right-wing' conspiracies. It is part of our growing intellectual indiscipline today that we seldom seem able to do the first properly without thinking we can get the whole matter over much more quickly by doing the second as well. We are in so great a hurry to brush aside people and arguments which stand in our way or make us feel ill at ease that we are inclined to confuse their opposition with our truth and their error. This is nothing else but a rejection of objectivity as a basis for inter-personal relations and it is this we have to avoid when we make none the less necessary remarks about the 'errors of rationalism'.

The error we call 'rationalistic' shows itself in theories of

[1] By such critics as Karl Popper.

human nature which play down the emotions, the sentiments, the unconscious, unconsidered sources of action, and play up the reasonable, deliberate, purposeful, and conscious sources. The same kind of error is made when the rationalist plans the lives of other men as if they could be made to conform to his rationalistic assessments by the imposition upon them of a carefully thought out, elegant piece of social planning. When the Stoics saw visions of a Cosmopolis, a world city, they did so by inference from arguments they cherished about the place of reason in human nature. They made no adequate provision for political realities, local passions, and the social inertia typical of so many people for so much of the time. On the other hand, such theoretical errors were not allowed to find practical expression. Critics of the French Revolution — men like Edmund Burke — took the view that the revolutionaries were, many of them, putting into practice the blunders of rationalistic theorizing about man and his relations.[1]

In this book we have used the methods of the intellect to defend the value of freedom, but at the same time we have had to be on our guard against rationalistic error. So in the first place we argued the essential variety of human experience as the condition giving rise to human freedom.[2] We made clear our opposition to all 'social engineering' aimed at reducing the variety and reducing all human experience to a few rational, logical types of expression.[3] But we must not be accused of the opposite error — the error of *irrationalism*. For if the rationalist is wrong in excluding the passions from his account of our nature, if he is still more wrong — vicious even — when he tries to govern as if such passions and such varieties of experience did not exist or ought not to persist, the irrationalist is wrong too: wrong not only to make his discovery of the passions exclude reason but to oppose all rational forms of social regulation such as the laws on the ground that they inhibit the passions or restrict spontaneity.

This brings us back to love. As a word for what Freudians and others sometimes call 'libido' or 'life force' and in so far as we are

---

[1] For an account of how the thinkers of the Enlightenment saw the function of 'reason' in relation to law, state and society, see E. Cassirer, *The Philosophy of the Enlightenment* (Boston, Beacon Press, 1951), ch. vi. This is a translation by Koelln and Pettegrove of *Die Philosophie der Aufklärung* (Tübingen, Mohr, 1932).

[2] See above, Part One.   [3] See above, Part Two.

taught to believe that social regulation not only restrains such force but harms us in doing so (by no means necessary conclusions from Freud's own work) love in this sense is on the side of the irrational, it is the enemy of reason and therefore, on the arguments set out earlier in this book, of both freedom and justice. For love now becomes the possibility of two sorts of demand: first, that others should have a certain kind of affection for us (and this, as a demand, we find comic); second, that we should be able to give free rein to passion (of one sort or another) and this, so far from being identical with freedom, is its negation and, as such, is as hostile to justice as it is to community.

For freedom here is the freedom of a somewhat from coercion and to be a 'somewhat' it is necessary that we see a person as rather more than the wind-tunnel for powerful passions. It is also necessary both in realizing freedom and in dealing with its consequences that men should be *answerable*; and it follows that if they are to be answerable with the minimum of coercion they should be so under laws which are not the commands of one man or a few, but are superior to all by way of rational agreement. This is why reason as regulator is indispensable to the social values and, despite the errors of rationalism, must be defended and practised against the confusions of irrationalism and its political expression, Anarchy. It may make sense to look to a future when government will 'wither away'. But given the state of human relations as they are at any one moment in history it only does make sense if you mean by 'anarchy' the reduction of coercion by the increase of rational co-operation. Otherwise, even given room enough to move, you can only mean the ultimate freedom of the few heroes to dominate and rule the rest.[1]

[1] Thomas Carlyle said in his celebrated lecture on 'The Hero as Divinity', 'No nobler feeling than this of admiration for one higher than himself dwells in the breast of man . . .'; 'Society is founded on Hero-worship'; 'In all epochs we shall find the Great Man to have been the indispensable saviour . . .'. Carlyle's heroes were 'gods, prophets, priests, kings, poets, teachers' and they included Odin, Mahomet and Cromwell. (*On Heroes, Hero-Worship, and the Heroic in History*, ed. A. Mac-Mechan, Ginn & Co., 1901). Émile Montegut is quoted by Carlyle's editor as having this to say about heroes: 'Heroes are those men who draw into themselves and concentrate the qualities and thoughts of masses of men, who sum up an epoch or create it, and so render themselves immortal by making themselves the masters of their time', but we in our time are ill disposed toward the heroic except in the fantasies of stage and screen where such as passes for heroic quality may be disposed of at the touch of a switch or the drop of a curtain. It would be worth while pondering *why,*

We shall try now to make the connexion between love, irrationalism, and the social values a little more clear.

Family feeling

Several renowned social thinkers have chosen to make the family their point of departure. The French Revolutionaries, in *their* formulation of social values, spoke of *Liberté*, *Egalité*, and *Fraternité* — the third of the values having clear connexions with family feelings, with 'brotherliness'. Modern working-class movements in English-speaking communities sometimes require their members to address each other as 'Brother' and the more optimistic of social thinkers and dreamers have spoken of the 'brotherhood of man', the 'human family', and so on.

It is for the social scientist to relate such practices to emotional needs. Our business is with the concepts involved and their bearing upon the value of community.

Clearly references to the family as a model for community has one great advantage: we are reminded, as in Aristotle, not only of man's original sociality but of the fundamental, pre-rational, pre-conscious origins of human relations. If any individualist ever meant to claim that a man could be a man with no dependence whatever on others, then reflection on elementary biological facts ought to mend his ways. It would be very different, however, if we were asked to deduce from this that all human relations or at least all political relations are or ought to be of this order. We know that it was arguments of this kind in Sir Robert Filmer's *Patriarcha* which caused John Locke to write a whole treatise in refutation.[1] For once you start thinking of a political community

having in mind what was most likely the moral purpose of Carlyle's lectures. The other well-known exponent of the heroic in recent times was Nietzsche, who hated what he regarded as the 'self-dwarfing' of European morality (see *Beyond Good and Evil*). Nietzsche praised 'nobleness', which implied, he thought, the 'unalterable belief that to a being such as "we", other beings must naturally be in subjection'.

[1] John Locke, *An Essay Concerning Certain False Principles*, now generally called the *First Treatise on Civil Government*, is meant here. (Dent, Everyman's, 1924, together with the *Second Treatise*.) For Sir Robert Filmer see Sabine, *HPT*, ch. xxv. Filmer was a royalist who suffered severely during the Civil War. He based his argument for Divine Right on the authority God was supposed to have given Adam. This was inherited by Noah, who sailed up the Mediterranean and allotted the three continents of the old world to his sons, Shem, Ham, and Japheth. The absolute authority of these patriarchs was handed on to all kings and governments (whether monarchical or by governing assemblies). 'There is', he wrote, 'and always shall be continued to the end of the world a natural right of a supreme father over every multitude.'

as a family, the sovereign as a father, the subjects as dependent children, it is obvious that laws will take on the status of paternal commands, the chief virtue may well be obedience, and all rational criticism of the way things are done will be stifled with something like that old-established retort: 'Father (or mother) knows best'.

Our objection, of course, is not merely that the analogy between State and family is a very limited one but that whatever may have been true of the primitive tribe our large, complex, political communities are meant to be communities of mature, relatively equal adults not of children to be protected by powerful parents. This is why we make freedom a value and voice our suspicions of all apparent tendencies to paternalism in government.

After all, even a proper biological family is judged to be a failure in our society if the children 'never grow up' — that is, never leave the protective authority of their parents for a world of their own in which they make their movements their own acts. It would be odd, therefore, if we were to find the family a satisfactory model for that community into which we escape from the restrictions of family life. But of course in spite of ourselves (as the psychologists will assure us) we do hanker after the protection we enjoyed as children, the immunity we had then from responsibility, the sense we had then of being enveloped within a love which was not only well-disposed toward us but also (so far as we could see) well able to look after us. It would come as no surprise, therefore, if social thought favoured such models of human relations partly because men hope to find somewhere, in community, what they have long since lost in family.

The difficulty is to issue all the necessary warnings against 'love' as a social value without seeming to be coldly unappreciative of what is undoubtedly one of the supreme if not the supreme human good. To be not merely well disposed toward someone but to care for his interests not only 'as if' they were your own but because they are your own, this is a disposition as blessed in the giver as in the receiver, though best of all, perhaps, where it is in both and is wholly reciprocal. No wonder people want to say 'God is love'. What more could men desire than to know that the universe itself was disposed toward them in this way despite all evidence to the contrary.

But 'love' in this sense — as the kind of disposition to be met with sometimes between two people whether in friendship or in family life — even this beatitude not only cannot be extended beyond the intimate, personal relation, but even there may easily deteriorate into or become confused with types of relation we would not so readily approve. What is sometimes called 'love' because the person who is said to feel it undoubtedly has strong feelings and does set out to serve another's interests may seem to the psychologist an unlovely attempt by the 'lover' to retain in his power a person upon whom he has become dependent against all justice and all attempts to achieve freedom. It is enough that the word 'love' can be used for such relations: this is enough to put us on our guard against careless extensions of the word as a value to wider systems of relations.

Consider for a moment the function of civil laws in relation to the intimate feelings of family love and see what this has to show us about the usefulness or otherwise of 'love' as a guide to the community value. It is not the case that marriage is always regarded by the civil law as a contract, though in some societies this is the case. That is, the partners do not always enter into a legal agreement laying down their rights and obligations and giving their written consent on the understanding that if too much is asked or not enough given the contract will then be regarded by the law as at an end. Nevertheless, very few societies indeed, even where 'romantic love' is regarded with something like reverence, act as if they thought the powerful passions which might move two people toward marriage were an adequate basis even for their relations let alone for those of their children. 'Love' between potential fathers and mothers is regarded by some as desirable but not necessary; by others as undesirable, an impediment to wise choice (best made by the parents); by others as both desirable and necessary, but even by these seldom as sufficient. Seldom, that is, as sufficient basis for all future relations deriving from the marriage.

So when children are born. The love of parents is regarded as highly desirable, even necessary, but never as sufficient. Less and less so, it might be said. It might be said that all too little is now left to parents in the care of children, but that is not the point we have to make at the moment. The point is that love is nowhere regarded as an adequate basis for human relations. Nor could it be any more than any other strong feeling, since civilisation itself could hardly begin let alone continue without recognition that the feelings by themselves were inadequate. Since it is accepted that our civilizing work necessitates regulation, we are therefore driven back once more to reflection on the principles upon which we regulate and this calls for a value of community quite distinct from any spontaneous social sentiment.

It is easy to go wrong here — to make so much, for instance, of the rational provision the law may make for the care of children that we overlook the possibility that a parent's love, however ill-informed, may in the long run do far more for the child's good than any amount of professional social service. This is why in any model of community we construct we must make every possible allowance for the value of freedom, for we do not know enough to back our laws and plans against all contradiction and there is some reason for saying that the more we truly 'know' the more likely it is that we shall see the sense of an 'open' as opposed to a 'closed' community.

Patriotism and philanthropy

Two well-known and widely used names for social sentiments call for distinctive comment: the first is patriotism, the feeling people have for their own nation; the second is philanthropy, a name for more general 'love of man'. The question is what place we should allow to such sentiments in the discussion of community.

Of patriotism more will be said when we discuss the nation as community. The importance of patriotism is that it can be the basis for a morality. That is, the patriot (his sincerity assumed) has a sentiment which commits him to interests of some breadth and generality and this requires moral effort to resolve conflicts between these and his own narrower interests, moral argument to discuss such issues with others. 'Love of country' is a misleading phrase, since it may mean what it says: affection or sentiment for the natural beauties and familiarities of a territory or what is normally meant by 'patriotism'; a communal sentiment powerful enough to override most if not all personal considerations. The least a moralist can say about patriotism is that the patriot is a better man than the 'wretch concentred all in self'[1] the poet

---

[1] Sir Walter Scott (1771–1832), *Innominatus*.

contrasts with him. Objections to patriotism arise partly from the association of this sentiment with bellicosity or 'jingoism'[1] — to this and to grave doubts about the viability of the nation-state as a proper model for the future community.

Before we try to discount patriotism, however, we have to ask what we discount with it. Patriotism itself is not a proper object for rational criticism any more than are love or family feeling. The proper method of criticism is to inquire, first, whether the 'nation' in any given example of patriotism is a subject of values and secondly whether, consequently, the disparagement of patriotism may at the same time be an abandonment of such values. If, on the other hand, we decide that whatever the future of wider systems of relations the nation in a given case has been and may yet be a viable organization for the defence and propagation of what we mean by the social values, we may find that patriotic feeling is a powerful support of the social values whereas decline in patriotic feeling may be nothing more noble than a decline of responsibility for those values.

'Philanthropy' has this danger among others. Of course it goes without saying that we 'ought' to have kindly feelings toward other men, though not, one would have thought, indiscriminately. But the criticisms we would want to make of what sometimes passes for philanthropy are, first, that a 'kindly feeling' may easily take the place of thought and action — in other words, help to dress up sentimentality to look superior to moral and social action. This is the first criticism. The second is that so-called philanthropy is sometimes offered in place of patriotism — as true philanthropy might well be — with every sign, however, of its requiring less of the philanthropist than patriotism ever required of the patriot.

The first of these objections is a special form of the objection we have had throughout this chapter to the use of 'love' where some more precise definition of the community-value is called for. Some people will refuse to face unpleasant facts about their fellows rather than disturb their peace of mind, the serenity of their

[1] 'Jingoism', a name for blustering nationalism, comes from a music-hall song by G. W. Hunt, popular around 1878 when England was thought to be on the verge of war against Russia in support of the Turks:

> 'We don't want to fight; but by Jingo, if we do,
> We've got the ships, we've got the men, and got the money, too'.

Supporters of the Russians at the time were called 'Jingoes'.

sentiments. 'Kindly feeling' in this sense may explain some permissiveness, for instance, between parents and children: far better to feel kind feelings than to have to take painful action. In dealing with world-wide relations, for instance, it may prove more comfortable to accept the worst that is said about your own nation by its enemies first and then to dissociate yourself from the nation in the name of philanthropy second, rather than to sift and sort out criticism and take a stand somewhere. If sentimentality is the enjoyment of feeling as such without the effort of thought or action, then we must suspect the feelings which call for less action, prefer those which call for more. As for love, we may find the views of Jean-Paul Sartre acceptable on this point:

... there is no love apart from the deeds of love; no potentiality of love other than that which is manifested in loving ... no genius other than that which is expressed in works of art...[1]

Philanthropic sentiment may be submitted to this test.

Marriage and family

We said that family feeling was hardly a suitable basis for the government of large, complex communities of mature people. We refused to follow those who have used the family as a model for government. Yet the fate of the family as an institution is of such obvious importance that we are bound now to consider one or two typical arguments which prevail either for its dissolution or in its defence.

The proposition that the family 'must go' inferred from statements about the 'failure' of family life may be taken first. We will pass over for the moment the difficulties involved in saying that any institution so deep-rooted in the primordial needs of man as the family 'must go'. We will confine ourselves instead to the notion of the family as a 'failure'. To make sense this must mean no more than that a given number of families are failures and this in its turn as implying that in such families people are unhappy or injured in some way because of conditions created by or identical with the family. That this is the case we do not doubt. It is not our business to deal with the evidence for such arguments, but we accept that it is so. More, by reason of arguments used throughout

[1] J.-P. Sartre, 'Existentialism is a Humanism', in *Existentialism from Dostoevsky to Sartre*, ed. Kaufmann (Meridian, 1957).

this book we now take the view that marriage is no more and no less 'indissoluble' than the resolution of its partners. This brings us to the second commonplace statement made about marriage.

'Marriages are made in heaven' is the kind of thing Christians and others say in opposition to divorce and to maintain the indissolubility of marriage. We cannot enter into debate with the theological bases for such propositions, but for our part we would say that this is a viewpoint fraught with some danger to the very institution it seeks to protect. 'Indissolubility' is a quality of all promises; it is the very nature of promise-making (as we have seen)[1] that it should intend to maintain reliable personal relations. Permanence lies in the determination of those who make such promises. To suggest it lies elsewhere — in metaphysical space or divine authority — is to detract from the responsibility of the partners. On the other hand, to propose seriously that a promise is meant to override all possible conditions in the future is to outdo the most extreme rationalist in ignorance and defiance of the nature of things. It is as misconceived to mean this by a promise as it is for a social planner to lay down long-term conditions for a community and insist on maintaining these however wrong he is proved by events.

So to promise that a partnership shall continue 'in sickness and in health' is reasonable; we know about sickness, we can foresee that and take it into our reckoning. Indeed *not* to take this into promise-making would be to make promising of no value since that kind of condition is what human love is intended to face and contend with. So with 'for richer or poorer' — this again represents conditions of a kind secondary in the scale of values to the love which we know from experience surmount such obstacles. But when promise-making includes such phrases as 'for better or for worse' the moralist is bound to pause. Can any moral agent seriously be asked to commit his life and others' on such conditions, when it can truly be said to be 'worse' that a relation should be sustained than that it should be ended? Of course there are many ways in which this phrase can be interpreted to suit those who have an interest in the indissolubility of marriage, but as it stands is is open to the most absurd glosses and represents indeed the reduction of promise-making to self-contradiction. For any two

[1] See above, Chapter 9.

persons who promise to harm each other would ordinarily be regarded as vicious or insane. And indeed some marriages have been sustained which suggest that this is no idle possibility.

On the other hand, and to return to the first statement, no social philosophy can contemplate easily the submission of marriage to some crude utilitarian test. Not, that is, if this means a superficial hedonism in accordance with which two people would be encouraged to think of a marriage as disposable as soon as uncomfortable, challenging, or failing to give a surplus of pleasures over pains. Even when the marriage consists only of husband and wife (with no children to make a family) there might be as much moral loss as gain from such a view. For whatever interest heaven has in the matter, 'selves' — and marriages — are *made* partly by the making over of limitations and frustrations just as they are made — and in the case of marriages, unmade — by recognizing failure, by admitting insuperable obstacles.

If people are free and responsible, then as partners in marriage they must be left to make the decisions which make the marriage — and make themselves. But by the same tokens social servants and social philosophers have also to make decisions in their work which influence the education of those who are not yet expected to be responsible but who, when the time comes, may be weakened or strengthened by what has been said to them by teachers and mentors. The task of marriage- and family-making is nothing but a poignant concentration of the whole career of free men. The aspect of it which concerns us is this: we have both to insist that the family be freely created, freely sustained, *and* reject any suggestion that this can be done without effort to maintain inter-personal reliability and fulfil love.

Not that we should make too much of what our arguments can do — or too little. As the most powerful force making for successful and happy marriage is a passion which can become enduring love, so the need for enduring love and the wisdom it inspires is, of course, infinitely more effective than any moral education need hope to be. On the other hand, intellectual confusion and sheer stupidity to say nothing of the wayward impulses of passion itself are the untiring enemies of human fulfilment. It is the task of civilizing activities such as philosophy to contend with them. As we are not human solely by reason of our intellect, neither are we human solely because we have passions like other animals. Philosophy is part of the struggle to give form and order to creative forces without denying them.

We have then no way out of the task. We cannot go back to old dogmas and teach children capable of maturity that all they have to do is obey and conform to ancient commands. But we may contend that the old beliefs and traditional imperatives contained a wisdom which, once appreciated, can come to our aid without them. We have taken some steps in this direction by speaking of the 'primary conventions' — the many-sided value of truth in personal relations. We have taken some steps by starting to think about the 'self' and its integrity. We must not now rush headlong from such premises to conclusions which underpin the old dogmatic prohibitions — prohibitions, for instance, on passion enjoyed outside marriage, prohibitions on divorce. But if we have reason to believe in the good in the kind of marriage our society has upheld and if at the same time we have some confidence in the ability of each generation to make that good its own, by and large, then we must pay the price of freedom and allow some, if they will risk that good, to lose it altogether, or, which is also likely, to come to it only by ways which traditional moralists would condemn without a hearing. Or, in brief, we may both teach the good of monogamy *and* acknowledge not only that men may reject it but that they may come to it in their own way.

This approach does not prevent our thinking out and teaching, if we will, the evil of, say, promiscuity. But we would have with the same insistence to tackle the risks and evils of a bad marriage. In any case, the issues for the teacher do not always or even most of the time lie in a choice between monogamy and promiscuity. The questions most frequently asked have to do with intercourse between the sexes before marriage (and this is not necessarily promiscuity) and divorce when a marriage is unhappy. As moralists we would be inclined to say that promiscuity would deprive a man of responsible freedom. Premarital intercourse, on the other hand, is important to morals when we look at it in terms of inter-personal reliability and the bearing of this on integrity.[1] Decisions of this nature have to take account of such facts as the

---

[1] Premarital intercourse could be defended on the ground that (under certain conditions) it was more likely to ensure inter-personal reliability.

difference between what a woman may feel after intercourse and what a man may feel — he may lose interest in her by the same experience which arouses her interest in him to the point where her 'self' is threatened if he does not help her care for it.

But our interest at present is as social philosophers. We have to say that if parental responsibility for children is eroded, if the family by degrees ceases to be a viable unit of human relations quite apart from the goods of human love which might be lost, we cannot foresee clearly enough what would become of human life in all its variety to say with confidence that this would help the values to which we are committed. Therefore, as social servants, we have to do whatever education can do both to preserve the good of the family and to learn what we can about likely alternatives if the family loses its place.

QUESTIONS FOR DISCUSSION

1. What arguments are there against adding to a Declaration of Human Rights the 'right to be loved'? (Arguments *for* might turn for support to J. Bowlby, *Child Care and the Growth of Love* (Penguin, 1953), part I, chs i, iv; pt II, ch. vii.)

2. Discuss the relative dangers of 'rationalism' and 'irrationalism' in politics. Read G. Wallas, *Human Nature in Politics*, 4th ed. (Constable, 1948) introduction and ch. i; M. Oakeshott, 'Political Education' (in *Philosophy, Politics and Society*, 1st series, ed. Laslett, Blackwell, 1956).

3. Granted that family feeling is suspect as a model for relations between government and subject what objections (if any) have we to it as an ideal of social relations more generally? Read: J.-P. Sartre, *Existentialism is a Humanism*; J. Barzun, *The House of Intellect*, chs vi, vii, viii.

4. Can we now dispense with patriotism?

5. Is 'free love' a contradiction? What would constitute a responsible marriage vow? (That is, taking 'love' as the name for the emotion which may precede sexual intercourse *plus* the responsibilities intercourse might be shown to create, whatever else it might mean.) Does effective contraception dispose of the 'need' for vows? (Do not neglect Huxley's *Brave New World* for models of alternative arrangements between the sexes.)

29

Contract and Community

WHEN in December 1620 the Pilgrim Fathers went ashore from
their boat, the *Mayflower* at what was to be Plymouth, Massa-
chusetts, it must have seemed to some that here was a social
thinker's dream come true. The New Englanders and indeed the
Virginians could carry out in practice what thinkers like Plato and
Sir Thomas More could do only in imagination.

To them the land that they occupied was 'tabula rasa' on which they
could write what they willed, without hindrance from the forms and
traditions of an older society.[1]

William Bradford, one of their number, and a future governor of
the colony, saw in the venture 'a great hope and inward zeal of
laying some good foundation ... for the propagating and
advancing the gospel of the Kingdom of Christ'.[2] He admits there
were 'strangers' among them who had made 'discontented and
mutinous speeches' on the voyage, men who said 'that when they
came ashore they would use their own liberty, for none had power
to command them . . .'[3] and this itself, perhaps, modifies the hope
of 'building from the ground up'. For in the compact entered into
by the colonizers before they left the ship there is a reminder that
they are loyal subjects of King James and an undertaking to plan
the settlement 'for the glory of God and advancement of the
Christian faith and honour of our king and country'.[4] There could
be no rule and order without some recall of the past, some
dependence upon symbols of power and authority, though they

[1] Nye and Morpurgo, *History of the United States* (Penguin, 1955), vol. i, pp. 39 f.
[2] William Bradford, 'Of Plymouth Plantation', in *American Puritans*, ed. Perry
Miller (Doubleday, 1956, from the edition by Samuel Eliot Morison published by
Knopf, 1952).
[3] Ibid.   [4] William Bradford, op. cit.

were now far distant, affording no physical protection to the small company.

The Pilgrims then 'solemnly and mutually in the presence of God ... covenant and combine ourselves together into a civil body politic, for our better ordering and preservation and furtherance of the ends aforesaid',[1] agreeing to enact 'just and equal laws ... unto which we promise all due submission and obedience'. The compact was signed and Mr John Carver confirmed as governor for that year.

The Pilgrim Fathers were not the only colonists who translated social contract theory into fact. What we have to do is to appreciate the concept of human relations that 'contract' implies or advocates before we attend to the objections, the limitations of the concept.

The 'Independents'

In Part One of this book we illustrated in several ways the importance of the relation men construct between themselves and their universe as a whole and the connexion between this and their social philosophy. If, for example, your king is one of the gods 'and the land's representative among the gods',[2] as to some ancient Egyptians, then corresponding views will be taken of authority, of the political organization of your relations with other men. Or if you see your relations with the universe as a whole as dependent not on the political authority, the king, but upon priests and a hierarchy of priests, or in some other way as dependent both on sacred and on secular authority then again your political and social philosophy will take account of such a 'universal relation'.[3]

Now the view of the universal relation which dominated the New England Puritans also had a prominent part to play in contract theory elsewhere. The view, that is, of the sectarians we

[1] Bradford, op. cit. p. 19: the *Mayflower Compact*. For the Puritans' place in the founding of America see T. J. Wertenbaker, *The Puritan Oligarchy*, (New York, Grosset & Dunlop, 1947). On social contract and the Puritans see J. Gough, *Social Contract*, 2nd ed. (Oxford: Clarendon Press, 1957), ch. vii.

[2] Frankfort and others, *Before Philosophy* (Penguin, 1949), p. 73.

[3] Some Christian writers argued from man's sinful condition to the absolute authority of the secular power. See, for instance, an account of St Gregory the Great in R. W. and A. J. Carlyle, *A History of Mediaeval Political Theory in the West*, vol. I, part iii, ch. 13. 'It is from the doctrine of St Gregory the Great that the religious theory of the absolute and irresponsible authority of the ruler continually drew its strongest arguments, both in the Middle Ages and later' (ibid., p. 153).

usually call the 'independents'. The name itself is significant. The teachings of Robert Browne are representative.[1] He taught that every church member is a spiritual person, having some of the qualities in him of 'king, priest and prophet'. Congregationalism, the movement which grew from Browne's teachings, made each local group of believers autonomous, though it modified 'independence' by making voluntary fellowship between the churches fundamental. Browne repudiated the national, Anglican Church because all citizens were compelled to belong to it by law whereas, on his view, the 'universal relation' (as we call it) was decided by divine election and membership of the independent churches was possible only by religious experience and the acceptance of the covenant.

Brownist 'independence' in religious matters was not by any means as revolutionary or as anarchic as some religious movements: he did not repudiate the authority of the civil magistrate but merely sought to limit it. Nevertheless, the social philosophy implicit in this movement is radically different from that implicit in other Churches such as the Episcopalian and the Presbyterian. For in Episcopalian theory authority is both hierarchical and rooted in the past, in the long tradition supported by the Apostolic Succession, while Presbyterians (literally, those ruled by 'Elders'), while abolishing the entire episcopal system and substituting election, nevertheless favoured a strong central government of the Church after the example of Calvin in Geneva. The Presbyterians,[2] all the same, shared with the Independents a view of the Church as based upon a covenant and a compact rather than upon a formal creed, an authoritative declaration of orthodox belief.

These two things have to be taken together — the notion of covenant and compact and the Independents' abolition of hierarchical and traditional authority in order to see the importance of their views for social philosophy. If we were mainly interested in political thought, we might concentrate on the form of church government; but for social thought in the broader sense (and as the context of political ideas) we have to attend to the stress upon

---

[1] Robert Browne (1550–1633), *Booke which sheweth the Life and Manners of all true Christians; A Treatise of Reformation without tarrying for Anie*, etc. Browne was a kinsman of that Lord Burghley to whom Richard Hooker — Locke's mentor — sent the written copy of his *Laws of Ecclesiastical Polity* in defence of the National Church.

[2] 'Presbyter', from the comparative degree of the Greek adjective 'old'.

personal, religious experience, the personal covenant with God as well as the group compact to constitute a church.

As the new science was to learning in general, so were such movements as the Brownist to man's special relation with the universe as a whole. Both were individualist.[1] Individualist and, we could say, modernist, since it repudiated institutions rooted in tradition; individualist, modernist, and democratic since it set up small, independent communities within which each counted for one. In such groups face-to-face, direct democracy was possible. The Church as a voluntary association of like-minded believers was not only a model for such secular intentions as the 'Mayflower Compact', it was itself a concrete community based upon contract.

Yet the Independents were individualists only in a very relative sense: relative, that is, to their sectarian demands for freedom from episcopal and secular interference.

Like most religious minorities, they were more zealous in claiming toleration for themselves than in vindicating it for others.[2]

They matter to us because they demonstrate contractual society, but they do it at a time when social philosophy in our sense is impossible without some use of the language, symbols, and institutions of religion. Such symbols and institutions severely limit the range given to human freedom and set very narrow frontiers to the 'community of meaning'. Toleration of the sects is a means to the end of religious reform. In making contract a basis for human relations, however, they set in motion a logic which will not respect their sectarian aims.

The idea of 'contract'

If we are to think of constructing community on a basis of contract, several conditions, obvious enough once stated, are necessary. In stating them, however, we shall find ourselves drawing attention to more general concepts.

To contract is to 'draw together';[3] a contract is a means or instrument of drawing together. Legal usage apart it follows that a

[1] On the relative contribution of science and puritanism to individualism see A. D Lindsay, *The Modern Democratic State* (Oxford, 1943), vol. i.

[2] Sabine, *HPT*, ch. xxii.

[3] 'Contract' from Latin *contractus*, past part. of *contrahere*, 'to draw together', 'to conclude a bargain'.

condition of social space or separation is necessary in order to talk about contracting such space. This may be one reason why though it makes sense to talk of a contract for marriage (that is, a bringing together of two persons hitherto separate, perhaps unknown), it makes much less sense to try talking of a contract within marriage between two partners who are already so intimately associated as to constitute no space between them. This is one way in which we can put the objection people 'in love' have to a contract for marriage — as they are already as close and inseparable as they feel themselves to be, to talk of 'contracting' the space between them is both meaningless and offensive.

When, on the other hand, total strangers have need of each others' services the space between them can be reduced by a contract — an instrument defining complementary needs.

This notion of separation or social space was also necessary to freedom. Freedom, in fact, consists in there being such separation. But the distance once created, the separation achieved, it is possible for each, holding himself apart, to conceive deliberately the conditions under which he would wish to reduce the space, to modify it. Contract is a concept of human relations proper only to some degree of mutual awareness and of freedom.

Again, this 'drawing together' is a matter of degree. It is not, of course, possible to end all separation between two individuals without ending the individuals and therefore the relation between them. Stomach, lungs, brain, sex glands, nerve centres, constitute an integrated system which cannot be merged with others in the manner of a modern commercial 'merger'. Organic realities apart, where love between two people leads to the suppression by one of the distinctive qualities which attracted the other and made their love exciting the relationship has been drastically altered and may even cease to exist as a concrete relation between two distinct persons. Contract does not mean annihilation of social space but its reduction or modification and where *justice* prevails this is carried out strictly in the interests of each alike.

The idea of contract can be seen, then, as an alternative to two other conditions in neither of which would it be so satisfactory to talk of human *relations*. In the first state where people are unknown to each other or, known or unknown, have no working, recognizable participation in common ends, it may be useful for social scientists, nevertheless, to talk about relations between them on the ground that they are members of the same community, subject to the same institutions, and so on. But 'relations' in this sense may be said to be abstract or formal rather than concrete and material. Contract realizes such relations. In the second state, where one man or one group is so much under the influence of another as hardly to have an identity, a recognizable, separate self, we may indeed speak of relations — even as we speak of relations between master and slave, husband and dominated wife, or wife and hen-pecked husband; but contract may be contrasted with such unsatisfactory relations, since it presupposes a certain equality, a sharper separation, and excludes (under certain conditions of 'justice') the absorption of one into the other.

In one sense contract may seem to repudiate *trust*. In another sense it is inconceivable without trust and can be seen, therefore, as an alternative to coercion.

It is the legalization of contract which seems to repudiate trust. A 'gentleman's agreement' can be contractual and as such seems entirely founded upon trust — upon inter-personal reliability or truth. But when the gentlemen take legal advice and submit their understanding to formularization and supervision by others, it seems obvious that however great the trust between them a limit to trust has been recognized. This need not be so, of course. It may merely mean that the partners realize that in due course more people are going to be involved in the agreement and its consequences; that social space will intervene and increase and will have to be bridged by some more or less precise statement of aims and intentions, rights and obligations.

'Trust', in any case, does not have to mean unconsidered assumptions or taking for granted that a relation will develop and produce desirable results without an effort. The gentleman's agreement is still an agreement, a drawing together, an effort of the will and a more or less deliberate attempt to 'pin each other down' by promises. Promise-making assumes promise-keeping, and both are attempts to exercise a degree of moral surveillance over the conduct of each partner, whether or not the law is brought in.

Nor does legal contract bring an end to trust. On the contrary, there would be no point in making a contract without some degree of expectation that each would fulfil his part in the agreement *without* constant surveillance. Where a contract is an exchange of services the basic, logical structure of the agreement is hypothetical: if you do this and that, I will do thus and thus, otherwise not. The legal authority will intervene if there is debate about whether the conditions have been fulfilled and such intervention is imperative where the contract is such that one partner has no service he can withhold in order to induce the other to do his part. (This is the case, for instance, where goods bought on credit rapidly deteriorate or are consumed before they are paid for.)

Even so the law can not always make up to the one who has been cheated or disappointed for the failure of the other. This underlines the part that trust must play in contractual relations — trust, not in the sense of a gullible, 'starry-eyed' belief in other people's goodness, but in the rational good sense of men who may be expected to understand that their interests can in the long run best be served if they keep their word or honour their bond.

Contract, in short, belongs to a state of human relations in which we can detect such qualities as we ordinarily mean by 'maturity' and, perhaps, 'responsibility', 'morality'. We have in some tangible ways to be considered 'grown up' before relations of this sort are possible. A society in which men were unfit for such relations would have to have proportionately more external authority for the conduct of its day-to-day affairs.

All this, however, has to do with the idea of contract rather than with the theory of social contract.

The social contract[1]

Social contract theorists wanted to ground relations between men in large communities on some such conditions as those we mean by 'contractual'. Sometimes 'unwillingly' because the theorists were more interested in supporting existing authority than in limiting it — you had to obey the government, they would

[1] On social contract now see J. Gough, op. cit. Hobbes's theory of contract seems more interested in securing submission (see *Leviathan*). Locke's theory is more concerned to remind governments of their obligations but we have to remember that he did not have a theory of governmental but only of original contract (see also above, Chapter 13 and for the distinction between governmental and original contract see Gough, op. cit.).

argue, because you have agreed to do so in return for certain benefits and the emphasis was on the need to obey. In other cases they were more interested in criticizing government. They were reminding rulers that their power rested on a popular consent which could be withdrawn if the government did not do its job properly.

We distinguish two distinct types of contract theory: governmental contract by which was understood a contract between a society already constituted and its rulers, and pure contract, thought to be the basis upon which society itself rested. Most modern objections are to pure contract as a theory of the origins of society. If pure contract was intended to be anthropology or sociology, the objection is sound. If, however, pure contract was a demand that community become more and more a 'community of meaning' — that its adult members should be expected to interpret their relations rationally and responsibly — there is an aim in the theory we share. Others have objected to governmental contract on a view of the State which we in our turn are bound to reject — the view of the State, that is, which Hegel among others propagated. It is surely better to insist that those who rule do so on clearly defined conditions of service to the community than to allow them to wrap themselves around with the mystique of a divinely created authority.

On the other hand, much more forceful objection was raised against pure contract theory by people who wanted to take much the same view of society as a whole that lovers might take of their relations or members of the same family of theirs. Community was too close, too intimate, to speak of contract; too spiritual to be associated with the ends commonly associated with contractual relations. Here are two distinct objections. We will take the second first.

It is true, of course, that when we speak of contract in ordinary dealings we usually mean an agreement of a commercial sort; we contract to buy and sell, to make profits or to earn wages. On the face of it there is no reason why one should not speak of contract for other and more exalted ends, but the question then arises whether such ends may not be frustrated rather than furthered by the contractual instrument. We will return to this in a moment when we have commented on the other kind of objection.

This is the objection that where relations admit of no intervention by others, where they are already intimate there to talk of contract is out of place. It would further be held that membership of a community — the nation, for example — either is or ought to be of that order. We are here in the kind of difficulty we anticipated earlier when talking about love. For though as we shall show we may agree that the contract is an *inadequate* model of what human relations might be, and even an inhibition to the development of some relations, it may, on the other hand, be a desirable alternative to overmuch talk of 'solidarity' and 'togetherness'. The most powerful objection to social contract as a basis for political obligation is this: if it refers to an actual agreement in the past, then it cannot bind new generations who took no part in the proceedings. At the same time, the strong feelings of community which some people have or which more have at some times do not constitute a sufficient reason for denying the separation, the individual freedom, of those who from time to time may want to have nothing to do with the community. Strong feelings of belonging are all very well in small groups which are also free associations; but we need to be protected against them in large communities where our liberty to resign and go somewhere else is purely nominal. In order to withstand them it might be better to insist on institutions which make provision for each member to be treated as if he were a contractual partner to be consulted with rights and obligations defined and not a member of the corporate body to be embraced and smothered by the whole, however benevolent this whole might be.

Community and 'meaning'[1]

The phrase 'community of meaning' has been used several times both in this chapter and elsewhere. We propose now to explain it

[1] Ferdinand Tönnies (1855–1936) puts forward a theory which the English title does not represent but which is relevant to the use of 'community' in this book. He conceived of two kinds of social relation based upon two types of human willing — *Kurwille* (rational will) and *Wessenwille* (natural will). *Gesellschaft* is an ideal type of society which embodies the *Kurwille*; *Gemeinschaft* is a complex embodying *Wessenwille*, of which the mother's love for her infant is an example. If its members think of the community as a gift of nature (or God) created by supernatural will then such a community is *Gemeinschaft*. Where consciousness of authority arises from class relations this is *Gesellschaft*. See *Gemeinschaft und Gesellschaft*, trans. C. P. Loomis as *Community and Society* (Michigan State University, 1957). In this book 'community of meaning' resembles Tönnie's *Gesellschaft* in certain respects though no identity is intended, neither is the distinction he makes accepted here.

in order to suggest why the contract approach to human relations in large communities may have a limited usefulness, but *only* a limited usefulness.

This phrase has been employed deliberately in order to contrast the interests of social science with those of social philosophy. For the sociologist, for instance, is properly engaged in explaining the 'meaning of community' according to the criteria and the terminology of the methods he finds adequate to his descriptive or explanatory function. Social philosophy, on the other hand, is engaged in a much less precise and indeed endless task — that of working out concepts by which the given social systems may be progressively permeated, so to speak, with understanding. Rousseau put this perversely when he talked about finding an association 'in which each, while uniting himself with all, may still obey himself alone, and remain as free as before'.[1] Besides, when it comes to devising forms of association the scientist is as concerned as the philosopher. None the less, Rousseau is not altogether that wide of the mark — we do engage in a constant and unending attempt to construct conceptual systems within which men may make the community given them at birth 'their own' and its laws in some degree their own will, and all 'models' of community, all social and political ideals, may be tested in terms of this aim.

Now 'contract' has at least the virtue of serving this aim by introducing into the concept of human relations the possibility of something more than vague consent to social regulation. Whatever happened to the New England Puritans, the men of the *Mayflower* facing a hostile land they proposed to conquer (with motives not altogether different from those of the imperialistic monarchs who issued charters for colonization in the previous century) were confronting the business of living together as free and responsible adults accepting the implications of independence. They were relieved of the immediate authority and also the protection of their 'dread sovereign, King James'. As William Bradford remarked, standing 'half amazed at this poor people's' condition, 'they had now no friends to welcome them nor inns to entertain or refresh ... no houses, much less towns to repair to ...',[2] but only themselves and what they could make of their co-operative effort.

[1] Rousseau, *Social Contract*, bk. i, ch. 6.   [2] William Bradford, op. cit.

Contract by comparison with the notions of paternal care and submission in the 'family' image of community, does suggest a mature acceptance of responsibility. It is a better starting point than vows of obedience and unquestioned loyalty *or* non-responsible, individualistic schemes for 'making what one can and getting out'.

But it is only a starting point. So long as we think of a relation with another only in terms of carefully catalogued rights and obligations we set limits to our relation and reduce it to a calculated mechanism scarcely more 'human' than a relation with a machine. Such a view may undoubtedly do violence to the kind of facts the sociologist represents by 'sociality'. What is more to the point, for us, is that it may inhibit the realization of whole ranges of possibility in human relations just as a carping, calculated exchange of services between husband and wife would impoverish the marriage and inhibit its development.

In short, we need constructive concepts of community which will retain what contract theories tried to put in the place of less mature notions of dependence but at the same time not shut us in with our tabulated rights and duties; on the contrary they will leave ample room for creative development of all the possible varieties of social life. The rest of this book is taken up with such concepts of community but first we have to consider what is involved in having such concepts and using them for social action.

QUESTIONS FOR DISCUSSION

1. Was the 'Mayflower Compact' strictly the *beginning* of a society? If not, in what sense *was* it a beginning? (The footnotes on pp. 329 f. are relevant.)

2. H. S. Maine (*Ancient Law*, 1861) said that the development of society has been 'from status to contract'. Discuss the advantages of the contractual model of human relations in terms of (*a*) freedom, and (*b*) community.

3. Go back to the discussion on 'meaning' in Part One. Read the reference to Tönnies on p. 337. Discuss the usefulness of the term, 'community of meaning', in planning social reconstruction.

M

30

Utopia

THE man who invented the name 'Utopia' ('No Place') was Sir Thomas More, Lord Chancellor of England from 1529 to 1532. While he was King Henry VIII's envoy in Flanders some years before he sketched a description in Latin of an imaginary island governed by a 'wise and good constitution' with few laws, 'where virtue hath its due reward, and yet there is such an equality that every man lives in plenty'.[1] The idea of constructing an imaginary society for the purpose of criticizing contemporary institutions and proposing better ones is, of course, as old as Plato's *Timaeus* and *Republic* and it is used by many writers after More. The method is a simple one.[2] Like the *Mayflower* you sail right away from all prevailing customs, laws, institutions, and settlements, but you sail in a different direction. More's Raphael Hothlyday seems to have sailed in the wake of Amerigo Vespucci,[3] but the lands he speaks of are as remote from the later, Puritan settlements in way of life as they were from the England of Henry VIII. Naturally; for *Utopia* is a work of art, not a travel-book or a work

[1] Thomas More, *Utopia* (Cassell, 1909), p. 62.

[2] For other uses of the Utopian method see the description of Sparta in Plutarch's Life of Lycurgus (a mixture of fact and fiction). 'Methinks', he says, 'all Laconia looks like one family estate just divided among a family of brothers' (*Plutarch's Lives*, trans. Dryden, revised by Arthur Hugh Clough, New York, Modern Library). The legendary *Atlantis* has been used for Utopian purposes — for example by Francis Bacon (1626). For other examples see: Hobbes, *Leviathan*; Filmer, *Patriarchia*; Rousseau, *Social Contract*; Campanella, *Civitas Solis*; Harrington, *Oceana*. On Campanella see A. Gray, *The Socialist Tradition*, ch. iii (*b*). In the same chapter there is comment on More. For a criticism of Utopian thinking not mentioned in the text see J. Bowle, *Politics and Opinion in the Nineteenth Century* (Jonathan Cape, 1954), bk. i, ch. 6. See also Karl Mannheim, *Ideology and Utopia* (Routledge, 1954).

[3] Vespucci (1451–1512). More calls him *Americus Vesputius* (*Utopia*, p. 14). On his own account Vespucci is supposed to have reached the American mainland eight days before John Cabot, that is, on 16 June 1497.

in anthropology. The method is to use imagination so to embellish moral judgement as to dramatize the contrast between what is and what might be.

It is, therefore, a little odd to hear a modern historian dismiss More's *Utopia* as 'the dying utterance of an old ideal',[1] expressing the 'futility of a moral aspiration that cannot make its account with brute fact'. For Sir Thomas More in his own whimsical way put all this much better. Raphael Hothlyday, giving reasons why he would not serve at Court, says,

> If . . . I should talk of these or such-like things to men that had taken their bias another way, how deaf they would be to all I could say!

> There is no room for philosophy in the courts of princes.[2]

The author in his imaginary reply says that this is perfectly true if Hothlyday will insist on assaulting people 'with discourses that are out of their road' instead of making the best he can of admittedly bad conditions in ordinary society. Then comes Hothlyday's objection to the charge that his Utopian talk is impracticable.

> . . . such discourses as mine, which only call past evils to mind and give warning of what may follow, have nothing in them that is so absurd that they may not be used at any time, for they can only be unpleasant to those that are resolved to run headlong the contrary way; and if we must let alone everything as absurd or extravagant — which, by reason of the wicked lives of many may seem uncouth — we must, even among Christians, give over pressing the greatest part of those things that Christ hath taught us . . .[3]

Here, then, is the first and more commonplace objection to what we may now call Utopian models of community and here is a reply to it by the inventor of the name. We shall in a moment go into this objection more thoroughly and then we shall turn to another — the objection that such models are not so much futile as dangerous (and we may well take the view that they can't be both).

'Ideal' and 'real'

Are Utopian models of community futile? The very name 'Utopian' has now to be watched, for it has come to mean 'futile'

---

[1] Sabine, *HPT*, ch. xxii. [2] More, *Utopia*, p. 57.
[3] Ibid., p. 59. For a criticism of More see Alexander Gray, op. cit., ch. iii.

(mainly under Marxist and positivist influence)[1] so that the question as we have put it is misleading. For if we immediately understand by 'Utopian' 'impossible' or 'fantastic', then there is no point at all in asking whether models which are Utopian (in this sense) are useful. Nevertheless, with Thomas More's clearly expressed intentions in mind it does make sense to ask whether constructive models, ideals of community, are futile and this is what the question means.

But even the word 'ideal' tends to beg any question in which it is used today. 'That's all right as an ideal, but . . .' is the ordinary critic's way of dismissing any attempt to abstract from undesirable conditions in order to show what might be or what ought to be. And here is the danger of wholesale rejection of Utopian models — we may by contempt for this way of thinking deprive ourselves of a variety of experience not only satisfying but essential to social progress.[2]

What does it mean to say, 'That's all right as an ideal, but . . .'? What it seems to mean is that in the model, the proposal put forward about how things could be, there are desirable qualities, but that these are either known to be unattainable or they have been advertised in a form which makes them incompatible with prevailing techniques. If the second is the case, then we have a criticism either of these techniques or of the way the models have been constructed. As for the first possibility, it is difficult to be clear immediately how people can *know* that qualities admittedly desirable are strictly unattainable. What we do know with a fair amount of certainty is that there are in any given social structure plenty of reasons why people should *resist* change, plenty of interests vested in the *undesirable* qualities which the Utopia shows up.

More himself, a dozen years before Henry VIII's demands over Anne Boleyn came to a head, wrote that the Utopians would not allow a husband to put away his wife for no fault other than that her body has grown old or deformed. 'But Henry was no Utopian', as his biographer has said.[3] It was More himself who,

[1] For a comment on the relation between Marxism and positivism see H. B. Acton, *The Illusion of the Epoch.*

[2] 'Progress', that is, as distinct from mere change.

[3] Francis Hackett, *The Personal History of Henry the Eighth* (New York, Horace Liveright, Modern Library edition, 1929), iii. 6.

with a kind of justice, lived out the 'ideal' of the Utopians in this respect to the point where it cost him his life. Does this demonstrate the futility of Utopian thinking? If so, it demonstrates at the same time the futility of *all* moral judgement which opposes the brute facts of social organization or political power.

This is the difficulty in this objection to *Utopia* or any similar way of taking an interest in community. Must one select the 'brute facts' which are to be ignored or denied? How is the moralist to know which facts are 'brute' and which have some chance of yielding before adequate moral persuasion? We cannot now inquire too closely into what constitutes a brute fact or indeed any gentler, more civilized kind of fact. (One philosopher, for instance, defines fact as 'the source and context of signs to which we react successfully'.)[1] But we are entitled to distinguish between the historian's hindsight which enables him to say that a 'Utopia' was not the 'authentic voice of the age that was coming into being'[2] and the moralist's obligation to make clear at all times in the most effective way he can what he sees to be the defects in his society and the standards by which he has judged it. We are assuming that some Utopian writings have in fact been systematic attempts to express moral judgements upon contemporary society.

What could make the expression of a moral judgement futile, that is, worthless? Surely only the failure of the mode of expression to convey the judgement.[3] This is not usually the complaint people make against Utopias or other modes of expressing what they call 'ideals'. They usually complain not that they have not been able to understand but that the 'ideal' is too far away from the 'real', that it will not persuade, that it has not the support of sufficient people, and so forth. None of these complaints seem to us to have anything to do with the worth of the judgement or, for that matter, of its mode of expression.

A Utopian model or other 'ideal' could be said to be worthless,

---

[1] S. Langer, *Philosophy in a New Key* (Harvard University Press, 1951), p. 267.

[2] Sabine, *HPT*, ch. xxii.

[3] Here is a selection of readings on moral judgement in addition to those recommended earlier: S. Zink, *The Concepts of Ethics* (Macmillan, 1962), ch. i; B. Mayo, *Ethics and the Moral Life* (Macmillan, 1958), part i, ch. 4; part ii, ch. 6; P. Nowell-Smith, *Ethics* (Penguin, 1954), part ii; S. Toulmin, *Reason in Ethics* (C.U.P., 1960); C. L. Stevenson, *Ethics and Language* (New Haven, Yale University Press, 1944). L. J. Binkley, *Contemporary Ethical Theories* (New York, Citadel Press, 1961), is a relatively easy introduction to contemporary British ethical theory.

however, if the judgement it expressed were itself deficient. But we have to be clear about the *kind* of deficiency or rather about what we consider makes a moral judgement of low quality if not actually 'worthless'. Questions about moral judgements — their validity, objectivity, and so on — are central to ethics or moral philosophy and too complex to be dealt with here. We are entitled, however, to lay down one minimal condition for the worth of a moral judgement: a moral judgement has some worth if in making it a man is giving as faithful an account as he can of the good as he sees it and the shortcomings of his society as these seem in terms of this good. Not to make such judgements prompted by one's moral experience might itself be immoral as a failure in interpersonal reliability. To make such judgements carelessly or with no respect for one's own experience of the good would be a worthless activity, certainly; and it is by some such tests as these that Utopian models might well be judged, not by their apparent failure to 'reflect the times'.

We turn now to the objection that models of community (if Utopian) are not futile but dangerous.

Utopianism as 'art'

A city will never know happiness unless its draughtsmen are artists who have as their pattern the divine . . .[1]

This is Plato's Socrates speaking. He goes on:

They will take as their canvas . . . a city and human character, and first they will make their canvas clean — not at all an easy matter. . . . They will not consent to lay a finger on city or individual, or draft laws, until they are given, or can make for themselves, a clean canvas.

If the *Republic* is the classic example of a Utopia, this passage and what follows is a very good example indeed of a Utopia-maker explaining his methods or at any rate the methods which ought to be used. Note the 'clean canvas' and recall what was said at the beginning of the last chapter about the New World and the Puritans.

A moment ago we were defending such works as More's on the ground that it could be regarded as the expression of a moral

---

[1] Plato, *Republic*, vi. 500 *d*.

judgement; it would be more difficult, we suggested, to defend failure to make such a judgement and, we might now add, impossible to defend the suppression of all such judgement-making on the ground that it was futile. Nor indeed may we condemn the making of moral judgements on the ground that they are dangerous. All criticism is dangerous to someone, or to some institution, or to some interest. Danger by itself is an inadequate criterion of evil, an insufficient cause for suppression. Judgements are meant to be dangerous to the things they condemn, just as they are meant to be helpful to the ends or values they approve. It would be misleading, therefore, to assess such Utopianism as Plato's solely or even principally in terms of the danger it presents to, say, a liberal or 'open' society.

But suppose now we look at such a Utopian model as indeed Karl Popper does both as a work of art and also as the blueprint for radical, social reconstruction.[1]

You can make moral judgements and you can express such judgements in such works of art as a dramatic dialogue or a fictional tale. The writings of men like More and Plato take this second course. The problem then is to distinguish the different criteria to which the different kinds of activity (moral judgement and work of art) are subject, and then to determine whether the criteria proper to the one have to any extent trespassed upon the criteria proper to the other. So, for instance, the objection often made to 'commitment' in modern writing is that this means moral or political judgement, and that the making of such judgements in a poem, a play, or a novel is a breach of the rules proper to art. We are considering the matter the other way round: when men put their moral judgements into art forms do these offend the rules to which moral judgement is subordinate?

Obviously there would be no problem if you made no distinction between morals and art, between the pursuit of the good and the creation and enjoyment of the beautiful. It is arguable that Plato — in the *Republic* at any rate — did *not* make much of such a distinction, for while on the one hand he had a low opinion of artists and of art as 'a poor child of poor parents',[2] he nevertheless (in the passage quoted just now) talks of political thought as if it were

[1] K. Popper, *The Open Society and its Enemies*, vol. i, ch. 9.
[2] Plato, op. cit. x. 403.

comparable to painting or draughtsmanship. Why should the distinction be important, whether he recognized it or not? Because in art we not only *allow* the artist complete mastery of his material in pursuit of his idea, we *expect* this. But in moral judgement extended into a model of community the 'materials' will be other men and women, living and yet unborn: so far from allowing these to be used as artists' material we have strong and fundamental objections to doing any such thing. This our discussion of freedom and justice has shown.

Yet this moral objection to the Utopian's art can surely no more apply to a piece of writing as such than to a novel, a drama, a painting, a symphony, or any other work of art which claimed to depict human life not as it is but as it might or, in the author's concepts, ought to be? The objection to Utopian writing can only arise when we have reason to suppose that the author and his friends mean to use the work of art as a programme of revolutionary social reconstruction, as a blueprint for a new order.

> Do you agree [asks 'Socrates'] that our words concerning city and constitution are not mere pious prayers ... but are somehow practicable ...?[1]

When he goes on to say that in order to build such a city it is necessary to send all those over ten years of age into the country, 'and so get the children out of the moral influences of their parents ...', it is hardly surprising that social philosophers who have lived through Adolf Hitler's 'final solution' and Josef Stalin's 'purges' should take fright and condemn the Utopian 'art' as a totalitarian weapon.

Utopians and engineers

The weight of Karl Popper's case against Plato and other 'enemies of the Open Society' is that the Utopian model lends itself to what he calls 'Utopian engineering'. By 'social engineering' he means all social activities which 'in order to realize some aim or end, consciously utilize all available technological knowledge'.[2] He does not object to social engineering provided it is what he

---

[1] Plato, op. cit. vii. 540.
[2] K. Popper, *The Poverty of Historicism* (Routledge, paperback ed., 1961), ch. iii. The quotations which follow are from this section.

calls 'piecemeal'. 'Piecemeal' engineering regards the ends of such social action as 'beyond the province of technology'; it recognizes that only a minority of social institutions are consciously designed, the rest having 'just "grown" '. The piecemeal engineer may have his own dreams or ideals for the community but he does not believe in the method of re-designing the community as a whole. In fact in respect of ends his techniques are neutral and may be used for totalitarian as well as for liberal purposes.

By contrast the 'Holist' or 'Utopian' engineer aims at re-modelling the whole society in accordance with a definite plan or blueprint. The difference between the Utopian and the piecemeal engineer is not precise but rests on two very different points of view. Utopians regard the 'piecemealers' as too modest, whereas they are themselves 'haphazard and clumsy', using piecemeal methods without the caution and self-criticism of the piecemealer.

Thus the difference between Utopian and piecemeal engineering turns out ... to be a difference not so much in scale and scope as in caution and preparedness for unavoidable surprises.[1]

What Sir Karl Popper means by 'Utopian engineering' is a set of ideas about society and of methods for social action hostile to the social values to which we are committed.[2] Therefore we would ourselves have to avoid any constructive concept of society inviting action for the wholesale reconstruction of human relations. But this notwithstanding, and leaving aside the question whether, in fact, there have been Utopians of this kind, we will not shun all 'models' simply because some, or even all, can be said to be dangerous.

Let us now say something about the need for such constructive concepts. We are opposed to a censorship which would check even the most fanciful creative effort intended to show up the possibilities of human community. If we are to allow each other the freedom without which creative ideas will not flourish, we must take a chance; we must run risks. Then again, if we are to discuss the general qualities of communal life, either to say what we think is desirable or merely to disapprove of what we think

[1] Ibid., p. 69.
[2] How far we are justified in calling Plato (or anyone else) a 'holist' engineer in Popper's sense is another matter.

M2

undesirable, we shall find it hard to do this without saying something like this: 'Imagine a society in which all laws are of such-
and-such a nature'; or 'Surely it would be better if all institutions
to do with social welfare had these characteristics and those . . .',
and then we shall be doing something like the Utopian writers of
Sir Thomas More's kind were doing. We do not have to give an
account of 'ends' in the sense of some perfect state or condition of
society we regard as beyond improvement — this would offend
the values we defend. We do have to discuss ends in the sense of
general conditions or kinds of relation if our engineers (be they
never so piecemeal) are not to run amok and manufacture ends for
us which have the merit only of suiting their techniques.

Social philosophy is particularly interested in this kind of
discussion. If Utopian or for that matter any other models of
community can be half as dangerous as writers like Karl Popper
fear then all the more reason why social philosophers should work
at them critically and replace them, if possible, by others more in
keeping with their values. Certainly they must not be put off by a
general disapproval of all systematic, constructive concepts of
community.

On 'modelling'

If an architect plans a whole estate[1] so that the people who buy
the houses will, without realizing it until it is too late, be forced to
have much more communal life than they would have chosen for
themselves, we can see in the original model something of what
we have to fear from Utopians if we care for freedom. Suppose a
whole town or a great city is similarly planned with comparable
built-in provision for certain 'values'? True, it could be argued
that only the inanimate materials have been 'moulded', but there
is a clear intention that this work of art should 'mould' people,
too. Is this kind of engineering 'piecemeal' or not? Suppose, now,
that certain social services are also constructed upon models which
have been thought out by a few and into which have been 'built'
arrangements which favour some qualities in human relations and

---

[1] An example of this kind of planning was recently described (on the whole,
approvingly) in *New Society* (28 Jan. 1965). The architects, a firm of private builders
and a local New Towns' Commission 'have between them imposed a highly social
pattern of living on twenty-five families who . . . were looking for nothing more than
privacy and domestic isolation'.

depress others. Is it hard to believe that this kind of thing happens in our modern communities? But if it *does* happen, how do those who make such models conclude that some qualities are good, others not good, some values preferable to others, some ends desirable, others not desirable? By what expertise are they qualified to reach such decisions and build them into models upon which some areas of our social life, however small, are planned?

Such modelling, if it goes on at all, must be for the most part an activity uninformed by discussion over anything like the area it is meant to influence, for there is little provision made in our professional education for discussion of values. If we get into the model-making business as social philosophers, how shall we go about it? We have been going about it all through this book by discussing social values, by preferring some to others, by certain explicit arguments and other implicit assumptions. In the first part of the book we took up a position in favour of the *variety* of human experience. This is a general argument against the kind of 'modelling' Karl Popper, among others, condemns. The variety of human experience was a condition within which it became possible to talk about freedom, but the value of freedom, we saw, could be argued in different ways with specific implications for human society. Taking freedom as our base it was possible to exercise some kind of critical control over ideas of justice and what was said about freedom and justice in turn provides now the conditions within which we can construct any concepts of community we find desirable.

There was a kind of model in the social contract theory. Rude men would say it resembled the model of a market-place or a stock exchange, but we found it preferable at least to the family model. One thing is certain: we cannot from the premises we have laid down go in for any concept of community which does not have built into it arrangements for encouraging an increase in responsible freedom. Some people might say this itself made a model inconceivable. For how can you model a community made up of people who are required by the model itself to be capable of changing whatever you lay down? So be it. If that rules out models, so much the worse for them, but there is no need to say so. Others would say that in our insistence upon the concept of responsibility we are reviving the 'paradox of freedom', but this is something to debate later on.

'Utopias' so called have, by definition, been abstractions from all or almost all the conditions with which any real community is familiar. As works of art this may not disqualify them but we prefer concepts not far removed from what would seem to most ordinary people in the range of the possible. So we shall begin with the nation and the nation-state, go on to international ideas, to democracy and 'open society' and only then do justice to the earlier discussion by an attempt at a less familiar construction — that of the 'responsible' society. The question throughout will be this: in which of these conceptual models are we able to see most possibility of a 'community of meaning'?

QUESTIONS FOR DISCUSSION

1. Read the quotation from More's *Utopia* on p. 341. Discuss the arguments for and against this kind of imaginative writing, (*a*) as social criticism directed toward social action, (*b*) as art. This may seem to raise the question whether commitment to certain social values makes for good art. Read E. Fischer, *The Necessity of Art; A Marxist Approach*, trans. Bostock (Penguin, 1963), chs i–iii.

2. Read K. Popper, *Poverty of Historicism* (Routledge, 1957), iii. 21. Can you have satisfactory 'engineering' whether 'piecemeal' or 'wholesale' without models of some sort? (The answers to such questions will lie partly if not wholly in the criteria of what is 'satisfactory'.)

3. In a footnote to p. 348 an example is given of a model which guided building construction in a deliberate attempt to inveigle people into a particular way of life. Suppose we either (*a*) approve of the ends and of the means, or (*b*) whether we approve or not, do not see how else architects can work, at what point would we say that planning of this kind began to be (i) illiberal, and/or (ii) controllable? Imagine a whole new town planned on the same principle. Imagine all towns reconstructed in this way. Discuss the implications for the ethics of social reconstruction.

1

The Nation

SCHOOLS in many lands make the nation the model of community. Flags are saluted; oaths of allegiance sworn; anthems sung; history books re-written to show the greatness of the nation; wherever effort is needed or improvement called for appeal is made to pride in *being* American, French, Turk, Arab, Jew. Of course in such ceremonies and such formal social education 'nation', 'race', 'state' may be mixed up as no sociologist would permit. The educator, however, is not a sociologist — at least not while he is teaching. Social servants are not social scientists — at least not while they are serving. Social service is practical — it aims at making changes and achieving ends. We may not like the way people do their social service — we may turn sick at the thought of flag-waving and drum-beating — but if work is to be done we still have to turn sooner or later from analysis, from classification, from observation, to action. When action is thwarted by inertia, lack of effort and co-operation by others, or when the whole field of action, the community, is threatened unless the community itself will resist alien government, for such reasons at least, let alone for the sake of social sentiments, ways have to be found of moving those we wish to serve to act together in their own interest. 'The nation' might be seen as a device, an image which we can justify solely on such practical grounds.

The nation as 'myth'
In Part One of this book we noticed two uses of the word 'myth'. One was for the 'mythopoeic' thought of an era 'before philosophy', before objectivity, before the conceptual separation of man from his universe, of the individual from his group; the other was for a deliberate use of such thought-forms for the

purpose of criticizing and regulating human conduct and human relations — as in the biblical myth of the Fall and the Myth of Protagoras. Protagoras' pragmatism[1] could be used to justify the use of such myths in social education on the ground that by such means men would come to attach the right value to having the beliefs and conforming to the conventions of their particular group. Plato, in the third book of the *Republic*, proposes to use such a myth in order to make the citizens of his ideal community 'care more for the city and for each other'.[2] They are to be taught that they have all come from the same origin but differ in their qualities: those fit to rule have gold in them, the auxiliaries silver, farmers and other craftsmen iron and copper, and though for the most part children will be of the same stuff as their parents gold might bring forth silver or silver gold, and so on.

Plato's opponents have, of course, no difficulty in falling upon this as evidence of his evil intentions, the more so as translators use such phrases as 'necessary lies' and 'noble falsehood'[3] in Socrates apology for this device. His defenders, on the other hand, point out that all three classes would believe the myth and that 'it is meant to replace the national traditions[4] which any community has, which are intended to express the kind of community it is, or wishes to be, its ideals, rather than to state matters of fact'.[4] In such defences of Plato's political myth we are up against a principle difficulty with all models of community and the model of the Nation in particular.

To start with the general difficulty, the notion of indoctrinating a population with 'falsehoods' however 'noble' does not have to be demonstrated as immoral — the very use of the word 'falsehood' assumes this. In our own arguments, for instance, we have made much of the 'truth conventions' and these require that interpersonal truth take account of objectivity. We have had in modern political action scandalous examples of the use to which political myth can be put. Georges Sorel,[5] a leader of the French Syndicalist movement, used the myth as a body of images which had the

---

[1] See above, Chapter 7.   [2] *Republic*, iii. 415.   [3] Ibid. 412.

[4] H. D. P. Lee, quoting Cornford in the Penguin Classics edition of the *Republic* (1955).

[5] Sorel (1847–1922) *Réflexions sur la violence*, trans. T. E. Hulme and published by Allen & Unwin, 1915, as *Reflections on Violence*. For comment see J. Bowle, *Politics and Opinion in the Nineteenth Century*, ch. x; A. Gray, *The Socialist Tradition*, ch. xv.

power to evoke sentiments. Sorel was impressed by Rousseau's
success as a 'myth maker': the fantastic myth of the 'general will'
simply succeeded in justifying the old State. In his *Reflections on
Violence* Sorel's attack on concentrated State power makes use of
the myth of the General Strike. This was to lead to violence ending
the stupefying humanitarianism of the European nations and
reviving their energy. Sorel admired Mussolini. The Italian Duce
and his Fascist theorists took over Sorel's notion of the political
myth.

'We have created our myth,' said Mussolini, '... a faith, a
passion. It is not necessary that it shall be a reality ... it is a goad,
a hope, a faith. ... Our myth is the nation, our myth is the
greatness of the nation.'[1] Obviously any resemblance between
what we mean by 'models of community' and what was meant by
such people as Sorel and Mussolini is enough to put us off all
such models. Two comments may be made here to show the
difference.

The first comment has to do with the general difficulty. It is this.
The myth as it has been understood and used in recent political
thought violates deliberately and systematically not only existing
institutions but also the efforts men have been making for
centuries to give reason its place in human relations, to check
irrational and violent action, and to make of community something
like 'community of meaning'. People living in a world of 'myths'
said Sorel, 'are secure from all refutation'. But if the model of
community not only claims to show the kind of community we
wish to be, but also makes the extension of responsible freedom
and the methods of critical, rational discourse its foundation, then
this, so far from resembling Sorel's myth, overthrows it. All we
are doing, in fact, is to state our opposition to the irrational myth
and the call to violence as forcefully as we can.

But can the 'nation' serve such ends? This brings us to the
second comment on the modern myth and also the particular
difficulty of the nation as a model.

The comment is this. Myth-makers like Mussolini will only talk
of the nation in terms of the State.

---

[1] A speech at Naples quoted by Sabine, *HPT*, from Hermann Finer's *Mussolini in
Italy* (1935). For a general treatment of the myth in politics see E. Cassirer, *The Myth
of the State* (Doubleday, 1955; 1st ed. 1946).

A nation, as expressed in the State, is a living ethical entity only in so far as it is progressive.

Fascism is totalitarian and the Fascist State, as a synthesis and a unit which includes all values, interprets, develops and lends additional power to the whole life of a people.[1]

Of the State in relation to the nation more will be said below, but we submit now that it is one thing to make the State — the organization of political power — 'a unit which includes all values' and another to set up as a deliberate corrective to such 'myths' a model of the community apart from, and in some sense superior to, its political organization.

'Nation' is a name given to concrete social experiences. My passport gives me 'national status' ('charter'-wise) as 'British subject, Citizen of the United Kingdom and Colonies'. It happens that my national and my political status can be linked in this way without difficulty. But there is more to national experience than legal and political classifications. The two may, indeed, fail to come to terms. An Arab who sees himself as belonging to the Arab *nation* (as distinct from the race) may have trouble from time to time in reconciling this with the policies of the nation-state which grants him political and national status. For these latter purposes he is Iraqi, Egyptian, Jordanian, Tunisian, and so forth. But he knows what he means by his claim to belong to the Arab nation. He means his language, his Islamic faith, the memory of an Arab Empire which straddled southern Europe, a common history, a common hatred, perhaps for Israel, and all manner of customs shared with men living along the coasts of the Levant, the southern Mediterranean, east of Suez, and south into Africa. These experiences distinguish him from Europeans, Americans, Chinese. However one gives an account of them to make them whole one speaks of the 'nation' and this is no myth — if indeed by 'myth' we mean 'fiction' or 'falsification'.

'Myths' and 'wholes'

At the same time it is hard for people in the habit of analysing experiences and giving accounts only of those which can be

[1] Benito Mussolini, 'The Doctrine of Fascism', trans. E. Cope and quoted in H. Kohn, *Nationalism, its Meaning and History* (Princeton, Van Nostrand, 1955), p. 172.

quantified and related experimentally to sensory data to know what to do with such a concept as 'nation'. We are up against a difficulty we noticed when talking about the variety of experiences (in Part One) and later in trying to say how 'self' could be understood in giving an account of freedom. To observe is one thing; to participate, another. There are a number of activities and characteristics in any given community which can be observed and classified together as 'nationality', but this will not be an adequate account of what people mean by 'belonging to the nation'; it will not adequately present the experience of participating in nationhood. As for creating or helping to create such experience (as we would do, for instance, in a school where children are encouraged to take pride in nationhood), this *is* participation. Observer's language will not do this for us. All we can do is to prepare ourselves for participation when the chance comes by asking whether we are justified in using this concept or, if not, how else we are going to construct our relations with each other.

Before we do this let us recall how Edmund Burke used this idea of the nation. For in his writings we can begin to see the difference between the nation as a constructive concept of the kind we mean by a 'model' and the nation-state as a myth to be used for political ends.

Rousseau glorified community in an abstract way using 'general will' as his model. But Burke meant by 'the nation' no mythical entity but the concrete community, its traditions, history, institutions, and way of life. Where the men of the Enlightenment before the French Revolution treated reason as a faculty which could sweep away all existing forms of social life and 'begin again', Burke saw the traditions of the nation as the repository of civilization, to be conserved.

... a nation is not an idea only of local extent, and individual, momentary aggregation; but it is an idea of continuity, which extends in time as well as in numbers and space ...[1]

Of the constitution he says:

... it is a choice not of one day or one set of people ... it is a deliberate election of the ages ... made by what is ten thousand times better than

[1] E. Burke, *Reform of Representation in the House of Commons* (1782), in Bohn's edition of the *Works*, vol. vi.

choice. . . . The individual is foolish; the multitude, for the moment, is foolish, when they act without deliberation; but the species is wise, and, when time is given to it, as a species it always acts right . . .[1]

Burke does not always make a clear distinction between the nation, the society, and the State. Yet what he says about 'the State' he would undoubtedly have intended for the nation. Scorning the notion of the State as a purely commercial contract he says:

. . . it is a partnership in all science; a partnership in all art; a partnership in every virtue, and in all perfection . . . not only between those who are living, but between those who are living, those who are dead, and those who are to be born . . .[2]

Here is the nation as a 'whole', giving continuity and therefore greatly extended meaning to the lives of its members. The nation as Burke sees it is somewhat like the Church as the Christian sees it — a community transcending the limitations of time and space.[3] So, S. T. Coleridge,[4] who shared Burke's interest in the nation, brings together nation and Church in what some people have likened to a Platonic 'idea'. It takes an effort of intellect and imagination to see things this way — a knowledge of history, a refinement of aesthetic sense — but a man with such equipment is seldom the responsibility of teachers or other social servants. He is able to conceive of a social whole and to take steps toward establishing community of meaning. The question is what to do when confronted with those who have no such sense of community.

We will now consider some objections to the idea of the nation as a model for community.

National sovereignty

The national model is said to *fracture* community; it cuts across the lines of communication by creating 'artificial' frontiers. But are not all frontiers artificial? And Burke, presumably, would

[1] Ibid.

[2] *Reflections on the Revolution in France* (O.U.P., World's Classics), p. 106.

[3] The Church 'Militant and Triumphant'. See, for example, a hymn written by Charles Wesley (1707–1788):

> One family we dwell in Him
> One church, above, beneath,
> Though now divided by the stream,
> The narrow stream of death . . .

[4] S. T. Coleridge. See J. Bowle, op. cit., ch. iii.

argue that as 'art is man's nature'[1] so the bare fact that men have in some sense made the nation is very far indeed from constituting an objection to the idea of the nation. If 'the nation' is a suitable concept of community, that is because it rests upon real community already — community of a sort not easily to be found in other associations.

But the objection is that the nation is an obstacle to international peace; it sets up tensions, for instance, through economic competition; it is a focus for war; it is a wasteful concentration of human effort.

Part of the force of such objections derives not from the idea of the nation but from that of national sovereignty. By 'national sovereignty' we mean the right a nation may claim to have the last word not only on domestic matters but also on issues affecting other nations. National sovereignty is possible only when the nation is also a nation-state. The difficulty arises from a comparatively recent conviction that all nations should also be nation-states — that is, that the nation should have its own political organization, its military forces, the right to make its own laws and conduct affairs with other nations as equals, having no law above their own 'sovereign' will.

Today most nation-states recognize that sovereignty in this sense must be subjected to drastic modifications if the world is not to live in a disastrous 'state of nature'. Even if we did not admit our economic and technological interdependence, the more powerful states know too well the consequences of using their power freely to insist on literal interpretations of sovereignty. On the other hand, the 'cold war' between great power groupings and the use made in this war of nationalist and anti-imperialist sentiments has (ironically) encouraged smaller nations to push the claims of sovereignty, at times, further than the great powers dare go and this, often enough, within the protection of the United Nations Organization — the nearest we have gone to world government.

Yet there is no necessary difficulty here. It is possible to maintain both that nation-states should manage their own affairs and that they should do so within the wider community, under law. There is no more difficulty in saying this than in maintaining that grown

[1] E. Burke, *Appeal from Old to New Whigs*, Works, vol. vi.

men of sound mind should manage their affairs with the assumption that this *means* that they will co-operate with others or not violate others' interests.

'Sovereignty' is the trouble-maker here. It belongs to the State rather than to the nation as such. Yet since the nation and the State are so closely linked, and since the values we associate with our own nation may be dependent on national independence, we need to look first to these values before reaching conclusions about the nation as community *and* before abandoning altogether the implications of national sovereignty.

Nationalism

Nationalism is a state of mind, in which the supreme loyalty of the individual is felt to be due to the nation-state.[1]

Nationalism is also the chief objection many have to the nation as a model for community. If we mean by 'nationalism' loyalty to the nation-state and this above all other loyalties, then nationalism is nothing but the abandonment of all values save one — the value of the nation as an end in itself. Freedom and justice, for instance, would at best come second in our concerns.

The indifference of nationalists to personal freedom is well-known today but the distinction was not always so clear. In the nineteenth century, for instance, the freedom of nations to become sovereign states was regarded by some liberals with the same passionate determination as they gave to the cause of individual liberty. We now know that a nation can achieve independence without enlarging the personal liberty of its people. The demand for collective freedom from an invading foe or an occupying foreign power attracts powerful sentiments. More, there is no doubt at all that many people have felt unfree simply because they were ruled by men not of their nation. This brings a powerful sense of release when the foreigner is expelled, however brief the duration of this feeling.[2]

---

[1] H. Kohn, op. cit., p. 9.

[2] Just how brief those who have lived through the heady phase of independence and its remote aftermath are, perhaps, more aware than those who see only the first days after a revolution. This writer had such an experience in the Republic of Iraq between the years 1958 and 1962. A book by an 'unknown' British expatriate, 'Caractacus', entitled *Revolution in Iraq*, and written in the best-selling days immediately

But the only persons *bound* to be less restrained when nationalism succeeds are those who enjoy political power. There is no reason at all why they should then dispense freedom generally and so cut down their own power. On the contrary, where a foreign power may have protected minorities in its dominion, native rulers in the new nation-state may oppress them. Justice as well as freedom may be endangered by the independence of the nation-state.

In the second place, then, there is no necessary connexion between nationalism and justice. On the contrary, worship of the nation-state may lead to collective violence against other nations, as in the wars of Napoleon, or to totalitarian oppression of the nation's own members, as in the Fascist nationalism of Hitler's Germany. When Hegel said that the State was the 'realization of freedom' he was threatening the value of freedom as we have explained it here in a way that has appealed to many nationalists.

... Truth is the Unity of the universal and subjective Will; and the Universal is to be found in the State. . . . The State is the Divine Idea as it exists on Earth . . .[1]

It is a fact of common moral experience that a man is more likely to 'find himself' in service to others or in membership of a group serving a common cause than he is, say, in self-contemplation and solitary indulgence. But the nationalist, manipulating philosophers like Hegel, draws from this the moral that all men ought therefore to be bundled into the collective 'good', willy-nilly, and the power which is to 'bundle' them should also be the cause they serve, the end to which they offer up their individuality. When the nation is dedicated to such views as these it is right to have very grave doubts about its suitability as a model of community.

Yet we had better understand how such an objection is to be argued. For we are not committed to individualistic concepts; we *are* committed to the value of community. The objection is that nationalism identifies State and nation, that the State is primarily a power organization and that while power is only another name for ability to get things done it is by the same definition *not* a primary

after Kassem's assumption of power made much more interesting reading four years later in the hours before Kassem was murdered by his compatriots. (*Revolution in Iraq*, Gollancz, 1959.)

[1] F. Hegel, *Lectures on the Philosophy of History*, 1822, trans. Carl and Paul Friedrich in *The Philosophy of Hegel* (New York, Random House, 1953).

value but the proper servant of primary values. Submit to it unquestioningly and you give up asking about the right of might; you say instead that might is right, and this is the abandonment of value. To be sure that the nation can be used at all as a model of community we have to be able to see it as a subject of values. But by the same argument we may be led to admit the need for loyalty to the nation.

National values

So far from being able to get rid of those social facts and experiences we call 'national' a great deal of the talk about our sociality may well support the conclusion that we are to some degree national animals. If this is true any attempt to deny nationality would be to some degree a denial of integrity. Marxists, of course, would put 'class' in the place of 'nationality' but that is not the point we are debating now. Neither 'class' nor 'nationality' taken as facts of our nature are themselves values. Only when we take the nation as a model of community, as an extension of certain ideals of the community, does this become the case. We may then be doing no more than relating to our own community some such values as we have been discussing here.

Values such as freedom and justice cannot be shut up inside any one political organization. The whole point of seeking such values is that in doing so we are laying down communication with people who may not belong to the given groups of race, nation, social class, and so forth. So if you make 'nation' the arbiter of values as the jingoist did when he said, 'My country, right or wrong . . .', you have in fact given up values altogether. And the same would apply to any *unquestioning* loyalty to a group, whether the group is the nation, the social class, the political party, or a religious sect. Yet at the same time it may well be that one nation is more inclined than another to commit itself to certain values, even to the point of using its political organization, the State, in their defence. This is a possibility to have in mind when talking about 'internationalism' as if it were obviously and without further explanation a better model of community than the nation. For, on the one hand, people can abandon national loyalty without any commitment to social values and use internationalism as a reason; and, on the other hand, being loyal to a more-or-less concrete community called the nation is conceivable; loyalty to 'internationalism' does not immediately make sense unless we translate this into 'loyalty to the United Nations Organization'.

This possibility, too, needs thought. For while undoubtedly UNO could be seen as a subject of values, that is, we could explain our overriding loyalty to this organization in terms of such values as peace, welfare, and so forth, we must not forget that a large number of those who direct the affairs of such an organization owe primary allegiance to their own nation-state and that these nation-states are not of necessity committed to our social values. Involved in this consideration is the question about war, but as this has nothing directly to do with models of community we will leave it.

The nation by itself is inadequate as a model but it may be that no other will make much sense except as it can be seen as an extension or modification of values which have grown up within the nation; just as all other models may in the last resort pale into abstractions unless they can command the kind of loyalty and deep, half-conscious sentiment which the nation can command.

QUESTIONS FOR DISCUSSION

1. What are the ethical objections to Sorel's teaching about the political myth? (See all the footnotes on this for comment and criticism.)

2. Read the quotations from Burke and the summary of his views on the nation. Discuss the moral value of such a concept and (*a*) of teaching it positively, (*b*) disparaging it among children.

3. Read H. Kohn, *Nationalism, its Meaning and History* (Princeton, Nostrand, 1955), part i. Suppose it makes sense to call one's own nation a 'subject of values', does this commit us to be nationalists in order to defend these values? If so, to what degree and in what circumstances? If not, to what have we subordinated such values in refusing to espouse the cause of the nation against others?

32

Democracy

IN a certain city attractive to tourists the best cuisine was always to be found at one Costello's restaurant. So famous was Costello's that no visitor to the city would eat elsewhere; no other hotel, no other restaurant, let alone the smaller eating-houses could do worthwhile business with tourists. One night — so the story goes — hoteliers and *restaurateurs* met to discuss their troubles. A plot was formed. By early dawn every hotel and restaurant, every café down to the humblest, back-street *trattoria*, was decorated with the sign 'Costello's'. As well-informed tourists began to arrive, asking for Costello's, they were directed by cab-drivers and others in the pay of rival *restaurateurs* to many different places where food and service ranged from the incredible to the intolerable. Yet when some of them met on boats and planes later each could maintain with equal conviction that he had eaten 'at Costello's, of course' and none dared confess he had found the experience unsatisfactory.

'Democracy' has suffered something of the fate which befell the original Costello's. Once it was thought to be the proper name for special institutions constituting a distinct form of government; but the reputation the word acquired from, say, 1917[1] onwards robbed it of distinction in two ways. In the first place, people began to call their governments 'democratic' irrespective of their political institutions; in the second place, others well disposed toward democratic government will nevertheless use 'democracy' as a 'hurrah' word for all or nearly all aspects of social life they approve and wish to have others approve. Left in this state the word 'democracy' is of no more use as a guide to community than

---

[1] '1917'; President Woodrow Wilson's speech in the American Congress calling for a world made 'safe for democracy'.

the name Costello's became, in the story just related as a guide to good food. To start a discussion on whether or not we approve of 'democracy' would be about as useful as it would be for half a dozen tourists after leaving that city to discuss whether or not they thought Costello's deserved its reputation without first settling which Costello's they were talking about.

Our question must then be *not*, 'What is democracy?' as a preliminary to asking, 'Do we approve of it?' but 'What conditions or qualities are indicated by different uses of "democracy" and which of these suit a model of community compatible with our values?'[1] (We might ask 'Where is the *original* Costello's?', or start all over again and ask 'Where can I find the best food and service in town?')

People and power

The Greeks made the word 'democracy'[2] out of two other words, *demos*, which came in time to mean roughly the 'people', that is, the majority of citizens, and *kratos*, which had to do with strength, power, or authority. This gives us some right to insist that the word 'democracy' ought only to be used for a community in which the majority of people, of members, have power or authority in their own government. We would then be deploring the use of the word to indicate, let alone approve, other constitutions lacking popular government. This seems a tidy arrangement, though it may not be so easy to prove that, for instance, a 'people's democracy' in Eastern Europe has not in some sense 'popular government'. We will keep to this meaning for the time, however, in order to discover whether 'democracy' (in this sense) is a suitable model for community.

We have already had something to say about majority rule.[3] As a way of getting representatives elected or reaching decisions about laws and policies majority rule had, we said, certain

[1] An example of the procedure Karl Popper describes as definition 'from right to left' (*Open Society*, vol. ii, ch. 11). So, instead of asking, 'What is democracy?' (thus preparing the way for Popper's 'essentialist' definition) we ask what qualities those are in government to which we attach the name 'democracy' (a 'nominalist' definition).

[2] For one approach to the difficulties of the word 'democracy' see T. Weldon, *The Vocabulary of Politics* (Penguin, 1953), ch. iv. Weldon's approach is typical of linguistic analysis, in its virtues and in its limitations.

[3] On majority rule see above, Chapter 15.

advantages over other forms of government by the tests of freedom. But by itself, with no further qualifications, this is not obvious. There is no reason, for instance, why majority rule should not go along with secret police and other oppressive machinery. John Stuart Mill drew attention to the tyrannical power of majority opinion and this is surely no less a possibility when such opinion can use the vote and the machinery of legislation. Over-simplifying for the moment, and taking the demand for popular government to be met when every citizen has a vote and can call his representatives to account at frequent intervals, we are bound to admit that this is preferable to a system in which governments cannot be called to account without violence; but we are also bound to question whether this takes us very far towards an adequate concept of community.

It is a point to insist on at some risk, for democracy in this sense has not always been approved and we run the risk of seeming to side with those who favour government by *élites* and so forth when we express dissatisfaction with popular government. Nevertheless, the alternative is to abandon value altogether.

The procedural device we call 'majority rule' is a way of reducing debate about qualities to a quantifiable conclusion. When the frankest possible discussion has taken place, let us say, between all those whose interests are directly concerned in the development of European unity and when no agreement can be reached about the admission of another State or the constitution of a proposed federation, the question of principle, of value, of quality is put aside and 'in order to get on' the disputants vote. Let us remember that if there was a genuine disagreement in the first place about a principle or an end to be pursued this dispute remains. What has been resolved is not the original subject of debate, 'Is it desirable to admit Ruritania?', 'Ought we, as a federation, to insist on habeas corpus and refuse admission to nations which imprison for political reasons?', but another question altogether, 'Can we now take action?' Voting settles the second question with or without settling the first.

Unless we are to say that whatever a given majority in any 'democratic' group decides is *right*, whatever ends it addresses itself to by voting good or even the best — unless we are prepared to say this we must also be prepared to say that popular government by itself is not a model for community, though it may well be an indispensable part of such a model. But let us be clear what would be involved in saying that the popular vote answers the question about quality or value as well as the procedural question about decision. For this is by no means an impossible position and it is certainly one which has some comfort in it. The comfort is in the relief it brings, always supposing the kind of people who worry about matters of value are also the kind of people who can accept the majority decision as an end to their worries. It is more likely that those who take refuge in the vote either do so because they are disinclined to worry, or because they have good reason to expect that the vote will go their way. Neither expectation is satisfactory to what we have called the truth-conventions.

If the majority vote is always right as well as (under the law) decisive, then we are back at the position we deplored in the last chapter as nationalism — we are back at 'might is right'; and it has been remarked that some such agreement has prevailed between nationalism and democracy at least since the time of the French Revolution. The trouble is that such facile respect for popular government overlooks obvious preliminaries to decision which no individual in his right mind would overlook when making a decision by himself. I do not for one moment suppose that a course of action is right or for the best simply because I have embarked upon it; any defence of it that I put up would be based upon what went before and by way of preparation. Such preparation includes a number of conditions not all necessarily and immediately related to the decision. For example, I inform myself about the situation, I consult other people, and I refer my decision before I make it, if I have time, to a number of criteria among which may well be moral values or moral rules of some generality if the decision is of the kind to provoke them.

Yet even so, and even if I have made such preparation to the best of my ability and the limit of my resources, I do not therefore assume that it *must* be right or is bound to be the best. That would be to assume far too much not only for my own abilities and my ways of preparing but for human knowledge itself both as information (fact-collecting) and as evaluating (relating general principles to particular circumstances and relating facts to ends and aims). Since decision by many people is much more complicated, calls for still more organization and selection, and puts a much wider gulf between general principles (on which we may also differ) and decision, it is curious to find people supposing that what is so open to doubt and uncertainty in individuals must be beyond doubt and wholly certain when carried out by large, complex groups.[1]

The power of the people, if genuine, is a power to act and decide; it does not include the power to be right, the power to know what is best even for the majority. This rests on conditions comparable to those governing personal decision. In estimating popular government as a model of community we are driven back to those conditions. We are driven back to all that is implied in making people 'free' from coercion and therefore able to live in a community which is also a community of meaning.

Collectivism

But many people use words like 'democracy' and even talk about popular power while making no institutional preparation at all for realizing this power. From the time of Rousseau onwards there has been a tradition of political thought, called by J. L. Talmon 'Totalitarian Democracy', and which he describes as 'a dictatorship resting on popular enthusiasm'.[2] Earlier we ruled out uses of 'democracy' which did not allow for the *power* of the people and we meant power of the concrete sort, manifested and deployed through such institutions as the vote and the election. But 'power', too, is a slippery word. It is possible to make people feel powerful simply by bringing them together, infecting them with mass hysteria, and making speeches about the 'nation' or the 'party', then sending them home while you get on with making decisions in which they have had no say whatsoever.[3] More; it is possible to corrupt the word 'freedom' and to argue that this 'losing oneself in the crowd' is a kind of liberation (which is true)

---

[1] On the relation between organization of knowledge and freedom see F. Hayek, *The Constitution of Liberty*, part i.

[2] J. L. Talmon, *The Origins of Totalitarian Democracy* (Secker & Warburg, 1952), p. 6 (reference is to the Mercury Books edition, 1961).

[3] The obvious example is the National Socialist régime in Germany before 1945. For one study of Adolf Hitler's methods see A. Bullock, *Hitler. A Study in Tyranny:* Cynics may find some faint resemblance to what goes on in parliamentary democracies at a reasonable interval after the General Election.

superior in value to the freedom from coercion which enables a man to make his own decisions and achieve a certain dignity (which we would say is not true). Nationalism, as we saw, has this kind of appeal. Combine the passions of unquestioning nationalism with this notion of liberation from 'self' by absorption in the collective and you have a model of community indeed and one, at that, which some people would be prepared to call 'democracy'.

For it is quite possible to argue that a collectivist community of this kind is serving the *interests* of the majority provided you leave out of these 'interests' a man's interest in governing himself. We said that this was what a utilitarian account of human good could lead to and this is certainly how collectivism could defend itself. Again, the dogma of human sociality with which we began Part Four could easily lend itself to such a concept of community. If from the premiss 'man is a social animal' we proceed to deduce the evils of 'social space' and individuality, the good of 'togetherness' and the 'sense of belonging', we are all set for a model of community which could easily today call itself 'democracy' — easily, that is, if slipshod habits of speech go with slipshod thinking and valuing. It may very well be that the growth and development of social services in our Western world could aid in this process provided the social servant is convinced that 'maladjustment' is the worst of evils, 'mental health' the supreme good and inclusive of 'lack of tension' disagreement, conflict, and nonconformity.

Why should we resist such developments, if indeed they are taking place? What is our objection to collectivism? First let us be clear what it is that we are objecting to. By 'collectivism' now we mean a model of community in which the supreme good is indicated by such words as 'solidarity', 'cohesion', 'unity', the 'common purpose' and where such words refer to the whole range of social and personal action. By collectivism we mean a community where what matters is not so much the preparation for decision as the decision itself; not so much that the majority participate in it as that their interests are served with the maximum of efficiency. By collectivism we mean a community where despite this concern for the majority interest the whole matters more than the parts and this is revealed in a discouragement of difference, a distaste for free, critical discussion, a preference for overall plans, and a dislike of individual divergence or nonconformity.

Enough has been said earlier about freedom and justice to indicate the main lines of objection. We will add now that collectivism is not, in our view, a model of *community*; for it leaves out of its design adequate provision for constructing community of meaning. By 'community of meaning' we understand something which can develop in a family as relations are regulated less and less by the will of one or two more and more by common agreement about means and ends. On the other hand, community of meaning may *create* a free association — a religious sect, a literary coterie, a political party. But by the same tokens the association may grow and persist and its institutions remain long after community of meaning has declined or been replaced by some other and more complex organization of interests. In the large political community nationality may, as we have seen, provide an area of meaning, yet hardly enough to mark out the lines for desirable development or progress. In our terms what is called for is an arrangement whereby more and more people will achieve that meaningful integrity we have called 'selfhood' and still find it both possible and desirable to take some positive part in the life of the community as a whole. Individualism was a denial of this because it tried to pursue selfhood without respect for community. Collectivism is repulsive for the opposite reason: it asks us to conceive of community of interests, but omits the requirements of selfhood, by making the collective the end and by asking us to abandon all interests which cannot be reconciled with this end.

'Open' society

Some people talk of 'open' society as their model or as signifying the qualities they approve in human relations. Further, some seem to relate 'open' society and democracy, with 'democracy' signifying the political organization best disposed toward that kind of society.[1]

What is 'open' society? 'A completely "open" society', according to one writer, 'would be a society whose modes of behaviour were entirely determined by a rational choice between possible alternatives and whose adaptations were all ... conscious and

[1] For example, Karl Popper opposes 'democratic social reconstruction' (i.e piecemeal social engineering) to Utopian social engineering. Elsewhere he describes Socrates as 'champion of the open society and a friend to democracy' (*The Open Society*, vol. i).

deliberate.'[1] This is contrasted with the closed society in which no one would be aware of making a choice. This writer says that such an open society has never existed and will never exist—a bold statement — but he says that the concept is useful, since we can speak of 'relatively closed and relatively open' societies.

Henri Bergson's closed society is an exclusive and excluding group 'on the alert for attack or defence'.

Such is human society fresh from the hands of nature. Man was made for this society as the ant was made for the ant-heap.[2]

Open society is represented by all mankind. The social instinct is always working for a closed society, but the open soul embraces all humanity. Yet both drives and both kinds of morality to which they give rise and therefore both the closed and the open society derive from sources more fundamental than society itself — biological or life forces.

Sir Karl Popper contrasts 'magical', 'tribal', and 'collectivist' society with the open society in which individuals are confronted with personal decisions. The closed society may appropriately be likened to an organism, its members being linked by semi-biological bonds, and by touch, smell, and sight. But in the open society members may be observed striving to rise, socially; class struggle may be observed; and this is a situation unsuitable to the organic model. It is true that the process tends toward abstraction — toward the abstract society in which the business of life could be conducted without any face-to-face relations at all. But what matters is in fact that between laws on the one hand, taboos on the other, there is 'an ever-widening field of personal decisions with its problems and responsibilities'.

Many of us make rational decisions concerning the desirability . . . of new legislation and other institutional changes . . . decisions based upon an estimate of possible consequences, and upon a conscious preference for some of them. We recognize rational personal responsibility.[3]

There can be no doubt that Karl Popper both prefers the open society and recognizes that its development is not inevitable. Steps

[1] E. R. Dodds, *The Greeks and the Irrational* (University of California Press, 1956), p. 255, n. 1. The context in which this arises is 'The Fear of Freedom' and the open society of the third century before Christ in Athens.

[2] H. Bergson, *The Two Sources of Morality and Religion* (Macmillan, 1935), ch. iv.

[3] K. Popper, *The Open Society*, vol. i, ch. 10 (all references are to the 2nd edition).

must be taken. Methods must be preferred and insisted upon. The end is not yet and the issue by no means certain. It is true that attempts to restore the tribal society are misguided, that the tribal society for which men who fear freedom may yearn *cannot* be restored, but such attempts have been made and will be made again and the making of them is to be deplored.

Some of the marks of the open — or opening — society resemble qualities we have already discussed: equal distribution of rights and obligations, equality before an impartial law and impartial courts, for instance. These show the connexion between the open society and democratic institutions. The same applies in some respects to Popper's use of 'individualism'.[1] Then again, his insistence that the State must protect such principles recalls the problem we raised when talking about the nation — the problem we have to face when once we can conceive of the nation, or the nation-state, as the subject of values committed in some sense to their protection.[2] Popper also includes a kind of negative utilitarianism or analgesic principle[3] as a criterion of his good society. We can say no more about this now than has been said earlier[4] but it does not seem to us a principle any more dependent upon an open than a closed society. All forms of community must protect the values for which they stand, which their institutions and ways of life represent, and such values are bound to include some measure of interest in pain-reduction; they could include total pain-removal without moving an inch in the direction of open society.

A more important characteristic stressed by Popper is that of individual choice and of what he calls 'critical rationalism'. The institutions of the closed society leave no room for personal responsibility, for there are few problems in this form of life and 'nothing really equivalent to moral problems'.[5] In the opening society, on the other hand, choices have to be made and these call for 'an attitude of readiness to listen to critical arguments and to learn from experience', which the writer calls 'critical rationalism'.[6]

The advantage to us of such an analysis is that it takes us further

[1] 'Individualism': ibid., pp. 100–4.
[2] 'Protection': ibid., p. 124; vol. ii, pp. 125, 160 f.
[3] 'Analgesic': ibid., p. 235, n. 6.   [4] See above, Chapter 9.
[5] K. Popper, op. cit., vol. i, p. 172.   [6] Ibid., vol. ii, p. 225.

than a lot of talk about democracy. It takes us further by making it possible for us to see what we have tried to see earlier in this book — that freedom requires more than democratic institutions can ensure. Free men and a free society rest upon personal qualities as well. The open society is far from being an easy commitment, effortless and painless. In the final chapter we shall try to show how this discussion of social values requires us to add to our own model of community rather more than concepts of democracy and open society alone suggest.

QUESTIONS FOR DISCUSSION

1. Read Benn and Peters, *SP*, ch. xv; T. D. Weldon, *The Vocabulary of Politics* (Penguin, 1953), ch. iv, sec. 2. How *ought* we to use the word 'democracy'? (Note: the word in italics is a warning against fallacy.)

2. Read the introduction to J. L. Talmon, *The Origins of Totalitarian Democracy* (Secker & Warburg, 1952). Discuss the objections to collectivism (*a*) from the point of view of freedom, (*b*) as relating to justice, (*c*) as proposing a model of community. Does such a discussion throw any light on the meanings of these terms?

3. Read K. R. Popper, *The Open Society and its Enemies*, ch. x. Compare the notion of the 'open society' with that of E. R. Dodds, *The Greeks and the Irrational* (University of California Press, 1956), p. 255, n. i, and Henri Bergson, *The Two Sources of Morality and Religion*, ch. iv. If society might be said to be moving in this direction (i.e. of Popper's 'open society'), what personal qualities would we expect to see developing or wish to see developed? (Consider again the final chapter of J. Piaget's *The Moral Judgment of the Child*.)

33

Responsible Society

'WHAT sort of people?'

Under this curious heading the British periodical, *New Society*, presented a short while ago the results of an inquiry addressed to some thousands of its readers.[1] A curious heading because it does not make clear which of several questions the inquiry is about. Consider the possibilities: 'What sort of people shall we become?' 'What sort of people are we?' 'What sort of people do we want to become?' 'What sort of people were we?' Those who answered the questions put in the inquiry would most likely have thought they were answering the third of these but, indirectly, they might have thought themselves concerned with the last or even with another: 'What sort of people do we intend to become?', though there was little provision in the inquiry to establish intentions. The authors of the inquiry professed themselves satisfied with the modest conclusion that 'when people had the chance to answer these questions they answered them in such-and-such a way'.[2]

Suppose an inquiry of this sort yielded the conclusion that at least 70 per cent of the population wished to be relieved of responsibility for the management of their own affairs whatever this might mean for personal freedom. Would this entitle civil and social servants to take appropriate action? By what arguments would we justify meeting such demands? Or how would we justify refusing to meet them? Whether or not we can answer these questions here the asking of them is a good way to approach what we want to add to such concepts of community as 'democracy' and 'open society'.

[1] *New Society*, May 1963.
[2] R. P. Kelvin, *New Society*, no. 32, p. 8.

Beyond democracy?

Some people think that to be 'democratic' a social (or a civil) servant must at all times obey the 'will of the people' or act only in accordance with a popular mandate. On the other hand, one interesting feature of the *New Society* inquiry was that fifty per cent of those who answered its questions (many of whom would have been social servants) said that they wanted 'more positive moral and religious leadership'. Did they see themselves as providing such leadership? Could they both make such a demand *and* take that view of the social servant's function sometimes regarded as the only genuine 'democratic' view? We shall argue that, on the contrary, the social servant who considers himself 'democratic' would be involved in contradiction if he did *not* refuse to accede to the kind of request we imagined a moment ago: if he did not, in such a case, 'lead' against the so-called 'majority wish'.

The methods of social service may be designed to increase the number of those able to manage their own affairs or to reduce them. For you cannot teach or otherwise minister with a view to maintaining a fixed proportion of responsible persons in society: to do that you would have to inhibit some and since there are many professions engaged in social service and large numbers of persons in each profession a general intention to inhibit some would lead to a general reduction in the number of those enabled to manage and of the area within which they could be autonomous or responsible. Now since democracy requires a majority, an overwhelming majority, to vote and to be consulted within any given democratic association, it also requires a majority to be capable of such participation. Therefore the social servant whose methods do not enable increasing numbers to take an increasing part in government of all kinds cannot call himself 'democratic'.

What, then, of the (fictional) vote for 'more protection' at the price of 'less freedom'? There is, of course, nothing to prevent an individual's arriving at some such concept of the good life and calling it 'freedom from responsibility': we all incline that way at times. What we are considering is the responsibility of social servants in reconstructions which would entail systematic reduction of responsible freedom. Our position is that nothing can be done in the name of democracy or on the authority of its principles which would withdraw its advantages either from those who consent to this or from those — possibly unborn — who do not.

Democracy is a set of political conditions created on and off through the centuries for purposes which we are now well able to understand. The vote may only be a device for reaching decisions where the need to act is greater than the need to resolve a conflict over values; but as such it deprives tyrants of an excuse to assert themselves when such a need arises. Consultation and representation have the task of delivering the many from servitude to the few and so enabling them to manage their own affairs. How, then, can we use the vote (or the researcher's poll) either to settle a question of value or to bring an end to all future voting, all future discussion and say we do it 'in the name of democracy'? How can we use consultation or our role as (in some sense) representatives to re-create servitude, however kindly, rejecting the wisdom of the centuries and denying to those yet to be the modes and the machinery of consultation which have been bequeathed to us? Above all, how can we say we do this 'on democratic principles'?

The value of this fictional situation is that it suggests the line we must take in refusing to be confused about leadership by spurious interpretations of what democracy means. Of course a social servant *can* choose to interpret his role as that of tool or instrument to those who sign his salary cheques or answer the questions the researchers ask. This has the advantage of sparing *him* the burdens of responsibility; but he cannot in doing so claim the support of a liberal or democratic heritage. Democracy to sustain itself must lead to responsible society and it can do so only through the leadership of those who see this and have the chance to act upon what they see.

Commitment

This leads us to speak of 'commitment'. For what we have said is that responsible society begins with the commitment of its servants. We are committed to the pursuit of responsible freedom. This entails our commitment to resist any conditions which reduce responsible freedom, including the imposition of other 'goods', however highly we may value them. The odd thing about such commitment is that it may well appear to others as non-commitment.

Compare, for instance, the commitment of an old-style, evangelical Christian — a Methodist, perhaps. The simpler Methodist evangelist of a generation or two ago had a very clear idea of the end he sought for other men as well as himself and for society. He would talk often of education and other social services as 'vanities' — futilities which could do no good and might do ill with men who had not been 'converted', undergone a 'change of heart', and set themselves on the way to 'holiness'. He might even preach with some particularity of the stages in religious experience through which men were required to pass, from repentance through conversion to sanctification. As for the reconstruction of earthly society, so far as this interested him at all what he demanded mostly was total abstinence from alcoholic drinks, gambling, sometimes dancing and other pleasures, total adherence to sabbath-keeping, strenuous prayer, bible-reading, and so on, and he would even take steps to bring legislators on to his side in these matters.

Compare all this with what we have called 'commitment'. As there is a sense in which all parental care may be said to have failed if the child at a given age is incapable of living without his parents, so, we are saying, all social service is corrupt if it does not enable those it serves to manage without it or at least enable them to do with less and less of other people's support. We are saying that no good we may do has value if it reduces the ability of those we serve to do good to themselves, and others. We are committed to what we called earlier the 'charter of freedom' and that is a very different kind of commitment in social service from the old evangelicals' or most others'.

But what commits us? In what role are we committed men — committed, that is, to this good of the responsible society and *therefore* obliged to restrain (in that role) any contrary commitments?

Surely we are not committed 'as' social scientists? Of course the social *reformer* 'must be prepared to assert a preference, to say "this is the kind of world I want to live in" '.[1] But does not being 'scientific' *mean* (among other things) being 'objective' and does

---

[1] D. V. Donnison, 'Reform and Therapy', in *Sociological Review Monograph No. 3*, ed. P. Halmos (Keele, University College of North Staffordshire, 1960). In the same monograph see also M. V. C. Jeffreys, 'Commitment and Objectivity'.

this not entail the 'bracketing' of preferences? The question is always important, but here specially because some who are disposed toward our kind of commitment too readily find themselves intimidated by some generalization of social science which they take to be an unanswerable, because 'objective', rebuttal.

> Unlike common sense, sociology is not a discipline bound to uphold the ethos of some particular order. It seeks maximum freedom from value suppositions.[1]

Well, that is just what we expect people to say who want to be thought of not only as 'scientists' but as scientists in the same sense as physicists are scientists. Nor do we dissent from the view that sociology is not 'bound to uphold the ethos of some particular order'. But is it not bound to take an interest in some kind of order, some sort of 'ethos'? Granted that the physicist is an observer of things and relatively well placed to be just an observer; just how easy is it *not* to be a participant as well when observing not things but people with whose habits and concepts one's own thinking, the very structure of one's thinking, is inextricably involved?

Now let us listen to another social scientist.[2]

> ... there is an ethical or political element in every theory or generalization in the social sciences. ... The social scientist might better picture himself as a learned lawyer in court, rather than as a scientist in a laboratory ...

The same writer goes on:

> Who can really doubt that the great advances in the social sciences have been made by people with a strong sense of commitment?

We will not debate that. Then:

> Objectivity need not be confused with neutrality. ... We are, as social scientists, inextricably involved in the fate of the un-things called people whom we observed.

In short, he says, the social scientist has to be both observer and participant — as we would certainly claim for the social philosopher.

---

[1] D. Martindale, *Nature and Types of Sociological Theory*, p. 5.
[2] B. Crick, 'What is truth in Social Science?' (*New Society*, no. 88, pp. 20 ff.).

If this is in any degree acceptable to social science, we certainly do well *not* to submit our moral commitments either to such fictional demands as the one we suggested might come from an inquiry into 'What sort of people?', or to any other theories or generalizations in the social sciences unless these have first been carefully examined with a view to uncovering their own commitments.

The commitment of the social servant as such at least has not this preliminary objection to meet. What we propose to do now is to summarize the commitment we have already sketched in general principles and then, finally, indicate areas of our social life within which such principles seem to have applications.

Principles: a declaration of intent

In the responsible society all laws, institutions, techniques in social reconstruction, methods in social service, must in addition to their particular ends and values satisfy one or both of the following conditions. They must serve to increase the number of those able to manage their own affairs. They must enlarge that area of human relations to which the individual's self-management commits him.

This is a 'declaration of intent', a formulation or re-formulation of the primary conventions upon which new federations (for example) could be constructed. We will comment briefly upon it.

Note, first, such words as 'enlarging' or 'increasing'. They are open to abuse. Any association could protest its intention to 'enlarge' or 'increase' the responsible freedom of its members: concrete tests are necessary. They lie beyond our competence here. On the other hand, such words have an advantage over some criteria for the good society. Unlike 'democracy', for instance, we are not obliged on such principles to turn our backs on states which have no parliaments, no two-party systems — or not for that reason alone. We in the West, once our principle is grasped, might look with more friendly eyes, with less self-righteousness upon other civilizations. At the same time, European nations now moving toward political union might use some such principle to *exclude* obviously repressive régimes which give no adequate proof of intent.

'Enlarge' and 'increase' are useful in criticizing the social services. They do not require us to carp at services which minister to the mentally sick, much less to talk as if we wish to reverse the progress of the past century in these fields. All we require to know is that the aim is wherever possible to enable the sick to become responsible for their own health and the well not to rely upon sickness to evade their freedom. 'Social work,' declares an almoner, 'is based on a simple philosophy which grants to the individual the right to direct his own life and go his own way at his own pace . . .'[1]

The first part of the 'declaration' has to do more obviously with social service as well as with the work of parents, priests, and others who deal with their fellows face to face. All successful social service — to the delinquent, the sick, the poor, to children, to students — has among its desirable consequences this of increasing the number of those able to 'manage'. The second part of the 'declaration' has special application to politics, to social engineering, to management, to labour relations, to international organizations, to part of the work of religious organizations. It asks for institutions to be constructed, agencies created, ways and means of communication to be advanced which extend the community of meaning and do so by creating positive links between self-management and responsibility for others.

For the remainder of this chapter we will pose problems, indicate situations wherein the general principles briefly introduced might be studied in order to see what their implications are in practice.

'Moral' education?

If all education is in some sense 'moral', in what particular ways do we suppose the declaration of intent can operate as a guide to its moral possibilities in a responsible society?

(a) Teaching methods

Centuries have passed since pedagogues like Rousseau, Pestalozzi, and their successors preached the links between freedom and educational methods. What is the position today and, more particularly, what have teaching methods to do with increasing the number of those able to manage their own affairs? We submit that there is one answer which is not adequate: the answer,

[1] Ruth Wilkes in *Social Work*, 20 Feb. 1964, p. 14.

that is, which protests that *all* teaching, irrespective of methods, is satisfying this principle in that it is equipping people to earn their own living. For while it is true that men cannot be said to 'manage their own affairs' if they are not capable of earning a living, merely to be able to perform a function in the economic organization and to receive wages is an end which can as well be achieved in a wholly 'closed' as in an 'open' society — achieved, that is, irrespective of the freedom and responsibility of the worker.

This is why we must discuss teaching methods and, in particular, the extent to which these *engage* the learner's judgement, his reason, his will, and these not only in mastering the subject-matter of the conventional disciplines but in evaluating, in making the kind of decisions 'moral' education implies. John Dewey said that through educational agencies 'a society transforms uninitiated and seemingly alien beings into robust trustees of its own resources and ideals'.[1] But not, we suggest, inevitably. If, as he said elsewhere, 'The problem of an educational use of science is . . . to create an intelligence pregnant with belief in . . . the direction of human affairs by itself . . .',[2] this might call for serious criticism of science in education when this excludes student-participation except in note-taking or information-gathering. This is what we mean by the importance of method to the responsible society. Can we look back upon our own formal education and claim that it provoked and engaged our judgement, that it prepared us by well-established habits for reasonable and decisive participation in the management of affairs?

(b) School government?

If school is not only a preparation for the responsible society but a part of such society, it follows that the regulation of school life is a very important part indeed of moral education. In criticizing school government we should have in mind all that has been said about law, about justice, and about freedom as responsibility. At the same time we should take care to appreciate the usefulness of those graduating terms, 'enlarge' and 'increase', in our declaration of intent.

Criticism on such terms may be as uneasy about the absence of

[1] John Dewey, *Democracy and Education* (Macmillan, 1961; 1st ed. 1916), p. 10.
[2] Ibid., p. 225.

any regularity in school life even if the students are supposed to participate in 'government' as it would be about regulations imposed from 'above' and 'without' (through local education authorities, for instance) with no genuine participation by students. For 'free discipline' might mean little more than government by caprice with some injustice seen to be done to members of the staff, while government by fiat of the Head is no government at all in terms of the responsible society.

Graduated or progressive responsibility is the test of good government in school — as elsewhere in the responsible society. But when students are given some part in government not only must it be genuine and issue in laws which will be maintained but it must be seen to be matched by the part teachers of all grades, too, have in government, otherwise the school becomes 'child-centred' in a way which deprives the child of moral education for a society composed of *all* ages.

These are suggestions about what some would regard as 'indirect' moral education. This is misleading: to engage children in these ways is to give them direct preparation for responsible society. Nevertheless, we have to consider the possibility of moral teaching, of preparation for responsible society as the special subject matter of men and women dedicated to this end. There is no time here to deal with the many questions which this raises. We confine comment to one suggestion only about the material for this kind of teaching in the hope that this will suggest other approaches and at least dismiss the objection that there is no such material.

All — or nearly all — the values that we have debated in this book as involved in social life have application in microcosm in one particular, closely concentrated, critical form of contemporary life in the West — life on the roads. Here men have power and here they enjoy freedom. Here natural law suggests itself and, at times, a 'state of nature' seems to prevail. Here on the roads beyond doubt positive law instructs co-operation for ends which (unless the law is at fault) all sane men can make their own. Here the driver can feel his moral judgement at work and can experience the alliance it can form with the Highway Code as well as with what we called 'the natural law'. So far, in many schools, primary education has confined itself to 'safety first' and 'kerb drill'. We suggest that through all the available media every possible social situation which the roads create and tangibly exemplify should be made over into teaching material for moral education. From some such starting point teachers at post-primary level can go on to relate the lessons learnt to such matters as the moral implications of technology, government (as exemplified in the school government) and the child's creation — partly through art — of his 'self'.[1]

Law, welfare, responsibility

Our purpose is to show responsibility as a value with particular, concrete expressions. For this purpose we take two kinds of relation and suggest (we can do no more) how certain sorts of law may increase or decrease the responsible freedom of those engaged in them.

(a) Parents and children

Recall now the discussion on permissiveness in Part Two.[2] Plainly we were uneasy about this concept and not at all happy that it should be mixed up with the general concept of freedom. Rightly or wrongly we concluded that parental permissiveness could too easily be confused with indifference and a permissive relation become a not-relation, a social non-entity. Put it another way and (on the basis of conceptual analysis) we concluded that permissiveness might be an abdication of responsibility by the parent and a failure in education for the child. Parents who behave in this way could not be said to be 'free' in any viable, social sense of the word and therefore laws which consent to their indifference consent also to the reduction of freedom by permitting the decline in responsibility.

If I am not called to account for what my children do in such a way and on such terms that I am bound to *feel* my accounting (and necessarily to feel it painfully) then the drive towards responsible freedom, already weak, becomes weaker. I could hardly 'care less' to quote a telling contemporary phrase. But if the laws of my society insist that I answer (because this is of the nature of law and

[1] Partly through art. For what seems to this writer an over-emphasis on the place of art see H. Read, *Education through Art* (Faber, 1958), and for a comment in keeping with the view taken here, see J. Barzun, *The House of Intellect* (Secker & Warburg, 1959), ch. i (at least).

[2] See above, Part Two, ch. 15.

of society) then whether I like it or not (and I certainly will not at the time) at least my 'sense of' being responsible is increased and I am required to think and feel more than I would otherwise have done. Since this is so it is possible that my child will soon know that at least I *care* what he does and expect him to answer to me. (Who will say that my wrath at a heavy fine for his delinquency is a worse thing for him than my continued indifference?)

The other side of this situation, of course, is the State's continuing encroachment upon the relation between parent and child and we must ask upon what criteria this is thought 'good', once it is understood that encroachment by the Central Authority even by means of social servants is likely to affect all and not merely those who can be said to have failed in elementary care of their children. Are we bedevilled by vague egalitarianism again? Or by the criteria of administrative efficiency? All we have to decide is what we are to say about such laws by the criteria of responsible society.

(b) Welfare and obligation

The other situation was referred to earlier in the complaint made by the Socialist, Beatrice Webb, against British welfare legislation.[1] She said that Lloyd George's reforms entitled people to help from the State 'without any corresponding obligation' to look after themselves. The fact that this criticism is made of European welfare legislation by its transatlantic critics, that in the United States there is often a clear failure in justice defended in the name of freedom makes it very difficult indeed to discuss this objection with the seriousness it needs. How can we both deal justly with men in sore need and not commit the gravest of all offences against them — reducing their autonomy, depriving them of capacity to be men? Certainly we have no reason to be intimidated by those who say that to ask such questions is to propose turning law into moral tutor; for the whole burden of our complaint, if it is a sound one, is that the State may already have done its moral re-education so well that it will be virtually impossible in the future to teach the larger part of the population to appreciate freedom.

Earlier[2] we considered the situation where students are endowed

[1] See above, Chapter 25, especially p. 284.   [2] See above, Chapter 22, Discussion.

by the State throughout their higher education (that is, by the community through taxation) with no corresponding obligation to serve the community later. A student in the United Kingdom, for instance, may complete an expensive course in medicine paid for by his fellow-countrymen and then emigrate to the United States or to Australia. A woman may be trained as a schoolteacher, marry immediately after her course has finished, and never teach at all. Our question is about what this does to the sense of being responsible, of belonging to a community, when 'rights' of a very expensive kind are granted without discrimination and no return is required, not even any modification of one's personal life or immediate ambitions.

Similarly protection has been built up for workers in some industries in some countries to a degree where they will now corporately resist technological developments of benefit to the whole community *not* in order to keep work but in order to keep the *same* work in the *same* place so that a 'good' which most moralists would rate pretty low in the scale of values is protected by laws which at the same time deprive the community of manifest benefits and the worker of enterprise and stimulus.

The conclusions we reach in discussing such situations matter less than the criteria we find ourselves handling in reaching them. The criteria in this case will have to reckon with the conditions which are more likely to make workers feel their responsibility to the community and estimate the connexion between their own standard of living and the contribution they make to industry.

(c) *Professionalism and community*

Professional groups have their own codes. We speak of 'professional ethics'. The rules involved are various. Among them, for example, are rules which have arisen in pursuit of the ideal of service to which the group is supposed to be dedicated. The most obvious example is the Hippocratic oath which is supposed to govern professional ethics among physicians and surgeons. But there are other rules in the professional code which have to do only indirectly, if at all, with service to the community. Their most obvious purpose seems to be to protect the member of the group from having to account for his errors and offences to the community. This may of course be a necessary protection of the service from vicious, ignorant or merely irresponsible attack from outside. But rules of this kind may also become sheer professionalism by which is meant the pursuit of immunity for its own sake, the pursuit of ease within the profession leading to lowered standards and virtual indifference in some cases to what is said or thought or suffered by the 'outsider'.[1]

Where a profession has to struggle for its existence by satisfying the public with its services professionalism in this sense is less of a danger. Accountability is 'built in' to the relation between the profession and the public. But with the growth of the civil services and of social services dependent upon government professionalism of the 'protective' kind may grow. We must apply to its rules wherever we meet them the tests of the 'declaration of intent'. Do such professional habits tend to increase the number of those who can be said to manage their own affairs? (Having in mind all this was seen to entail when we discussed freedom.) Do the rules enlarge the area to which autonomy commits a man?

To give one or two examples of possible situations, academic professionalism is manifested in an exclusive attitude to other academic fields, in a special language (often essential to research), and often in complete indifference to the 'public world'. This looks like failure in responsibility. Suppose that academic philosophers, for instance, can only talk to other philosophers and confess they have no interest in 'practical problems' — what are we to say of their discipline and of the money spent upon it by the public? (No foregone conclusions here.) Suppose again the author of *Parkinson's Law or the Pursuit of Progress*[2] is anywhere near the truth in his conclusions about the Civil Service. Do such institutions tend toward a responsible society? If not, let us try to specify the professional habits which are at fault and relate them to more personal, moral qualities.

For that is what all this discussion is meant to come to — a reappraisal of a very old discovery: that cities are, in some sense, the individual 'writ large'[3] and so, to particularize, a 'responsible'

[1] J. Barzun, op. cit., has some comments on professionalism in the academic world which are worth studying.

[2] C. Northcote Parkinson. The whole of this brief work (Murray, 1958) is worth reading now.

[3] We can say this without going all the way with Plato.

society is the kind of society its members deserve because they, too, have learnt the ways by which freedom in society requires certain qualities of them. No discussion of social philosophy which does not in this way point on (or back) to questions of morals just as surely to those of politics has done very much. That is why, in this chapter, we have thought it good to suggest a choice confronting us even if this does look, on reflection, like an over-simplification.

Propositions of the form 'either . . . or' are never more suspect than when they appear in moral contexts. Is that because they are always over-simplifications if not downright falsehoods? Or is it because (whatever may be said of some such alleged choices) the moral life is bound to face us with decision and, not liking it, we use every possible sophistry to escape? One thing is certain. Such decisions *are* uncomfortable. They can be painful. If one's notion of the good life is to avoid them, it is better either to stay away from reflection altogether or as quickly as possible equip oneself with some philosophical method which will dispose of every anxiety as soon as it can be put into words.

QUESTIONS FOR DISCUSSION

1. Must social science be both objective and neutral in respect of social values? (Or should the question be '*Can* it?'?) Read pp. 375f and what the almoner has to say, as quoted on p. 378.

2. Discuss the degree to which your own education has engaged your judgement, your rational participation. Compare what might be said in this respect of (*a*) scientific studies with (*b*) studies in the arts or humanities.

3. Discuss the government of schools you have known as preparation for responsible society. Distinguish here between (*a*) direct teaching on the good life and the good society, and (*b*) the organization of the school for the purposes of government.

4. Ought parents to be made more responsible or less so for the behaviour of their children? Whichever answer you give discuss the appropriate means.

5. What would make Beatrice Webb's 'corresponding ob-

ligations' for beneficiaries of the Welfare State 'to look after themselves' meaningful? Is it in the interests of (a) civil or (b) social servants that people should be made to feel more dependent upon them? Specify such interests, if so, and relate them to the social values of freedom, justice and so forth. (For the reference to Beatrice Webb see above, Chapter 25.)